Dedication

For my wife, Bonnie Myhre, and our daughter, Mary Anne,
and also for a few of my Yosemite companions:
Mary Burris,
plus Rudy Goldstein and Joan Castelli and their daughter Elizabeth

WILDERNESS PRESS • BERKELEY

YOSEMITE
National Park

A Natural-History Guide
to Yosemite and Its Trails

Jeffrey P. Schaffer

FIRST EDITION 1978
Second printing March 1982
SECOND EDITION 1983
Second printing January 1985
Third printing July 1986
Fourth printing April 1987
Fifth printing January 1988
Revised sixth printing September 1989
Seventh printing March 1991
THIRD EDITION June 1992
Second printing November 1993
FOURTH EDITION June 1999
Second printing July 2000
Third printing March 2002

Design by Margaret Copeland
Drawings, photos, and maps by author except as noted
Cover design by Larry B. Van Dyke
Topographic map in pocket revised and updated by author,
        based on U.S. Geological Survey overlays

Library of Congress Card Catalog Number 99-23703
International Standard Book Number 0-89997-244-6

Manufactured in the United States of America
Published by **Wilderness Press**
                1200 5th St.
                Berkeley, CA 94710
                (800) 443-7227
                e-mail *mail@wildernesspress.com*

Contact us for a free catalog. Visit our Web site at **www.wildernesspress.com**

♻ Printed on recycled paper, 20% post-consumer waste

Front cover photo: **Backpackers approaching Nevada Fall**
Back cover photo: **Yosemite Fall, seen from the Valley**
Title-page photo: **Liberty Cap and Nevada Fall, seen along Hike 78**

Library of Congress Cataloging-in-Publication Data

Schaffer, Jeffrey P.
        Yosemite National Park : a natural-history guide to Yosemite and
its trails / Jeffrey P. Schaffer. -- 4th ed.
            p.   cm.
        Includes bibliographical references (p.   ) and index.
        ISBN 0-89997-244-6 (alk. paper)
        1. Hiking--California--Yosemite National Park Guidebooks.
        2 Trails--California--Yosemite National Park Guidebooks.
        3. Natural history--California--Yosemite National Park Guidebooks.
        4. Yosemite National Park (Calif.) Guidebooks. I. Title.
        GV199.42.C22Y677   1999
        917.94'47045--dc21
                                                    99-23703
                                                    CIP

Contents

Acknowledgments

"I'm going to map all the trails of Yosemite and the adjacent area in one summer," I told a park ranger when I was beginning field work on the first edition back in 1976. I had to eat those words. Even if I hadn't had a three-month-long knee ailment, I would have been hard pressed to complete the field mapping in *two* summers. Fortunately, during the second summer I had Ben Schifrin, a first-rate mapper and observant naturalist, helping me. Ben, now a medical doctor living in the Sierra's foothills, wrote all the prose for Hikes 3–5, 9–10, and 12–14 and most of the prose for Hikes 2, 6, 8, and 11. He made helpful comments for other parts of the original edition and provided photographs for his section and other sections. For later editions I've revised Ben's sections based largely on prose in his *Emigrant Wilderness and Northwestern Yosemite,* also by Wilderness Press.

Supplying additional original prose was Thomas Winnett, a veteran backpacker and former publisher of Wilderness Press. In the original edition I borrowed his trail descriptions for about half of the trails in the Tuolumne Meadows 15' quadrangle, and also for a few sections in the Mono Craters 15' quadrangle, but later made changes in his prose to reflect changes in the trails and in the lands they traverse.

In order understand what really had occurred in the Sierra Nevada, geologically speaking, I reviewed virtually all relevant written research, plus in the 1990s I logged about 150 days in the range while personally examining glacial and uplift evidence. That evidence is considerable, amounting to a book larger than this one, published, in 1997, by Wilderness Press: *The Geomorphic Evolution of the Yosemite Valley and Sierra Nevada Landscapes: Solving the Riddles in the Rocks.* The "Acknowledgments" in that book cites persons who have aided me in that field work. Additionally, over the years I have benefited from geological discussions with Howard Schorn (Univ. of Calif., Paleontology, retired), and in the 1990s with David Jones (US Geological Survey, retired) and Jeff Middlebrook (a geologically literate Sierran backpacker). The uplift and glacial histories presented in the current geology chapter of this guidebook differ radically from all previous interpretations, particularly from those of François Matthes, Clyde Wahrhaftig, and N. King Huber, all formerly of the US Geological Survey. In particular, I first wrote (back in 1994) that Sierran uplift was much earlier than previously thought—so early that Sierran rivers had tens of millions of years to cut their deep canyons, which existed long before glaciers flowed through them. Other prominent geologists with whom I've corresponded, who now also share this early-uplift view, include Brian Wernicke of Cal Tech, Peter Molnar of M.I.T., and Jack Wolfe of the Univ. of Arizona.

For comments and criticisms on the original biology chapter, I am indebted in part to Dave Graber, a grad student at the Univ. of Calif. during the 1970s while at the same time being Yosemite's bear expert. Also, the late Dr. Carl Sharsmith of the Yosemite Association gave me a solid introduction to alpine wildflowers, and he reviewed an early form of this chapter. Thanks also go to Dr. Thomas Harvey of San Jose State University, who reviewed Hike 93, which deals with giant-sequoia ecology. That hike's description was based largely on work done by Harvey, Hartesveldt, and others. Finally, Len McKenzie, Yosemite's Chief Park Interpreter, read much of the manuscript's natural-history sections.

Giving me encouragement at every step of the way for the first edition was Ron Mackie, Jr., the Chief Backcountry Ranger, who not only shared Park philosophy and management problems with me, but also gave me a *carte blanche* that enabled me to do unrestricted field work in the Park. Ron also read all 100 hikes of the manuscript and made numerous valuable comments, particularly with regard to safety. Also, I would like to thank Les Arnberger, a former Park Superintendent, who contributed the Foreword to the original edition. Finally, I would like to thank my wife, Bonnie, for the moral support I received during the rigorous field work of the 1990s, and my daughter, Mary Anne, who at age 12 typed much of the latest draft.

Jeffrey P. Schaffer
June, 1999

Foreword to the First Edition

Like John Muir more than a century ago, thousands of people have begun to discover in recent years that going to the mountains is going home. Muir spent much of the last 46 years of his life reveling in the "glories" of the High Sierra, basking in its "measureless mountain days," marveling at its breathtaking land forms and intricate subtleties, and breeding a passion for the spectacular yet gentle attributes of this "Range of Light." It was a passion rooted in a boundless sense of wonder and a sense of community with the earth. His zeal and his eloquence nurtured the seeds of an emerging conservation ethic, and his influence was pivotal in molding others' perceptions of wilderness and solidifying the embryonic national park concept.

Today Muir's gift with words is again influencing the ways people perceive and use wilderness, for his written works have enjoyed a resurgence in popularity. The Sierra Nevada is a lodestone that lures a swelling tide of hikers and backpackers each year. They seek the solitude, the excitement, the adventure, the therapeutic qualities, the spirit of freedom—yes, perhaps an element of danger as well—that are inherent in wilderness. For many, a wilderness experience is an escape—from urban pressures, job stress, perhaps the environmental blight spawned by our culture. And, like Muir, they often find—as they should—that going out, they are really going in.

With the spiraling demand for wilderness use have come intensified problems and responsibilities. Wilderness managers have had to exercise the responsibility for its protection by imposing limits on the number of people permitted in the backcountry and some constraints on their activities there. Likewise, it is imperative that individual wilderness users accept those constraints and, as the Indian did, touch the earth softly to help insure that they don't degrade the resources they presumably go to the wilderness to enjoy.

Having logged more than a few miles on Yosemite's trails myself, I have personally discovered Muir's "tonic of wilderness," the balm that soothes the soul and brings spiritual refreshment and rejuvenation. I have also learned that, like a sponge, wilderness has a limited absorption capacity. Its tolerance for human impact is finite; it isn't everything to everyone. To Muir, Yosemite was a temple as sacred as any consecrated by man. Only with constant care and vigilance on the part of all who use the wilderness can the intrinsic qualities and values of this temple remain intact.

This book will provide you a bridge to Yosemite's wilderness. It will not only help you plan a safe and pleasurable backcountry outing, but will sharpen your understanding of Yosemite's physical and biotic character and the processes, both natural and cultural, that have shaped it and govern it today.

Primarily, though, this book is a hiking guide that will heighten your wilderness I.Q. and bring your experience in Yosemite into sharper focus. Perhaps at least one of these mountain trails will take you "home."

Leslie P. Arnberger
Superintendent
Yosemite National Park, 1974–1979

Part One

Introductory Chapters

Chapter 1

Introduction

Yosemite National Park certainly is one of the world's finest parks, and in the second half of the 20th Century it achieved international recognition. On any given day there may be visitors from dozens of countries, perhaps most of these arriving in tour buses. Yet for most out-of-state visitors, Yosemite may be but one scenic attraction among many on their list, and consequently they spend little time in the Park. They may visit only Yosemite Valley and Glacier Point, or, if their schedule permits, they may head up the scenic Tioga Road to Tuolumne Meadows and exit the Park at Tioga Pass.

This Yosemite guide is primarily a *hiking* guide, but if you plan to visit the Park for only one day, you'll hardly have time to get out of your vehicle. Given only one day, you can best sample Yosemite's greatness by driving across it. Starting in Oakhurst or Fish Camp with a full tank of fuel, first drive north up Highway 41 to the entrance station, head up to the Mariposa Grove (consider taking a free shuttle from Wawona), and then take a tram tour past the giant sequoias. Next, continue north from Wawona to the Glacier Point Road, which you take east up to Washburn and Glacier points. Backtrack to the main road and descend to Yosemite Valley. Park at the Bridalveil Fall lot and walk up the short path toward that fall (start of Hike 62). Then drive through the Valley and walk to the base of Lower Yosemite Fall (end of Hike 64). Leave the Valley, drive up to Crane Flat, then start up the Tioga Road. If the Mariposa Grove was too crowded and you passed it up, then just up the road branch left into a parking area and make a one-mile descent into the Tuolumne Grove of Big Trees, then return. Drive up into a red-fir forest, traverse the Yosemite Creek drainage, and then stop at Olmsted Point, recognized by the tourists and tour buses. It is worth it. Next, descend to nearby Tenaya Lake, seen from the point, and perhaps stop along it to savor its setting as well as to watch climbers ascend various routes on an adjacent domelike ridge. A few minutes beyond the lake, you enter Tuolumne Meadows, and if you have two-hours' time and considerable energy, make the unforgettable ascent to at least Dog Dome, if not to slightly higher Lembert Dome (both in Hike 45). Conclude your day by exiting via Tioga Pass, which in late afternoon or evening can have a backdrop of dramatic clouds.

Because this book's topographic map is also available separately, it contains all pertinent day-hiking and backpacking information. (In particular, all should be aware of disease-producing microorganisms—*Giardia lamblia*—see "Drinking Water"

Left: Half Dome and Yosemite Valley, viewed from Eagle Peak, Hike 69

1

on the back side of the book's topographic map.) Similar information exists in this chapter, as well as in the introduction to every hiking chapter. Hopefully, they will agree, although because the book and map have independent press runs, updates do not occur simultaneously. Therefore, if you find a discrepancy, go with the product (book or map) which has the more recent copyright date.

Purpose of This Book

Many people return to Yosemite time and time again to experience the appeal of its multifaceted landscape. For these hikers in particular, this book was written. Not being an equestrian, I use the term "hikers," but hopefully equestrians will find my book equally useful. I hope all users will benefit from this book in at least three ways. First, this book describes every single trail in Yosemite that is worth taking, and it also describes many trails just outside the Park. With this information, arranged in 100 hikes, you can leisurely *plan* your hike. Table 1, at the end of this chapter, will aid you in planning your hike, for with it you can see at a glance the basic characteristics of each hike. When you see a hike that matches your desires—say, a 2-day hike that is 10-15 miles long—turn to that hike and read its description. Often, photos included in the hike will give you a feel for the scenery.

Second, this book is a *guide*. Yosemite's trails are adequately signed, but if you are caught in a blizzard or are hiking a largely snow-covered trail, then directions may be important. In addition, there are a few places where a trail may not be obvious, and the text identifies these. This book also gives you advice you won't find on signs, such as avalanche dangers, significant bear problems, difficult fords, and potentially dangerous sections of trails.

Third, by stressing natural history, this book aims at increasing your *awareness, understanding, and appreciation* of the landscape you traverse. One avid hiker, Keith Schiller, decided to hike every trail in a previous edition, bringing dozens of friends and fellow Yosemite lovers with him to the Park. By the time he was nearing completion he became alarmed at deteriorating conditions in the backcountry, and resolved to help preserve Yosemite. He founded the East Bay Chapter of the Yosemite Fund. His friends became the initial nucleus for this all-volunteer organization, which by 1992 had raised approximately

$200,000 for the restoration of the Happy Isles area in Yosemite Valley. More importantly, in that year he conceived of, and saw established, the Yosemite license fund, which has raised considerably more, over 3 million dollars by the close of the century. (If you see a van with a YOSE GEO license plate, it's mine.)

While I don't expect every hiker or equestrian to become as motivated as Schiller, I nevertheless hope that they will gain some appreciation for the Park. Too many veteran hikers come to the High Sierra year after year and never extend their natural-history knowledge past the identification of a few prominent tree species. However, the more you know about the environment, the more you will appreciate, protect, and defend it. And you will develop a better feeling for man's role in it. For these reasons, natural history is stressed in this book's 100 hikes. In addition to trailside nature notes, this book goes into considerable detail about geology (Chapter 2), biology (Chapter 3), and history (Chapter 4). The remainder of this Chapter 1 offers information you'll need to make your Yosemite visit more rewarding.

On the Web

If you have access to the Internet, you might check it for various information on the Park, including road conditions, weather conditions, the Yosemite Association, the Yosemite Fund, and accommodations both in the Park and in surrounding areas. Several web sites contain various information, but the only site you may need, since from it you can access others, is: www.nps.gov/yose/.

Accommodations

Many visitors who stay overnight in the Yosemite area would like to do so in campgrounds, which are shown on this book's topographic map. Reservations are required for sites in Yosemite Valley's North, Upper, and Lower Pines campgrounds. Your chance of getting one of the 418 sites is slim, even when you phone early. The Valley also has Sunnyside Walk-in Campground, on a first-come, first-served basis. Your chance of getting one of its 35 sites is essentially nil. Other Park campgrounds requiring reservations are Crane Flat, Wawona (reservations May-September), Hodgdon Meadow (reservations May-September), and half the sites of Tuolumne Meadows. The Park's five other campgrounds, which are smaller and are open only in the summer season, are on a first-come, first-served basis. These are Bridalveil Creek, along the Glacier Point Road, and, from west to east on or near the Tioga Road, Tamarack Flat, White Wolf, Yosemite Creek, and Porcupine Flat campgrounds.

To make reservations, phone the National Park Reservation System at 800/436-7275 (7 A.M.-7 P.M. Pacific Standard Time) as early as possible within the given time frame. You can reserve up to five months in advance. For example, if you wanted to camp between June 15th and July 14th, you could reserve as soon as February 15th; between July 15th and August 14th, as soon as March 15th; between August 15th and September 14th, as soon as April 15th; etc. You can also make reservations online at: reservations.nps.gov. If you don't have a reservation, then try to show up at a campground by 10 A.M., the checkout time.

Other visitors to Yosemite National Park would like to stay at a hotel, lodge, or camp operated by Yosemite Concession Services. In Yosemite Valley these are the Ahwahnee Hotel, Yosemite Lodge, and Curry Village. The Ahwahnee Hotel, a world class hotel, charges fairly high prices (but nevertheless worth it!). Yosemite Lodge has comfortable rooms and is moderately priced. Economically priced Curry Village has rooms, cabins, tent cabins, and camping at its nearby Housekeeping Camp (concrete-walled, tarp-covered campsites), but most of its accommodations lack private baths. Yosemite Concession Services also operates the Wawona Hotel, near the Park's south border. This historic complex, which is open weekends only from after Christmas until early spring and daily for the rest of the year, is a cut above Yosemite Lodge in both ambiance and price. The company also manages spartan White Wolf and Tuolumne Meadow lodges, both open only during the summer season. White Wolf Lodge is about a mile off the Tioga Road, and is halfway between Tuolumne Meadows and Yosemite Valley. Tuolumne Lodge is near the east end of the meadows.

As with the Park's campgrounds, you ought to make a reservation as soon as possible, especially for stays between the Memorial Day and Labor Day weekends. To make reservations, which you can do *up to one year and one day* in advance, use the Internet at www.yosemitepark.com/lodging/, or phone 559/252-4848 (8 A.M.–5 P.M., seven days a week), or write to Central Reservations, Yosemite Concession Services, 5410 East Home Avenue, Fresno, CA 93727. The company also manages the backcountry High Sierra Camps. These are so popular that a lottery is held each December to determine the lucky relative few for the following summer. To enter the lottery, contact Yosemite Concession Services between September 1st and November 15th.

In addition to accommodations provided by Yosemite Concession Services, you can also lodge at two other locations. The first is The Redwoods, located in a private inholding in the Wawona area. It is composed of over 100 units, from one-bedroom cabins up to spacious six-bedroom homes, with prices to match. For reservations, write to The Redwoods, 8038 Chilnualna Falls Road, Wawona, CA 95389, phone 209/375-6666, or contact their website at www.redwoodsinyosemite.com. The second is Yosemite West, also on private land, but located just outside the Park, and it is reached from a signed road starting just south of the Glacier Point Road's junction with the Wawona Road. It too has a range of sizes (with matching prices), from studios, condos, cabins, and cottages up to spacious homes. For reservations, write to Yosemite West Reservations Office, P.O. Box 507, Bass Lake, CA 93604, phone 559/642-2211, or contact their website at www.yosemitewestreservations.com. From Yosemite West you can reach three popular destinations in under ½ hour: Yosemite Valley, Glacier Point, and Wawona.

Outside the Park there are private campgrounds and Forest Service campgrounds, plus dozens of motels, lodges, and bed-and-breakfasts—far too many to mention here. Especially if you are traveling from out of state, you likely will not find accommodations within the Park but instead will have to settle for a room in one of the Park's satellite towns—such as Sonora, Groveland, Mariposa,

El Portal, Oakhurst, Fish Camp, Bass Lake, Lee Vining, or Bridgeport—or for a room in one of a number of establishments along Highways 41, 120, 140, and 395. Mammoth Lakes, just southeast of the Yosemite area, is a vacationland unto itself, a bustling Lake Tahoe *sans* the lake and casinos. You can usually find all kinds of accommodations and services in and about this small city, plus lots of lakes, scenery, and trails nearby. On the Internet, check out www.yosemite.com for accommodations and services outside the Park.

Yosemite Activities Other Than Hiking

Horseback Rides: Just because this book is mainly a guide to Yosemite's trails doesn't mean that you have to hike to enjoy them; you can also ride horses along most of them. Weather permitting, from spring through fall you can ride horses in Yosemite Valley and Wawona, and in summer up in Tuolumne Meadows. In addition, there are pack stations located outside the Park, and these offer backpack trips into the Park and adjacent wildernesses.

Fishing: Originally, trout were native only to the Merced and Tuolumne rivers below their mid-elevation cascades. The vast majority of Yosemite's streams and virtually all its lakes were barren. Up to 1972 about 160 of the Park's lakes were regularly stocked with rainbow and brook trout, and, to a lesser extent, with brown, golden, and cutthroat trout. But in the late 1970s the Park Service greatly reduced the number of lakes to be stocked, then in 1991 completely stopped stocking them. Hence some of the once-stocked lakes may be barren. Certainly there will be fewer trout to catch. As one might expect, lakes close to Highway 120 and lakes along popular trails attract the most anglers, so you might do better to select a more remote lake or stream to fish in. However, avoid lakes at the higher elevations, such as those over 9000 feet. In Yosemite Valley, you can only do catch-and-release for the native rainbow trout, using only artificial lures or flies with barbless hooks. Bait is prohibited. Check the Park's latest edition of the *Yosemite Guide*, available at entrance stations, for more information. If you do fish, be sure you have a California fishing license if you are 16 or older, which can be bought in Yosemite Valley or in Tuolumne Meadows as well as in towns en route to the Park.

Swimming and Rafting: Many hikers swim in Yosemite's lakes, the warmer of which get up into the high 60s by midsummer. You can also swim in the Merced River through Yosemite Valley. Although the water temperature is cool, the often hot afternoon air temperatures are great for warming up afterward. There are a number of frequented river pools, ranging from lower Tenaya Creek in the east part of the Valley to the Cascades Picnic Area in the west part. During the summer, water temperatures tend to be in the low 60s at the east part and in the mid 60s at the west part. By driving out of the Park and down past El Portal, you may spot some of the Merced River's roadside pools, which can warm up into the 70s. Also check out the South Fork Merced River. There are some rockbound pools located just up from the river's covered bridge, as well as in spots upriver, while some are located beside and downriver from stretched-out Wawona Campground. In addition, Yosemite Lodge and Curry Village each have a large swimming pool open to the public.

If you want to raft, you must wear a life-vest, and you raft at your own risk. (Ironically, if you swim, which is more dangerous, you don't need one.) During late spring and early

Fishing at Lukens Lake, Hikes 23 and 24

Cooling off in Tenaya Creek

Boating: Nonmotorized boats are allowed in Tenaya Lake, whose strong afternoon winds are great for sailing. Kayakers and canoeists will favor the morning. Since the lake lacks a launching ramp, the size of the boat is limited to whatever you and your friends can carry to the lake's shore.

Bicycling: In the central and eastern parts of Yosemite Valley there are more than 12 miles of paved bike paths. Early in the third millennium there should be several more miles, these in the western part, which then will allow bicyclists to enjoy the Valley's scenery, from El Capitan east to Happy Isles and Mirror Meadow. You can rent bikes at both Yosemite Lodge and Curry Village. However, *rented* bikes are not allowed on the stretch of paved path up to Mirror Meadow.

Rock Climbing: Yosemite Valley is, in my biased opinion as a former Valley climber, the rock-climbing capital of the world. It offers over a thousand drug-free ways to get high. For the uninitiated or the novice climber, Yosemite Mountaineering School and Guide Service offers safe, affordable introductory lessons. For the more-advanced climber, it offers qualified guides. However, for the very difficult climbs (5.10 and above) the rate can be

summer high runoff, rafting on the Merced River or South Fork Merced River is prohibited (as is, wisely, swimming). Later on, drifting on an air mattress is relatively safe from Clark Bridge down to El Capitan Bridge. Rafting, however, is limited to a shorter stretch from Stoneman Bridge, just north of Curry Village, west to Sentinel Beach, opposite Leidig Meadow. The drawback of this activity is that once you've gone downstream, you have to get back to your starting point. However, if you park your vehicle at the west end of the Yosemite Lodge parking lot (don't use guests' spaces), you can take a shuttle bus upriver to the Clark Bridge (by the Pines Campgrounds), then inflate your raft or air mattress and make the leisurely 3 ½ -mile cruise down to the broad bridge below Yosemite Lodge. This is the seventh bridge beyond the Clark Bridge. In 1991 the Park Service stopped removing trees from the Merced River. Consequently, trees now obstruct a rafter's course. These snags, while upsetting to some rafters, increase the diversity of river habitats, which benefits both birds and trout.

Tenaya Lake water sports

On La Escuela, base of El Capitan

tory, photography, art, writing, day hiking, and backpacking. Some courses involve little exercise, others a lot, and some are family-oriented. For course information, contact the Yosemite Association at P.O. Box 230, El Portal, CA 95318, or phone it at 209/379-2321, or visit its web site at http://www.yosemite.org.

Other Activities: Many scheduled activities, such as nature walks and slide shows, are held each week. Consult the *Yosemite Guide,* a seasonal newspaper given to you at the Park entrances, or else check at Yosemite Valley Visitor Center, Tuolumne Meadows Visitor Center, Big Oak Flat Information Station, or Wawona Information Station.

With so many activities available in Yosemite National Park, it is unfortunate that most visitors don't stay longer to appreciate them. The Park is certainly large and varied. In Chapter 2, which is essentially about the Park's geology, we'll see just how complex its landscape can be. The Park's biology, discussed in Chapter 3, is even more intricate. Finally, every area has a history, and Yosemite's is presented in Chapter 4. Chapters 5-12, the remainder of your guidebook, make up Part Two: One Hundred Hikes.

hundreds of dollars per day. During the summer, the climbing service operates out of Tuolumne Meadows, while off-season it operates out of Curry Village in Yosemite Valley. I do not recommend rock climbing from about mid-November through mid-February due to stormy weather, ice-cold rock, and increased rockfall hazard.

Skiing: Both downhill and cross-country skiing are popular at Badger Pass, just off the Glacier Point Road. Lessons and rental equipment are available. The season is brief, at best from about Thanksgiving to early April. Cross-country skiing also is popular in Yosemite Valley, whose floor is typically snow-covered during January and early February. One can rent equipment in the Valley. Other cross-country ski areas with longer-lasting snow are Crane Flat and the Mariposa Grove.

Yosemite Association Field Seminars: The Yosemite Association offers a diverse array of courses from about February through October, but particularly during the summer season. There are courses in astronomy, geology, botany, zoology (especially birding), his-

Chapter 2
Evolution of the Yosemite Landscape

Padre Pedro Font, on the second Anza expedition, in April 1776, saw a distant range to the east, as other Spaniards had, but he was the first to give it a name: Sierra Nevada, or Snowy Range. John Muir would see the range almost a century later, in April 1868, but did not write about it until 1894, in his first book, *The Mountains of California*. In it he questioned the range's name, saying:

> *... after ten years spent in the heart of it, rejoicing and wondering, bathing in its glorious floods of light, seeing the sunbursts of morning among the icy peaks, the noonday radiance on the trees and rocks and snow, the flush of the alpenglow, and a thousand dashing waterfalls with their marvelous abundance of irised spray, it still seems to me above all others the Range of Light, the most divinely beautiful of all the mountain-chains I have ever seen.*

Although he doesn't explicitly say so, Muir could have added that the pastel colors of the High Sierra's granitic bedrock—generally light gray but almost creamy in places—made it more luminous than the dark, volcanic Cascade Range, the variegated, geologically complex Rocky Mountains, or the metamorphic, heavily vegetated Appalachian Mountains. But the high country of Yosemite and the rest of the High Sierra would not be very luminous if the overlying rocks intruded by molten "granite" had not been removed, if the volcanic rocks that blanket the northern Sierra had buried the entire range, and if glaciers had not developed on numerous occasions to remove the soil and create vast tracts of barren lands. If its complex geologic history had taken a different course, the Sierra Nevada might not have gotten its three national parks—Yosemite, Sequoia, and Kings. All three were set aside because of their groves of giant sequoias and because of their glaciated high country. Additionally, Yosemite National Park was set aside because of its renowned Yosemite Valley, arguably the world's most spectacular, which owes its origin not to special geologic processes, but rather to a unique pattern of major, generally vertical fracture planes in its granitic rock.

Today's masterpiece was long in the making, created over a few hundred million years. How was it produced? The modern answer is very different from that which we geoscientists (geologists, geographers, etc.) believed as recently as the early 1990s. Before then, most of us thought that the range was first raised to great heights during the Nevadan orogeny, which presumably lasted from about 160 to 155 million years ago. After that a several-mile thickness of various rocks was eroded by streams and rivers over tens of millions of years to greatly reduce the height of the range and to expose the formerly subsurface granitic rock. Then in the last 500,000 to 50,000,000 years—for lack of definitive evidence, geoscientists could not decide—the range was raised again to great heights. Finally, in concert with this postulated uplift, rivers steepened their gradients and so were able to erode very effectively downward, creating deep canyons, which in turn were made considerably deeper, more broad-floored, and steeper-sided through massive erosion by ensuing glaciers. In Yosemite Valley, a large, deep lake presumably formed after the last glacier retreated.

Nothing in this account is true, as I document in my book, *The Geomorphic Evolution of the Yosemite Valley and Sierra Nevada Landscapes: Solving the Riddles in the Rocks* (see "Recommended Reading and Source Materials"). This *"Riddles"* presents the history of geological research in the range as well as presents evidence of uplift and glaciation. It does not address the range's complicated history before about 80 million years ago. That has been largely revealed by the work of other geoscientists in the 1980s and '90s, working not only in the Sierra Nevada, but also around the world, where analogs of the early Sierra Nevada have been found.

Some of the range's relevant uplift and glacial evidence lies in Yosemite National Park, and where each is encountered along some of the hiking routes in this guidebook, I identify and describe it. For example, like the postulated-but-imaginary trans-Sierran river canyon at Deadman Pass, a few miles southeast of the Park, there is another equally imaginary river canyon near Rancheria Mountain, and I discuss it in Hike 14.

The Present as a Key to the Past

We can examine what geological processes are occurring today and apply them to the past. Along most of California, the San Andreas fault is the approximate boundary between the Pacific plate, on the west, and the North American plate, on the east. This primary fault is one of several nearly parallel major faults of the San Andreas fault *system.* Movement on these major faults is right-lateral—the block of crust on the west side of each fault moves north with respect to the block of crust on the east side. (In *right-lateral* faulting, the land on one side of the fault moves during an earthquake to the right with respect to an observer on the other side. It makes no difference which side of the fault the observer is on.) Currently the San Andreas fault exhibits the most movement, but in the past other faults were more active, and in the future still other faults probably will become more active.

About 5 million years ago, the direction of the Pacific plate's motion began to change, so that instead of its east edge sliding smoothly north past the west edge of the

North American plate, the east edge was increasingly compressed against it. The continental crust riding on the two plates, being of relatively low density, could not sink out of the way, so the compressive forces caused uplift, and the Coast Ranges were born. Because the major faults aren't perfectly parallel, irregularities have arisen. Where parallel faults tend to converge, as through west-central California, a block of submerged continental crust was raised thousands of feet above sea level to create the Santa Lucia Range, among others. But to the north, where parallel faults tend to diverge, a lowland developed, the San Francisco Bay. Notice that in the same fault system, opposite events can occur at the same time—compressional uplift here, extensional subsidence there. When right-lateral or left-lateral faulting is associated with compression and extension, the resulting motion is called, respectively, *transpression* and *transtension*. These motions occurred in the early Sierra Nevada, just as they do in the Coast Ranges today.

The Santa Lucia Range, growing in elevation above the Pacific Ocean, may one day be thrust east across the Central Valley, initiating another Sierran mountain-building episode

If the change in the direction of the Pacific plate's motion continues, the Coast Ranges will grow to rival the Sierra Nevada in only a few million years. Eventually the angle between the two plates may increase to the point that the Coast Ranges will be thrust across the Central Valley, obliterating it. If so, they will be compressed against the western Sierra Nevada, and this compression will cause an *orogeny*, or mountain-building episode. During it, the Coast Ranges will become attached, or *accreted*, to the range, which then will become a bit wider. This accreted belt of continental crust will be similar to previously accreted belts, each called a *terrane*—a usually complex, fault-bounded

IGNEOUS ROCKS

generally increasing oxides of silicon, sodium, and potassium	**Volcanic Rocks**		**Plutonic Rocks**	*generally increasing oxides of magnesium, iron and calcium; also, increasing melting point and increasing density*
	rhyolite	*approximately equals*	granite	
	rhyodacite	*approximately equals*	quartz monzonite	
	dacite	*approximately equals*	granodiorite	
	andesite	*approximately equals*	diorite	
	basalt	*approximately equals*	gabbro	

geologic unit (as opposed to a terrain—a geographical area). The compression that leads to accretion also causes a transformation in a terrane's rocks through increased heat and pressure, and through the movement of super-hot fluids. This compression is on a grand scale, resulting in *regional metamorphism*. Sedimentary rocks are metamorphosed to *metasediments*, volcanic rocks to *metavolcanics*.

While the continental crust can't sink, the denser oceanic crust as well as the dense, upper-mantle rock underlying both crusts can, and so an oceanic plate will dive under a continental plate, a process called *subduction*. With increasing pressure and depth, the diving plate will begin to undergo partial melting, and the melt, or *magma*, being of relatively low density, will ascend through the continental crust. As it ascends through preexisting rock of the upper crust, it alters the existing crustal rocks. This alteration is called *contact metamorphism*, since in these rocks it is greatest near the contact with the magma. In the Sierra, older rocks show signs of being metamorphosed two or more times. Magma that solidifies beneath the surface forms *plutonic* rock, and a body of this rock is called a *pluton*. In Sierra Nevada lands, most of this rock is light-gray *granitic* rock.

If magma reaches the surface as eruptions of ash or lava, it becomes *volcanic* rock. Voluminous eruptions can create a mountain range, such as the Cascade Range of Washington, Oregon, and northern California. That range is largely the result of an oceanic plate diving eastward beneath the Pacific Northwest. Together, volcanic and plutonic rocks are classified as *igneous* rocks, which are any that have solidified from a molten mass. The common types of igneous rocks are listed in the accompanying table.

Oldest Rocks

For decades a signed Highway 140 "oldest rocks" geologic exhibit stood along the east base of Ferguson Ridge about 10 road miles west of El Portal. However, 1980s research indicates that these rocks are a mere 245 million years old, plus or minus a few million years. The oldest rocks in the Park's vicinity are more than twice as old, having been deposited as sandy sediments around the start of the Paleozoic era (about 540 million years

ago). These quartz-rich sandstones later were metamorphosed to *quartzites*, which today straddle the Park's lightly visited northern-boundary lands. You can see them between Grace Meadow and adjacent Bigelow Peak within the Park, and between the peak and adjacent Bigelow Lake, just over the boundary in Emigrant Wilderness. Other ancient rocks, nearly as old, exist here in the Snow Lake pendant, and also about 3 miles to the southwest, in the Sachse Monument pendant, composed of small remnants between that summit and Lower Twin Lake.

A *pendant* is by definition a suspended object, which neither of these two is—nor are the several others located along the Park's periphery. Nevertheless the inappropriate term has stuck. There are a number of pendants in the range, and each is a part of a once quite extensive, but now mostly eroded away, terrane.

The oldest rocks of the Snow Lake and Sachse Monument pendants originally were sediments deposited on the ocean's floor off North America's west coast some 500+ million years ago. In addition to these sediments there are considerably younger ones, which like those at Highway 140's geologic exhibit are about 245 million years old. Between these are more than 250 million years of missing sediments. There are two other Park-borderland pendants with a similar age span, but they contain several units or formations of intermediate age. These are the Saddlebag Lake pendant, which extends north from Tioga Pass, and the northern Ritter Range pendant, which extends south from it. Their rocks have weathered to earth tones, which locally add color to our area's crest lands. Additionally, the mineral-rich soil they produce results in more plant species and in greater numbers than in adjacent granitic soil.

The Antler and Sonoma Orogenies

In the vicinity of Yosemite National Park, the early geologic record is too incomplete to permit a reconstruction. However, evidence elsewhere makes a reconstruction possible, and it indicates that in the Sierra, volcanism began about 420 million years ago (and has continued on and off until geologically recent time). Before the creation of the Sierra Nevada range proper, there were several periods of *arc volcanism*, eruptions produced by a curved line of volcanoes, such as Alaska's Aleutian Islands or the Ryukyu Islands between Japan and Taiwan. Just as a *back-arc basin*—the shallow South China Sea—separates that chain of volcanic islands from the coast of China, a similar basin separated a chain of volcanic islands in the vicinity of the Sierra Nevada from the coast of North America, located in today's Nevada. After initial sputtering, volcanoes began to erupt in earnest around 400 million years ago and did so until the Antler orogeny, which occurred about 365 to 350 million years ago. In the vicinity of today's range, existing sediments were metamorphosed as the chain of volcanic islands was thrust eastward, compressing, heating, and disrupting them.

After the Antler orogeny, which would have raised the compressed lands, they underwent extension, which caused them to sink and to become buried under accumulating marine sediments. After tens of millions of years the sea retreated and the upper marine sediments were eroded away through uplift, leaving about a 50-million-year gap in the geologic record. (The Santa Lucia Range, mentioned earlier, had a similar, if considerably more recent, uplift-extension-subsidence-uplift history.) Eventually, land in our area formed once again with a second round of arc volcanism, which began about 260 million years ago. This lasted at least until the Sonoma orogeny, which occurred from about 250 to 240 million years ago, around the time the Paleozoic era gave way to the Mesozoic era. As before, the orogeny was due to a chain of volcanic islands being thrust eastward.

During each orogeny North America proper grew slightly westward as masses of crustal rocks were compressed and metamorphosed and then became accreted terranes. Probably included among them are ones that later would be reduced to the Snow Lake, Sachse Monument, Saddlebag Lake, and northern Ritter Range pendants. Terranes do not necessarily stay in place; today in California (and elsewhere), some are on the move, riding passively atop the earth's plates (their motions are called *plate tectonics*). The terranes in today's Sierra Nevada became fixed because magma rose beneath them, solidifying to form a very stable basement composed of one or more plutons. The earliest

surviving plutons in the Sierra Nevada are located in its southern part. They are about 240 million years old and formed as the Sonoma orogeny was waning. The earliest ones in the Yosemite area are about 210 million years old, and are found east of the crest, close to their relatively contemporaneous volcanic rocks. You'll see these granitic rocks above the north shore of Lundy Lake, in middle Lee Vining Canyon near its Warren Fork, and at Kidney and Lower Sardine lakes.

The Nevadan Orogeny

For a third time the direction of motion of the oceanic plate became increasingly more nearly perpendicular to the North American plate, and another major compressional period began. This was the Nevadan orogeny, named after the Sierra Nevada, where its record is best preserved. Like earlier orogenies, this one metamorphosed the area's previously existing rocks, including those in today's pendants. The orogeny was quite protracted. Compression and uplift may have begun by 176 million years ago, peaked from 163 to 152 million years ago, and then continued in their waning stages until about 140 million years ago, if not longer.

During this orogeny, magma mostly intruded an assemblage of older rocks lying west of the Park, accreting them to western North America. These lands have been called the Foothills belt and the Foothills terrane, but research in the 1980s and '90s, particularly by David Jones of the US Geological Survey, suggests that this belt is composed of at least five terranes. Within the Park, plutonism was minimal. Only one Nevadan-orogeny pluton is known, a small one straddling the Park's northern boundary immediately west of Bigelow Peak. It is composed mostly of diorite and gabbro, both dark-gray rocks. During the orogeny's maximum, the Sierra Nevada was a minor length of a major range, a cordillera, which extended along the western edge of both North America and South America. If a new view of Sierran uplift is correct—one that involves detachment faulting—then the range's lands should have been higher than they are today. To discuss detachment faulting, we first have to elaborate on continental crust and how it reacts to stress.

Extension, Plutonism, and Volcanism

Each of the assortment of plates that comprises the outer layer of our planet is composed of crust atop underlying upper mantle. The crust can be either thin oceanic crust, thick continental, or both. The continental crust is thick enough so that about 6+ miles down the heat and pressure are sufficient to cause it to deform. The lower crust, which in the Yosemite area extends to a depth of about 25 miles, can slowly flow, up to several inches per year (about as fast as your fingernails grow). The crustal flow can be due either to flow in the underlying upper mantle or to flow deeper within the earth. The upper crust (the top 6+ miles), being brittle, cannot flow, and its base can only accommodate so much strain in response to underlying stresses before it breaks. A break, or *fault*, then grows upward from the base of the upper crust, generating an earthquake in the process. Where extension has been extreme, such as in the Great Basin, so much stress can develop that the base of the upper crust detaches from the top of the lower crust. This fairly horizontal breaking apart between the upper and lower crust is called a detachment, and the movement along it is detachment faulting. As we will soon see, this faulting played a very important part in the formation of today's Sierra Nevada.

Major changes were needed to create today's largely granitic range, and these were accomplished in part when the major compression that brought about the Nevadan orogeny gave way to major extension. Faults rifted the upper crust apart, providing space for ascending magma. Extension and plutonism went hand in hand, and from about 115 to 85 million years ago, plutonism occurred on an unprecedented scale. At first plutonism occurred in a north-south belt from north of the Park's northwest corner southward along its western boundary and beyond it to the edge of today's San Joaquin Valley. Over time the locus of magma generation migrated episodically eastward across the ancestral Sierra Nevada, perhaps in response to a shallowing angle of an east-diving oceanic plate. Consequently, granitic rocks east of the boundary, say in the upper part of the Merced Gorge and the west half of Yosemite Valley, are about 105 to 100 million years old. Those in its east

half are about 100 to 90 million years old, while those farther east, say around Tuolumne Meadows, are about 90 to 85 million years old.

The actual patterns of the spatial distribution and composition of plutons are complex. Some magma intruded older plutons, resulting in younger plutons partly displacing them. And some magma, working upward over millions of years, intruded and displaced outward newly solidified magma. This resulted in a nested, composite pluton called an intrusive suite, whose composition of magma has evolved over time. The largest one in our area, about 450 square miles, is the Tuolumne intrusive suite, which today is exposed over most of the eastern third of the Park, but also includes the eastern part of Yosemite Valley, Tenaya Canyon, Little Yosemite Valley, and most of the Illilouette Creek drainage. Its plutonism began about 91 million years ago and continued in surges until about 86 million years ago, and the magma's composition evolved toward increasing amounts of lighter-colored minerals (quartz and alkali feldspar).

During the 30-million-year period of abundant plutonism, volcanism locally dominated when extension and plutonism were minimal. Towering stratovolcanoes such as today's Mts. Shasta, Hood, and Rainier likely stood at various times above the range's core. During the last surge of magma in the Tuolumne intrusive suite, one large volcano rose high above what is now Johnson Peak, just south of Tuolumne Meadows. However, a more-impressive volcano straddled the Park's southeast border about 100 million years ago, centered on the Minarets caldera. A *caldera* is a large, more-or-less circular basin at the center of a large volcano. The Minarets caldera was giant, about 18 miles across from near Chiquito Creek northeast to Thousand Island Lake, and 14 miles across from near the San Joaquin River northwest to Washburn Lake. Over its existence this eruptive center produced an estimated 360 cubic miles of ash and lava. This volume is enough to bury the San Francisco Bay metropolitan area under about 1100 feet of deposits, the Los Angeles-Orange counties metropolitan areas (excluding the San Fernando Valley) under about 1700 feet, or the San Diego metropolitan area under about 6600 feet!

Magmatism waned on in the Sierra Nevada until about 80 million years ago, when the oceanic plate greatly increased its velocity and shallowed its angle of diving. The result of these changes was that the locus of magma generation shifted far east of the range, and it ultimately caused a mountain-building episode in the Rocky Mountains, the Laramide orogeny. The Sierra Nevada now had a core composed of dozens of generally light-gray plutons. These, however, typically lay several miles beneath a largely volcanic landscape—definitely not the Range of Light. More change was in order.

Sierra Nevada Uplift

In 1990, after four months of field work examining evidence of past glaciers in the Stanislaus River drainage, I realized that the giant glaciers there—as large as the ones in Yosemite Valley—had barely eroded the granitic landscape. Along the North Fork Stanislaus River, past glaciers had cut, at best, a narrow stream channel just a mere 30 feet below the base of a remnant of a 23-million-year-old rhyolite deposit. This observation conflicted with the widely held view that glaciers in the Sierra Nevada (and elsewhere around the world) had performed tremendous erosion. Furthermore, this deposit and other old, dated deposits just

above the floors of other canyons suggested that they had been almost as deep as they are today. For example, just above Hetch Hetchy Reservoir about ¼ mile west of Rancheria Falls, there is a small deposit, left here 9½ million years ago, at 4500 feet elevation. These indicate that the ancient Tuolumne River canyon was already about 3000 feet deep. But because these remnants lie on slopes, they do not represent the ancient canyon's floor, only its lower slopes. The floor would have been lower, and the ancient canyon would have been almost as deep as the modern one. In short, the range's major canyons, including the Merced River's Yosemite Valley, have been deep for 20+ million years.

This conclusion posed a problem with regard to uplift. Over the last 20+ million years, geoscientists believed that the Sierra Nevada had been tilted westward, raising crest lands in our vicinity by about 11,000 feet. Because it was tilted as a rigid block, a point one fourth up from its base would have been raised one fourth this amount, or about 2750 feet; a point one-half up from its base would have been raised one half, or about 5500 feet; and so on. Today the canyon floors of the Tuolumne and Merced rivers at the halfway point are about

Small volcanic remnants about ¼ mile west of Rancheria Falls

2000 feet elevation. But since some 5500 feet of uplift supposedly has occurred at that point, the canyon floors initially must have been about 3500 below sea level—an impossibility. (Geoscientists got around this by assuming that over this period the canyons had been deepened by thousands of feet. There is no evidence to support this; all evidence indicates less than 100 feet. Indeed, this erroneous view of Sierran uplift originated as a miner's tale told California State Geological Survey members in 1862, a year before any of them had set foot in the range!)

In 1990, when I was reaching my conclusions, Peter Molnar of M.I.T. wrote an article. It proposed that in the last few million years the world's mountain ranges rose exponentially faster, which caused human brains to evolve exponentially larger. The article was a spoof, written because he was fed up with so many geoscientists asserting that their favorite mountain range had risen in Quaternary time (about the last two million years). The Sierra Nevada is no exception. As I document in my *"Riddles"* book, there have been many attempts to prove major uplift in the last few million years, and not one of them stands up to scrutiny. In that book I also offer three field methods—not artificial constructs—to quantify this uplift, and each indicates no measurable uplift for tens of millions of years.

The Quaternary-uplift/major glacial erosion myth of the world's glaciated ranges originated in the 1840s. "What started the Ice Age?" early geologists asked. The only answer available to them was that before glaciation the world's major ranges were low and their canyons were shallow, but then the ranges rose, creating glaciers and starting the Ice Age, and the glaciers over time deepened and widened the canyons. Plate tectonics was unknown back in the 1800s, and the answer lies with it: compression of continental crust leads to uplift and the creation of ranges. Because the ranges must have been low before this uplift, their canyons would have been shallow. Hence today's deep canyons must have been excavated first by invigorated mountain rivers and then perhaps even more by the ensuing glaciers.

Earlier I said that about 80 million years ago an oceanic plate greatly increased its velocity and shallowed its angle of diving, and that where extension is extreme the base of the upper crust will separate from the top of the lower crust along a detachment fault. As the oceanic plate beneath the Sierra Nevada greatly increased its velocity and shallowed its angle of diving, it would have imparted severe stresses on the crust. Through extension the lower crust would have thinned as it stretched laterally, and a detachment fault would have developed between the lower and upper crust. In perhaps only a few million years—this figure based on rates of detachment-fault movements elsewhere—the upper crust would have been removed from the Sierra Nevada, exposing mainly the upper parts of plutons but also some lower remnants of metamorphic terranes. Where did the range's upper crust go? I suggest that it was faulted west with respect to the lower crust, and then was transported northward as one or more terranes along a right-lateral fault system. We know that in the past other terranes originating south of California were transported on such faults to northern lands.

With the removal of the upper crust, the lower crust of the Sierran block would have risen, although not to its original height, which is why the pre-faulted range should have stood higher. The Sierran crustal block, supported by underlying mantle, is similar to a block of wood floating in water. This may float, say, about ½ inch above water, and if you saw off the part protruding above water, the block will rise, due to the removal of the weight of the upper ½ inch. However, it will rise less than ½ inch. An ice cube melting in water is another useful analog. Be aware that since the raised lower crust no longer had the weight of the upper crust upon it, it now experienced less pressures and lower temperatures and so became brittle, capable of fracture.

Conventional wisdom requires that Sierran uplift is greatest where the crust is thickest. Consequently, because elevations are greatest along the crest, the crust should be thickest beneath it and should thin westward. However, 1990s seismic studies show that the crust thickens westward, and in our vicinity it is thickest—about 25 miles—near the western boundary of Yosemite National Park. Therefore, by conventional wisdom, uplift should have been greatest there, producing the highest elevations near El Portal. In 1997 David Jones suggested that uplift actually was greater in the western part of the range than at the crest, about 10 miles versus 4. This conclusion is based on the mineralogy of granitic rocks exposed at the surface. Each mineral forms at certain pressures and temperatures, so by knowing the minerals now exposed at the surface, we can estimate the original depth at which they solidified. As I mentioned above, during the Nevadan orogeny the Sierra Nevada was part of a much longer range. Two parts of it were what are now southern California's Transverse Ranges and Peninsular Ranges, the latter extending south to the tip of Baja California. Mineralogical studies in them show that they had uplifts of similar timing and magnitudes to what we now envisage for the Sierra Nevada.

Origin of a Modern Sierra Nevada

Uplift of the lower crust in response to removal of the upper crust created a range that resembled today's, one of a similar size and of similar elevations. Uplift also created the Sierra's crest and therefore the valleys east of it. The foremost ones are, from north to south, the Truckee-Lake Tahoe basin (no lake until about 2 ¼ million years ago), Mono Basin, and Owens Valley. These three (and others) have been considered youthful because faulting and volcanism have occurred in each in the last few million years. However, 1990s mapping and dating of Owens Valley faults demonstrated that some of the faults are extremely old—Mesozoic in age—active when the ancient Sierra Nevada was growing through terrane accretion. Additional evidence of the valley's antiquity comes from measuring how fast its granitic bedrock is weathering, which in the Alabama Hills, below Mt. Whitney, is about 7 feet per million years. If the Owens Valley began to form only 3 to 4 million years ago (the commonly cited dates), then only 21 to 28 feet of weathering has occurred along the resistant ridges that today descend thousands of feet from the Sierra crest. These ridges have changed very little in this period, so back then the valley already was very deep.

The extensional forces that led to the birth of the modern Sierra Nevada and its east-side basins also fractured the range's recently raised bedrock. It was about then, some 80 million years ago, that the range's modern rivers originated on the newly created surface, cutting into what was once lower crust and hav-

ing their courses dictated in part by recently formed fractures, or *joints*. These also dictated the courses of some tributaries, particularly north of the Tuolumne River, where linear canyons are the rule, not the exception.

The composition of bedrock can also influence the development of a landscape. For example, if Yosemite Valley had been carved in diorite instead of granodiorite and granite, it likely wouldn't be part of a national park today (and the Sierra Nevada wouldn't be "the Range of Light"). Diorite does not form massive cliffs, and where it forms summits, they tend to be low hills, such as Ackerson Mountain, south of Camp Mather, along the road to Hetch Hetchy. Diorite also does not form impressive domes such as Mt. Starr King, North Dome, and Half Dome.

Joints are more important than the composition of bedrock, and good evidence for this is in western Yosemite Valley and the adjacent upper Merced Gorge. In this area are the Rockslides, which are a veneer of talus derived through rockfall from minor, upper diorite cliffs to cover minor, lower ones. Diorite here has fractured into many small pieces and has weathered much more readily than does the more-massive granite. However, the situation is more complicated than that. In actuality only the western part of the cliffs above the Rockslides is diorite, the eastern part is granite, the same bedrock that makes up El Capitan—one of the world's most resistant monoliths—and also the part of the upper Merced Gorge west of the Rockslides. So there are three very different landforms created in this granite: the enormous vertical walls of El Capitan, the highly fractured, minor cliffs of the eastern part of the Rockslides (and those on the opposite walls), and the V-shaped upper Merced Gorge. When it comes to directing the evolution of the Yosemite landscape, the alignment and spacing of joints are more important than the type of bedrock.

Evolution of Yosemite Valley

At the start of the Cenozoic era 65 million years ago, the dinosaurs had met their demise, and small, primitive mammals, including our ancestors, had inherited the giant-free kingdom. At this time the granitic Yosemite Valley was continuing to evolve under warm, wet climates. These generated intense chemical

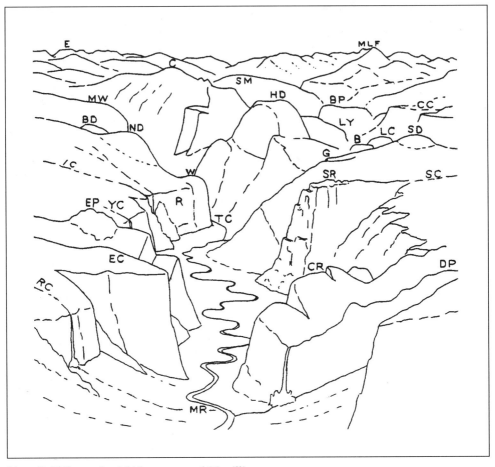

Yosemite Valley as it might have appeared 33 million years ago

weathering, which causes deep subsurface weathering, such as in the highly fractured bedrock floor of Yosemite Valley. However, weathering was minimal on essentially joint-free monoliths such as El Capitan and Half Dome, which had already come into existence. Some 65 million years ago, the main difference from today's lands was that the river canyons were shallower. In contrast the topographic features above the canyon rims resembled their modern equivalents.

By around 65 million years ago the Merced River may have cut down to about 5600 feet elevation (versus about 4000 feet today). The river, having encountered joint-free granitic bedrock in the upper Merced Gorge west of the Valley proper, greatly slowed its rate of incision. In the Valley signif-

icant subsurface weathering should have begun in its highly fractured bedrock floor. If so, then the river would have had a low gradient and it would have meandered across the Valley's river sediments, which lay atop decomposed bedrock. Even back then the Valley was developing a generally broad U-shaped cross profile of steep slopes and a flat floor—one characteristic of today's equatorial and tropical granitic ranges.

If the Merced River bed's estimated elevation is more or less correct, then at the start of the Cenozoic era the summit of El Capitan would have been about 2000 feet above the west end of the Valley, while the summits of Sentinel Dome, Glacier Point, and Half Dome would have been, respectively, about 2500 feet, 1600 feet, and 3200 feet above the east end. These estimates suggest that the Valley had achieved at least half of its present depth by then. The lower part of Tenaya Canyon would have achieved a similar depth. All of the Valley's major features that today rise above 5600 feet elevation were recognizable, and the slopes of these features were about as steep as those of today's, governed by similar joint patterns. Lower Brother and Lower Cathedral Rock barely protruded above the Valley's floor.

Since this time, weathering and erosion have removed only about 100 feet of bedrock from the most resistant summits. Broad uplands, where forested, had a higher rate of denudation. Consequently, 65 million years ago they would have been perhaps 200 to 500 feet higher than today's, so the domes would not have projected as much above their surrounding lands as they do today. Just as the Merced River should have encountered resistant bedrock in Yosemite Valley around this time, it also should have encountered resistant bedrock in Little Yosemite Valley. Then from that valley's west end the river would have plunged down to the east end of Yosemite Valley via two small falls—the incipient Nevada and Vernal falls—and a series of rapids, cascades. Other Valley falls existed, especially Upper Yosemite Fall, which could have had about two thirds of its present 1410-foot height. Also, today's 1612-foot Ribbon Fall back then may have achieved a similar proportion. In like manner, Hetch Hetchy Valley had achieved similar proportions and had developed incipient Tueeulala and Wapama falls. The Grand Canyon of the Tuolumne River was not so grand, but east of it the broad, flat Tuolumne Meadows area resembled its modern equivalent.

Throughout the first half of the Cenozoic era Yosemite Valley continued to deepen, but only slowly, since the Merced River was quite ineffective at incising through the massive bedrock west of the Valley. The jointed bedrock floor of the Valley weathered over millions of years, eventually producing deep basins of decomposed end-products of the granitic bedrock. Both immediately above and below the Valley the Merced River's gradient was much higher, and its gradient was irregular (stepped). Also, during this time, the slopes and cliffs of Yosemite Valley were subject to slow retreat due to mass wasting, which was governed by the spacing and pattern of joint planes. The rate of rockfall generally was too slow to produce talus slopes.

All of the falls in Yosemite Valley proper should have achieved their full heights by the time the climate changed profoundly 33 million years ago. Overall the climate became cooler and drier, and rates of chemical weathering decreased substantially. By this time, Yosemite Valley may have reached 80% of its width and more likely reached its full depth and then some—the floor is now higher thanks to a couple hundred feet of glacial deposits. Resistant summits such as El Capitan, Middle Cathedral Rock, Sentinel Dome, North Dome, Half Dome, and Mt. Starr King stood only about 10 to 30 feet higher than today's summits. The same would apply to lesser features, such as Mt. Broderick and Liberty Cap, which now would have achieved close to their modern size, and their southwest faces would have projected perhaps some 200+ yards beyond their present location. Similar reconstructions apply to other similar faces. The forbidding, exfoliating northwest face of Half Dome, instead of being slightly concave, would have been slightly convex, much like its back side. Royal Arches was an ordinary cliff, somewhat like its western continuation, neither having significant arches.

Over the 32 million years that had elapsed since the start of the Cenozoic era, the Merced River had cut down through resistant bedrock to perhaps about 3800 feet elevation just west of Yosemite Valley. In the Valley the river meandered across a flat floor, at perhaps 3850 to 3900 feet elevation, so the Valley was slightly deeper than today's, and slightly narrower. In modern tropical lands, subsurface weathering can extend 2000 feet down through bedrock, and beneath the Merced River such weathering may have locally extended to this depth by this time.

Virtually all of the Valley's major features existed, including Lower Yosemite and Bridalveil falls. Back then you could have used today's topographic map of the Valley to navigate along its forested floors, up its forested recesses and side canyons, which would have lacked talus slopes, and across its forested uplands. The same applies to the rest of the Sierra Nevada from about the northern border of Yosemite National Park southward. The lands have evolved only a relatively minor amount over the last 33 million years, and you could have used today's topographic maps without getting lost. North of the Park's border, violent rhyolitic eruptions were beginning to occur, and in time most of the northern Sierran landscape would become buried under various volcanic deposits.

Late-Cenozoic Volcanism and Faulting

It is possible that the violent rhyolitic eruptions which occurred just north of the Park some 23 million years ago may have resulted in fairly sizable ash-fall deposits within the Park. However, since ash deposits are readily erodible, they don't last unless they are buried by, say, a lava flow. This did not occur, and not surprisingly no remnants of the nearby rhyolitic volcanism have been found in the Park. In the northern Sierra, another period of volcanism—one largely of andesitic and basaltic lavas—began about 20 million years ago and climaxed about 10 to 9 million years ago before waning. Major eruptive centers were located as far south as the lands around the northern Yosemite boundary. Although no major volcano stood within the Park, there was at least one just north of it, which produced volcanic deposits in sufficient quantity to bury much of the Park's lands north of the Tuolumne River. Locally the deposits were as much as 2000 feet thick, this amount based on remnants on and around Rancheria Mountain, northeast of and above Hetch Hetchy Reservoir. Earlier I said that a small deposit was left on a lower slope of Hetch Hetchy Valley 9½ million years ago. This indicates that in the valley the deposits originally were at least 4500 feet thick. Indeed, they were thick enough to fill the canyon below Hetch Hetchy to its rim; deposits at one time may have extended as far east as Tuolumne Meadows.

Most of these volcanic deposits were readily erodible and would have been carried away by streams before major glaciers advanced westward from the Sierra crest. What the streams missed, the glaciers got most of. Rancheria Mountain has considerable deposits because its summit area is quite broad and relatively flat, and therefore was little affected by stream erosion, and because it stood above the glaciers. Fortunately, glaciers failed to remove all the deposits, allowing us to reconstruct the topography here some 9 to 10 million years ago.

While voluminous volcanic deposits were burying most of the Park's northern lands, a small eruption occurred about 9.4 million years ago along the Tuolumne River about a mile upstream from Glen Aulin. Today part of the original basalt flow remains, and because its columnar lava resembles that in Devils Postpile National Monument, the flow carries the unofficial name of Little Devils Postpile. This basalt flow, beside the south bank of the river, is important: it shows that in the last 9.4 million years the river has incised only a few feet through the resistant, massive granite that the basalt rests on. Giant glaciers repeatedly advanced through this area, yet—as elsewhere in the Sierra Nevada—they were impotent at eroding through such resistant bedrock. In addition to the Little Devils Postpile flow there has been only one other late-Cenozoic eruption in the Park. This is a vent that produced a small basalt flow about 3½ million years ago just south of Merced Pass, close to the Park's southeast boundary. Beyond the boundary, in the heavily glaciated San Joaquin River drainage, are abundant, larger flows of similar age, and like the Little Devils Postpile volcano, they testify to the inability of glaciers to erode through the resistant granitic bedrock on which they rest.

Little Devils Postpile

Faulting often accompanies volcanism, and since volcanism within the Park has been minor, so has faulting. The only identified faulting is in the vicinity of the Snow Lake pendant, which is near the southern end of major late-Cenozoic volcanic eruptions. Several faults appear to have been active there about 9 million years ago and possibly later. The greatest faulting, however, lies east and southeast of the Park, in Mono Basin and Long Valley, where major volcanic activity began 3½ million years ago, as did major faulting. Both are active in the area today, presenting geological hazards to the communities of Lee Vining, June Lake, and Mammoth Lakes.

Multiple Glaciations

By around 15 million years ago the modern Mediterranean climate of California had set in, complete with the cold coastal current and relatively dry summers. In these last 15 million years both chemical and physical weathering have been minimal, and summits such as Yosemite Valley's El Capitan and North Dome

have experienced only a few feet of denudation. Unglaciated, granitic Sierran lands 15 million years ago had achieved topography nearly identical to today's. The main difference appears to have been slight canyon deepening by the major rivers, such as the Tuolumne and the San Joaquin, whose glaciated canyons may have deepened by tens of feet, or perhaps even by 100 feet, but not much more.

Glacial landscapes developed best near the crest of the Sierra Nevada, but this was due more to mass wasting, particularly earthquake-induced rockfall, than to glacial erosion. The principal role of an alpine, or mountain, glacier in any of the world's glaciated ranges is to transport the products of mass wasting, not to erode by abrading and plucking, which is minimal where the bedrock is resistant, as in most of the Sierra Nevada. Indeed, glaciers failed to remove some pre-glacial volcanic flows and deposits on the floors and/or lower slopes of the South Yuba, North Stanislaus, Tuolumne, South San Joaquin and Middle Kings river canyons. Nevertheless, glaciers did remove loose rock, soil, and vegetation to

The highest glacial deposit above Yosemite Valley may be this one atop Turtleback Dome. Glacier Point and other high points along the Valley's rim never were glaciated.

expose vast tracts of fresh, generally light-colored bedrock—the final step in transforming the range into John Muir's Range of Light.

The range's earliest glaciation may have occurred as early as 15 million years ago, when the climate cooled and Antarctica first developed a major ice cap. Glaciers may have been restricted to the heads of canyons below high peaks. In each glacial episode, cold climates would create myriad freeze-and-thaw cycles of ice, which pried rock from steep walls to collect below as talus. As the walls gradually retreated through rockfall, the heads of canyons became broader. The canyon heads are called *cirques*, the small glaciers that occupied them are called *cirque glaciers*, and today there are several recently formed ones in our area, the most notable one lying beneath the shady north slopes of Mt. Lyell. Not all of the early glaciers were small. For example, there were worldwide glaciations at about 5.6 and 5.2 million years ago, and during them *valley glaciers* could have extended many miles down the Sierrra Nevada's principal canyons.

Glaciation began in earnest by 2 million years ago, if not ½ million years earlier, and the upper lands may have been glaciated about 3 dozen times. There is very little evidence of most of these glaciations, and those occurring before 200,000 years ago collectively are called pre-Tahoe, since they preceded the well known Tahoe glaciation. On the east side of the range, the Sherwin glaciation, which lasted from about 900,000 to 800,000 years ago, produced the largest known glaciers. On the west side, the few old, remaining boulders left by glaciers probably were left by Sherwin glaciers.

By about 2 million years ago, the lands of the Sierra crest already may have experienced much glaciation, which would have widened the heads of canyons into cirques. However, the range has "cirques" in *unglaciated* lands. Additionally, the cirque that holds Clark Fork Meadow, just north of Sonora Pass and the Park, had already formed when it was buried under volcanic deposits about 20 million years ago. These features suggest that the Sierra's cirques may be quite old and may not have been widened that much by glaciation. Glacial deepening definitely was minimal, for had much occurred, the cirques would not hang above the floor of the canyon just beyond it, as most of them do.

The rate of mass wasting greatly increased late in the Cenozoic, judging from the excess amount of post-glacial talus present today. In similar unglaciated landscapes, such as the southern Sierra's Dome Land Wilderness, talus is nearly absent, although the area lies relatively close to east-side faults. The current rate of rockfall production in Yosemite Valley appears to be great enough to fill it to the rim in 20 million years (at today's volume of space between the rims above the sedimentary floor, not the bedrock floor). This great increase in rate is due to several causes. First, and perhaps least important, was the Valley's gradual deepening over time, which led to taller cliffs that had more surface area from which rocks could fall. Second, during glaciations, there would have been some minor glacial abrasion of loose wall rocks. Third, with the development of east-side faults came earthquakes, which dislodged the Valley's wall rocks. Fourth, after each glacier left the Valley, post-glacial pressure release triggered accelerated exfoliation, generating a great amount of mass wasting. The most impressive slabs to fall were the ones that resulted in Royal Arches. Finally, the overabundance of talus in the Valley's deep recesses may be due to a misperception. Geoscientists have assumed that all of today's abundant talus formed after the last glacier left the Valley, about 14,000 years ago. However, rather than being carried away by glaciers, preexisting talus in these recesses was instead buried by them, and hence much, if not most, of the talus had already accumulated before the last glaciation, not after it. Therefore its average age is much more than we have imagined; and its rate of production is much less.

Just before the first major glaciers developed in the Sierra Nevada about 2 million years ago, Yosemite Valley had widened, mainly through rockfall from its cliffs, to perhaps 90% of its present width. Since then, its walls, on average, have retreated as much as 150 or so yards, also mainly through rockfall, not glacial erosion. The resistant summits were only about 1 to 5 feet higher than today's. Where the pre-glacial bedrock floors were fractured, glaciers removed the loose rocks, and lakes formed when the glaciers retreated. The largest lake was one that formed in Yosemite Valley, presumably after the Sherwin glaciation. At the head of Merced Gorge, west of the Valley, it may have been 1900 feet thick; at the east end, about 2400. While enormous, this glacier still did not overtop Glacier Point or other parts of the Valley's rim, except for Royal Arches and Washington Column. When this glacier retreated from the Valley, it could have left a shallow 8-mile-long lake, one extending west to Pulpit Rock. After the Sherwin glaciation, the following glaciers were smaller, perhaps due in part to a rain shadow that began to develop in response to the rapid uplift beginning in central California's coastal ranges. These smaller glaciers deposited more sediments than they removed, so after each successive glaciation there was a thicker layer of sediment, and therefore a slightly higher Valley floor.

Two of these post-Sherwin glaciers were larger than the others, the Tahoe and Tioga glaciers, which existed, respectively, about 200-130,000 and 30-15,000 years ago. These two were larger than previously supposed, advancing to the lower part of Merced Gorge, about 6 miles beyond the last end moraine (a deposit left by the retreating Tioga glacier) by Bridalveil Meadow. Also, both glaciers were thicker than previously supposed, especially in Little Yosemite Valley, where they were about 2000 feet thick, not 1000. As in all other glaciated canyons studied so far, the Tahoe glacier was slightly larger than the Tioga glacier, although in Yosemite Valley the Tioga's ice

surface was slightly higher than the Tahoe's simply because some sedimentation had occurred between the two glaciations, giving the Tioga a higher base, and hence a higher ice surface. After the Tioga glacier left the Valley about 15,000 years ago, there was at best a swampy floor, not a lake. The greatest change between then and now was the significant accumulation of talus, generated mostly through depressurization of the Valley's lower slopes when the glacier rapidly left them, after having exerted force against them for some 20,000 years. Myriad slabs exfoliated over this time span, and even today there are thousands of cracks, many of them active, some even noticeably widening over just a few years, to the consternation of climbers. Yet without this depressurization and resulting crack formation, the glaciated Sierra Nevada would have far fewer climbing routes.

The Uniqueness of Yosemite Valley

Yosemite Valley has been hailed as perhaps the premier example of what a glaciated canyon should look like. It certainly was glaciated. Its Tahoe glacier was about 1200 feet thick near El Capitan and about 1600 feet thick up-valley near Glacier Point, and was about 33 miles

Angular shapes, rounded in time, abound in and around Yosemite Valley. The heavy lines depict master joints—large fractures in the granitic bedrock. These vertical joints are more susceptible to erosion than is unjointed rock, and deep valleys with steep-sided walls result. Not all joints are along vertical planes and neither are all Valley walls. Photo of Half Dome shows its joint-controlled front and back faces.

long. While large, it paled in comparison to the Tahoe glacier in the Grand Canyon of the Tuolumne River, which was about 3500 feet thick near Hetch Hechy's dam, over 4000 feet thick up-canyon around Pate Valley, and about 58 miles long (it may have flowed 2-3 miles past the Tuolumne/Cherry confluence). Despite the enormity of the glaciers, they barely widened and deepened the floor of their canyons. Most glaciated canyons in the Sierra and elsewhere do not look like Yosemite Valley. Most do not have nearly perfectly flat floors and most do not have steep-to-overhanging cliffs. The Valley's expansive, flat floor is easily explained: it is not bedrock, but rather is the top of sediments left by glaciers and by the Merced River between glaciations.

Yosemite Valley is unique because of the pattern of variations—in size, spacing and orientation—of its joint planes ("joints" for short). Joints are often linear, usually parallel fractures in bedrock. Most of the Sierra Nevada is granitic and possesses joints, as do other types or rocks such as massive sandstone, which in Utah's Zion National Park is cut by a rectangular grid of streams (and it has glacial features—such as cirques, hanging canyons, and broad floors—despite the *absence* of glaciation). But Yosemite Valley has a unique pattern of variations in its joint system.

Without the overabundance of joints in the bedrock floor of the Valley, deep subsurface, tropical weathing never would have occurred. The east end of the Valley would have been just like many other glaciated canyons having two major joining canyons—very little downcutting. Furthermore, Yosemite Valley has steep-sided walls (with over 1000 difficult climbing routes up them) because its walls are governed by the presence of vertical joints. Glaciers didn't make the walls vertical—their contribution was minor; the walls were already quite steep long before glaciation.

In like manner, parts of Tenaya Canyon and of the Grand Canyon of the Tuolumne River may stay V-shaped almost indefinitely, for they lack this important control. I should note here that the *spacing* of joints is also important. If joints are closely spaced, the rock is more easily excavated—witness Indian Canyon and the Rockslides. In contrast, the hulking, vertical-walled monolith of El Capitan is essentially joint-free, although at

one time it had been bounded by several major, vertical joints before it backwasted to its present state.

North of the Tuolumne River, Yosemite's backcountry is a fantastic landscape of straight, joint-controlled canyons. An easy way to visualize the effect of joints in controlling the development of a landscape is to drive up the Glacier Point Road and get a bird's eye view of Yosemite Valley and its environs. Your first stop should be at Washburn Point, from which you look directly across at Half Dome. Note that it is not really half of a dome, as its name implies, for it is rather symmetrical, the southeast face being about as tall and as steep as the northwest face. The steepness of these two faces are in large part controlled by vertical, northeast-trending joints. These vertical joints were more closely spaced along the northwest face, and glaciers took advantage of this, cutting the face back by about 500 feet. However, contrary to what Josiah Whitney had proclaimed in the 1860s, at no time in the dome's history did a northwest half of the dome fall into Tenaya Canyon.

Below and to the right of Half Dome you'll look down—from Washburn Point—on Mt. Broderick and Liberty Cap, both also bounded by vertical, northeast-trending joints. Glaciation has substantially enlarged the joint that separates the two monoliths, although it is instructive to note that although these two features were likely glaciated perhaps three dozen times, neither was eroded away nor was the gap between them transformed into a broad canyon. Had they been laced with joints, they would not be standing today.

The same joint that governs the southeast face of Liberty Cap also governs the cliff that Nevada Fall leaps over. Vernal Fall is also governed by a vertical joint, but it trends northwest, not northeast. If such vertical joints had been closely spaced, then glaciers would have been able to cut through them, creating cascades, not falls. Like Half Dome, Mt. Broderick and Liberty Cap, Panorama Cliff is governed by vertical, northeast-trending joints, and if you were way down on the trail to Vernal Fall, you could look toward our viewpoint and identify many major, parallel joint planes between Illilouette Fall and Glacier Point.

Before driving on to Glacier Point, look at Mt. Starr King, on the horizon east-southeast of you. It is rounded on all sides—a true dome, unlike most so-called domes. If it is so rounded, does that mean it is not controlled by joints? Not really. Mt. Starr King appeared on the Yosemite landscape by 65 million years ago, if not earlier. It was almost certainly bounded by vertical, intersecting joint planes, and back in its early days it may have looked somewhat like Mt. Broderick, below you, looks today. Time and weathering, however, have taken their toll, weathering faster at the edges than at the faces, and even faster at the corners than at the edges.

From Washburn Point continue down to the Glacier Point parking lot and walk out to unglaciated Glacier Point. The 1200-foot-dead-vertical cliff below you is governed by a major joint, but the curving Glacier Point Apron, below it, lacks joints and has been very resistant to erosion. It's been planed down by glaciers perhaps a maximum of several hundred feet, or perhaps only tens of feet.

From Glacier Point you can easily see how Half Dome got its name, for it certainly looks as if there had been a northwest half of the dome, which would have fallen into Tenaya Canyon. Looking up Tenaya Canyon, note that it is distinctly **V**-shaped in cross profile, not **U**-shaped, as a glaciated canyon is supposed to be. However, there are no major vertical joint planes in this canyon, so a "Yosemite Valley" never developed. Above the canyon stand North Dome and Basket Dome, both rounded like Mt. Starr King and both having a similar history.

Below North Dome is Washington Column, which is distinctly separated from Royal Arches by a large, vertical fracture. Royal Arches is a beautiful anomaly. An arch can form on a granite face when an exfoliating sheet of granite breaks loose, leaving a curved scar at the place of attachment. However, more often than not, an arch does not form. On Half Dome's southwest slope, facing us, you'll see a giant half arch. Looking northwest, you'll see a light-colored scar just west of the lower part of Upper Yosemite Fall. That rockfall, perhaps 1000 tons in mass, occurred in June 1976, leaving no arch, though a considerably older one, above and right of it, did. The reason for the massiveness of the uppermost arch of Royal Arches seems to be that the joint planes are widely spaced. Had they been closely spaced, only thin slabs of rock would fall or be quarried away by a former glacier.

The Holocene Epoch

The last 10,000 years have been classified as the Holocene epoch, which is misleading, for it implies that the glacier-dominated Pleistocene epoch is behind us. Notwithstanding global warming through man's zealous production of greenhouse gases, nothing could be farther from the truth. There will have to be a lot of future movements of the earth's giant plates before the ocean's circulatory patterns are sufficiently changed to permit substantial warming of the northern latitudes. We are only in a short-term interglacial period similar to a preceding, major one that lasted from about 130,000 to 120,000 years ago.

Since 15,000 years ago, the unofficial start of the Holocene for the Sierra Nevada (when its glaciers had all but disappeared), the Yosemite landscape has changed very little. The massive face of El Capitan has weathered back only ¼ inch, if even that, though parts of it have spalled rockfalls. Rockfalls generally occur in winter and early spring, as water works its way behind large flakes, freezes and expands, and thereby pries the flakes loose. While all flakes are initially formed through unloading, they can be pried loose by processes other than freezing water. On March 26, 1872, John Muir, Galen Clark and others witnessed massive rockfalls due to the distant Owens Valley earthquake. A sufficient tonnage of rocks fell from Liberty Cap to temporarily dam the Merced River just above the brink of Nevada Fall.

Lightning can be another cause of rockfalls. A large-scale rockfall is unlikely to result, but in June 1976 a lightning bolt broke off a 220-foot-high 1000-ton slab from Upper Yosemite Fall's massive wall. Finally, from the 1930s, especially during the '60s and '70s, climbers drove countless pitons into thousands of cracks, briefly accelerating the natural rate of exfoliation.

Major rockfalls occur every few years in Yosemite Valley. The largest one identified is the prehistoric fall that dammed Tenaya Creek to create Mirror Lake, estimated to be about 15,000,000 cubic yards. The 1987 Middle Brother rockfall, perhaps the largest historic one, pales in comparison at about 800,000 cubic yards. Fresh rockfall sites on cliffs are easy to identify, since they expose fresh rock. Over decades, medium-gray lichens grow over the exposure, blending it in with the rest of the wall. Without lichens, Yosemite Valley would have walls mostly creamy or light gray.

While rockfalls built up talus slopes in Yosemite Valley and other parts of the Park, rivers and creeks worked ineffectually at removing them. Rivers and creeks were also ineffective at cutting through bedrock, and they typically have carved only a foot or so into it in the last 15,000 years. Examine the brink of Vernal or Nevada fall and see just how little erosion the Merced River has done.

By the start of the Holocene epoch, all of the Sierra's Tioga glaciers had disappeared. However, a minor period of glaciation began about 1250 A.D. and became pronounced from about 1550 to 1850 A.D. This was the historic Little Ice Age, and John Muir was the first to discover a real glacier in the Sierra Nevada, not just a year-round snowfield. This was the Merced Peak glacier, which Muir had discovered in 1871. By late 1977, a severe drought year, all traces of ice and snow had disappeared. With continued climate warming, this may be the fate of the few remaining Sierran glaciers.

Before closing this chapter, we should look at the origin of Yosemite's meadows. It had long been assumed that High Sierra meadows once were lakes that had developed after Tioga glaciers had disappeared.

According to this view, a lake was gradually filled in with sediments until at last a meadow existed. François Matthes had proposed it for his Lake Yosemite—the most extreme example. But sedimentation, it turns out, is a very slow process in the Sierra Nevada, and most lakes formed back then are still lakes today. The average Sierran lake typically has between 10 and 20 feet of sediments—about one foot of deposition per thousand years.

Actually, as Spencer Wood has shown, many of the High Sierra meadows, such as Tuolumne Meadows, were forested up to at least the start of the Little Ice Age, when colder conditions developed and the level of ground water rose, drowning the trees. We can therefore be thankful for the Little Ice Age, for without it we wouldn't have the many meadows from which we can view the snow-clad High Sierra landscape. The view-packed Yosemite Valley meadows are also in existence largely due to the presence of a high water table. The meadows once were much more extensive, covering about 745 of the Valley's 1,141 acres, but they were greatly reduced by humans in part due to the lowering of the water table in order to reduce both flooding and mosquitoes, two problems that plagued early tourism. Humans locally can be powerful agents of geologic change.

The Lyell Glacier, as it appeared around 1880

Chapter 3
The Living Yosemite

Who can forget his or her first visit to Yosemite—the enormous granite cliffs of El Capitan and Clouds Rest, the leaping, dashing waterfalls, the domes of Yosemite Valley, Tenaya Canyon, and Tuolumne Meadows, the rusty, metamorphic peaks above Dana Meadows? Of these features only the waterfalls move, and none are living. For most visitors, memories of living forms—except for giant sequoias (Hikes 18, 19, 92, and 93)—are likely to take a back seat to the inanimate landscape, although many out-of-state visitors will be duly impressed with the size of some conifers. But despite the barren peaks, cliffs, and canyon walls, Yosemite is predominantly a landscape of forest green. Along all but a few of the Park's trails, conifers shade your way. In this chapter we'll delve into the "Living Yosemite"—the assemblage of plants and animals which we too often take for granted. We'll look at its *ecology*, the relations between organisms and their environment. Because humans too are an organism, we'll also look at them.

Driving up Highway 41, 120, or 140, you can't help noticing that the natural scene changes with elevation. The most obvious changes are in the trees, because they are the largest organisms and unlike most animals they are readily observable. When you pay close attention, you notice that not only the trees but the shrubs, wildflowers, grasses, and animals also change with elevation. You might wonder why you don't see the same species in Tuolumne Meadows that you saw in Yosemite Valley. Climate is probably the foremost limiting influence on species' distributions, but there are others. In the following pages we'll also look at the roles that topography, soil, fire, and organisms play in regulating the distribution of plant and animal species.

Climatic Influences

Of all influences, temperature and precipitation are probably the most important. The pertinent climatic data for Yosemite National Park and the lands to the west and east of it are summed up in the following table. The climatic sites are arranged from west to east in ascending order to Mt. Dana, then in descending order on the Sierra's steep east slopes down to Mono Lake. Note in this table that temperature decreases with increasing elevation, and that precipitation increases only up to mid-elevations, beyond which it decreases slowly to the crest, then rapidly beyond it.

Ellery Lake seems to be an exception. Its high precipitation figure is due to storm winds whipping through Tioga Pass, spreading out, and depositing their snow downcanyon around this lake. In like manner,

Table 1. Climatic data along a west-east transect of the Sierra Nevada

Site (plant community)	Elevation		Average annual temperature		Average minimum temperature in January		Average maximum temperature in July		Average annual precipitation		Growing season
	feet	meters	°F	°C	°F	°C	°F	°C	inches	cm	months
Merced (valley grassland)	160	50	63	17	36	2	98	37	12	30	9
Mariposa (foothill woodland)	2000	610	58	15	32	0	94	34	30	77	7
Yosemite Valley (ponderoas pine forest)	3970	1210	53	12	25	-4	90	32	37	94	6
Mariposa Grove (ponderoas pine forest)	6000	1800	48	9	20	-7	80	27	45	115	5
Crane Flat (sugar-pine/lodgepole-pine forest)	6200	1890	48	9	20	-7	80	27	45	115	5
Tenaya Lake (red-fir/lodgepole-pine forest)	8149	2484	43	6	17	-8	72	22	40	102	4
Tuolumne Meadows (mountain meadow)	8600	2620	39	4	15	-9	70	21	35	89	3
Tioga Pass (subalpine forest)	9941	3030	36	2	10	-12	60	16	30	76	2
Mt. Dana (alpine fell-fields)	13053	3978	32	0	0	-18	55	13	25	63	1½
Ellery Lake (subalpine forest)	9489	2822	37	3	10	-12	60	16	35	89	2
Mono Lake (sagebrush scrub)	6400	1950	48	9	20	-7	84	29	14	36	6

stormy winds whip up the deep Middle Fork San Joaquin river canyon, cross the low Sierra crest, and deposit a thick mantle of snow in the Mammoth Mountain ski area, giving it one of the longest lasting ski seasons in the state.

Because much of a winter's snow remains through late spring—and some remains throughout summer—most of Yosemite's vegetation has an adequate water supply. In fact, the presence of the subalpine meadows is due to too much water, for conifers aren't able to survive in these seasonally water-saturated soils. However, on the rocky slopes of Mt. Dana, the Dana Plateau, and other alpine slopes, the snow often melts before the start of the growing season. On these dry slopes, then, the wildflowers are often dependent on summer thunderstorms for moisture. The winter snow on these slopes serves a different purpose for their perennial wildflowers: it buries and protects them. In extremely cold winter winds the equivalent wind-chill temperature can easily drop below –40°F (–40°C).

Physiographic Influences

The topography indirectly affects the distribution of plants and animals. As we have seen, a change in elevation means a change in temperature and precipitation, and irregular topography can create uneven distribution of snow. Well-named Snow Flat is at about the same elevation as Tuolumne Meadows, yet because it lies south of Mt. Hoffmann, it receives about twice as much snow as Tuolumne Meadows, which lies just north of the Cathedral Range. This range creates a "rain shadow" on its north side so less precipitation falls over the meadows. The Sierra crest creates an even greater rain shadow, which explains why Mono Lake, in the table, has such a low precipitation—about 30% of the maximum figure.

Topography also affects vegetation in other ways. A north-facing slope, because it receives less sunlight than a south-facing slope, is cooler, so evaporation and transpiration on it are less. Consequently, it can support a denser stand of vegetation. This denser stand produces more litter, which results in more humus, so ground water is retained better. In one soil survey conducted by the author, about 60% of a soil's weight on a north-facing slope was due to water, whereas on a nearby south-facing slope, only about 5% was due to water. This was an extreme case, but, nevertheless, it helps one to visualize why north-facing slopes tend to be heavily forested while south-facing ones tend to be more open and sometimes brushy. At mid-elevations we see red and white firs on the shady slopes and Jeffrey pines and huckleberry oaks on the sunny ones.

Edaphic Influences

Yosemite's soils are derived primarily from granitic rocks. The decomposition of these rocks creates the soil that High Sierra hikers are so familiar with—gravel-size pieces of feldspar and quartz with a few flecks of mica and hornblende. On mid-elevation slopes these weathered minerals can accumulate to produce a deep, well-drained soil, which will support a moderately dense forest of pines and firs, such as on slopes along much of the Tioga and the Glacier Point roads. In soils that are extremely porous, a pure stand of Jeffrey pines can develop, as in volcanic soils of the Mono Basin, east of the Park. Where a gravelly Sierran soil is also shallow, drought-tolerant shrubs replace pines.

It is the dark minerals of granitic rock that are important in supplying certain elements to plants. These dark minerals often are the first part of the bedrock to decompose, and the products are often carried as ions in solution, only to be deposited lower down. Hence richer soils exist in flat areas, where these nutrients accumulate. Dense forests, particularly lodgepole forests, then develop, provided that the ground water is low enough. Where ground water saturates the soil for a few weeks or more, meadows develop.

A small fraction of Yosemite's soils are derived from metamorphic rocks, which are found mainly along the Park's highest elevations. At these heights an alpine plant definitely thrives better on the resulting metamorphic soils than on adjacent granitic soils. This is because metamorphic bedrock fractures into smaller pieces than granitic bedrock does, thus creating a greater water-storage capacity for plants. Furthermore, this rock is much richer in dark minerals, so it yields a more nutrient-rich soil. And, being darker in color than their granitic counterparts, metamorphic-derived soils absorb more heat, which is very important to plants at these alpine altitudes.

A final point to be made about soils is that in the range there were a lot of thick soils before glaciers removed them, and this altered the distribution of at least one notable species, the giant sequoia. In the fossil record it is associated with red firs, but today it grows mostly with white firs. Why did the sequoias switch allegiance from red firs to white firs? They didn't. There is an obvious explanation for this "switch," and it was unwittingly first put forth, in rudimentary form, by John Muir in 1876: glaciers overran most of the trees, eliminating them from their preferred habitat, the red-fir belt. Glaciers removed the belt's deep, preglacial, groundwater-rich soils, and the modern, postglacial ones, while adequate for red firs, are too water-deficient for sequoias. They do grow in one almost pure, shady, red-fir grove in the southern Sierra, the Atwell grove, which, extending up to 8800 feet in elevation, is the range's highest grove. They grow there because the slopes never were glaciated.

Biotic Influences

Soils can affect the type and amount of vegetation, but vegetation can also create and change soils. A soil is more than just a combination of loose, moist sand and gravel—it also has an organic component. Each year the Merced River deposits sterile silt, sand, and gravel at the south end of Washburn Lake. Grasses and sedges take root in these new accumulations and stabilize them. Then, as these plants die over the years, they add an organic component to the sediments, converting them to soil. As the soil develops here, it becomes ripe for invasion by willows, which further modify the new soil. These trap more sediments, and they add detritus to the soil, enriching it and making it more suitable for other species. Additionally, transpiration by both herbs and shrubs helps to lower the water table: aspens and lodgepole pines can now invade. In this way, a sterile beach eventually becomes—through activities by a *succession* of plant species—a rich forest soil.

Animals also influence the development of soils and thus affect the development of vegetation. Most of the Yosemite landscape stands above the range of the lowly earthworm, but at mid-elevations, nature has other soil processors. Foremost among these is the industrious pocket gopher, who works year-round, even in the cold of winter when other rodents are either hibernating or living off their stored cache of food. Winter is actually a safer time for the gopher to work, for it can burrow along at the base of a snowpack without danger from its summer predators—hawks, owls, gopher snakes, weasels, badgers, foxes, and coyotes. After the snow melts, the gopher's winter tunneling appears as "gopher ropes." (After a gopher digs a tunnel through the snow, he later fills it with soil from his diggings in the ground beneath the snow. When the snow melts, this core of soil is then exposed, looking like a piece of thick rope.)

In a mountain meadow a gopher population will churn up tons of soil each year. This process has numerous benefits all leading to the development of a richer soil. To a much lesser extent, burrowing and digging by ground squirrels, moles, badgers, and coyotes also contribute to soil development. And we must not forget the decomposers—bacteria, fungi, lichens, invertebrates, and even a few plants, without whom dead plants and animals would continually accumulate until the entire forest lay smothered beneath their mass. Decomposers, which are usually minute and unseen, busily convert dead plants and animals into litter and humus. However, because too much litter and humus can prevent seedling germination, fire is an integral part of the ecosystem in all but Yosemite's subalpine and alpine areas, which are too sparse to support forest fires.

It has been said that the giant sequoia might not be around today were it not for the roles played by fire, the chickaree (Douglas squirrel), and a cone-boring beetle, all three aiding with the dispersal and germination of seeds. Momentarily we'll overlook the role of fire and concentrate on the roles of organisms. More than 150 species of insects depend in part on the giant sequoia, and it is very dependent on one beetle. This tree is not alone in this respect. In Yosemite, insect species outnumber plant species about ten to one. Without insects, most wildflowers would disappear for lack of pollination. Then too, wildflowers receive aid from birds and rodents in the form of seed planting and seed dispersal. Even preying on plants is beneficial; otherwise plants would

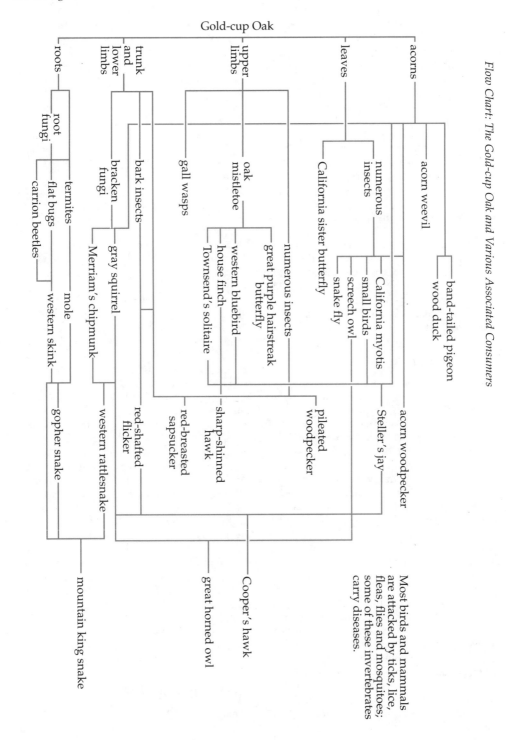

Flow Chart: The Gold-cup Oak and Various Associated Consumers

undergo a population explosion, cover the earth, and die in their own debris.

An example of the complexity of plant-animal interaction is shown in the following flow chart, which shows some of the plants and animals that either directly or indirectly depend in part upon the gold-cup oak (also known as the canyon live oak). The lines show who eats whom. For example, the mountain king snake, at the bottom right, preys on the western rattlesnake, the gopher snake, and the western skink (among others not shown). The gopher snake also preys on the western skink, and also on the mole. The mole feeds on termites, and so on. The list of plants and animals could be extended indefinitely. If one were to remove the oak's parasitic mistletoe, perhaps the oak population would increase, but then, the animals that feed on the mistletoe and the animals that in turn prey upon them would be adversely affected. Whenever you tamper with one of nature's components, you affect the whole system.

The Role of Fire

The presence or absence of ground fires can really alter the system, for it significantly alters the populations of ground-dwelling plants and animals and everything associated with them. Fires were once thought to be detrimental to the overall well-being of the ecosystem, and early foresters attempted to prevent or subdue all fires. Until 1971, fire suppression was a general, though sometimes contested, Yosemite policy. This policy, however, led to the accumulation of thick litter, dense brush, and overmature trees—all prime fuel for a holocaust when a fire inevitably sparked to life. It also led to a change in the distribution of plant and animal species and encouraged root rot (see Hike 66).

Foresters now know that *natural* fires should not be prevented, but only regulated. These fires, if left unchecked, burn stands of mixed conifers—such as those found in Yosemite Valley—about once every 10 years. At this frequency, brush and litter do not accumulate sufficiently to result in a damaging forest fire; only the ground cover is burned over, while the trees remain generally intact. Thus, through small burns, the forest is protected from going up in smoke. Ultimately, however, stands of trees mature, the trees die, logs accu-

mulate on the ground, and major fires occur, such as the 1988 Yellowstone fires.

Some trees are adapted to fire. The giant sequoia, for example, releases its seeds after a fire, as do numbers of conifers, shrubs, and wildflowers. Seeds of the genus *Ceanothus* are quick to germinate in burned-over ground, and some plants of this genus are among the primary foods of deer (see Hike 8). Hence, periodic burns will keep a deer population at its maximum. With too few burns, shrubs become too woody and unproductive for a deer herd. In like manner, gooseberries and other berry plants sprout after fires and help support a variety of different bird and mammal populations.

Without fires, a plant community evolves toward a *climax*, an end stage, of plant succession. Red and white firs are the main species in the climax vegetation that is characteristic of the Sierra's mid-elevations. However, a *pure* stand of *any* species invites epidemic attacks and therefore can be unstable. In the past, pure stands of Yosemite's lodgepoles have been severely attacked by lodgepole needleminers—the larval stage of a moth—which turned the living stands into "ghost forests."

Fire is also beneficial in that it unlocks nutrients that are stored up in living matter, litter, topsoil, and even rocks. Vital compounds are released in the form of ash when a fire burns plants and forest litter. Fire also can heat granitic rocks enough to cause them to break up and release their minerals. In one study of a northern coniferous forest it was concluded that the weathering of granitic rock in that area was primarily due to periodic fires. A post-fire inspection in Yosemite can reveal that fires do get hot enough to cause thin sheets of granite to exfoliate, or sheet off, from boulders.

Natural, periodic fires, then, can be very beneficial for a forest ecosystem, and they should be thought of as an integral process in the plant community. they have, after all, been around as long as terrestrial life has, and for millions of years have been a common process in most of the Sierra's plant communities.

Biogeography

We have just delved very briefly into the influences regulating the distribution of plants and animals. Of course, not every species is equally affected by these influences. And therefore

Plate 1. Some common Yosemite trees—all conifers
Top row (l. to r.): *foothill (gray, Digger) pine, Jeffrey pine, whitebark pine*
Middle row: *western juniper, incense-cedar branches, mountain hemlock*
Bottom row: *red fir, red fir cone (top) and western white pine cone, western white pine (silver pine)*

Plate 2. Some common Yosemite shrubs
Top row (l. to r.): *chinquapin, tobacco brush, pinemat manzanita*
Middle row: *mountain ash, thimbleberry, mountain spiraea*
Bottom row: *red mountain heather, bog kalmia, Labrador tea*

Plate 3. Some wildflowers of foothill woodlands and ponderosa-pine forests
Top row (l. to r.): *Indian pink, mountain dogbane (Indian hemp), miner's lettuce*
Middle row: *Lemmon's catchfly, mountain violet, common madia*
Bottom row: *fireweed, nude buckwheat, California stickseed*

Plate 4. Some wildflowers of Jeffrey-pine forests
Top row (l. to r.): *mountain pride (Newberry's penstemon), pussy paws, sulfur flower*
Middle row: *Mariposa tulip (lily), spreading phlox, wavy-leaved (Applegate's) paintbrush*
Bottom row: *scarlet gilia (desert trumpet), single-stemmed senecio, mule ears*

34

Plate 5. Some wildflowers of red-fir/lodgepole-pine forests
Top row (l. to r.): *western spring beauty, bleeding hearts, branched false Solomon's seal*
Middle row: *spotted coralroot, pinedrops, snow plant*
Bottom row: *white-veined wintergreen, dwarf lousewort, California Jacob's ladder*

35

Plate 6. Some wildflowers of creeks, springs, and bogs
Top row (l. to r.): *ranger's buttons (swamp white heads), cow parsnip, leopard lily*
Middle row: *elephant heads, common monkey flower, crimson (red) columbine*
Bottom row: *wandering daisy, arrow-leaved senecio (butterweed), broad-leaved lupine*

Plate 7. Some wildflowers of meadows
Top row (l. to r.): *sticky cinquefoil, corn lily, monument plant (green gentian)*
Middle row: *hiker's gentian, shooting star, marsh marigold*
Bottom row: *yarrow, meadow penstemon, Gray's lovage*

Plate 8. Some wildflowers of subalpine forests and alpine fell-fields
Top row (l. to r.): *alpine gold (hulsea), timberline phacelia, shaggy hawkweed*
Middle row: *flat-seeded rock cress, Newberry's (alpine) gentian, mountain sorrel*
Bottom row: *rock fringe, sphinx moth and Davidson's penstemon, alpine saxifrage*

every plant and animal has its own *range, habitat*, and *niche*. The range is the entire area over which an organism may be found. Some species have a very restricted range; others, a very widespread one. The giant sequoia, for example, occurs only in about 75 small groves at mid-elevations in the western Sierra Nevada. An organism's habitat is the kind of place where it lives. The habitat of the sequoia is typically a gently sloping, forested, unglaciated, periodically burned slope that has abundant ground water. An organism's niche is the functional role it plays in its community. For example, the sequoia provides food and shelter for dozens of insects that utilize the tree's needles, branches, bark, and cones, and additional organisms benefit from soil changes created by the sequoia's roots. At the same time, the sequoia receives essential aid from the chickaree, from a long-antennaed beetle, and from fire (see Hike 93). Thus the niche is a give-and-take relationship.

The sequoia's range, though not really large, is great compared to that of a few alpine species such as the snow willow. This "shrub"—usually less than an inch high—is found on only a few old, nearly flat surfaces on or close to the Park's northeast boundary. Animals, having the ability to move, generally have greater ranges than plants, though the Mt. Lyell salamander has a spotty, subalpine range about equal in north-south extent to that of the giant sequoia. An isolated population of this animal survives atop Half Dome (Hike 80).

Some plants and animals have tremendous ranges. For example, the squirreltail is a grass that grows in dry, open habitats from the Park's alpine fell-fields down to the Park's lowest elevations. Outside the Park, it descends to sea level, and its range extends from Mexico north to British Columbia and east to Texas and South Dakota. Some other far-ranging plants growing throughout much of Yosemite are bracken fern, pretty face (golden brodiaea), comb draba, Brewer's lupine, wavy-leaved paintbrush, woolly sunflower, and yarrow.

In the animal kingdom, the mule deer (see Hike 8), mountain lion, coyote, badger, long-tailed weasel, California ground squirrel, and deer mouse are mammals that range through much of Yosemite. Many birds seen in Yosemite have migrated, if not from the south, then from the lowlands, and they follow the development of a food supply that occurs higher and higher as the winter snowpack retreats. In most of the Park you can expect to see the American robin, dark-eyed junco, Brewer's blackbird, northern flicker, white-crowned sparrow, chipping sparrow, American dipper (water ouzel), red-tailed hawk, and northern harrier (marsh hawk). Reptiles and amphibians, despite their limited mobility and their disadvantageous cold-blooded circulatory system, do include a few well-adapted species that have broad ranges. Seen from the foothills up into the subalpine zone are the western fence lizard and Pacific treefrog. The western rattlesnake is also widespread up to about 7000 feet, and a few individuals have made it up to the subalpine zone. Thus, some plant and animal species can adapt to environments and competitors better than others. Most of Yosemite's plants and animals have a more restricted distribution, each living in only several of Yosemite's seven plant communities, and some species live in only one community. We'll now look at some species found in the Park's communities.

Plant Communities and Their Animal Associations

When you hike in the mountains, you anticipate seeing certain plants and animals in a given habitat. You quickly learn, for example, that junipers don't grow in wet meadows, but corn lilies do. Corn lilies, in turn, don't grow on dry rock slabs, but junipers do. Likewise, you would expect to find garter snakes in wet meadows and western fence lizards on the dry rock slabs, but never the reverse. Thus you could group plants and animals by their habitat. In this book, this classification is based on the dominant *plant* or *plant type* of a habitat simply because plants are the most readily observed life forms. Such a group of life forms is called a plant community, even though it includes animals as well as plants.

Because animals move, they can be harder to classify. Birds, for example, typically have a wide—usually seasonal—range, and therefore may be found in many plant communities. In the following list of communities, a species is mentioned in the community in which you, the visitor, are most likely to see it. In addition, only the more prominent and/or diagnostic species are mentioned. To mention all would fill an entire book—Yosemite Valley *alone* has about 400 species of grasses and wildflowers and thousands of species of insects! Common names, particularly among wildflowers, vary from book to book, so I have attempted to use either the common names appearing in authoritative texts or in popular guidebooks that I feel are the most accurate. To save space, grasses, ferns, lower plants, trout, and invertebrates have not been included.

The following plant communities are listed in approximate order of ascending elevation and decreasing temperature. These plant communities aren't the final word in plant-animal classification, since each community could be further subdivided. For example, Lionel Klikoff identified eight vegetational patterns in the subalpine Gaylor Lakes area (Hike 46), near Tioga Pass. Each pattern is the result of a different set of microenvironmental influences.

Table 2. Yosemite's Plant Communities

1. Foothill Woodland

Trees: foothill (gray, Digger) pine, knobcone pine, blue oak, interior live oak, tanbark oak, California buckeye, red willow, arroyo willow, black cottonwood

Shrubs: scrub oak, poison oak, Parry manzanita, whiteleaf manzanita, chaparral whitethorn (ceanothus), yerba santa, toyon, western redbud, spice bush, bush poppy, bush monkey flower, mock orange, chaparral currant, bitter gooseberry

Wildflowers: Indian pink, soap plant, California poppy, miner's lettuce, Chinese houses, purple milkweed, star flower, western buttercup

Mammals: gray fox, bobcat, spotted skunk, ringtail, brush rabbit, Merriam's chipmunk, Botta's pocket gopher, dusky-footed wood rat, Heermann's kangaroo rat, brush mouse, pinyon mouse, ornate shrew, small-footed myotis (bat), western pipistrelle (bat)

Birds: California thrasher, wrentit, bushtit, plain titmouse, scrub jay, rufous-sided towhee, western bluebird, Nuttall's woodpecker, Hutton's vireo, Bewick's wren, blue-gray gnatcatcher

Reptiles: common king snake, racer, striped racer, ringneck snake, western whiptail, southern alligator lizard, Gilbert's skink

Amphibians: foothill yellow-legged frog, California slender salamander, California newt, arboreal salamander

Where seen: sunny slopes about and below Hetch Hetchy Reservoir, Arch Rock-El Portal area, lower Alder Creek trail

2. Ponderosa-Pine Forest

Trees: ponderosa pine, incense-cedar, black oak, sugar pine, white fir, interior live (gold-cup) oak, Douglas-fir, giant sequoia (restricted distribution), California laurel (bay tree), big-leaf maple, Scouler's willow, mountain (Pacific) dogwood, white alder, black cottonwood

Shrubs: whiteleaf manzanita, mountain misery, western azalea, American (creek) dogwood, buckbrush, deer brush, Sierra gooseberry

Wildflowers: broad-leaved lupine, harlequin lupine, narrow-leaved lotus, black-eyed Susan, common madia, scarlet monkey flower, blue penstemon, evening primrose, bleeding hearts, wild ginger, false Solomon's seal, mountain dogbane (Indian hemp), umbrella plant (Indian rhubarb), mountain violet, waterfall buttercup

Mammals: black bear, raccoon, striped skunk, gray squirrel, long-eared chipmunk, big brown bat, hairy-winged myotis (bat)

Birds: Steller's jay, black-headed grosbeak, western tanager, Townsend's solitaire, acorn woodpecker, white-headed woodpecker, downy woodpecker, band-tailed pigeon, purple finch, solitary vireo, Nashville warbler, black-throated gray warbler, MacGillivray's warbler, winter wren, violet-green swallow, screech owl, spotted owl, golden eagle

Reptiles: California mountain kingsnake, rubber boa, gopher snake, northern alligator lizard

Amphibian: ensatina

Where seen: Yosemite Valley, Cherry Lake, Mather R.S., Pate Valley, Alder Creek trail, Wawona, Merced, Tuolumne, and Mariposa groves

3. Jeffrey-Pine Forest

Trees: Jeffrey pine, red fir, white fir, incense-cedar, sugar pine, western juniper

Shrubs: huckleberry oak, greenleaf manzanita, snow bush, tobacco brush, sagebrush, squaw wax currant, curl-leaved mountain mahogany

Wildflowers: mountain pride (Newberry's penstemon), Bridges' penstemon, showy penstemon, Gray's lupine, single-stemmed senecio, coyote mint (mountain monardella), mule ears, Sierra wallflower, jewel flower (streptanthus), spreading phlox, scarlet gilia, pussy paws, sulfur flower, nude buckwheat, Leichtlin's Mariposa tulip (lily), Sierra sedum

Mammals: Sierra Nevada golden-mantled ground squirrel, mountain pocket gopher, bushy-tailed wood rat

Birds: mountain quail, fox sparrow, green-tailed towhee, Townsend's solitaire, olive-sided flycatcher

Reptiles: western fence lizard, sagebrush lizard, western rattlesnake

Where seen: El Capitan, North Dome-Indian Ridge, old Kibbie Lake trail, lower West Walker River, slabs above Lake Vernon and Agnew Lake. At most of Yosemite's rocky or dry-gravelly mid-elevation sites; widespread on the Mono Basin's higher slopes.

4. Red-Fir/Lodgepole-Pine Forest

Trees: red fir, lodgepole pine, western white (silver) pine, white fir, mountain hemlock, aspen, Scouler's willow, MacKenzie's willow

Shrubs: bush chinquapin, pinemat manzanita, mountain spiraea, Labrador tea, red heather, Sierra-laurel, Sierra gooseberry, sticky currant, service-berry, bitter cherry, mountain ash, Lemmon's willow, mountain alder

Wildflowers: white-veined wintergreen, pinedrops, snow plant, spotted coralroot, meadow rue, Richardson's geranium, arrow-leaved senecio (butterweed), larkspur, monk's hood, crimson columbine, fringed lungwort (mountain bluebells), alpine (tiger) lily

Mammals: red fox, porcupine, marten, chickaree (Douglas squirrel), lodgepole chipmunk, western jumping mouse, dusky shrew, little brown myotis (bat)

Birds: blue grouse, dark-eyed junco, mountain chickadee, red-breasted nuthatch, golden-crowned kinglet, Williamson's sapsucker, Hammond's flycatcher, Cassin's finch, evening grosbeak, red crossbill, goshawk, great gray owl

Where seen: generally found between 6500 and 9000 feet—the elevation traversed by the bulk of Yosemite's trails; it is the most widespread plant community in the Park. Most accessible sites: Tioga Road from Crane Flat to Tuolumne Meadows, and White Wolf, Pohono Trail, Badger Pass, Chiquito Pass

5. Mountain Meadow

Shrubs: arctic (alpine) willow, shining (caudate) willow, Eastwood's willow, Sierra willow, western blueberry, dwarf bilberry, bog kalmia

Wildflowers: corn lily, Jeffrey's shooting star, cow parsnip, swamp onion, carpet clover, Leichtlin's camas, marsh marigold, Lewis monkey flower, primrose monkey flower, Lemmon's paintbrush, alpine paintbrush, Sierra penstemon, meadow penstemon, slender cinquefoil, sticky cinquefoil, Drummond's cinquefoil, pussytoes, elephant heads

Mammals: Belding ground squirrel, white-tailed hare (jack rabbit), montane meadow mouse, water shrew

Birds: white-crowned sparrow, Brewer's blackbird, mountain bluebird, spotted sandpiper

Reptile: mountain garter snake

Amphibians: Yosemite toad, Pacific treefrog, mountain yellow-legged frog

Where seen: Tuolumne Meadows, Dana Meadows, Lyell Canyon, Grace Meadow, Kerrick Meadow, McGurk Meadow, Mono Meadow, Moraine Meadow, Lukens Lake, Cathedral Lakes, Dog Lake, Middle Gaylor Lake, Washburn Lake, Emeric Lake

6. Subalpine Forest

Trees: whitebark pine, lodgepole pine, western white pine, mountain hemlock

Shrubs: bush cinquefoil, arctic (alpine) willow, Eastwood's willow, Mono willow, Sierra willow, red mountain heather, white heather, Labrador tea, alpine gooseberry, sticky currant

Wildflowers: Sierra wallflower, Davidson's (timberline) penstemon, Coville's lupine, Coville's columbine, mountain sorrel, rock fringe, Lobb's eriogonum, cut-leaved daisy, alpine saxifrage, pink alum root

Mammals: pika, yellow-bellied marmot, white-tailed hare (jack rabbit), alpine chipmunk, ermine (short-tailed weasel), little brown myotis (bat)

Birds: Clark's nutcracker, pine grosbeak, mountain chickadee, mountain bluebird, black-backed woodpecker

Amphibians: Mt. Lyell salamander, Yosemite toad

Where seen: most high lakes and passes, including Dorothy Lake, Peeler Lake, Benson Pass, Virginia Pass, Summit Lake, McCabe Lakes, Gaylor Lakes, Tioga Pass, Mono Pass, Ireland Lake, Vogelsang High Sierra Camp, May Lake, Ten Lakes, Buena Vista Peak, Post Peak Pass, Fernandez Pass, upper Chain Lake

7. Alpine Fell-Fields

Shrubs: snow willow, arctic (alpine) willow, bush cinquefoil, alpine prickly currant

Wildflowers: sky pilot, alpine gold (hulsea), Brewer's draba, Lemmon's draba, Sierra draba, dense-leaved draba, cushion phlox, Davidson's penstemon, cut-leaved daisy, dwarf alpine daisy, sticky locoweed (oxytrope), Sierra podistera, oval-leaved buckwheat, Muir's ivesia, alpine (pygmy) lewisia

Mammals: pika, yellow-bellied marmot, alpine chipmunk

Birds: rosy finch

Where seen: most of the Sierra crest from Matterhorn Peak south, including Mt. Dana, Dana Plateau, Parker Pass, and Donohue Pass; also Mt. Hoffmann and Red Peak Pass

The Ahwahnechee

One animal that could be found in all of Yosemite's plant communities was *Homo sapiens*—aboriginal natives of Yosemite Valley. Calling themselves the Ahwahnechee, these people roamed the Yosemite landscape for food gathering, trade, or tribal interactions. Generally, however, they found most of what they needed right in Yosemite Valley. Annually they burned the vegetation on the Valley's floor, and this was a tradition that had definite benefits. Foremost, it maintained the oak population, and acorns from black oaks alone made up about 60% of their diet. Fire also reduced brush and kept the forests open and parklike, thus reducing the chance of ambush. Today Yosemite Valley holds far more *Homo sapiens* (humans) than its resources could feed. We, however, carry in our own food or buy trucked-in foods. The Indians had to make do with the resources on hand, not only for food, but for all aspects of survival. They made extensive use of the Valley's resources and the resources of other nearby plant communities. The following table, based on work by a former Park naturalist, Will Neely, gives one an idea of just how extensively they utilized the plants. Animals—both vertebrates and invertebrates—were also extensively utilized.

Table 3. Indian Uses of Yosemite Plants

Food

Acorns and large seeds: black oak, sugar pine, western juniper. When black-oak acorns were scarce, then the following were used: canyon live oak, interior live oak, foothill pine, buckeye, pinyon pine (east of the Sierra crest)

Smaller seeds: bunchgrass, western buttercup, evening primrose, clarkia (farewell to spring), California coneflower

Bulbs, corms, roots: Mariposa tulip, pretty face (golden brodiaea), common camas, squaw root, Bolander's yampah

Greens: broad-leaved lupine, common monkey flower, nude buckwheat, California thistle, miner's lettuce, sorrel, clover, umbrella plant, crimson columbine, alum root

Berries and fruits: strawberry, blackberry, raspberry, thimbleberry, wild grape, gooseberry, currant, blue elderberry, western choke cherry, Sierra plum, greenleaf manzanita

Drinks: whiteleaf manzanita, western juniper

Medicine

Yerba santa, yarrow, horse mint (giant hyssop), Brewer's angelica, sagebrush, showy milkweed, mountain dogbane, balsamroot, California barberry, fleabane, mint, knotweed, wild rose, meadow goldenrod, mule ears, pearly everlasting, California laurel (bay tree)

Soap

Soap plant, meadow rue

Rope and Twine

Mountain dogbane (Indian hemp), showy milkweed, wild grape, soap plant

Baskets

Redbud, American (creek) dogwood, bigleaf maple, buckbrush, deer brush, bracken fern, willows, California hazelnut

Bows

Incense-cedar, mountain (Pacific) dogwood

Shelter

Incense-cedar

Western Humans in Yosemite

In the late 1850s tourists, homesteaders, and entrepreneurs began to flock to Yosemite Valley in increasing numbers. By 1864 the Valley was set aside ostensibly for "public use, resort and recreation," but also to protect it from these people so that future generations could enjoy it. The surrounding high country, however, was not protected, and sheep (and cattle to a lesser extent) were driven up into virtually every High Sierra meadow. Tuolumne Meadows in particular was severely overgrazed by sheep, resulting in deterioration of its soils. Overgrazing was certainly detrimental to the native fauna and flora, but by the mid-1890s grazing had been virtually eliminated from all parts of the Park except Yosemite Valley, where a dairy herd grazed, as did everyone's horses. Fruit orchards displaced native vegetation.

All the introduced animals together with their masters inadvertently brought in unwanted alien plants, insects, and associated diseases. Galen Clark, the Park's first guardian, noted that in the 30 years that passed after the Park was first created, the luxuriant native grasses and flowering plants of Yosemite Valley had decreased to only one-fourth of their original number. Part of this was due to grazing, part to other causes, and part to the new plant competition.

Overgrazing on the Valley floor resulted in trampled soil and bare spots, both inviting invasion by ponderosa pines and incense-cedars. Prohibition of fires insured the survival of young conifers which, as they matured, shaded out the once co-dominant black oaks. Finally, lowering the water table through blasting and ditching hastened this conifer invasion of the meadows. Throughout the 20th century the Valley's plant community has been largely a dense conifer forest with neatly defined, gardened meadows, not an open conifer-oak woodland.

Thanks to the Yosemite Fund (which you should join), the underfunded Park Service is now able to reverse some of the past damage. It has aided endangered peregrine falcons, great gray owls, and bighorn sheep, and has restored some meadows to more natural conditions. But how does one deal with the top predator, man?

The millions of annual visitors often has been perceived as the foremost threat to Yosemite's fauna and flora. However, the most pernicious threats usually go unseen and are beyond the control of the Park Service: man-induced global warming, increasing atmospheric pollution, upper-atmosphere ozone depletion, and habitat loss in middle and lower elevations of the Sierra Nevada and elsewhere in the Americas. The latter is of particular concern for Yosemite's birds, which in the fall typically migrate to lower elevations or to lower latitudes, such as to Central America. But everywhere the mounting human population is destroying habitat and the life it once held. For example, each person added to California ultimately causes enough habitat destruction to destroy, on average, up to one ton of animals, plants, and micro-organisms—something to ponder.

Chapter 4
Humans in Yosemite

The Thursday morning had been icy, and at times the horses of the Mariposa Battalion found themselves chest-deep in snow. Coaxed on by the spurs or verbal commands of their mounted riders, the horses progressed north toward the unknown-but-rumored Yosemite Valley. Descending through deep drifts, the battalion's 50-60 men suddenly emerged from forest cover on the western brink of the Valley's south wall. Early rumors about the Valley had not prepared the men for the breathtaking view now before them. Later recalling that profound moment of discovery, Lafayette Bunnell wrote: "The grandeur of the scene was but softened by the haze that hung over the valley—light as gossamer—and by the clouds which partially dimmed the higher cliffs and mountains. This obscurity of vision but increased the awe with which I beheld it, and as I looked, a peculiar exalted sensation seemed to fill my whole being, and I found my eyes in tears with emotion." Momentarily forgetting that there were here to round up hostile Indians, the doctor continued: "I have here seen the power and glory of a Supreme being: the majesty of His handywork is in that 'Testimony of the Rocks.' That mute appeal—pointing to El Capitan— illustrates it, with more convincing eloquence than can the most powerful arguments of surpliced priests." The day was March 27, 1851, and though about 100 million visitors viewed the Valley by the close of the second millennium, many of today's visitors share similar emotions on their first encounter.

Leaving their viewpoint, which they quickly named Mt. Beatitude (today's Old Inspiration Point), the battalion descended to the floor of Yosemite Valley and, after a brief reconnoiter, set up camp near the edge of Bridalveil Meadow. That night, at the suggestion of Dr. Bunnell, the Valley was christened "Yo-sem-i-ty," which the good doctor felt was the name of the tribe of Indians living in it. Later they discovered that the Miwok Indians inhabiting it called it "Ah-wah-nee" and called themselves the "Ah-wah-ne-chee." However, the name "Yo-sem-i-ty" stuck, though its spelling was changed to "Yosemite" in the first published account of the Valley, which was written by Lieutenant Tredwell Moore for the January 20, 1854, issue of the *Mariposa Chronicle*.

The Mariposa Battalion, under the leadership of Major James D. Savage, was certainly the first group of white men to see *and* enter the Valley. Joseph Reddeford Walker, crossing the central Sierra Nevada under threatening weather during the autumn of 1833, may have *seen* the Valley, for his party came to the rim of a deep canyon whose walls appeared to be "more than a mile high." The Valley was certainly viewed and *possibly* entered by William P. Abrams and his companion on

October 18, 1849, for his description accurately portrays some of the Valley's landmarks. Nevertheless, it was members of the Mariposa Battalion who first publicized its existence.

Chief Teneiya and the Ahwahnechee

Of course, Yosemite Valley was first discovered by the Indians. Just how many bands of Indians visited or resided in the Valley is unknown; however, the last band to live there was the Ahwahnechee, under the leadership of Chief Teneiya. Growing up with his mother's tribe, the Mono Indians, he spent much of his youth in the Mono Basin, but as a young man founded his own band and in the early 1800s moved west across the Sierra crest, probably via Mono Pass, to take up residence in Yosemite Valley. Before dying, an old "medicine man" counseled the young chief against the horsemen (Spaniards) of the lowlands, declar-

Indians gathering acorns in Yosemite Valley

National Park Service

ing that if they should enter Ahwahnee, he and his tribe would be the last Indians to live in their beloved Valley. The prophecy was self-fulfilling, for his braves attacked the outpost of James D. Savage, whose site was located along the mouth of the South Fork Merced River. Today it is passed by motorists driving east along Highway 140 up toward El Portal.

Savage and his men were not driven away; rather, he returned to the area as Major Savage of the all-volunteer Mariposa Battalion, entered the Valley in spring 1851 and burned the Indian settlements (see "The Ahwahnechee" in Chapter 3 for a look at Indian life). By June, Chief Teneiya and his band were captured by troops under Captain John Bowling and were escorted to a reservation near Fresno. Life there was unpleasant for the chief, and he made it unpleasant for others, so with some relief the reservation's officials let him return to the Valley on his own recognizance. Unfortunately, a group of eight miners who entered the Valley in the spring of 1852 were attacked by the chief's braves, and hostilities were renewed. Realizing that troops would soon be sent, Teneiya and his band fled the Valley and took refuge with his blood relatives, the Mono Indians. The band apparently returned to the Valley around summer or early autumn in 1853, but then Teneiya's braves returned to the Mono village, stole some horses that the Monos had stolen from ranches, and returned to the Valley. Fired with anger over the way the Ahwahnechee had violated their hospitality, the Monos pursued and killed most of the Ahwahnechee, including Chief Teneiya. The Valley was now safe for tourists.

The Early Tourists

Few Californians believed the first accounts of Yosemite Valley. When Dr. Bunnell wrote an article describing the height of the Valley walls as 1500 feet (half their true height), a San Francisco newspaper correspondent suggested he cut his estimates in half. Enraged, Bunnell

Upper House, built in 1858, later converted to Cedar Cottage

tore up his manuscript. Lieutenant Moore, mentioned earlier, thus produced the first published account, in January 1854. However, local Indian trouble instilled fear in potential tourists, so the first ones did not visit the Valley until the 1855 season. Among them were three men who would contribute to the Valley's history: James Hutchings, Thomas Ayrers, and Galen Clark.

Word of the beauty and grandeur of Yosemite Valley spread quickly, perhaps due to James Hutchings more than anyone else. In June 1855 he organized and led the first tourist party to Yosemite Valley, bringing along artist Thomas Ayrers to record their discoveries. No sooner than he had returned to Mariposa, Hutchings wrote up his adventures, which were published in the July 12 issue of the *Mariposa Gazette*. In 1855 California as a state was but five years old and, largely due to the clamor of the Gold Rush, it was an area of interest to many persons in the eastern states. Hutchings' article was copied in one form or another in a number of journals and newspapers, which, if nothing else, diverted readers' minds from the serious, burning issue of slavery.

Hutchings was not content to sit idle after his one article, and in July 1856 be began to publish a magazine, *Hutchings' Illustrated California Magazine*, which was devoted to the scenery of California. The first issue contained a lead article on "The Yo-Ham-i-te Valley," illustrated by none other than Thomas Ayrers. Later, Hutchings elaborated on this article, producing "The Great Yo-Semite Valley" in a series of four installments, from October 1859 to March 1860. These installments then immediately appeared as part of his book, *Scenes of Wonder and Curiosity in California,* which stayed in print well into the 1870s.

During 1856, when Hutchings first began his magazine, Thomas Ayres returned to Yosemite Valley to produce more sketches. These were highly detailed, though not true to form; rather, they exaggerated the angularity of the Valley's walls and the size of the Valley's falls. Nevertheless, Ayres, who also began to write about Yosemite, underestimated the height of the falls, as had most of his predecessors.

Commercialism first came to Yosemite in 1856. In that year Milton and Houston Mann— 2 of 42 tourists to see the Valley in 1855—completed a toll path up the South Fork Merced River and over to the Valley floor. They charged $2.00 per person—a large sum in those days—but they were later bought out by Mariposa County, and the path became free. Today you can more or less parallel this historic route by first walking up the South Fork Merced River trail, then ascend the Alder Creek trail (Hike 82), and hike from Wawona up to Bridalveil Creek (last half of Hike 83).

Next, Hike 72, from Bridalveil Creek to Dewey Point, and Hike 71, from Dewey Point to Yosemite Valley, complete the course.

The Mann brothers needed a way station along their trail, so they convinced Galen Clark, who had just built a cabin in today's Wawona area, to tend to the needs of the tourists. He did this with kindness, and his spirit of devotion to Yosemite profoundly imbued travelers with a similar reverence for this mountain landscape. The impact Clark made on others was far greater than one would expect from a quiet mountain man. Meanwhile, a simple structure, later called the Lower Hotel, was being completed as the first tourists rode down the Mann's still-fresh trail into Yosemite Valley. Other trails and hotels quickly followed and tourism increased.

Yosemite Becomes a Park

The Civil War began in April 1861, just months after Hutchings' *Scenes of Wonder and Curiosity in California* appeared. With America locked in Civil War, it is a wonder that anyone visited Yosemite. Still, some people did, and a few of these helped to get park status for Yosemite Valley. A highly influential Unitarian minister, Reverend Thomas Starr King, who had visited the Valley in 1860, saw that homesteading and commercial pursuits in it might be harmful, and he was the first—through his nationwide audience—to press for a public park. Photographs of the Valley were taken in 1861 by C. E. Watkins, and these, together with geographic and geologic data gathered by the Whitney Survey of California, provided legislators with favorable evidence backing King's exhortations.

The call of Yosemite eventually lured Fredrick Law Olmsted, the country's foremost landscape architect, to Yosemite in 1863 and he too noted that the Valley and the Mariposa Grove of Big Trees were both being ruined by commercial interests. Though young, he was already very influential, and he convinced Senator John Conness of California to introduce a Park bill in the Senate. The bill, not being controversial in the war-torn Congress, easily passed in both houses and was signed by President Abraham Lincoln on June 30, 1864. The bill deeded Yosemite Valley and the Mariposa Grove of Big Trees to the State of California "for public use, resort and recreation," and these two tracts "shall be inalienable for all time."

It is one thing to create a park on paper; it is another matter to bring it into existence. In September, California's governor proclaimed a board of Yosemite commissioners, which did not come into existence until 1866. The commissioners appointed Galen Clark as the Park's first guardian, a position he hold on and off through 1896. However, the commissioners at first lacked authority to evict homesteaders, and an 11-year battle ensued. Josiah D. Whitney, who was the first director of the California State Geological Survey, feared that "Yosemite Valley, instead of being 'a joy forever,' will become, like Niagara Falls, a gigantic institution for fleecing the public." Expressing his concern in his 1870 *Yosemite Guide-Book*, he continued:

Instead of having every convenience for circulation in and about the Valley,—free trails, roads, and bridges, with every facility offered for the enjoyment of Nature in the greatest of her works, unrestrained except by the requirements of decency and order,—the public will find, if the ownership of the Valley passes into private hands, that opportunity will be taken to levy toll at every point of view, on every trail, on every bridge, and at every turning, while there will be no inducement to do anything for the public accommodation, except that which may be made immediately available as a new means of raising a tax on the unfortunately traveller.

National Park Service

Horse stage on Big Oak Flat Road in 1903

In part he was writing against Hutchings, who like others had hoped to gain homesteading rights to 160 of the Valley floor's 2200 acres. In 1875 the claims of the early settlers were resolved. Hutchings, like three other pre-Park land owners, lost his ownership, but he was in part compensated with a State grant of $24,000 for the improvements he made on the Upper Hotel, which he had purchased just months before President Lincoln signed the park bill. Hutchings lost his hotel, but still profited from his book, which continued to attract tourists. In 1877, just after his land loss, Hutchings published a second guide, *Hutchings' Tourist Guide to the Yo Semite Valley and the Big Tree Groves* for 1877, which amazingly was very factual and not vindictive toward the Park commissioners. (An interesting sidelight in that book is that he speculated on the Valley's origin. Having lived in it extensively and having experienced floods, rockfalls, and the 1872 Owens Valley earthquake, and knowing Muir's pronouncements on glaciation, he put virtually all of it together, except for the important role of past tropical weathering, a discovery that would not be published until the following year. Nevertheless, *proper*, certified geoscientists totally ignored his views, for, as I have been told, if you don't have a Ph.D. in the field, you are unqualified to make observations. Consequently, for over a century the public has been insulted with gross misinterpretations on the Valley's origin. The only detailed account, François Matthes' US Geological Survey Professional Paper 160, published in 1930, was written to fit his professor's views, not the field evidence, and much of his mapped glacial deposits do not actually exist. My chapter 2 is based on verifiable field evidence, not imaginary, but until the USGS says otherwise, Matthes' monograph—and later USGS spinoffs—will remain the Valley's geologic Bible.)

In 1880 the reigning Park commissioners were ousted, new ones were appointed, and James Hutchings replaced Galen Clark as the Park guardian! Hutchings was a man who could get things done—usually for the *good* of the Park. Back on May 10, 1869, the transcontinental railroad had been completed, and during the 1870s a flood of settlers poured into California. These people were potential tourists, but the lengthy *horseback* ride to

Yosemite Valley was a deterrent. However, in the mid-70s, three stagecoach roads were built to the Valley: the Coulterville Road (June 1874), the Big Oak Flat Road (July 1874), and the Mariposa (Wawona) Road (July 1875). Tourists now came in droves, and this influx resulted in an increase of hotels and services in Yosemite Valley, which were more or less regulated by the commissioners. Still, these men were concerned over the Valley's deteriorating condition, as shown in their 1880 report:

1. Most of the available land is under lease for pasture and garden purposes.

2. The enclosed fields are being invaded by willows, wild roses, and other growth, to the damage of their value and of the beauty of the Valley.

3. The upper portion of the Valley, which has been set apart for the convenience of campers [first camp established in 1878], is largely overgrown with willows and young pines. The views are obstructed, the pasturage destroyed, and the appearance injured.

4. There is no practicable and unobstructed carriage road around the Valley, near the base of the cliffs. At present all who attempt to make the circuit of the floor of the Valley, must pass through gates and fields, lose some of the finest views, and be subjected to annoyance and loss of time.

Creating a National Park

While Yosemite Valley was being subjected to the detrimental effects of tourism, the surrounding countryside fared no better. Although this land was supposedly protected under Federal jurisdiction, its meadows were subjected to overgrazing by sheep (and to a lesser extent by cattle) and its forests to depletion by loggers. This rape of the landscape was first noted by a young Scotsman, John Muir, who visited Yosemite Valley in 1868 and decided to stay. His exploration of the High Sierra, first while working as a shepherd, convinced him of the damage being done by humans and their animals. In the mid 1870s he criticized both shepherds and loggers, but to no avail. Lumber was needed to build

California's growing communities, and wool export had become big business, with more than 20 million pounds produced annually.

Muir's protestations generally fell on deaf ears until 1889, when he met Robert Underwood Johnson, who was editor of the very influential *Century Magazine*. Muir took Johnson on a tour of Yosemite's highlands, including Tuolumne Meadows, and showed him the damage done by "the hooved locusts" as well as by loggers. About camping at Soda Springs in these meadows, Johnson later wrote:

> One conversation that we had beside the campfire at Soda Springs had an important sequel, for it was here that I proposed to Muir that we should set on foot the project of the Yosemite National Park. Our camp on the Tuolumne was outside the limitations of the Yosemite Valley reservation. It did not by any means include the headwaters of the streams which fed the three great falls, the Yosemite, the Nevada, and the Bridalveil. On account of the denudation by sheep the winter snows, having no underbrush to hold them, melted in torrents early in the spring, so that there was comparatively little supply for the waterfalls during the summer months. This was all explained to me by Muir, whereupon I said to him, 'Obviously the thing to do was to make a Yosemite National Park around the Valley on the plan of the Yellowstone [National Park, created in 1872]'

As any seasoned Yosemite visitor knows, Yosemite's falls greatly diminish in summer, sheep or no sheep. This is because the Sierra's post-glacial soils are young, sparse, thin, and gravelly, and so hold little ground water. Furthermore, the Tuolumne River never dries up but, as Johnson himself says, it does not feed the falls! The falls are fed by drainages that received very little grazing. But back then (as today) *accurate* environmental assessments were not performed; rather, the public needed to be motivated by whatever means it took (and, some argue, the ends justify the means). Therefore, that Muir was wrong was not important. What mattered was that his sheep argument was convincing, and he wrote some articles for the *Century Magazine* which coin-

cided, conveniently, with a Park bill introduced in Congress. The Yosemite Act of October 1, 1890 easily passed without opposition, for communications in those days were still poor—the sheep and lumbermen out west probably knew little, if anything, about the Act. but even if they had known, they wouldn't have been able to organize a lobby against it, for the Act was passed too quickly. This Act withdrew lands from "settlement, occupancy, or sale" and protected "all timber, mineral deposits [none in Yosemite], natural curiosities or wonders, and their retention in their natural condition." This included protection against "wanton destruction of the fish and game and their capture or destruction for purposes of merchandise or profit."

Yosemite Under the Fourth Cavalry

What the Yosemite Act failed to stipulate was how the newly formed Yosemite National Park should be administered. Hence it was, like Yellowstone National Park before it, put under Army jurisdiction. Troops of the Fourth Cavalry, led by Captain Abram Wood, arrived in the new park on May 19, 1891, and set up camp in Wawona, *not* in Yosemite Valley, for that part of the Park still lay under state jurisdiction. Troops were allowed into the Valley, but they had to camp at its west end, in Bridalveil Meadow.

One of several major problems confronting Captain Wood and his men was the problem of sheep grazing. Each year about 100,000 sheep had been led up into Yosemite's high meadows, but now this practice was illegal. Wood lacked the legal authority to arrest the trespassing sheepmen, but he devised a technique that discouraged them: his men would escort these herders "to another part of the Park for ejectment, this march consuming four or five days; and after they are ejected it takes as long to go back to their herds. In the meantime the sheep are alone, and the forest animals are liable to destroy or scatter many of them. When the owner awakens to this fact, he takes more interest in the doings of his herders and gives them orders not to enter the Park under any circumstances." The herders, however, grew more wary and took their sheep into more remote parts of Yosemite. The sheep problem, therefore, did not come under control until the late 1890s, and at least one herder drove sheep into Yosemite until the 1920s.

To aid in their pursuit of herders, the troops established a network of trails. Because these trails were faint and obscure, they were made easier to follow by blazing trailside conifers with a conspicuous **T**, or trail mark. None of the original **T**s remain today, but the symbol stuck, so that even in recent decades trees along Yosemite's trails were **T**-blazed.

At the end of 1896, an aging Galen Clark, who had earlier been reappointed Yosemite guardian, resigned, and was replaced by an inept guardian. Yosemite Valley began to have increased problems, and the Army, whose jurisdiction lay outside the Valley, could do nothing about them. John Muir had earlier seen the need to incorporate the Valley into the Park, in 1892 had organized the Sierra Club, and had become its first president. With 181 other charter members he pressed for this goal and others, and in 1906, after much lobbying, saw the ceding of Yosemite Valley and the Mariposa Grove to the Federal Government. However, a price was paid: the area of Yosemite National Park was substantially reduced. (Today, however, more lands are protected than in the 1890 Act, due to the creation of three buffer areas around the Park: the Ansel Adams, Hoover, and Emigrant wildernesses).

The Hetch Hetchy Reservoir

Though Muir and the Sierra Club could claim partial victory with the creation of a unified, if reduced, Yosemite National Park in 1906, they had another serious problem to confront. In 1901 the city of San Francisco had applied for permission to dam Hetch Hetchy. "Dam Hetch Hetchy!" Muir exclaimed. "As well dam for water-tanks the people's cathedrals and churches, for no holier temple has ever been consecrated by the heart of man." Secretary Hitchcock of the US Department of the Interior concurred with Muir and denied permission. But the city persisted and, despite continued opposition by the Sierra Club and others, it succeeded in obtaining water rights with the passage of the Raker Act in late 1913. The new Secretary of the Interior favored dams.

Cavalry F Troop on the Fallen Monarch giant sequoia in 1899

National Park Service

Construction began, Hetch Hetchy's granite was dynamited for rocks to make the dam's core, and the canyon's floor was cleared of timber. Part of this timber was used in the dam's construction, but an additional 6+million board feet of timber logged *inside* the Park was also used, adding insult to injury. The project was completed in 1923, but in 1938 the dam was increased by 85 feet to its present height. This reservoir could have been located down-canyon, just outside Hetch Hetchy, but a lower location would have resulted in reduced hydroelectric power. I wonder: if the road to Hetch Hetchy had extended up-canyon, providing access to the Grand Canyon of the Tuolumne, would the city have built an even greater hydroelectric project there?

Exit the Army

With the passage of the Raker Act in 1913, conservationists took a decisive defeat in their battle to save Hetch Hetchy. Muir died shortly afterward, perhaps of heartbreak, though certainly of old age. Just before he died he expressed hope that "some compensating good must follow [from the Raker Act]." It did—in the form of a new spirit of conservation, of a growing national awareness that Americans must preserve the land, not exploit and destroy it. This mounting consensus probably played a significant part in the creation of the national park Act of 1916—though in addition Europe was already at war, America was talking war, and the Army probably wanted all its troops out of the nation's parks.

When the Fourth Cavalry left Yosemite, they left behind an impressive record. They had driven sheep and cattle from the Park, had helped to settle property disputes, had laid the foundation for today's trail system, had mapped the park in substantial detail, and had even planted trout in the Park's lakes (this, however, would adversely affect the lake's native fauna). Many of the cavalry's troops are commemorated today by their names lent to dozens of the Park's backcountry features, such as Rodgers and Foerster peaks, Benson and Smedberg lakes, Fernandez and Isberg passes. For Yosemite, the cavalry had by and large "come to the rescue."

Dawn of the Automobile Era

While the intrusion of dammed water into Hetch Hetchy raged as an issue from 1901 to 1913, another intrusion faced the Park administrators. In 1900 the first automobile entered Yosemite Valley, stirring up dust and controversy, and soon proponents squared off on both sides of the automobile question. The final decision came in 1913: automobiles would be allowed in the Valley. Thus when the fledgling National Park Service took over administration in 1916, they were faced with a rising tide of tourists. America had entered the era of the automobile, the airplane, the transcontinental telephone, and the Eastman (Kodak) camera.

Faced with a rapidly growing clientele, Park administrators turned most of their attention to upgrading services. New trails were built, and old ones were brought up to modern standards. In 1916 Tuolumne Meadows Lodge was built, as were camps at Tenaya and Merced lakes, followed in 1924 by precursors of the rest of today's High Sierra Camps. Also in 1916 the Tioga Road was opened to the public, and that summer 600 automobiles entered the Park from its east side. Existing roads were paved, widened, and realigned while others were built. The All-Year Highway (Highway 140) opened in 1926 and assured that food and supplies could by transported to Yosemite Valley year-round—when major floods and rockfalls didn't temporarily close it! Herds of dairy cows had left the Valley's meadows in 1924, only to be replaced with hordes of automobiles. This flood spelled an end to the Yosemite Valley Railroad, which had started service in 1907. Many drivers drove their autos into the meadows, so in 1929 the Park Service cut roadside ditches—barriers that stopped the practice. Campgrounds were now in forest groves, away from the meadows that had been so important to the previous generations of horseback tourists.

The Yosemite Museum opened in the same year as the All-Year Highway, just four years after the creation of Yosemite's first Park Naturalist position. The early naturalists relied heavily on work done under Joseph Grinnell and Tracy Storer of Cal Berkeley's Museum of Vertebrate Zoology. Their 1914-20 field work resulted in the 1924 752-page *Animal Life in the Yosemite*. In 1930, François Matthes' monograph on the evolution of the Yosemite landscape was published. Both were declared classics, and the former, based on extensive field evidence, certainly was. The latter, based of faulty theory at the expense of field evidence, was not, and finally in the 1990s was exposed for what it actually was: a highly believable, but very erroneous, artificial construct.

When the Yosemite Museum was opened in 1926, the "urban" center of Yosemite Valley was still in the "Old Village," between today's Sentinel Bridge and the Yosemite Chapel. Gradually the Park's headquarters and Valley's stores were moved to the area around the museum, for this site was sunnier, considerably warmer in winter, and less subject to flooding. Also in 1926, work was begun on the Ahwahnee Hotel, which opened with festivities on Bastille Day, July 14, 1927. Steven T. Mather, the National Park Service's first Director, presided over the ceremonies.

Of greater importance was the end to Park logging. More than ½ *billion* board feet of timber—mostly sugar pines—had been logged from World War I until 1930, when John D. Rockefeller, Jr. and the Federal Government split the cost of buying out the Yosemite Lumber Company (some of the logged land can be seen along part of Hike 83).

During the Depression years, numerous persons were employed in CCC, CWA, and PWA projects that added refinements to the human imprint on the Yosemite landscape. World War II temporarily put an end to future projects and during it the Park served as an R & R site for almost 90,000 battle-weary troops.

The Postwar Years

After VE and VJ days, America engaged in a pursuit of the good life, and this included traveling in ever-increasing numbers. About ⅔ million tourists visited Yosemite in 1946, and by 1954 the number had grown to 1 million. In 1956 the National Park Service embarked on a 10-year "Mission 66" program, whose goal was to "assure the maximum protection of the scenic, scientific, wilderness, and historic resources of the National Park System in such ways and by such means as will make them available for the use and enjoyment of present and future generations." By the end of this program, in 1966 (the 50th anniversary of the NPS), Yosemite was receiving about two million visitors a year.

Hikers and car-campers continued to inundate Yosemite in following years. On the three-day "summer" weekends—Memorial Day, Fourth of July, and Labor Day—as many as 50,000+ visitors, half of them youths, crammed into Yosemite Valley. Whereas campers used to leave their belongings out on tables day after day, to do so now was to invite theft. By 1970 the Valley scene had become ugly, with thefts, drugs, rapes, fights, riots, and even murders.

However, 1970 also marked the start of a series of projects based on research done in the Mission 66 program. One was to remove vehicles from the congested east end of the Valley and replace them with a free shuttle bus system. With the start of the third millennium, they will be removed from all but the westernmost part of the Valley, and then, hopefully, will be completely removed a few years later, once alternative public transportation has been set in place. Realizing that a complete ban on vehicles was years away, the Park Service took an intermediate step to reduce the Valley's noise and violence. During the early and mid-70s it gradually converted the campgrounds

The 1970s "John Muir Freeway," 8 lanes wide, through Tuolumne Meadows

over to a fixed-site plan, which reduced the camper population to several thousand instead of tens of thousands. Tranquillity began to return to the Valley.

And what of the backcountry? Likewise, it too had a population explosion, driven in part by lightweight backpacking technology which made carrying food and gear into the wilderness easier than ever. The backcountry, like Yosemite Valley, developed local areas of congestion—mostly in Little Yosemite Valley and at easily reached lakes off the Tioga Road. The wilderness permit came to the Park in 1972 as an initial step to monitor use. In succeeding years, rangers attempted to direct hikers away from popular destinations, and soon initiated a quota system, which set limits to backcountry sites. The quota system spread through the Sierra Nevada, to the satisfaction of many, but to the annoyance of others. For example, on any given day only a trifling number of hikers can ascend Mt. Whitney, the highest summit in the Lower 48 States. In contrast, anyone can ascend Mt. Kosciusko, the highest summit in Australia. Why? The Aussies built a first-class trail, and a number of outhouses, to handle the traffic. And in Austria the mountains have hundreds of heavily used "huts" that have minimal environmental impact. Thus while we Californians can visit many foreign countries and have ready access to their mountains, the reverse is not true for foreigners coming to the Sierra Nevada and expecting to hike say, the John Muir Trail.

During the 1970s the number of Yosemite visitors temporarily stabilized at about 2-2½ million per year. However, the '80s saw an upswing, which continued into the '90s, when annual visitation hovered around 4 million per year. How could the Park Service address the needs of all these visitors and still protect the natural integrity of the Park? Back in 1980 a range of solutions were proposed in the *General Management Plan* (GMP). However, given the Federal deficit, the GMP was unaffordable. Still, during the '80s some points in the GMP were implemented, including: the asphalt parking lot in front of the Visitor Center was removed; several miles of bike paths were constructed; sewage treatment was upgraded; the warehouse and reservation functions of the Yosemite Park and Curry Company were relocated to Fresno; most of the Park was given wilderness status; and

bighorn sheep were introduced back into the Park. But most of the plan was not implemented, and in 1989 the Park Service produced the *Draft Yosemite GMP Examination Report*, which stated why the 1980 GMP wouldn't work and why it should be changed. Predictably, this enraged certain environmental groups. However, the GMP had treated the Park as a closed system, which it is not. Any grand solution for the Park, for the Lake Tahoe Basin, for the Mother Lode, or for any other designated area must address a much larger area, and must address it in great complexity. A start in this overdue, holistic, ecological approach was made in the mid-90s with the publication of the 2800+ page *Status of the Sierra Nevada*, a Congressional study by the Sierra Nevada Ecosystem Project, based at the University of California, Davis.

The Park celebrated its centennial as a national park in 1990. It was not the Park's best year. January brought a flood of letters, mostly negative, on the *Draft Yosemite GMP Examination Report*. In March a rockslide briefly closed Highway 140. The Tioga Road, opened on May 17, was twice closed by late-season snow. July 14 saw a downpour in Yosemite Valley. Then from August 7 through 21, lightning-caused fires ravaged western Park lands, burning over 24,000 acres and destroying most of the homes of the private inholding known as Foresta; Yosemite Valley visitors had to be evacuated. On October 1, the Park celebrated its official 100th anniversary. However, because of Federal budget uncertainties, Park campgrounds and visitor centers were closed for two days. As part of the 1990 Centennial Celebration, three speeches were presented by noted speakers. Rather than being celebrations, they were criticisms of what was wrong with the Park, with pleas to return it to its natural condition.

The Park—particularly Yosemite Valley—can never be returned to the pristine condition seen by its discovers, the Indians. However, certain beneficial changes can be made, and are being made, thanks in particular to the Yosemite Fund, which in its first 10 years, 1988-1997, raised $11½ million for about 100 projects. What the Federal Government could not do, the private sector did. Mother Nature also helped, with "the flood of the century" in the first few days of January 1997. Expensive damage to structures on the Valley floor

ensured that they would not be rebuilt. To preserve Yosemite National Park in the third millennium will require the cooperation of all
branches of the government and all aspects of
the private sector, including input from communities along the highways to the Park. One
hopes the Park can be managed in such a way
that it will instill in each new visitor the same
awe and reverence that were experienced by
those who first laid eyes on it.

Part Two

One Hundred Hikes

Selecting Your Hike

If you know what area you want to hike in, turn to the appropriate geographical section and review its hikes. The 100 hikes in this guide are found in Chapters 5-12, and these eight chapters are arranged more or less from northwest to southeast. If you are skilled at using a topographic map, then the one enclosed with this book should help you envision the Park's geography encountered along its trails. (Hikes sometimes mention elevations of peaks, passes, or lakes, and these elevations are taken from 15' topographic maps, not this book's less-detailed Park map.) If you are unfamiliar with the Park or are uncomfortable at map interpretation, you can use Table 1 to decide what hike is best for you. For each hike in this table, the following basic information is given, which should help you narrow your selection to just a few possibilities.

Recommended hiking time: This is the length of time that I feel is best for a given hike walked by the *average* hiker. You may want or need more time or less time. Elevation, topography, and hiking duration were taken into account in arriving at these recommended times, for a hike will be more exhausting if it is at high altitude, if it involves lots of ascent and descent, or if it is long and therefore requires an initially heavy backpack. Generally, most of this book's backpack trips require only 8-10 miles of walking per day—a travel rate designed to give you ample time for many stops. John Muir would have found this meager distance disgraceful, and the recommended hikes in *his* 1912 guidebook generally required an output of 25 miles per day over rugged terrain. At that rate, however, you see little more than peaks and domes, and you can't absorb the myriad sights, sounds, odors, or feelings experienced by hikers intimately aware of their surroundings.

Grade and difficulty: The information in this column tells you how hard your hike will be. The numbers refer to each hike's mileage, as follows: 1: 0.0-4.9 miles; 2: 5.0-9.9 miles; 3: 10.0-14.9 miles; 4: 15.0-19.9 miles; 5: 20.0-29.9

miles; 6: 30.0-49.9 miles; and 7: 50.0+ miles. The letters refer to the total elevation gain you must climb: A: 0-499 feet; B: 500-999 feet; C: 1000-1999 feet; D: 2000-3999 feet; E: 4000-6999 feet; F: 7000-9999 feet; and G: 10,000+ feet. Total gain is not the elevation difference between your trail's high and low points (that is net gain); rather it is the vertical distance you'll have to climb along your entire trip, both going and returning. The ratings are for the minimum distance and do not include any side hikes that are suggested in the hike's description, which are extra.

The words "easy," "moderate," and "strenuous" describe the difficulty of the hike, given the recommended hiking time. Of course, you can decrease the difficulty of most hikes by taking longer to do them.

Hiking season: This is the period of the year you should be able to drive to a trailhead and then hike an essentially snow-free trail. On the higher trails you may experience snow flurries, but your trail will be covered by only a few inches of snow, not a snowpack. Should you choose, you can hike early in the season, when trail use is light or nil, but then be prepared for some route-finding problems due to

Left: *Two hikers descending Half Dome's cable route*

57

parts of the trail being under snow. In Yosemite Valley you can hike year round, for it is unlikely you would get lost even with a foot of winter snow on the floor. You may not find the trail, but then, you won't have to, if the snowpack is firm enough for cross-country hiking or skiing.

Hiker use: "Light," "moderate," "heavy," or "very heavy" is used to describe each trail's popularity. This gives you an idea of how many people to expect. On heavily used backpack trails, campsites may be in short supply on weekends though probably not on weekdays. Some of this book's hikes have sections that vary significantly in usage. For example, Hike 14's first day traverses to heavily used campsites near Rancheria Falls, but on the second day it leaves virtually everyone behind. Later, it joins the moderately used Pacific Crest Trail, then takes the lightly used Jack Main Canyon trail to Moraine Ridge, beyond which you descend on a moderately used trail. Therefore, overall its use should be moderate, but I have given it a light designation, based on my own subjectivity, since along its two lightly used sections I felt truly alone.

Can swim and fish: This is fairly obvious. Usually where you can swim you can also fish, typically in one or more lakes seen along the trail, but also in the Tuolumne, Merced, and South Fork Merced rivers. If you can do only one of these two activities, then the table says which one. For example, Harden Lake (Hike 20), is too shallow to support trout, but is an enjoyable, relatively warm swimming hole. In contrast, on a walk up along Tenaya Creek to Mirror Meadow (Hike 66), you can fish, but the creek is unsuitable for safe and enjoyable swimming.

Exceptionally scenic: Yosemite as a whole is very scenic, but some trails are more scenic than others. The criterion used for this category is that a hike is classified "exceptionally scenic" if the views alone justify taking it. Hikes that are not rated exceptionally scenic are still worth taking unless your sole concern is spectacular mountain scenery.

Other Pre-Hike Information

Once you have narrowed your potential hike down to a few choices, you can turn to them and read their descriptions to see which one is best for you. At the start of each hike is certain basic information: distance, grade (already discussed), trailhead, and introduction.

Distance: Distance is given in miles, not also in kilometers, since trail signs give mileage only. Included with the distance is the type of hike: round trip, loop trip, semiloop trip, and one-way trip. A *round* trip is not a circular one, but rather is one on which you hike to a destination and return the way you came. A *loop* trip is one on which you wind across the terrain and return to your trailhead without having to retrace any of your route, except perhaps for a small part of it. A semiloop trip is a combination of the two: it has at least one significant segment on which you'll have to retrace your steps plus at least one loop. A *one-way* trip is one on which you hike in one direction, ending somewhere away from your starting point. On this kind of hike you'll usually have to be dropped off by someone who later meets you at trail's end. Or, if you and your friends have two vehicles, you can leave one at the start and the other one at trail's end.

Mileages are based on my data, and they often disagree, usually slightly, with signs. Signs aren't always consistent. If you were to record all the mileages on signs and then determine the distances along segments between trail junctions, you would find that some segments have two or more distances. Which to use? I use my own, based on my own detailed mapping of the trails and then measuring the length of the trails as drawn on topo maps. There are map distortions in every topo map, so my distances can be off. Nevertheless, they are accurate enough for hikers. Along an actual 10.0-mile trail I may come up with 9.8 to 10.2 miles.

Trailhead: The trailhead is where you park your vehicle and start your hike. Included in this section for each route are all the necessary driving directions to get to the trailhead. Virtually all the roads are in good-to-excellent condition except when snowbound. At the end of this section is a letter/number combination in boldface type—for example, **F3**—which gives you the location of the trailhead on this book's topographic map.

Introduction: This section tells you briefly what you can expect. It is useful in your decision of what trail to hike.

Wilderness Permits

For overnight stays in the backcountry, you need a wilderness permit. If you are visiting from November through April, there are no reservations; you register in person. For the appropriate location to register, see the "Wilderness Permits" section at the start of each hiking chapter (Chapters 5-12). For the rest of the year you can make reservations, although for most trails and destinations, you can probably do so successfully in person, since their quotas likely will not be full. However, popular destinations, such as Lyell Canyon, the Cathedral Lakes, the Vogelsang Lake area, and Little Yosemite Valley, can easily reach their quotas, especially for overnight trips beginning on a summer weekend. Therefore, you might want to get a permit well in advance, especially if you are hiking on a summer weekend.

You can get a permit from 24 weeks to 2 days in advance of your trip date. You can also get a permit by calling the Wilderness Center at 209/372-0200 (press 3), but the reservation phone lines are often busy, and you may not get through. Therefore, you are encouraged to make your request in writing. Written requests are processed simultaneously with phone requests. Write to: Wilderness Permits, P.O. Box 545, Yosemite, CA 95389. Include the following in your request: name, address, daytime phone, number of people in party, method of travel (i.e., ski, snowshoe, foot, horse), number of stock (if applicable), start and end dates, entry and exit trailheads, and principal destination. Include alternate dates and/or trailheads. A $3 *per person* non-refundable processing fee is charged for all reservation requests. Payment by check or money order should be made to the Yosemite Association. Credit card payments are accepted with valid card number and expiration date. For wilderness information, you also can go to the wilderness website at www.nps.gov/yose/wilderness.

Yosemite's trails may be marked with "T" blazes, "i" blazes, or "ducks"

Table 1. Summary of this guide's 100 hikes

Hike	Recommended hiking time	Grade and difficulty	Hiking season	Hiker use	Can swim and fish	Exceptionally scenic
Chapter 5: Trails of Yosemite's North and West Backcountry						
A. Trails approached from the north						
1	1 day	4D-strenuous	mid July-mid Oct.	Moderate	No	Yes
2	6 days	7F-moderate	mid July-mid Oct.	Moderate	Yes	No
3	2 days	4D-moderate	July-October	Heavy	Yes	No
4	6 days	7F-moderate	July-mid Oct.	Moderate	Yes	Yes
5	2 days	3D-moderate	July-October	Moderate	Yes	Yes
6	3 days	5E-moderate	July-mid Oct.	Moderate	Yes	No
7	2 days	4D-moderate	July-September	Moderate	Yes	Yes
B. Trails approached from the west						
8	4 days	6E-moderate	mid June-Oct.	Moderate	Yes	No
9	2 days	4D-moderate	mid June-Oct.	Moderate	Yes	No
10	1 day	3D-moderate	May-November	Heavy	Yes	No
11	4 days	5E-moderate	mid June-Oct.	Moderate	Yes	No
12	4 days	6F-moderate	July-mid Oct.	Light	Yes	No
13	5 days	7G-strenuous	July-mid Oct.	Light	Yes	No
14	7 days	7G-strenuous	July-mid Oct.	Light	Yes	No
Chapter 6: Trails of Yosemite's West-Central Lands, between the Tuolumne River and Highway 120						
15a	½ day	1C-strenuous	April-November	Light	Yes	No
15b	1 day	2B-easy	April-November	Light	Yes	No
16	½ day	1B-easy	May-November	Light	No	No
17	2 days	4D-moderate	June-October	Light	No	No
18	2 hours	1B-moderate	May-October	Moderate	No	No
19	2 hours	1B-moderate	June-October	Heavy	No	No
20	½ day	2B-easy	June-October	Heavy	Swim	No
21	2 days	5D-moderate	July-October	Light	No	No
22	2 days	5E-strenuous	June-October	Moderate	Yes	No
23	½ day	1A-easy	July-October	Moderate	Yes	No
24	2 hours	1A-easy	July-October	Moderate	Yes	No
25	2 days	3D-moderate	July-mid Oct.	Heavy	Yes	No
26	½ day	1B-easy	July-mid Oct.	Heavy	Fish	No
27	1 day	2D-strenuous	July-mid Oct.	Heavy	Fish	Yes
28	3 days	5E-moderate	July-September	Light	Yes	No
Chapter 7: Trails of Yosemite's West-Central Lands, between the Tioga Road and Yosemite Valley						
29	1 day	2C-moderate	May-November	Light	Yes	No
30	½ day	1B-easy	late June-Sept.	Light	Yes	No
31	1 day	4D-strenuous	late June-Sept.	Light	Yes	Yes
32	1 day	3C-moderate	July-October	Moderate	Fish	No
33	1 day	2D-moderate	July-October	Light	No	Yes
34	1 day	2A-moderate	July-October	Light	Fish	No
35	1 day	3B-moderate	July-October	Light	Fish	No
36	2 hours	1A-easy	late June-Oct.	Moderate	Yes	Yes
Chapter 8: Trails of the Tuolumne Meadows Area, north of the Tioga Road						
37	1 day	2B-easy	July-mid. Oct.	Light	Yes	No
38	1 hour	1A-easy	late June-mid Oct.	Heavy	Fish	Yes
39	2 days	3C-easy	July-mid. Oct.	Heavy	Fish	Yes
40	6 days	7F-moderate	July-early Oct.	Heavy	Yes	Yes
41	4 days	6F-moderate	July-mid. Oct.	Moderate	Yes	Yes
42	7 days	7G-strenuous	mid July-September	Moderate	Yes	Yes
43	5 days	7G-strenuous	mid July-September	Moderate	Yes	Yes
44	2 days	3D-moderate	July-mid. Oct.	Heavy	Yes	Yes
45	½ day	1B-moderate	July-mid Oct.	Heavy	Yes	Yes
46	1 day	2C-easy	July-mid. Oct.	Moderate	Yes	Yes

Chapter 9: Trails of the Tuolumne Meadows Area, south and east of the Tioga Road

47	2 days	3D-easy	July-mid Oct.	Heavy	Yes	No
48	1 day	3D-strenuous	July-mid Oct.	Moderate	No	Yes
49	2 days	5E-strenuous	July-mid Oct.	Moderate	No	Yes
50	½ day	2C-moderate	July-mid Oct.	Heavy	Yes	Yes
51	2 days	5D-moderate	July-mid Oct.	Heavy	Yes	Yes
52	4 days	6D-easy	July-mid Oct.	Heavy	Yes	Yes
53	½ day	2C-moderate	July-mid Oct.	Light	Yes	Yes
54	½ day	1C-moderate	July-mid Oct.	Heavy	Yes	No
55	½ day	2A-easy	July-mid Oct.	Heavy	Fish	Yes
56	4 days	5E-moderate	July-mid Oct.	Heavy	Yes	Yes
57	2 days	5D-moderate	July-mid Oct.	Heavy	Yes	Yes
58	3 days	5D-moderate	mid July-September	Heavy	Yes	Yes
59	1 day	2C-moderate	July-mid Oct.	Moderate	Yes	No
60	2 days	5D-moderate	mid July-September	Light	Yes	Yes
61	½ day	2D-strenuous	July-mid-Oct.	Heavy	No	Yes

Chapter 10: Trails of the Yosemite Valley Area

A. Valley Floor

62	½ day	2B-easy	April-December	Moderate	Yes	Yes
63	½ day	2A-easy	April-December	Moderate	Yes	Yes
64	2 hours	1A-easy	April-December	Moderate	Yes	Yes
65	2 hours	1A-easy	April-December	Moderate	Fish	No
66	2 hours	1A-easy	April-November	Heavy	Fish	Yes
67	½ day	2A-easy	May-November	Moderate	Fish	Yes

B. North Rim

68	½ day	2D-strenuous	late May-early Nov.	Heavy	No	Yes
69	1 day	3E-strenuous	late June-October	Moderate	No	Yes
70	1 day	4E-strenuous	July-October	Moderate	Fish	Yes

C. South Rim

71	1 day	3D-moderate	mid-June-mid Nov.	Light	No	Yes
72	1 day	3C-moderate	July-mid Oct.	Moderate	No	Yes
73	2 hours	1A-easy	late June-mid Oct.	Moderate	No	Yes
74	2 hours	1B-moderate	late June-mid Oct.	Heavy	No	Yes
75	1 day	3D-moderate	July-mid October	Light	Fish	Yes
76	2 hours	1A-easy	mid June-October	Heavy	No	Yes

D. East of Valley

77	2 hours	1A-moderate	April-November	Very heavy	No	Yes
78	½ day	2D-strenuous	June-early Nov.	Very heavy	No	Yes
79	2 days	2D-moderate	June-October	Very heavy	Yes	Yes
80	1 day	4E-strenuous	mid June-September	Very heavy	Yes	Yes
81	3 days	5E-moderate	mid June-mid Oct.	Heavy	Yes	Yes

Chapter 11: Trails south and east of the Glacier Point Road

82	½ day	2C-moderate	mid April-mid Nov.	Light	No	No
83	3 days	6E-moderate	mid June-October	Light	Fish	No
84	2 days	3C-easy	July-mid October	Heavy	Yes	No
85	2 days	4D-moderate	July-mid October	Moderate	Yes	No
86	4 days	6E-easy	July-mid October	Moderate	Yes	No
87	1 day	2C-moderate	late June-mid Oct.	Heavy	No	Yes
88	6 days	7G-moderate	July-early October	Moderate	Yes	Yes
89	5 days	6F-moderate	July-early October	Moderate	Yes	Yes
90	1 day	2D-moderate	May-November	Moderate	No	No
91	4 days	5E-moderate	July-mid October	Moderate	Yes	No
92	1 day	4D-strenuous	June-November	Light	No	No
93	½ day	2C-moderate	June-November	Moderate	No	Yes

Chapter 12: Trails of Yosemite's Southeastern Backcountry

94	2 days	4E-moderate	July-October	Light	Yes	No
95	2 days	3D-easy	July-October	Heavy	Yes	No
96	3 days	5E-easy	July-October	Moderate	Yes	No
97	3 days	3D-easy	July-October	Heavy	Yes	Yes
98	6 days	6F-moderate	July-early Oct.	Moderate	Yes	Yes
99	2 days	4D-moderate	July-mid Oct.	Moderate	Yes	No
100	3 days	5E-moderate	July-early Oct.	Moderate	Yes	Yes

Chapter 5

Trails of Yosemite's North and West Backcountry

Introduction: There are so many trails leading into Yosemite's north and west backcountry that their descriptions could easily fill a book. Actually, in past years they have helped to fill four small books: *Pinecrest, Tower Peak, Matterhorn Peak,* and *Hetch Hetchy* High Sierra Hiking Guides, published by Wilderness Press. Of these, only Hetch Hetchy is still in print, though in 1990 *Pinecrest* and *Tower Peak* were replaced by Dr. Ben Schifrin's *Emigrant Wilderness and Northwestern Yosemite.* The *Matterhorn Peak* guide contained only two routes not described in this Yosemite guide. One is through awe-inspiring, although lakeless, Buckeye Creek canyon, which offers a long way in to the backcountry. The other is up a trail south from Mono Village to a use trail that climbs south to a saddle above the head of Spiller Creek canyon. These two routes are shown on this book's map, along with many other undescribed trails outside the Park.

The trail description in this section includes the shorter and more-desirable approaches. All the trails within Yosemite's north and west backcountry are described. This area's landscape is characterized by many parallel or nearly parallel canyons, which, generally, speaking, get progressively deeper toward the east. Many of the canyons lack trails, and the Park's management is to be applauded for keeping them that way. In the author's opinion, this Yosemite backcountry and the adjacent Emigrant Wilderness together contain the finest assemblage of cross-country routes to be found in the Sierra Nevada—a last stronghold for the true wilderness experience.

Supplies and Services: Absolutely everything you'll need for a Yosemite outdoor experience can be purchased in the western-foothills town of Sonora. This includes full backpacking and mountaineering gear, available at the Sierra Nevada Adventure Company. Supplies in Bridgeport, on Highway 395, are also quite complete, and each of these towns has at least one hospital. Limited supplies can also be purchased in smaller settlements such as Groveland, Pinecrest, Strawberry, Dardanelle, Lee Vining, and Mono Village. Mono Village, a large resort, has one of the best backpacker-oriented stores to be found in any Sierra mountain resort.

Wilderness Permits: If you want to reserve a permit, rather than get one in person, see the "Wilderness permits" section on page 59. In person, for Hikes 1 and 2, get your permit at the Summit Ranger Station, located at the Pinecrest "Y." For Hikes

Left: *North Peak reflected in Greenstone Lake, along Hike 7*

3-7, stop at the Bridgeport Ranger Station for permits if you're coming from the north. It is on Highway 395, about ½ mile south of Bridgeport. Those driving from the south on Highway 395 may prefer to get a permit at the Lee Vining Ranger Station, on Highway 120, 1.2 miles west from the Highway 395 junction. For Hike 7, permits are also available at the Saddlebag Lake Resort, near the trailhead. Those following Hike 8 should stop at the Groveland Ranger Station in the small community of Groveland, about 14 miles before the Cherry Lake turnoff. For Hikes 9-14, use either the Information Station at the Park's Big Oak Flat Entrance Station, or use the Hetch Hetchy Entrance Station, by the Mather Ranger Station. The latter is open from about early April through late October.

Campgrounds: For Hike 1, if you are driving up from the west, use Baker Campground, located just off Highway 108 about 9.2 miles before Sonora Pass. If driving from the east, use Leavitt Meadow Campground, on Highway 108, 7.1 miles west of Highway 395 and 8.0 miles east of the pass. Also use this campground for Hike 2. For Hikes 3 and 4 use any of the five campgrounds along Twin Lakes Road or use the private campground in Mono Village. For Hikes 5 and 6, camp at Virginia Lakes Campground, just yards from the trailhead. Saddlebag Campground is best for Hike 7, since it is only a minute's walk from the trailhead parking area. Sawmill Walk-in and Junction campgrounds are along the Saddlebag Lake road, and five more campgrounds are along Highway 120 between Highway 395 and Tioga Pass. For Hike 8 use Cherry Valley Campground. From the major intersection near the trailhead parking area go left 0.5 mile west up Road 1N04, then branch right and go 0.5 mile to the campground's entrance. For Hikes 9-14, you could spend the night at Dimond O Campground, about 5.6 miles north on Evergreen Road, which begins from Highway 120 just 0.6 mile before the Park's boundary below the Big Oak Flat Entrance Station. *If you have a wilderness permit*, you can stay at the Hetch Hetchy Backpackers Campground, located on the loop road by the O'Shaughnessy Dam trailhead.

HIKE 1

SONORA PASS TO KENNEDY CANYON CREST

Distance: 16.4 miles round trip

Grade: 4D, strenuous day hike; no trailside campsites

Trailhead: Drive up Highway 108 to Sonora Pass and park at the signed Pacific Crest Trail parking area, whose entrance is about 250 yards west of the pass. Trail begins in map section **H1**.

Introduction: This alpine route, an 8¼-mile segment of the Pacific Crest Trail completed in 1977, provides breathtaking panoramas of granitic northern Yosemite National Park and of the volcanic Sonora Pass area. Continuing southeast on the trail to Dorothy Lake Pass (reverse of Hike 42) is an extremely scenic way to enter Yosemite National Park.

Description: From the lower part of the parking area, the Pacific Crest Trail (PCT) traverses about 200 yards southwest over to a highway crossing just 50 yards north of Sonora Pass. We now begin a winding course up the crest of the Sierra Nevada. After only 250 feet of elevation gain the dominant lodgepole pines are mostly replaced by those harbingers of timberline, whitebark pines. We cross the crest, then dip to cross five closely spaced gullies, which contain our only permanent source of water. Beyond them we circle clockwise, climbing the well-graded trail up a cirque's rubbly headwall back onto the now-alpine crest. From it a panorama explodes into view, ranging from Peak 10641 in the southwest to Stanislaus and Sonora peaks in the north, and down into the West Walker River canyon in the east. Our climb south stays just a few yards east of the crest, and on the upper part of this ascent the narrow trail becomes quite exposed. Although this exposure on loose volcanic rock is generally not a problem in mid or late summer, it can be one before mid-July, when it is apt to be covered by an icy snowfield. Inexperienced mountaineers should not attempt this trail during that season, for then there are also two more hazardous trail sections.

Our 400-foot climb south ends above the 2-mile-high level, leaving one breathless but elated, for all the major climbing is now over, and the trail ahead is generally an easy, contouring route. Its ease is certainly an added plus, for with a full ⅓ less oxygen than at sea level, the rarefied atmosphere would hinder one's enjoyment if the trail were difficult. Your enjoyment can also be hindered if you haven't dressed for windy weather and if you haven't protected yourself—with hat, dark glasses, and sunscreen—from the more-intense ultraviolet radiation existing up here.

On west slopes within Emigrant Wilderness we contour south toward Leavitt Peak, the point where three crests unite. Dense waist-high clumps of whitebark pines sporadically paint the rusty alpine landscape with patches of green both before and after a crest saddle. At a second saddle the PCT crosses the crest, then makes a brief, steep switchback and descends gradually—seasonally across a lingering snowfield—to two glacial moraines at the foot of a glacial cirque. These two moraines were left by a glacier during the Little Ice Age. Because the volcanic rock there is so rubbly, it doesn't hold water, so we don't find a lake in the small, deep basin between the two moraines and Peak 11265.

From the moraines we climb steeply but briefly up to a cleft in a ragged ridge and are almost knocked off our feet by the overpowering view (or perhaps by a gusty wind). You can find higher passes in the Sierra Nevada, but hardly one with a view that surpasses the rugged, alpine view before us. From the cleft we skirt the base of the ridge, staying high above Latopie Lake, whose barren, rocky shore offers little consolation to the camper. The abundance of large blocks along our traverse testifies to the instability of the volcanic ridge above us, and the possibility of a rock avalanche is a real concern for early-season hikers. Their final concern will be just ahead, where this short stretch in early season could send an inexperienced hiker quickly down to—and over—the brink of a cliff above Latopie Lake. Luckily, this hazard can be avoided by first climbing southwest up to a level area below Leavitt Peak and then heading southeast on it to a gully.

Beyond the gully our trail descends gradually across a giant scree slope—the east side of Leavitt Peak. Its instability makes plant growth on it virtually impossible, thus making the landscape an austere one. Where the slope curves from southwest to southeast, you should leave the trail if you plan to "bag" Leavitt Peak, a loose but safe 800 feet of climbing above you. Otherwise, contour ¼ mile southeast back to the crest of the Sierra Nevada—actually a double crest that has the tendency to become very blustery. Your last 2¼ miles of trail also can be likewise, though most day hikers will experience pleasant weather. The volcanic slopes here are more stable than the ones we just left, thus you may see alpine gold and other high-altitude wildflowers dotting the landscape. Here volcanic rocks extend

The Sierra crest, including Tower Peak at far right, seen from jeep road above Kennedy Canyon

all the way down to the shore of Kennedy Lake, 2800 feet below us. By 7 million years ago, our once-granitic landscape had been buried in places to a depth of more than 3000 feet due to the outpouring of dozens of lava flows and other volcanic products. Along your ridge traverse be sure to stop at the three main-crest saddles, all only a few yards away from the trail. The changing views of glaciated Leavitt Creek canyon are well worth the small effort.

Our section of PCT ends at a switchback on a closed jeep road, and from here you retrace your day's course. Alternatively, you can end your hike by first following the jeep road 0.2 mile northeast up to a saddle to start a 2200-foot descent to Highway 108. You first take the main jeep road down to the outlet creek of Leavitt Lake, where you can find campsites among small stands of whitebark pines. You may find more-protective sites along the drivable road that descends 2.9 miles from the lake to a switchback along Highway 108. This junction is 3.7 miles below Sonora Pass. The more than 1100-foot climb from that junction up to 9556-foot Leavitt Lake makes a relatively easy backpack trip, although many will find the lake's treeline environs too cool, windswept, and shady.

HIKE 2

TOWER PEAK COUNTRY VIA WEST WALKER RIVER

Distance: 57.4 miles one way

Grade: 7F, moderate 6-day hike

Trailhead: Park one vehicle at trip's end at the Hike 1 trailhead. From adjacent Sonora Pass, drive a second vehicle 8.0 miles east down Highway 108 to Leavitt Meadow Campground. Park in the trailhead parking area immediately north of the campground. **H1.**

Introduction: This relatively low-level route into the heart of the Yosemite north country passes some justifiably popular fishing waters, then cuts cross-country for 2 miles to reach Tilden Lake, possibly the epitome of the verdant, pastoral north country. Our exit, via the famous Pacific Crest Trail, provides a rugged, spectacular alpine finale.

Description: From the trailhead the West Walker River trail drops east a few yards to bridge the wide West Walker River under a typical east-slope volcanic-soil forest association: robust, widely spaced Jeffrey pines, squat junipers, streamside Fremont's cottonwoods, and a sagebrush understory. East of the river, our well-trod path climbs briefly east past metamorphic rocks, then traverses briefly south to a west-dropping use-trail. From this junction we climb east momentarily to a low ridge and, 0.3 mile from our trailhead, reach an important junction. From it the older trail to Roosevelt Lake via Secret Lake continues east before climbing south. This trail is 0.6 mile longer than the newer trail, and its undulating route requires quite a bit more climbing and descending.

We take the newer trail, which swings south and quickly drops to an open, sagebrush-dotted bench on the east side of giant Leavitt Meadow. It stays along this side for 1.4 miles, keeping well above wide meanders of the West Walker River. Across it, one may hear the shouts of Marine mountain troops practicing rock-climbing techniques on a nearby cliff. Later, we pass the horse trail from Leavitt Pack Station, which is not a recommended route for backpackers due to a deep, dangerous ford of the river. Upon leaving Leavitt Meadow, we begin to climb, and in several minutes reach a junction with another Leavitt Meadow trail, coming in on our right, and then in several more minutes our trail tops out at a diminutive pond. Immediately beyond it we encounter a long, slender pond and just past it a junction with a trail that heads northeast to Secret Lake. Ahead, we traverse about 130 yards to a junction with the last Leavitt Meadow trail—the route one would take if one were to follow the meadow's westside road.

We continue south, going through a gulch between granitic bluffs. This easy walk leads quickly to the north shore of Roosevelt Lake, which, with its southern twin, Lane Lake, is heavily visited, but it makes a good lunch stop. Both of these small, shallow lakes—separated by a broad isthmus of sand of possible glacial origin—harbor trout and crayfish, as well as a teeming variety of insect and attendant bird life. In the past beaver felled lakeside trees, which became covered with plants—a verdure more commonly seen in the volcanic Cascade Range. The two lakes support an unusual abundance of life, perhaps supported by lake-bottom springs, whose source is nutrient-rich volcanic rocks just above to the east and southeast. Glaciers here were about 1500 feet thick, yet despite their enormity they lacked the erosive ability to remove all of the volcanic rocks that had once buried this ancient, granitic canyon.

The West Walker River trail passes some adequate camps on the isthmus between Roosevelt and Lane lakes, then climbs gently above the latter, returning soon to camps at its southern outlet. Here a newer trail branches from the older one, which can still be followed southwest down to the West Walker River to large, secluded campsites. The newer trail climbs, via switchbacks, southeast up volcanic tuffs to a rising mile-long traverse through open aspen groves and sagebrush flats on a bench east of the river. Later, we rejoin the old riverbank route and drop to a lodgepole-and-aspen grove that borders the river's inner gorge. Here, under a 400-foot bluff of solidified volcanic mud flows, we could share shaded campsites with cattle that range through this canyon.

We quickly leave this cooler haven to swing southeast across a side stream, then steeply attack a stretch that climbs over a chaparral-clothed spur. On it we have our first up-canyon views of Forsyth Peak. We then descend briefly to the Red Top Lake trail, branching west. Although they lie only 10-20 minutes from our main trail, Red Top and Hidden lakes are only lightly visited. Red Top Lake is rimmed by sickly lodgepole pines and has poor campsites in the adjacent dense forest. Hidden Lake, just beyond, is smaller, shallower, and less appealing.

From the trail junction we resume a pleasant streamside stroll south past good camps under sheltering lodgepoles. After ¼ mile the West Walker River's course becomes a 15-foot-deep gorge through jointed granodiorite, and we follow it closely on some dynamited tread. Just beyond this gorge, the old trail fords the river, but those on foot will prefer to stay on a newer trail, which continues along the east bank for another ½ mile to a junction. From it we head briefly north and cross the river via an easy, sandy ford.

On the far bank we find campsites, the west bank West Walker River trail, and the Fremont Lake trail, about 7¼ miles from the trailhead. This trail climbs steeply northwest ¼ mile in deep sand to Fremont Lake, the best bet for our first night's camp. Fremont Lake lay directly on the route of the pioneers' Sonora Trail route west to the gold fields. In fact, emigrants once had to lower the outlet level of this good-sized lake so that their wagons could pass around its lodgepole-and-juniper-lined western shore! Heavily used camps greet us at Fremont Lake's south end. Fishing for brook and rainbow trout is only fair.

The next morning, ignore lateral trails south from Fremont Lake to Chain of Lakes and Long Lakes. These trails are unpleasantly dusty, and when the latter lakes aren't nearly stagnant, they teem with mosquitoes (but, in all fairness, with trout too). Instead, return to the West Walker River. Here also ignore the longer, less-used west-bank trail, as it too is sandy, is mosquitoey in early summer, and later may reek of cowpies. Regain the east-bank trail, southbound, and climb moderately up a wooded gully and over a minor saddle to nearby Long Canyon, up which a trail ascends southeast 4 miles to shallow, subalpine Beartrap Lake. Leap Long Canyon's creek, then continue southward through a forested grove to Lower Piute Meadow. Keeping well back in the dry eastern fringe of lodgepole forest, our way turns south along that sandy grassland, then past it our trail undulates over small ridges to soon reach the Long Lakes trail, which branches west across a small, often moist meadow. After ¼ mile of easy walking, we pass the Cascade Creek trail, bound for the

Roosevelt Lake

Pacific Crest Trail, and continue up-canyon in a lodgepole forest.

After a mile of usually easy climbing, we level off at a junction near the north end of large Upper Piute Meadow. From here the Kirkwood Pass trail continues ahead along the side of the meadow. Our route branches right, south, and momentarily we cross the West Walker River and reach nearby the Forest Service's Piute Cabin. We now head out into stunningly beautiful Upper Piute Meadow, backdropped by graceful, sweeping Hawksbeak Peak. We head south around the meadow's perimeter, following tread that may be discontinuous. About halfway along this stretch, blazes mark a resumption of good tread, angling slightly uphill into a lodgepole forest. This leads quickly to a small, wetter meadow, then to a nice packer camp on the edge of lovely Rainbow Meadow.

With Tower Lake as an objective, we progress south up Tower Canyon, soon crossing its creek, and in ½ mile recrossing it. You might consider spending your second night along this ½-mile stretch, for camping is poorer at Tower and Mary lakes, both near treeline. Our trail crosses a tributary, then parallels the Tower Lake outlet creek midway to the lake. It then crosses this multibranched creek and climbs steeply to very steeply, up to the lake's outlet, at 9570 feet. Taking many breather stops on this ascent, the backpacker can admire the challenging buttress of Tower Peak's north ridge, to the south, or the fine crest of Hawksbeak Peak, to the east. In early fall this landscape, like Leavitt Meadow where we started, is painted a brilliant gold as the plants—here willows—change color. Tower Lake and its northern satellite are both tightly rimmed with bedrock, talus, and willows,

leaving only tiny spots for camping, the better ones at the satellite. Tower Lake supports a small population of beautiful golden trout. From here onward, the route ahead can be largely snowbound before mid-July.

Our route from here is cross-country. From the lake's south shore we climb south up to a conspicuous saddle. The climb, though steep, is fairly safe for experienced backpackers, the greatest danger perhaps being a careless twist of one's ankle. From the 10,150-foot saddle between Saurian Crest and Tower Peak we can gaze southwest down Tilden Creek canyon over barren, windswept Mary Lake to long, forest-girded Tilden Lake and its southern guardian dome, Chittenden Peak. Leaving this austere gap, we scramble easily down through a swale of corn lilies and willows to the clustered whitebark pines that afford the best camps above the inlet of Mary Lake, which may have some golden trout. Follow Mary Lake's rocky northwest shore to reach the outlet, then descend moderately through frost-shattered hummocks and a velvety alpine fell-field of reed-grass, rice-grass, and red heather to about 9420 feet, about ¼ mile below the outlet, where a poor, ducked trail begins to define itself. This use trail leads southwest, always quite near the west bank of raucous, dancing Tilden Creek, down through a step-ladder of delightful meadows and subalpine conifers. Once, at 9120 feet, Tilden Creek makes a small waterfall, and wildflowers explode across the moist slopes, overlooked on the east by mitre-capped Craig and Snow peaks. A long hour below Mary Lake, we traverse the final lumpy meadow to the head of lovely Tilden Lake.

A more-substantial trail follows the west shore of 2-mile-long Tilden Lake, which is con-

Upper Piute Meadow, Hawksbeak Peak above it, and Ehrnbeck Peak on the right

spicuously better clothed in lodgepole pines than is the east side, which is slabby and lacking soil. Almost half way along this narrow gem, we find a sandbar which offers the best swimming beach for miles around. Farther on, our lakeside path bends southwest and enters open subalpine meadows near the base of black-streaked Chittenden Peak. This summit, named for an early Yosemite boundary commissioner, is easily climbed and provides the best overlook of Jack Main Canyon. Rounding south of Chittenden Peak, we find some good camps under a lodgepole canopy, then reach the end of Tilden Lake's long outlet lagoon. Here we boulder-hop south to find the well-used Tahoe-Yosemite Trail. Even if you don't plan to camp at Tilden Lake, you may want to walk ¾ mile east on this trail for storybook views up-canyon, where Tilden Lake, when the water is calm, mirrors the cockscombed Saurian Crest. Excellent camps are also found here, near emerald shoreline meadows.

From the outlet of Tilden Lake, the cobbly trail drops moderately west along the slabby, boulder-strewn south banks of frolicking Tilden Creek, where a profusion of shrubs and herbs line our path, including spiraea, shooting star, willow, red heather, corn lily, rosy ever-

lasting, and senecio. Chittenden Peak's south face looms well above us, and we gain views west across the wooded trough of Jack Main Canyon to Schofield and Haystack peaks. Soon switchbacks appear to ease our way down into thickening forest, always near now-cascading, sometimes free-falling Tilden Creek. Below 8400 feet we turn south through sandy lodgepole forest and trace Jack Main Canyon downstream for ½ mile before stepping through a fringe of Labrador tea to the 70-foot-wide, shallow ford of Falls Creek. On the west bank we find a pleasant camp, and 80 yards later reach the Pacific Crest Trail and turn north. To complete the next three days' spectacular hiking along the PCT, see **Hike 42**. Should you first want isolated camping, head 0.1 mile south to a creek and ascend its south bank 1 mile west to Otter Lake, located on a subalpine bench with Little Otter Lake and over a dozen ponds and lakelets.

Doe and fawn at Tilden Lake

HIKE 3

UPPER KERRICK MEADOW VIA BARNEY AND PEELER LAKES

Distance: 18.6 miles round trip

Grade: 4D, moderate 2-day hike

Trailhead: From Highway 395 near the west side of Bridgeport, take paved Twin Lakes Road south 13.6 miles to the entrance to Mono Village at the west end of upper Twin Lake. Park within the village for a nominal fee. **E1-F1.**

Introduction: The Robinson Creek trail is the most popular route through the Hoover Wilderness and into the Yosemite north country, and justifiably so. This short, scenic trail leads quickly into breathtaking subalpine terrain, and glittering Peeler Lake, surrounded by frost-shattered and glaciated granite and windswept conifers, mirrors the region's grandeur. Intimate campsites beside its shore more than compensate for the day's tough climb.

Description: We begin in Mono Village, a private resort sprawling across the alluvial fan of

Robinson Creek at the head of upper Twin Lake. Although this resort contains a maze of roads and facilities, there is a well-signed way to the Barney Lake trailhead, at the resort's far, west end. Before starting up the Barney Lake trail, you might spend a few minutes at the head of Twin Lakes, especially in the fall when the Kokanee salmon run and hillside aspens turn first amber, then red. Twin Lakes lie behind curving recessional moraines, which were left near the end of the last, or Tioga, glaciation. Tioga lateral moraines form obvious bouldery, sagebrush-dotted benches high above both the north and south shores of Twin Lakes, indicating that the last glacier filled the canyon here to a depth of about 1500 feet! Summits to the north of Twin Lakes, from Eagle Peak to Robinson Peak and Sawmill Ridge, as well as Crater Crest and Monument Ridge to the south, are composed of former volcanic rocks and limestone that originated more than 200 million years ago. Volcanic eruptions ranged in composition from explosive rhyolitic lava to fluid basaltic lava, like those found east of the Park today. During the Nevadan orogeny all these rocks were metamorphosed, then later were metamorphosed again with the much later intrusion of magma from below, about 85 million years ago, which solidified to form our canyon's walls of Cathedral Peak granodiorite.

Follow signs to reach the start of the Barney Lake trail, branching right, away from the pretty meadow and its tantalizing glimpses of granitic parapets south up Blacksmith and Horse creeks. The trail, if vague when you hike it, quickly becomes well defined, in a bare-floored Jeffrey-pine forest. Your level path then strikes west, staying north of Robinson Creek under a canopy of white fir, Jeffrey pine, Fremont cottonwood, and aspen. Presently you walk under the scarp of a small roche moutonnée (an asymmetric knoll), where Basque shepherds carved their names on aspen trees early in this century. Then after a few minutes of walking you reach a persistent stream, chortling down through wild-rose shrubbery from the basin between Victoria and Eagle peaks.

Afterwards, the trail winds gently up through more-open terrain, where bouldery ground moraine and alluvium support sparse conifers, sagebrush, manzanita, and barley. Soon the cobbly, dusty path comes close to

Robinson Creek, where its waters veer north around a jutting granitic promontory, and here the canyon, and our vistas, open up. As our path continues on a westward course, well above lodgepole pines in locally beaver-dammed Robinson Creek, we note the sweeping aprons of avalanche-scoured slope-wash that descend south from ruddy Victoria Peak, contrasting sharply with the spidery cliffs of light-hued granodiorite that form the sharper crests of Hunewill and Kettle peaks, guardians of the upper Robinson Creek basin. Here, the dry surroundings are mule ears, relieved by patches of gooseberry, mullein, rabbitbrush, and some curl-leaf mountain mahogany. At 7600 feet we pass through a grove of aspens, then amble through more sagebrush and boulders to the Hoover Wilderness boundary, about 2½ miles from Mono Village. From here a use trail cuts south to the mouth of Little Slide Canyon, up which can be seen the smooth granitic buttress called the Incredible Hulk, as well as other incredible, but unnamed, rock-climbing goals. Minutes later we re-enter white-fir cover, and can stop for a drink beside tumbling Robinson Creek. This is a good rest spot for the climb ahead.

When you are ready to assault the canyon headwall, gear down to accommodate more than a dozen well-graded switchbacks that lead north through head-high jungles of aspen, bitter cherry, serviceberry, snowberry, and tobacco brush, staying always within earshot of unseen Robinson Creek. Above 8000 feet we step across a rivulet merrily draining the slopes of Hunewill Peak, a welcome respite that furnishes flowers of American dogwood, giant red paintbrush, Labrador tea, fireweed, aster, Parish's yampah, and Gray's lovage to delight the eye. Still climbing, we return momentarily to the creekside, where industrious beavers at times create a small pond, then we climb rockily, bending south, in a gully under aspen shade. Half our ascent is behind us when we level out to step across a branch of Robinson Creek that drains the 10,700-foot saddle to our west. About a yard or so beyond this creek, the easily-missed use trail to South Fork Buckeye Creek branches west through a tangle of aspens and creek dogwoods. Just a few yards later, where Robinson Creek can be repeatedly plugged by small beaver dams, a level use trail branches south along the outlet stream of Barney Lake, with adjacent campsites. This short spur trail joins the paralleling main trail at the northwest corner of Barney Lake, where a sandy beach, good after a swim, makes a fine spot for a lunch break.

About 4½ miles from Mono Village, 14-acre Barney Lake, at 8290 feet, is nestled in a narrow, glaciated trough, rimmed on the east by the broken, lichen-mottled north spur of Kettle Peak. The western shoreline, which our trail follows, is a dry talus slope mixed with glacial debris. Here, a pair of switchbacks elevate the trail to an easy grade some 100 feet above Barney Lake's inlet. Below, beavers have dammed meandering Robinson Creek, drowning the meadow and a grove of lodgepole pines. Farther southwest, cirque-girdled Crown Point dominates the horizon, with Slide Mountain behind its east shoulder, while Kettle Peak flanks to the east, topped by a gendarmed cockscomb.

After a few minutes, we descend several short switchbacks, wind through broken rock and past avalanche-twisted aspens, over two freshets draining Cirque Mountain, then come to a ford of Robinson Creek, about ¾ mile past the lake and about 2½ miles before Peeler Lake. This crossing can be a wet ford in early season if industrious beavers have widened the ford by damming the creek in the meadow just downstream. Rainbow and brook trout of handy pan size occur here, as in Barney Lake. From the far bank, we climb easily south in a pleasant forest of lodgepole pine, red fir, western white pine, and a new addition, mountain hemlock, which reflects our higher altitude. The trail soon leads back to the west bank of Robinson Creek, which we cross (using a log, if one is handy). Next the trail crosses the cascading stream from Peeler Lake, beside which one might rest before ascending a long series of switchbacks just ahead. The first set of gentle, well-engineered swithchbacks traverses a till-covered slope to about 8800 feet, where we level off momentarily for a breather before darting north for a steeper ascent. The vistas east to stunted whitebark pines growing on rough, ice-fractured outcrops of Kettle Peak offer good excuses to stop frequently on this energetic climb. Eventually we come to a small saddle at 9195 feet, which has a trail bound for Rock Island Pass and Slide Canyon.

Those bound for Peeler Lake now turn northwest, walking moderately up in mixed open forest, to a small, shaded glade beside Peeler Lake creek. We step across this stream twice before switchbacking south moderately up into a narrow gully. The wind can pick up as we ascend it, a sure sign that we're nearing the ridgetop, and sure enough, about 8 miles from Mono Village, Peeler Lake's often windswept waters soon come into view, behind car-size granodiorite blocks that dam its outlet. A short descent leads us below this talus to dynamited trail tread on the lake's north shore, where its startling blue lake waters foreground rounded Acker and Wells peaks, in the west. Most of the good campsites, under conifers, are found as we undulate rockily into forest pockets along the north shore—though the east shore has some fine ones too, if a bit out of the way. The lake margin, mostly rock, does have a few stretches of meadowy

Deeply cleft Crown Point rises more than 3000 feet above Barney Lake

Ben Schifrin

beach, where one can fly-cast for rainbows and brookies to 14 inches.

Leaving Peeler Lake near its northwest end, the path climbs slightly to a granitic bench dotted with bonsai-stunted lodgepoles plus sedges and ocean spray, where views back across the outlet show serrated Peak 11581 rising east of Kettle Peak. Now a short descent leads to the signed Yosemite National Park boundary, beyond which pocket meadows covered with dwarf bilberry and sedge gradually coalesce into the northeastern arm of Kerrick Meadow. Soon our path ends in this meadow at a junction, from which the Buckeye Pass trail goes north and the Kerrick Canyon trail (**Hike 4**) goes south.

<hr>

HIKE 4

KERRICK CANYON/ MATTERHORN CANYON SEMILOOP

Distance: 53.9 miles semiloop trip

Grade: 7F, moderate 6-day hike

Trailhead: Same as the Hike 3 trailhead. **E1-F1.**

Introduction: Matterhorn Canyon, named for 12,264-foot Matterhorn Peak, which dominates its head, is the most spectacular canyon in the Yosemite north country. Here former glaciers slightly modified the 13-mile-long trough, giving it a dazzling array of smooth cliffs and aprons, capped with lofty, frost-riven peaks that now support lasting snowfields. Cozy conifer groves make the canyon bottomlands eminently hospitable to campers. After traversing through equally interesting Kerrick Canyon, which has less relief but a marvelous assortment of flanking domes, this hike follows a portion of the Pacific Crest Trail to find Benson and Smedberg lakes, both with good fishing. It then traverses a major part of Matterhorn Canyon, and then passes right under the spiry Sawtooth Ridge at the head of little-visited Slide Canyon.

Description: Follow the Barney Lake trail (described in **Hike 3**) up from Mono Village

past Barney and Peeler lakes, spending your first night at the latter, then descending the next morning to the north arm of Kerrick Meadow. Here, about 9¼ miles into your trek, you start south on the Kerrick Canyon trail. Kerrick Meadow, covering a vast ground moraine at the head of Rancheria Creek, is a frost-hummocked expanse of sedge, rice-grass, reed-grass, and dwarf bilberry, quite typical of Sierran subalpine meadows. Numerous young lodgepole pines encroach upon the grassland, but can die if the soil gets too boggy, as happens in years of abundant snowfall.

Head down-canyon along the path, which can be rutted up to 2 feet deep in the delicate turf, and soon cross the seasonal headwaters of Rancheria Creek. Now you descend easily, ambling along the west margin of Kerrick Meadow, over slabs and dry terraces, typical habitat of sedges. At times a profusion of birds flit among the open lodgepoles near our route: yellow-rumped warblers, American robins, mountain bluebirds, white-crowned sparrows, northern flickers, dark-eyed juncos, and Brewer's blackbirds. Lemmon's paintbrush and alpine gentian blossom in early summer.

After about 1½ miles from the previous junction, we come to another one, with the Rock Island Pass trail, which is an alternate route for our return trip. Still gently descending, we pass through a lodgepole grove, then emerge at the northern end of an even larger meadowed expanse, rimmed on the west by 400-foot bluffs. Long views south down upper Kerrick Canyon are topped by Piute Mountain and other dark, rounded summits near Seavey Pass. After 1½ miles of rolling, sandy trail, our route crosses a trio of low moraines, then cuts close to an oxbow in 20-foot-wide Rancheria Creek where the broad canyon pinches off above a low hillock. In this area you'll find the north-flowing outlet creek of Arndt Lake. This lake, ¾ mile south, has good campsites. About 13½ miles from Mono Village, it is a good destination in itself, away from sometimes overly popular Barney and Peeler lakes.

Presently Rancheria Creek's banks become a broken gorge, and we drop rockily down, only to strike another sandy meadow, this one with a flanking cluster of steep domes. Our path soon leads out of this lupine-flecked flat, down through a bouldery salient of lodgepoles to yet another meadow. Down this we amble south, soon to walk right along the sea-

Rock-rimmed Peeler Lake and the Buckeye Ridge   Ben Schifrin

sonally muddy bank of meandering Rancheria Creek. At the next curve, about 2 miles below Arndt Lake's creek, we cross our creek to a clump of lodgepoles on the east bank, and continue down-canyon. Presently a master joint in the Cathedral Peak granodiorite bedrock directs Rancheria Creek briefly east, and we follow its splashing course down over broken, porphyritic (large-crystal) bedrock slabs, then back west on another master joint for ½ mile on shaded slopes to a junction with the Pacific Crest Trail (PCT)—**Hike 42.**

Bound for Seavey Pass, 0.7 mile away, our route climbs sometimes steeply up the sandy-cobbly PCT into a dome-girded ravine, at the top of which we glimpse a small pond rimmed with corn lilies and other flowers. The PCT now bends southeast and ascends to the Rancheria Creek/Piute Creek divide, then briefly drops southwest to another gap, the real Seavey Pass.

From this point, our path winds its way down over open benches, soon coming upon a large tarn with vistas over the confusing array of rust-stained cliffs surrounding Piute Creek to Peak 10060 and Volunteer Peak, which form the horizon. From this pond our route switchbacks west down a shaded draw, then turns steeply southeast, negotiating sometimes brushy slopes first north of, then south of a cascading stream. Glimpsing our second day's goal, Benson Lake, we finally reach the valley bottom, a sometimes-swamped tangle of wil-

lows and bracken ferns under lodgepoles and firs. At the floodplain's south end, some 2¾ miles from Seavey Pass, is the Benson Lake spur trail. The 0.4-mile-long spur to Benson Lake ends at a broad, sandy beach—once the lake has dropped a foot or so—and campsites lie just back from the shore. Along the shore you have vistas over the mile-long lake to brushy domes at the outlet. Angling here is for large rainbow and brown trout.

Our third morning finds us retracing our steps to the PCT, where we turn southeast across wide Piute Creek via fallen logs, then climb up into the morning sunlight to a brushy saddle. A short distance later our route strikes the creek that drains Smedberg Lake, which poses a difficult ford in early summer, usually best solved in the thicket of aspens just upstream. South of that stream the path climbs rockily up, often at a steep gradient, before crossing the creek twice more, in easier spots, along a more moderate ascent in a tight canyon walled by tremendous bluffs. Once again south of the creek, our route tackles a steep hillside, via moderate switchbacks under increasing numbers of mountain hemlocks. Red heather forms a discontinuous, showy understory here. Almost 700 feet higher, but still under the stony gazes of precipitous Peak 10060 and Volunteer Peak, we find a trail branching southwest to shallow Murdock Lake, about ½ mile away. It is a recommended destination for those desiring some isolation,

Finger Peaks (left) and Sawtooth Ridge (center), from 9300 feet in Matterhorn Canyon   Ben Schifrin

which is usually lacking at Smedberg Lake. Even more isolation lies at more appealing Rodgers Lake, and by climbing east ⅓ mile on the PCT, we reach a meadowy junction with a trail that departs south to that lake, vaulting a ridge along its mile-long course (see **Hike 14** for details on Murdock and Rodgers lakes).

To reach Smedberg, the PCT over the next mile switchbacks down, then up to a slabby, polished bench overlooking the lake's south shore. Named for an Army cartographer who, with Lieutenants Benson and McClure, mapped the Yosemite backcountry in the early 1900s, 30-acre Smedberg Lake is dotted with low, grassy islets and rimmed with light granite, strips of sedge-and-bilberry meadow, and pockets of conifers. Pan-size rainbow trout are common in its shallow waters, which reflect a sweeping face of streaked granite over the east shore, and the brooding vertical profile of Volunteer Peak on the south. Most camps are found on the west and north shores, and remote camps exist above its northwest and northeast shores in the vicinity of, respectively, Surprise and Sister lakes.

We leave Smedberg Lake by curving south into a hummocky, boulder-and-meadow vale, then soon step across one of its three inlet creeklets to climb northeast toward Benson Pass, an even 2 miles past the lake. The first rise is moderate, under open mixed conifers; then we level out in a small meadow before the last, earnest climb to the pass. Near the top, some of the sandy trail is very steep, but it is soon behind us, and at the pass, sparingly inhabited by whitebark pines, we stand in coarse granitic sand, catching our breath to views west to Volunteer Peak and northeast over Doghead and Quarry peaks and beyond to Whorl Mountain and Twin and Virginia peaks.

A steep stretch rapidly leads us from Benson Pass down to a gravelly flat; then it becomes a switchbacking descent, under pleasant shade, to the hop-across ford of Wilson Creek in a steep-walled trough. This is a classic glaciated, hanging tributary canyon, widely believed to be hanging because its glacier could not erode downward as fast as the larger glacier in the main canyon. Such is not the case. In resistant bedrock, such as that found in our range, glaciers of all sizes eroded very little; all tributary canyons were hanging before glaciation. Turning down-canyon, the PCT alternately traverses dry openings and lodgepole forests as we cross Wilson Creek twice more. Soon the gentle-to-moderate descent resolves itself into some two dozen tight, rocky switchbacks as hanging-valley Wilson Creek canyon debauches itself into deeper Matterhorn Canyon. Bottoming out a few minutes later, we turn up Matterhorn Canyon through dry, sandy, lodgepole-filled flats and pass a large camping complex just before the wide, cobbly ford of Matterhorn Canyon creek. On the east bank, 4½ miles from Benson Pass, is a trail starting up the canyon.

Leaving the PCT, we start north for a 6-mile ascent to Burro Pass, and if you aren't camping near the ford of Matterhorn Canyon creek, you ought to consider doing so higher up in the canyon. At first our trail climbs imperceptibly, passing some nearby good camps, and keeping near the large creek past sandy meadowlands. Views within this steep-walled trench are dominated by soaring Peak 10400+, above the canyon's west slopes. In about 1½ miles we enter an open, bouldery stretch, then cross Matterhorn Canyon creek via boulders to a small, lush meadow, later recrossing the creek at a horseshoe bend. About 200 yards later, we see evidence of past winter avalanches which, descending from high on Quarry Peak, decapitated trees even as they flowed across the canyon and part-way up the opposite wall. The massive east face of Quarry Peak, composing part of our canyon's west wall, offers rock climbs up to 10 pitches long in the summer months.

About ¾ mile farther upstream, we ford again to the west side, then wind into a boulder-strewn, talus-footed meadow. Willows line the streamside, intermittently making way for rapidly thinning forest patches. Our gently ascending sandy path passes a few very nice, remote camps, your last desirable camping opportunity. Ahead it's pretty much open going, with Burro Pass clearly in sight, the low point on a light ridge, with Finger Peaks on the west and massive Matterhorn Peak on the east. Standing behind Burro Pass, the jagged Sawtooth Ridge slices into blue skies and billowing afternoon cumulonimbus clouds. Above 9800 feet, under an arc of jagged peaks

that stretches from Matterhorn Peak to Whorl Mountain and its unnamed overhanging outlier, the tread becomes steeper, crossing a delicate alpine fell-field sometimes replete with Lemmon's paintbrush, Sierra penstemon, and pussy paws. Soon the cobbly, rip-rapped trail becomes steeper still, and resolves into a chaos of eroded, miniature switchbacks through broken granite forming the final slope of Burro Pass, which at nearly 10,700 feet is just over 2 miles high.

Up here, where the air pressure is only 80% that at sea level, one has a well-deserved rest after the short but arduous ascent. From our vantage point with a 360° panorama, aptly named Sawtooth Ridge, to the north, throws up a picket line of fractured granite gendarmes, culminating in 12,264-foot Matterhorn Peak. East of us, massive Twin Peaks loom beyond an unnamed peak, dwarfing Whorl Mountain and its 11,920-foot outlier, which together spawn a textbook rock glacier. Vistas back down the trough of Matterhorn Canyon stop at the exfoliating slopes of Quarry Peak, save for a real treat on a clear day, when over its east flank peek Clouds Rest, Quarter Domes, and Half Dome, all near Yosemite Valley. Before our view southwest is blocked by the shoulder of Finger Peaks, we see Doghead

Evening view from Rock Island Pass: Kettle Peak above Snow Lake

Peak, the tip of Volunteer Peak, and distant Central Valley smog. West of Burro Pass, Slide Canyon curves down into pine-clad lower slopes from a pair of beautiful, little-visited alpine lakelets occupying a bench under the gaze of Finger Peaks.

Leaving Burro Pass, our trail drops steeply via rocky switchbacks, often obscured by long-lasting snowfields, to hop across infant Piute Creek in spongy alpine-meadow turf. It then follows that raucous, bubbling stream west on a sometimes steep descent into clustered whitebark pines, which soon become an open forest. Soon we hop to the south bank of Piute Creek, then wind through a delicate, boggy meadow before recrossing just above an excellent campsite, complete with small waterfall, in mixed conifers. Leaving this camp, the trail stays farther from the creekside and descends, sometimes via moderate switchbacks, into denser forest. Fair camps are found all the way down to the campsites in willow-understoried forest on the floor of Slide Canyon, our trail's low point along Piute Creek. Truly remote, essentially pristine, trailless camping lies along the creek down this canyon—a worthy layover day.

Now the trail begins to go gently up in sun-dappled forest, and soon switchbacks moderately near a small branch of Piute Creek. From here we can look down-canyon to view the feature that gave the names to this canyon and the mountain south of us—the Slide. This feature was first noted by Lieutenant Nathaniel F. McClure, while mapping the Yosemite north country:

> After traveling three and one half miles down the canyon, I came to the most wonderful natural object that I ever beheld. A vast granite cliff, two thousand feet in height, had literally tumbled from the bluff on the right-hand side of the stream with such force that it not only made a mighty dam across the canyon, but many large stones had rolled far up the opposite side.

McClure somewhat overestimated Slide Mountain's 1600-foot wall, but he understated the magnitude of the rockfall. About 2½ million cubic yards fell, some boulders the size of small houses, and the debris cut a swath across Piute Creek about ¼ mile wide, and rolled almost 200 vertical feet up the far bank!

After a few switchbacks we find ourselves atop the rim of Slide Canyon, on a sloping subalpine bench. Here we step across the small stream we've been paralleling, then ascend more steeply west into a rocky gulch. This climb presents ever-improving panoramas east to Burro Pass and the headwaters of Slide Canyon. Our trail climbs north up the gully, then descends gently south into a spongy, boulder-rimmed stepladder meadow. The final rise from this vale to the 10,460-foot saddle dividing the Piute and Robinson creek drainages proceeds on frequently steep, always cobbly tread. Possibly the most interesting view from this windy col, about 4 miles beyond Burro Pass, is to the northeast, over the head of Little Slide Canyon, guarded by the Incredible Hulk and north beyond to the ruddy metamorphic caps of Buckeye and Flatiron ridges.

Leaving behind the Yosemite National Park boundary, our trail leaves the col by first descending a half dozen moderate switchbacks to a stream-braided, marshy terrace fed by an unmapped snowfield in the hollow north of Slide Mountain. At the lower end of this flat lies a small tarn, which we skirt to the south, and then we descend rockily in a maze of head-high whitebark pines and talus blocks along its outlet stream. Soon the way becomes even steeper, plunging north, losing 500 feet elevation via excruciatingly rocky switchbacks, to another pocket meadow, where we cross to the stream's west bank. Below, we trace the sharp western lateral-moraine crest, left perhaps by a Little Ice Age glacier from Slide Mountain. It descends to upper Robinson Creek, as do we, where in a sandy, willowed flat we meet a junction, about 1½ miles from the col, with the Rock Island Pass trail.

Here anglers and hikers who desire a more secluded alpine campsite may turn southwest toward Rock Island Pass. Their route up along the steep southern slopes of Crown Point succumbs to gentle switchbacks and rewards one eventually with a grassy knoll at 10,260 feet, affording a breather and views over the Sierra crest to the Sawtooth Ridge. Then the trail angles briefly down past snug, sandy camps to sedge-rimmed Snow Lake, containing both rainbow and golden trout. Almost everyone who reaches here, especially photographers, will want to ascend the short, meadowed distance from Snow

Lake's inlet to broad Rock Island Pass, 1½ miles from the previous junction, for lake-reflected vistas of frost-fractured Kettle Peak. Some hikers may decide to descend the moderate trail 2 miles west from the pass down through a quiet subalpine forest to meet the Kerrick Canyon trail at the lower end of Kerrick Meadow, then exit Yosemite National park via Peeler Lake, adding an extra half day to their journey.

Back at the Rock Island Pass trail junction in the sandy flat, our route turns downstream, through talus boulders and willows. Across the stream, 100 yards east, sits a large, pretty tarn, well worth the side trip for the ecological lessons, views, and secluded alternative camping to sometimes-crowded Crown Lake. This lakelet sits on a meadowed bench between granite hillocks. Its outlet stream used to flow northeast, directly down to the head of Crown Lake, but it now starts northwest down into the willow-choked meadow traversed by our trail, then goes around a rocky knob before heading down-canyon. Possibly, rapid growth of the thick bilberry, sedge, and rush turf surrounding the tarn blocked the original outlet and elevated the lake level until the water found the northwest outlet. Also, frost-heaving of the dense sod during spring months may have closed off the old outlet and further elevated the lake rim. Note that it is markedly higher than the surrounding meadow.

Leaving this interesting lakelet, we return to the Robinson Creek trail and descend east via gentle switchbacks to the sodden meadow on the west shore of Crown Lake. The path circumvents the meadow to reach Crown Lake's north outlet, from where use trails lead to the only legal campsites, in grouped whitebarks and hemlocks above the lake's rocky east shore. Anglers will be pleased to find a self-sustaining fishery of rainbow trout.

The next leg of our descent leads to the two small Robinson Lakes, on a 9200-foot bench under towering Crown Point. First we hop Robinson Creek just a minute north of Crown Lake, then descend more and more steeply under open conifer shade. One-half mile below our first ford, we jump back to the west bank, just above the larger Robinson Lake, where we get nice views north over its shallow, rainbow-breeding waters to Hunewill and Victoria peaks. Meager camps lie on the isthmus between the two Robinson Lakes,

although if you camp here, you should look for more ecologically correct ones farther from their shores.

Leaving the isthmus, our trail swings west along the north shore of the swampy, grassy western lakelet, then climbs through a chaos of mammoth talus blocks—the terminal moraine of the Crown Point cirque glacier. One-third mile of dynamited trail through this jumble ends under the quiet shade of a pure mountain-hemlock grove that lines a gully containing a seasonal creek. We hop the creek here, turn northeast, and soon climb to a sunny col to meet the Peeler Lake trail. From here we retrace our first day's steps downhill all the way to Mono Village at upper Twin Lake.

HIKE 5

VIRGINIA LAKES AND GREEN CREEK BASIN

Distance: 14.8 miles with side trip to West Lake; one way

Grade: 3D, moderate 2-day hike

Trailhead: Turn west off Highway 395 at Conway Summit, 12.3 miles north of Lee Vining or 12.8 miles south of Bridgeport, onto Virginia Lakes Road. Follow it 5¾ miles to Virginia Lakes Campground road. Continue straight ahead on a road, not turning into the campground proper. Reaching an overlook close beside the east shore of Big Virginia Lake, park in the large loop, and find the signed trailhead near a toilet structure at its east end. **F2.**

Green Creek roadend is reached by Green Creek Road, which meets 395 4.4 miles south of Bridgeport or 8.4 miles north of Conway Summit. Follow it 8.9 miles west to Green Creek Campground and a large trailhead parking area, with toilet and water spigot, in a pine forest. **F2.**

Introduction: Between them, the Virginia Lakes and Green Creek basins hold over 20 assorted, trout-abundant lakes that are easily visited. In addition, this area provides interesting geological lessons, multihued panoramas of crumbling peaks, and seasonally an unmatched parade of wildflowers.

Description: From the parking area the Blue Lake trail climbs easily west, first rounding above the shore of pretty, but crowded, Big Virginia Lake, then entering a stand of aspens. In a minute or two, we turn northeast, and ascend briefly to a stand of pines, where we find a junction with a horse trail branching right, east, down to a pack station at Trumbull Lake. We turn left and start gently uphill, under a sparse subalpine shade. Our trail parallels an unused mining flume in a narrow ravine, quickly passes north of first one and then a second tarn, and reaches the Hoover Wilderness boundary. Moments later Blue Lake comes into view, cupped in steep slopes of ruddy-brown hornfels—a metamorphic rock that lacks foliation. Where our path nears the outlet of Blue Lake, there is a small grove of pines, an adequate camp, and a profusion of wildflowers. Elsewhere, as we see while climbing gently above the north shore of Blue Lake, the terrain is composed of talus or moraines, supporting a sparse but lively ground cover of paintbrush, penstemon, buckwheat, and antelope brush. Rickety spires of rusty-weathered Dunderberg Peak loom high to our north, spalling rockfall, resulting in talus that is home for yellow-bellied marmots, who study our ascent.

At Blue Lake's western headwall our way climbs steeply, stopping for a moment at a 9950-foot overlook, then rounds an immense talus fan to the verdant banks of Moat Lake's outlet stream, which descends merrily from the north together with its steeply clambering use trail. Now under the prow of a light-colored crag guarding Moat Lake, our trail switchbacks southwest up a forested hillside, presently to find the Gold Start Mine. One more switchback brings us to the outlet of Cooney Lake, which occupies a low bench in this austere timberline upland. Good camps are found south of the inlet in wind-tortured knots of whitebark pines. Here views open to our trip's high point as barren Burro Pass (a local name) saddles the western horizon, its metamorphosed tuffs looking cream-colored against the surrounding, darker, metamorphosed lavas, such as Black Mountain, to our south.

About 1¼ miles into our hike, we leave often windy Cooney Lake and ascend gently west into a rocky-meadowed draw. Here we easily step across infant Virginia Creek via rocks and logs to find a second, rolling bench, harboring a clutch of small lakelets—the Frog Lakes—named for once numerous mountain yellow-legged frogs, which share the cold, shallow waters with small eastern brook and rainbow trout. We swing south of the meadowy, lowest Frog Lake, then ascend on lush alpine turf to the largest and highest lake, where good camps are found among scattered whitebark pines.

The next riser on our staircase ascent is steeper than those before, and has even less tree cover. Finally, the trail resolves into red-sandy switchbacks, reaches an overlook of the highest Frog Lake, then leaves the last whitebark pines behind for a true alpine ascent along the west wall of a cirque. The relatively warm, mineral-rich, easily weathered, water-holding metavolcanic soil here supports an abundance of alpine wildflowers rarely seen elsewhere along a trail in such numbers:

Blue Lake trail and Frog Lakes, view northeast from near Burro Pass

robust, blue-bugled Davidson's penstemon, sour-leaved mountain sorrel, furry-leaved alpine gold, showy skunk-leaved polemonium, and ubiquitous, yellow-headed sulfur flower. After a burst of switchbacks you gain 11,110-foot Burro Pass, then can gaze back down Virginia Creek over your 3.2-mile toil. By walking north just a minute from the trail's high point, you can also view the Hoover Lakes at the base of Epidote Peak. In the northwest, Summit Lake occupies the saddle under Camiaca Peak's avalanche chutes, backdropped by the dark, brooding temple of distant Virginia Peak.

From the barren, windswept crest, we make an initial descent south, then momentarily switchback northwest toward Summit Lake. Beside the trail you'll see tight clusters of whitebark pines, the largest cluster offering emergency shelter if you're caught in a blizzard. Our trail switchbacks northwest down through a small, stark side canyon to a sloping subalpine bench, which gives our knees a rest before we hit the third set of switchbacks. After about a 1.4-mile descent from Burro Pass, we arrive at a small bench with a trail junction. From here the Virginia Canyon trail drops briefly southwest before climbing ½ mile to Summit Lake (see **Hike 6**).

The Green Creek trail turns northeast, down over gravelly slopewash past a tarn (look for dainty, violet alpine speedwell) to an excellent overlook down-canyon to the Hoover Lakes. Beyond, light-granitic Kavanaugh Ridge shows over the massive shoulder of Dunderberg Peak. We drop to step north across East Fork Green Creek, then gently descend over orange, cobbly schist around the north shore of the larger upper Hoover Lake. Its wide rocky outlet stream poses only minor difficulties, below which we find lower Hoover Lake and an old trail going southwest to windy camps on the upper lake's east shore. Lower Hoover Lake, which our trail traverses via the talus-strewn lake, has in the past contained rainbow, brook, and brown trout.

Below the lake and 1.2 miles past the trail junction, we drop easily over willowed benches, then circle above less-visited Gilman Lake to cross East Fork and Green Creek once again, via logs, in a stand of hemlocks and whitebark pines. Soon afterward, our descent ends and our route rises gently past easily recognized outcrops of conglomerate rocks. Soon

Hoover Lakes, view down-canyon

we pass a short spur trail to Gilman Lake, followed closely by small, green Nutter Lake. Camps lie below our trail in subalpine conifers at Nutter Lake's west end. A short northwest climb from the lake on a mat-manzanita patched slope next presents East Lake, largest of the Green Creek lakes, spread 100 feet below us under the iron-stained talus skirts of crumbly Epidote Peak, Page Peaks, and Gabbro Peak. We round above East Lake's rocky, open-lodgepole-forested east shore on a descent past two small ponds to the extensive camping complex at the rock-dammed north outlet, about 3.2 miles from the last junction. Fishing is good here for rainbow trout.

Departing East Lake, we step across the small outlet stream, then drop gently through dry, open lodgepole cover, taking a few switchbacks, to recross East Lake creek some 140 vertical feet lower. A short dogleg leads from this rockhop to another one across the same stream, in a lusher assemblage of lupine, monkshood, alum root, meadow rue, and columbine. Regaining the west bank, we stay near the stream's chorus all the way down a chain of short switchbacks, ending finally near shaded camps clustered beside West Fork

Green Creek. These camps are just yards east of Green Lake's log-strewn outlet, where fishing is good for rainbow and brook trout. A log bridge leads us north across the stream and past an old mining cabin to a junction, 4.8 miles below the last, where our route turns right, down Green Creek. A highly recommended side route is to traverse about ¼ mile west through forest cover to a junction along the north shore of Green Lake, then climb via short switchbacks 1⅓ miles to West Lake. By not taking it, you will cut about 3 miles from this hike's total distance. That lake is perched on the northeast edge of a corrugated bench that contains the smaller Bergona Lake and Par Value Lakes and a number of isolated campsites among sparse forest. Unlike at Green Lake, along the edge of the bench you have views both down into the main canyon as well as up to the encircling ridges.

From the brushy, morainal shoulder northeast of Green Lake, the 2½-mile-long Green Lake trail first drops northeast on dusty tread through low aspens and tobacco brush. Some 200 feet lower in elevation, in pleasantly shaded lodgepole and aspen groves, we come to parallel West Fork Green Creek in fantasy-jungles of early-season wildflowers: tiger lily, rein orchid, checker, giant paintbrush, columbine, larkspur, sweet-cicely, monkshood, and blue-eyed grass. This damp, gently descending path crosses numerous streams, some of them mapped, and then we leave the Hoover Wilderness and descend more steeply on morainal slopes via 12 open switchbacks. Below them, we tread through another forest grove, then climb a small juniper-clad ridge where an old mine shaft lies 50 feet north of our sandy path. We quickly leave this dry saddle and descend steeply down to Green Creek and the meadowed parking area, just 160 feet after a rocky turnaround.

HIKE 6

VIRGINIA LAKES TO VIRGINIA CANYON VIA SUMMIT LAKE

Distance: 21.9 miles by shortest (round trip) route

Grade: 5E, moderate 3-day hike

Trailhead: Same as the Hike 5 trailhead. **F2.**

Introduction: Virginia Canyon is the easiest-to-reach classic glacier-smoothed subalpine gorge of the Yosemite north country. As well as its own pleasant, sunny lodgepole forests and ever-changing Return Creek, it offers a variety of more-rugged alpine options to avoid retracing one's steps on the return trip.

Description: Follow the trail described in **Hike 5** up past the Virginia Lakes, over 11,110-foot Burro Pass, and steeply down a long procession of switchbacks to the Green Creek trail, on a gravelly, whitebark-pine-dotted bench just above 10,000 feet near East Fork Green Creek. With 4.6 miles behind you, you turn southwest and drop momentarily to cross four small freshets in a seasonally verdant meadow where tiny yellow club-moss ivesia plus daisies, Lemmon's paintbrush, and monkey flower all float in a sea of purple-mist grass and alpine timothy. A steep, cobbly ascent ensues, paralleling Summit Lake's outlet stream. Soon the climb moderates, and we note the avalanche slopes of Camiaca Peak straight on as our ascent over dry sedge flats and benches passes numerous good hemlock-bower campsites. Nearing Summit Lake's usually windswept outlet, we level off. Campsites are few here, and a tent is advisable, for the scattered whitebark pines offer little wind protection. Sunset views, however, can be quite spectacular. Angling for small brookies is fair.

Continuing on, we curve west along Summit Lake's north shore, alarming "picket-pin" ground squirrels in dry flats of Brewer's reed-grass and sagebrush. Summit Pass, on the Yosemite National Park boundary, barely rises above the 10,205-foot lake. As recently as 16,000 years ago, a lobe of the massive Virginia Canyon glacier flowed east across this pass and the Summit Lake basin to augment the East Fork branch of the Green Creek glacier. Until the next glaciation the lake is slowly diminishing in size as winter and spring avalanches carry loose rocks and detritus down into it. Standing at the pass, you can readily identify Virginia Peak, a pointed metamorphic summit that rises above the summits of Stanton Peak and Gray Butte, both south of it. Broad, deep Virginia Canyon, which frames distant Mt. Hoffmann, is a classic example of glacial topography, yet it has been only modestly widened and deepened despite repeated episodes of glaciation over the last 2 million years.

As we descend into the Park, Summit Lake's stunted whitebark pines quickly yield to well-formed lodgepoles and a sagebrush ground cover. After a mile's descent and almost 7 miles into our trek, we meet a junction with the Virginia Pass trail, a highly recommended return route that will be described after the description of Virginia Canyon. From this 9850-foot junction the down-canyon trail immediately crosses Return Creek and descends moderately-to-gently through a lodgepole forest for 4 miles before reaching the Pacific Crest Trail (PCT) at 8540 feet. Most of this canyon, like much of the Park's granitic terrain north of the Tuolumne Meadows lands, is composed of Cathedral Peak granodiorite, which solidified in the earth's crust about 85-90 million years ago. Marking our down-canyon progress is an ever-changing view of Shepherd Crest, on our left, whose steep-sided north slopes harbored glacierettes during cold periods of the Little Ice Age. Near the junction of the PCT (**Hike 42**) you'll find many campsites, popular with backpackers and bears, above both banks of Return Creek. In early season this creek is dangerous to cross, and you had best camp on the west bank.

One recommended exit route, so as not to retrace one's steps, is to link this hike with **Hike 7**, for an enjoyable subalpine sojourn at McCabe Lakes. Otherwise, backtrack 4 miles up the Virginia Canyon trail to the junction at 9340 feet, and either retrace your steps to your trailhead or start up the Virginia Pass trail. This trail initially is on the east bank of Return Creek, but crosses the stream thrice on its northbound ascent. After 1.2 miles, the trail dies out at 9850 feet, in a thick meadow turf where a stream falls down from an unnamed lake under the red pyramid of Virginia Peak, to our west. One could easily ascend about 400 feet to this lake for nice, secluded camping.

From where the trail dies out, you have a 700-foot elevation gain north up steep, open treeline slopes of sagebrush and whitebark pines to 10,540-foot Virginia Pass. Views here are breathtaking. South down wooded Virginia Canyon, the spiry western Cathedral Range, Half Dome, and Clouds Rest can be seen, bordered on the east by the tips of Mt. Conness and North Peak and the north scarp of Shepherd Crest. More to the west, the upper cirque is guarded by Gray Butte, Stanton Peak, Virginia Peak, and the towering, gendarme-bristled south slope of Twin Peaks. In the northeast, Glines Canyon slopes to forested Green Lake, while the rolling sageland around Bodie marks the horizon. Spend a few minutes examining the metavolcanic schists at often windy Virginia Pass. Note that striations in this hard rock indicate that a lobe of the Virginia Canyon glacier flowed from west to east across this col, as one did at Summit Pass.

Leave this instructional gap at its southeast end, from where a use trail starts steeply north down into Glines Canyon. Poor switchbacks soon come into play over a slope of moraine and talus, and then we level off momentarily in a rocky meadow at 10,230 feet. Here *southbound* hikers will want to look for the vague path along the left-hand margin of the meadow, near the first cluster of whitebark pines. Everyone should look for the hexago-

From Park boundary, view east across Summit Lake to Dunderberg Peak, on left

nally-patterned rock rings that have been heaved up by repeated frost action in this soggy flat. Down-canyon hikers will find a resumption of trail along the east side of West Fork Green Creek, which tumbles musically down through Sierra willows, dwarfed pines, red and white heathers, and baby elephant heads. Next, we veer away from the stream for a short while and then drop steeply to a marshy flat, where we rejoin the creek. Here lies a mammoth boulder of marble that is slowly dissolving, and its minerals are precipitating on cobbles lying downstream, causing the stream bed to appear ghostly white.

Across the meadowy flat we turn momentarily up along Green Creek, then hop north over it just below eye level with another meadow. Our steep descent continues, now under scattered-to-moderate mountain hemlocks that frame vistas of Peak 10880, on the north canyon wall. Soon a denser hemlock forest on steeper slopes blocks all views, and we come to the ruins of an old stamp mill, in a lush herbaceous jungle. An upward jog a minute later finds a ruined log cabin in a field of fireweed capping a viewful promontory; yards behind it is a collapsed adit, on the contact between two differing schists. From this site we switchback north down to cross two streams, the second being the outlet from Par Value Lakes, in a patch of swamp onion, yarrow, and dusky horkelia. Just above us lie the ruins of a water-powered, eight-crucible, rocker-arm "Ideal Stamp Mill pat. Oct 8 1899," and a "No. 3 Dodge Rock Brkr" from the Parke and Lacy Co. Old prospect pits dot both hillsides.

Below this amazing testament to strong backs and hopeful, ingenious minds, our trail sidehills down near scattered lodgepoles, then enters a deeper forest with trail-encroaching hemlocks. The creek stays within easy earshot, and we eventually walk along an old wagon road that supplied the mine. Near the head of Green Lake, our path finally becomes gentle and reaches some excellent campsites, in duff-floored lodgepole-and-hemlock forest. To reach the northeast end of Green Lake, from where the Green Creek trail may be followed northeast for an easy exit, or the East Lake trail may be climbed back to the junction below Summit Lake (see **Hike 5** for both routes), our trail heads north around the west side of 50-acre Green Lake. Numerous

creeks create a boggy path. From Green Lake's north shore, our sometimes overgrown path climbs up some 50 feet to a dry, mule-ears-and sagebrush bench, where we meet the descending West Lake trail (see the last part of **Hike 5**).

HIKE 7

McCABE LAKES VIA SADDLEBAG LAKE HINTERLANDS

Distance: 16.7 miles, semiloop trip to Lower McCabe Lake; only 8.1 miles if cross-country hike to Secret and McCabe lakes is omitted

Grade: 4D, moderate 2-day hike, or moderate 2B hike if the cross-country hike is omitted

Trailhead: Drive 2.1 miles north on Highway 120 from Tioga Pass, then 2.4 miles northwest to Saddlebag Lake. **F3.**

Introduction: By adhering to official trails you won't find a quick way in to the McCabe lakes. Knowledgeable hikers, however, reach Upper McCabe Lake in only several hours by taking this described partly cross-country route. Since the crest route above Secret Lake can be dangerous, hikers inexperienced at mountaineering should not attempt to climb it. Be prepared for a sudden summer snowstorm. Chances are you won't be caught in one, but if you are, don't attempt to return to Secret Lake and don't attempt to hike cross-country to Roosevelt Lake. Rather, do as the rangers suggest and take the trail from Lower McCabe Lake west 2⅓ miles down to the Pacific Crest Trail, then south 7 miles on it to Glen Aulin High Sierra Camp, and from there continue on the trail out to the Tioga Road in Tuolumne Meadows. Bus service runs along this road, so you can get a ride to the start of the Saddlebag Lake road.

One need not do the cross-country. If you stick to the basic semiloop—Saddlebag Lake to Helen Lake and back—you will visit some of the Sierra's finest scenery and will do so without any climbing risks.

Description: By Saddlebag Campground is a fairly large trailhead parking area for those hiking north into the Hoover Wilderness. You can get both a wilderness permit and a fishing license at close-by Saddlebag Lake Resort. The resort's store sells fishing supplies and a few groceries, and its cafe serves breakfast and lunch, but not dinner. The resort also rents small boats, and on weekdays as well as weekends Saddlebag Lake often has quite a population of anglers in hot pursuit of the lake's brook, rainbow, and Kamloops trout. If you want to fish here, great, but get off this large lake in a hurry if a thunderstorm approaches—lightning kills. The resort also provides scenic trips on the lake plus water-taxi service to the lake's far end. The water taxi will pick you up at your own pre-arranged time.

To get to the lake's far end, you could hike along the closed road that parallels the east shore, but a better, shorter alternative is to hike on a trail that parallels the west shore. From the trailhead parking entrance you can see a road descending to the base of the lake's dam, then climbing to the dam's west end. Head there, where the trail begins—a blocky tread cutting across open, equally blocky talus slopes. This metamorphic-rock talus may be uncomfortable to walk on, but from an alpine plant's perspective it is better than granitic-rock talus. Metamorphic bedrock fractures into smaller pieces than granitic bedrock does, thus creating a greater water-storage capacity for plants. Furthermore, it is much richer in dark minerals, so it makes a more nutrient-rich soil. And, being darker in color than their granitic counterparts, metamorphic-derived soils absorb more heat, which is very important to plants at these cool altitudes.

About ½ mile north of the dam, our trail bends northwest and Mt. Dana, in the southeast, disappears from view. Shepherd Crest, straight ahead, now captivates one's attention, in tranquil reflection across the early morning waters of Saddlebag Lake. Among willows and a seasonally fiery field of Pierson's paintbrush, our trail ends near the lake's north end, and we climb west to the east shore of Greenstone Lake. In the early morning a breathtaking, colorful reflection of North Peak mirrors across the placid waters, beckoning photographers to linger. Following the lake's shore north, we quickly meet the closed mining road that water-taxi riders will be hiking on, and above this shore our narrow road enters the Hoover Wilderness. Southwest

View southeast from crest: Secret Lake, Steelhead Lake, Saddlebag Lake, and pointed Mt. Dana

across Greenstone Lake a granite wall sweeps up to a crest at Mt. Conness, in whose shade lies the Conness Glacier. Our tread climbs northwest, and then at the "Z" Lake outlet creek bends west over to relatively warm Wasco Lake.

Beyond the first tarn north of Wasco Lake, our trail enters the drainage of northeast-flowing Mill Creek. Then just past the second tarn we come to a junction with a former jeep trail, the start of interesting side trips. We take this trail, which descends north to the south shore of Steelhead Lake, bends west, then starts a climb south up a linear gully. Growing in its moist confines are seasonally profuse clusters of Suksdorf's monkey flowers. Typical of many alpine plants, their stems are greatly reduced, thereby making their one-inch-long yellow flowers seem greatly oversized. You could continue up the gully, then branch southwest to easily reached snowfields below North Peak, but we climb west from the gully to nearby Potter Lake. Its outlet creek immediately cascades noisily into deep Steelhead Lake, and near the cascade are ledges from which brave souls can high-dive into that lake's chilly depths.

Our route to the McCabe Lakes is now essentially cross-country, although we'll be following a use trail for most of the way. Just northwest of Potter Lake is a low, broad

North Peak and more distant Mt. Conness (center), from Steelhead Lake

bedrock ridge that separates Towser Lake from larger Cascade Lake. Start north up this bedrock, and soon you'll be climbing a faint trail up beside a Cascade Lake inlet creeklet. Eventually this trail crosses the creeklet and then parallels its west bank up to a granite bench that holds icy, barren Secret Lake. Hardly a secret, it sometimes attracts dozens of day-hikers on weekends.

Pausing at Secret Lake to survey your route up the headwall, you see three choices. Adept mountaineers can attack the wall directly, preferably keeping just to the right of the black, lichen-stained vertical streak on the headwall. Hikers who want to put out some extra effort to achieve certainty and lack of steep exposure can arduously pick their way up the scree north of Secret Lake to the lip of what looks like—but isn't—a lake basin. From there, they will traverse slightly upward to their left, under the solid face of the east end of Shepherd Crest, to the low point on the headwall divide. Probably most people choose a third way. From the south side of Secret Lake you walk directly up the increasingly steep headwall until, about halfway up, you come to a long ledge that slopes slightly up to the south. Ducks may mark this route, but they are not always easy to see. About 200 yards south up this ledge, you leave it and follow ducks almost directly up to the ridgecrest. Once on it, follow it north to the low point of the divide to

find the ducked route descending on the west side of the ridgecrest. From the crest's saddle—a shallow gap—you can see that an ascent up Shepherd Crest would be tedious but not really dangerous. While you're looking at it, note how icy winds have reduced the whitebark pines on its lower slopes to a knee-high ground cover. To the southeast, pointed Mt. Dana stands high on the horizon above Saddlebag Lake.

The descent from the saddle is easier and safer than the ascent. A ducked route starts among cropped whitebark pines and bush cinquefoils, then descends steeply southwest toward a large, seasonal pond on a flat bench. There can be several primitive, misleading paths down to this pond. The greatest danger—assuming you don't get way off route—is that of knocking loose rock down on your traveling companions. Beyond the pond you'll come to large, deep, windswept Upper McCabe Lake. Along its north shore are several cramped campsites among stunted whitebark pines—not much protection from wind or storms. Better campsites lie ahead, so boulder-hop the lake's wide outlet, climb due west ¼ mile up to a shallow gap on a glaciated spur ridge, then descend south a short ¼ mile to a shallow pond behind a low lateral moraine. Beyond the moraine's crest you drop steeply southwest through an ever increasing forest that boasts sizable lodgepole pines by the time you reach the north shore of deep Middle McCabe Lake. Since it lacks campsites, follow its outlet creek down to shallower Lower McCabe Lake, arguably the most photogenic of all three. Good campsites lie beneath lodgepole and whitebark pines, which grow on the moraine atop a buried bedrock ridge that dams this bouldery lake. The added presence of red heather and Labrador tea warns one that mosquitoes will be a pesky problem until late July. After your stay, return to Secret Lake and then descend to the south shore of Steelhead Lake to begin the last part of the Saddlebag Lake hinterlands.

From the shore of Steelhead Lake follow the former jeep road north alongside deep blue Steelhead Lake to its outlet. The road continues west above the lake's north shore to the Hess Mine, blocked with boulders. Higher up the road, however, is an unblocked mine that goes 50 yards into the mountainside. Just beyond it the road ends and there you have a commanding view of this "20 Lakes Basin," as it is sometimes called. The large, white horizontal dikes on North Peak stand out well, and pointed Mt. Dana pokes its summit just into view on the southeast skyline. On the west side of Steelhead Lake's outlet—Mill Creek— we go a few yards downstream, then scramble over a low knoll as we follow a faint trail that quickly descends to the west shore of tiny Excelsior Lake. At the north end we go through a notch just west of a low metamorphic-rock knoll that is strewn with granitic glacial erratics. A long, narrow pond quickly comes into view which, like many of the lakes, contains trout. Our trail skirts its west shore, then swings east to the north shore of adjacent, many-armed Shamrock Lake, backdropped by Mt. Conness.

Our ducked route—more cross-country than trail—now continues northeast over a low ridge, then goes past two Mill Creek ponds down to the west shore of Lake Helen. On a trail across talus we round this lake's north shore to Mill Creek, where our trail dies out just below the lake's outlet—which flows through a tunnel. We go 30 yards up to the tunnel, walk across it, and begin an east-shore traverse south across blocky talus. Don't take the tantalizing trail that follows the lake's outlet creek north; it quickly becomes very dangerous.

Adding warm colors to the dark metamorphic blocks are crimson columbines, white

Coville's columbines, and their pink hybrids. Two creeks empty into the lake's southeast end, and we follow the eastern one up a straight, narrow gully that in early season is a snow chute rather than a wildflower garden. Soon reaching the outlet of Odell Lake, we cross it and parallel the west shore southward while observing the lobes of talus just east of the lake. Like some other metamorphic-rock talus slopes in this glaciated basin, these developed lobes through solifluction—a slow downslope flowage of unstable, water-saturated rock masses.

Near the lake's south end an old route may still be seen climbing slightly before dying out. In contrast, our route drops to water's edge before climbing from the south shore up to Lundy Pass. At this gap our path can become vague, but by heading south down toward a pond, we soon reach the outlet of Hummingbird Lake and here an obvious trail tread resumes. This tread parallels the east side of the outlet creek ½ mile down to the closed mining road. Here you can descend to the water-taxi dock on Saddlebag Lake and wait for the boat if you made reservations for a return trip, or you can retrace your steps on the west-shore trail. Of course, for variety you can take the closed road back to the lake's south end.

CHERRY LAKE TO BOUNDARY LAKE VIA KIBBIE LAKE

Distance: 30.2 miles round trip, including two visits to Kibbie Lake and one to Boundary Lake

Grade: 6D, moderate 4-day hike

Trailhead: From Groveland drive east 13.6 miles on Highway 120 to paved Cherry Road 1N07, a.k.a. Forest Route 17, starting just beyond the highway bridge over South Fork Tuolumne River. (A spur road right, immediately before the bridge, leads briefly down to the popular Rainbow Pool day-use area—a refreshing spot to visit after your hike.) Take F. R. 17 5.3 miles to a junction with paved Hetch

Hetchy Road, a.k.a. F. R. 12, and branch left. Still on F. R. 17, go 17.6 miles to Cottonwood Road 1N04. The signed Cherry Dam parking area is just yards east down this road.

While you could start your hike from here, most people would prefer to save 4.3 trail miles and a 1200-foot ascent by starting at a newer trailhead. To reach it, drive across Cherry Valley Dam, then continue ½ mile beyond it to a T junction with Road 1N45Y. Turn left, north, up this good road, then down, in the next 2 miles passing a succession of signed trailheads and parking lots for, respectively, Lake Eleanor, Kibbie Creek-Flora Lake, and old Kibbie Ridge trails. Onward, the road climbs alongside Kibbie Ridge, just a short distance below the old trail. Three switchbacks eventually lead up to a deadend at 5580 feet. Here are a corral and a sign indicating the way to the Kibbie Ridge trail.

Be aware that during hunting season, one must park down by the reservoir. This closure is designed by Forest Service biologists to minimize intrusions on the large deer herds that migrate down Kibbie Ridge each fall. To avoid this increased hiking distance, plan to hike this route before late September.

Introduction: Among knowledgeable backpackers, the lower, less-trammeled Kibbie Ridge region of Yosemite is a favorite for early- and late-season weekenders. Deep forests and some little-fished lakes are their rewards. For the more adventuresome, the Kibbie Ridge trail is the fastest way in to Huckleberry Lake, in the heart of one of the most lake-blessed areas of the Sierra Nevada. At 4 miles distance, Kibbie Lake, the goal of the first day of backpacking, is close enough for comfortable day hiking.

Description: From the road's end, we start on a spur trail that leads east-northeast uphill to the nearby Kibbie Ridge trail. Just about a minute's walk down this main trail is Shingle Spring, with beautiful dogwoods and nearby camps. However, we take the main route north, gaining about 400 feet in elevation as it first climbs to a descending ridge and then curves east into cooler, forested Deadhorse Gulch. Just past its upper end we reach the main ridge and, in a conifer grove beside a small grass-choked pond, 1¼ miles into our hike, meet the 2¾-mile-long Kibbie Lake trail—our route.

Skirting this pond, we near a ridgetop open space freckled by mat lupine, streptanthus, buckwheat, and pretty face (golden brodiaea), the last species eaten by the Miwok Indians. Quickly our trail enters Yosemite National Park and drops on rocky tread sur-

Granite cliffs provide high-diving opportunities at Kibbie Lake

rounded by chaparral, lightly treed with Jeffrey pines, into a small canyon. We amble north through a sodden bottom land, passing the first lodgepole pines of our trip, which here, accompanied by white firs, form a dense canopy. Mountain dogbane (Indian hemp), branched Solomon's seal, bracken fern, Parish's yampah, violet, shooting star, and deadly bleeding hearts thrive in the shadows, enticing the traveler to linger in coolness. But mosquitoes, far and away the most numerous inhabitants of damp early-season forests, will no doubt urge you on!

The trail leaves the forest, climbing northeast onto granitic slabs mottled by huckleberry oaks to a 6500-foot saddle. The rocky route next descends to cross a tributary of Kibbie Creek under a south-facing dome that offers good rock climbing on its peeling skin. After the step-across ford, we closely parallel smooth, green pools on Kibbie Creek, which is lined by western azaleas, willows, and tall conifers. We pass a good camp on the right, then, just yards later, before a poor trail climbs up amid huckleberry oak to the right of a granitic outcrop to continue over slabs to the west shore of Kibbie Lake, our route angles down to a 30-foot rock-hop of Kibbie Creek. Across the ford, among lodgepoles, is a very good camp. Our trail turns upstream, climbing over blasted granitic ledges, the route indicated by rock ducks.

After passing ice-scoured lagoons presaging 106-acre Kibbie Lake, we reach its south shore, where camps are found in a lodgepole-and-Labrador-tea fringe. Kibbie Lake is named for pioneer H. G. Kibbie, who traveled throughout the Yosemite north country and constructed small cabins at Frog Creek in the Lake Eleanor vicinity, at Tiltill Meadow, and on Rancheria Mountain. Kibbie Lake is bounded on the west by gently sloping granite, while the east shore is characterized by steep, broken bluffs and polished bosses. The lake is mostly shallow, with an algae-coated sandy bottom, where distinctively orange-colored California newts may take your bait if a rainbow trout doesn't.

The next day, retrace your steps to the Kibbie Ridge trail and turn north on its duff tread. After dropping past Sand Canyon, you pass, in quick succession, a marshy flat, a creek with a good camp (at the Emigrant Wilderness boundary), and a switchback that leads up onto sparsely forested granitic slabs covered with "gruss," or weathered granite. Note how the massive roots of the Jeffrey pines loosen and fracture the peeling rock, hastening the development of soil. Soon re-entering red-fir forest, we climb steadily to Lookout Point, with vistas west of the deep cleft of Cherry Creek canyon. Next we pass Swede's camp—a corn-lily-filled meadow—and ascend to a large, warm, shallow pond. After skirting its sandy north shore, we climb under sparse mixed trees, often at a steep incline, to an open-ridgetop sand flat where we find the Yosemite National Park boundary. A steep path straight up the sandy ridge, blessed with fine panoramas east-southeast to Mount Conness, leads to the seasonally muddy, marsh-marigold-dotted vicinity of Sachse Spring, where there is a good camp.

Here you might stop, rest, and consider the ecology of the mule deer which make this area their home in the summer and fall months. Biologists studying the mule-deer herd in this area named it the "Jawbone Herd" after its winter range on Jawbone Ridge and along Jawbone Creek, some 12 miles below Cherry Lake. The mammalogists separated the herd into two distinct groups, the Clavey Unit deer, occupying the rich, brushy, volcanic-earthed Clavey River basin, and the Cherry Unit deer, ranging throughout the Cherry Creek drainage. Mule deer of the Cherry Unit must subsist in poorer conditions than Clavey deer, owing to the prevalence of forage-poor glacier-polished-granite terrain and lack of food-rich fire- or logging-caused brushy areas in the Cherry Creek basin. When springtime snows begin to melt, Cherry mule deer begin to drift from their winter range, following budding plants upward, keeping generally 1000 feet below the receding snowline.

By contouring along canyon slopes that are first to sprout new vegetation, most of the deer reach the prime summer range by late June. Once on the summer range, the deer fawn and fatten themselves on forbs and shrubbery. Deer populations are most dense between 6000 and 7500 feet, in forest fringes near meadows and brush. In this habitat, moderate summer deer populations reside below Lookout Point and Kibbie Lake, while deer are rare in higher elevations in the open, soil-deficient granite terrain. On Kibbie Ridge, as elsewhere, deer prefer the open, brush-floored

Jeffrey-pine community, and are less common in the shadier red-fir community. The most preferred browse species for Jawbone deer in summer months is snow bush, and huckleberry oak is also favored. Aspen and willows are desired foods for pregnant or lactating does, as well as young black-oak leaves and mountain misery.

In fall, prompted by the first snowstorms, deer in the Cherry drainage begin a downward migration, the highest deer moving first, and finally reach their winter range by early December. There are two main travel corridors followed by Cherry deer heading south to the winter range. One begins west of Emigrant Lake, heads north of Hyatt Lake to West Fork Cherry Creek and then down Hells Mountain, passing along the ridge west of Cherry Lake. The second migration route begins south of Emigrant Lake and bisects the region visited in this hike by traversing to Lord Meadow, then going east of Many Island and Kibbie lakes to lower Kibbie Ridge, between Cherry Lake and Lake Eleanor. Other park deer have similar migratory routes.

Rested, we continue east from Sachse Spring, on a trail that undulates on morainal material supporting western white pines and red firs. A large lakelet almost 0.2 mile off the trail offers good campsites along its south shore. Beyond a seasonal creek our route begins to descend onto open granitic slabs, a harbinger of typical Emigrant Basin terrain to come. Mercur Peak, at 8080 feet elevation, is a prominent dome in the northeast. Like many granitic features in the Park, it has exfoliated considerably due to a depressurization caused by the removal of the weight of the last major glacier, which had pressed upon it for thousands of years.

Coming off the slabs into a small lodgepole forest surrounding a murky tarn, we keep right, following blazes and ducks, then continue over sandy slabs on a bearing straight for Mercur Peak. Its summit, reached by an easy scramble up its south slope, provides a fine vantage point for examining the southern Emigrant Basin. In a lodgepole forest south of the peak our trail reaches a large tarn. You can camp here, although in early season the ground can be quite damp.

This tarn marks the start of a route to aptly named Many Island Lake. Proceed due south through lodgepoles and around early-season ponds to low-angle slabs bounding the north part of the basin that holds this lake. By keeping one's feet flat on the sloping rock and pointed downhill, one should have no difficulty descending a total of ½ mile to campsites flanking the summer-warm, shallow waters of Many Island Lake, which harbors rainbow trout.

East of the Many Island Lake cross-country route, the Kibbie Ridge trail passes through a narrow, joint-controlled gully to reach Styx Pass, where it leaves Yosemite National Park some 7¾ miles beyond the Kibbie Lake trail. We descend to better views of the North and East Fork Cherry Creek drainages, flanked by soaring domes and smooth aprons. Eight tight, rocky switchbacks decorated by clumps of sedge and of red Sierra onion bring us to a long traverse east to the Boundary Lake trail, 0.6 mile beyond Styx Pass. If not signed, this junction can be easily missed. It is encountered on a steep, broken slope of exfoliating granite right before one makes two small switchbacks and starts a traverse northwest down to Lord Meadow.

On the Boundary Lake trail we make a switchbacking ascent east-southeast toward a low point on the nearby crest. the ascent presently becomes less steep as it climbs through a jumble of lodgepoles and rocks to a forested tarn. From it a final rise takes us back into the Park, where we immediately confront a pair of seasonal ponds that in early season connect with Boundary Lake's north shore, 0.6 mile beyond the trail junction. Sandy flats with sparse conifers make for good camping on this side of the lake; the east shore has high bluffs. The trail around Boundary Lake's west side winds over granitic outcrops, through patches of huckleberry oak and stands of fir and pine. The undulating path keeps generally away from the irregular rocky shore, but sometimes we near the shore to find a snug camp near clumps of willows or Labrador tea. You can expect good fishing for rainbow trout.

At Boundary Lake's south end, we steer through a notched dome, then descend to a step-across ford of the outlet. On the south bank for a moment, we have telescoped views across the lake's slate-gray entirety to Gillett Mountain before we turn south down a joint gully to the marshy north end of Little Bear

Lake. Heading east of this islet-speckled, 25-acre, rainbow-trout fishery, we pass a fine camp on the north shore, then turn south behind a red-fir-and-lodgepole grove entangled in a marshy maze of bracken and manzanita, where the trail peters out. From the south end of Little Bear Lake you could extend your trip by descending ½ mile southeast to granite-cupped Spotted Fawn Lake, which has adequate camping in its north-shore lodgepole curtain and, like all the lakes of this area, has angling for rainbow trout. Those with considerable mountaineering expertise can continue cross-country a mile southeast to a brink above the Kendrick Creek canyon. Steep slopes and lack of trails make this canyon's half dozen lakes among the least visited in the Park.

Wherever you camp, when you leave, retrace your steps along Kibbie Ridge and then back to Kibbie Lake. This lake can also be reached by cross-country routes from either Many Island Lake or Little Bear Lake, both routes being shorter than retracing the trail. Since Many Island Lake drains into Kibbie Lake via Kibbie Creek, the cross-country route along that creek is easy to follow until the lake, where you will likely have to go up cliffs regardless of which way you go around the lake. To end your hike, retrace your steps to the trailhead. However, you can take an alternate way back to it, which is about 4 miles longer.

Rather than retrace your steps from Kibbie Lake, you can start at the camps by the lake's south shore and follow a lightly used path. This path strikes southwest, ascending gently to moderately through pleasant pocket meadows, then goes out onto pine-dotted slabs that give vistas southwest down Kibbie Creek. Above 6800 feet, the way becomes steeper, and we clamber south up rough switchbacks to the ridgetop, a pleasant, dry, red-fir forest floored with mat manzanita. Here we quickly cross the crests of three glacial moraines before our faint trail strikes a slightly more visible trail. (This gradually disappearing trail climbs about 2 miles northeast before completely vanishing about one mile west of Flora Lake.) At this trail junction we leave the morainal crest and follow now-better trail tread south, the way becoming very steep, bouldery, and open. In the southwest, former clearcuts with renewed vegetation—a boon for

deer—spread over the rolling topography above Cherry Lake.

As our descent becomes more moderate, once again in forest cover, we approach a seasonal creek, entrenched below us, angle southwest, and then descend often brushy, glaciated terrain for about a mile before we cross the creek. To avoid a smooth whaleback ridge, our trail skirts around its brushy base and then enters another shady forest. We walk southwest down the slopes of a large moraine and then, at its base, angle south and reach a ford of wide, potholed Kibbie Creek—a wet crossing until late summer. Beside the crossing large-leaved umbrella plant, or Indian rhubarb, whose stalks the Miwoks ate raw, grows along or in the creek. Across the creek you'll discover several small, gravelly campsites.

Beyond the wide ford, conifers gradually give way to canyon live oaks as we descend gradually southwest, but they reappear as the dominant plant form after a mile, where our bouldery trail veers south to begin a saddle-crest traverse of Kibbie Ridge, along the Park border. At the saddle's lowest point we reach a junction with the prominent Lake Eleanor trail. Those who want to spend one more night in the back country can drop east to the west shore of large Lake Eleanor, visible through the pine-and-black-oak cover atop Kibbie Ridge. From here, a good trail leads moderately down for ¼ mile to a trail junction, from where the left fork drops east to a shaded peninsula on 27,000-acre-foot Lake Eleanor. This reservoir was created by the city of San Francisco in 1918 to raise, by 35 feet, an existing lake. Travelers may desire to follow the right-hand trail south to the 60-foot-high, 20-caisson concrete dam. At its east end lies the Lake Eleanor NPS Station and a road that follows a part of the south shore of Lake Eleanor, then climbs south and east to Miguel Meadow, where the trail to Laurel Lake begins (see **Hike 9**).

When you want to return to your trailhead from the Lake Eleanor environs, go to the ridgetop junction above the lake and then start northwest down the Lake Eleanor trail to soon strike the trailhead's road. This you could follow north about 3¼ miles back up to the trailhead. However, if you go but 0.1 mile north on the road, you'll intersect a lower part of the Kibbie Ridge trail, which you can take 1¾ miles up to the trailhead.

Author's party assembling a backpackable drilling platform on Laurel Lake

HETCH HETCHY TO
LAUREL LAKE

Distance: 15.5 miles by shortest (round trip) route

Grade: 4D, moderate 2-day hike

Trailhead: Just 1.1 miles outside the Park's Big Oak Flat Entrance Station, leave Highway 120 and drive north 7.4 miles on Evergreen Road to its junction with the Hetch Hetchy Road. Turn right and go 8.4 miles to a junction left. Backpackers turn here, park in the obvious parking area by the road's start, then walk 0.5 mile on the road to O'Shaughnessy Dam. Day hikers continue driving 0.7 mile past the junction to the dam, beyond which is parking. **B3.**

Introduction: At 6490 feet in elevation, Laurel Lake is the lowest of any *large* natural lake in the Park, providing relatively warm swimming. Being lower, this conifer-ringed lake lacks the inspiring scenery of the Park's higher

lakes. But in compensation, there are many campsites above its lengthy shore, these allowing for secluded camping even when others are present. The lake is perhaps the most glacially significant one in the entire Sierra Nevada, for its sediments provide irrefutable evidence that most of the glacial deposits mapped during the 20th century were mapped in error.

Description: For those in shape, this hike can be done as a day hike. Backpackers, starting from their parking area, will add 1 mile to their round-trip distance. Everyone should start early in the morning, since the switchbacking route up from the reservoir is only partly shaded, and summer temperatures can reach into the 90s by noon. Carry sufficient water; in late season it's two or more hours before reaching water.

You begin by starting across the top of O'Shaughnessy Dam (3814 feet) at Hetch Hetchy Reservoir. Along this curving monolith, named for the Hetch Hetchy Project's chief engineer, we find bronze plaques posted here to commemorate those who made possible this intrusion on a national park, back in 1914, along with similar structures on Lake

Eleanor and Cherry Lake. Visitors today can look, but not touch (to protect San Francisco's hygiene, one must assume), so we can only gaze east over the 8-mile-long reservoir. The soaring canyon walls that remain standing above it are good reminders of what Hetch Hetchy Valley once was—a less-spectacular sibling of Yosemite Valley. Yosemite Valley, being a popular tourist destination, was saved from dam(nation), but Hetch Hetchy Valley, being quite unknown, was an easy victim. On the south wall, the prow of Kolana Rock soars 2000 feet above the reservoir, while to its north, tiered Hetch Hetchy Dome rises about 400 feet higher. In a shaded cleft on the dome's west flank, two-stepped Wapama Falls plunges an aggregate of 1400 feet. In early summer its gossamer companion, Tueeulala Falls, glides down steep slabs farther west.

Across the 600-foot-long dam, we enter a 500-foot-long tunnel blasted through solid granite when the original dam was raised 85 feet in 1938. Emerging from this bat haven, the formerly paved road traverses above the rocky west shore of Hetch Hetchy Reservoir in a pleasant grove of Douglas-fir, gray pine, bigleaf maple, and bay trees. Sour, blue-blushed California grape, shiny poison oak, and palm-like giant chain ferns grow in the shadier spots. Each of these plants was utilized by the Miwok Indians that visited in Hetch Hetchy. One mile into our route, we reach the junction with the Rancheria Falls trail (see **Hike 10**), just before our route's first switchback.

Keeping to the former road, we ascend moderately steep switchbacks and have better views up the reservoir of LeConte Point and the Grand Canyon of the Tuolumne River.

As we ascend, fairly open, lower slopes give way to oak-shaded slopes, then near the top to oak-and-conifer-shaded ones. The last of eight switchbacks swings north into a gully with a trail junction on a small flat. With about 3 miles and half of the elevation gain under your belt, you start up a trail through a partly burned forest of ponderosa pines, sugar pines, and other conifers. In ¼ mile you reach a mile-high creeklet which, although diminutive, usually flows through the summer. This is your first reliable water, and people have camped hereabouts.

Up the trail about 200 yards past the creeklet you'll see a shallow gully on your right. This is the start of a relatively easy 1½-mile-long cross-country route east to the brink of Wapama Falls. They are the only major year-round waterfall in the Park to lack a trail to its brink. The cross-country route, which I'll leave for you to discern, has been done by so many hikers that a faint use trail exists. Be forewarned that the route is dry, is in rattlesnake habitat, has locally dense brush, and has flower seeds that stick to socks and shoelaces. However, the view from the falls' brink is stupendous, and after about mid-July, Falls Creek has diminished enough in flow to permit a refreshing swim in a shallow pool just above the brink.

Unlike the former road you ascended, which maintains a nearly constant grade, your ascending trail varies, being locally steep, moderate, gentle, or even briefly down. You'll eventually climb 1000 feet above the creeklet before the serious climbing ends. About ½ mile beyond the creeklet, your trail curves east and levels off, and you may want to rest. Ahead the trail climbs north, then northwest, and then the serious climbing ends with a curve east to cross a crest of a lateral moraine. On this ascent look for linear deposits, which too are lateral moraines. Also look for flat near-trail bedrock exposures into which Indians drilled mortar holes and ground up black-oak acorns and sugar-pine seeds. Once on top, 4.6 miles into your hike, take a break; you deserve it. While resting, look around and read the following paragraph.

The moraine crest you've crossed is sharp and its rocks are fresh, indicating that it is of Tioga age. Immediately north of it is a shallow, linear lakelet, which holds water well into summer. It appears to be dammed by the moraine, but actually is dammed by bedrock buried under the thin deposits of your moraine. Immediately north of the lakelet is another lateral moraine, judged to be older, of Tahoe age, because it is broad and not sharp-crested, and has fewer boulders. Beyond it, glacial deposits extending up to Laurel Lake are even thinner and more amorphous, and hence judged to be very old, possibly of Sherwin age. By using these criteria, geologists identified and mapped three episodes of glaciation in Yosemite National Park and other glaciated lands west of the Sierra crest. The older the deposits are, the more weathered they become, yet if you look at formerly buried boulders exposed by Laurel Lake's outlet creek, you'll see they are fresh, not disintegrated. In 1993 I proposed that the location and shape of glacial deposits are dictated by topography and glacial physics, and that most of the Sierra's thin, amorphous deposits actually are young, that is, of Tioga age—not old, of Sherwin age. Laurel Lake was an ideal site to test which view was correct. Conventional wisdom called for hundreds of feet of lake sediments and a date of basal sediments some 800,000 years old. My interpretation called for 10-20 feet of sediments and a date no more than 16,000 years old. On August 20, 1994 my 5-man work party successfully penetrated 14 feet of lake sediments to extract basal sediments, sent them off to be dated, and soon received the results: Laurel Lake is only about 13,000 years old. Glacial deposits throughout most of the Sierra Nevada had been dated under the wrong assumptions.

Your hike ahead is now relatively easy. After rounding the linear lakelet's east end, the trail crosses the broad moraine's crest, drops momentarily, then ascends 0.4 mile through an open white-fir forest to a junction with a southwest-descending trail. Laurel Lake, though only ¾ mile northwest of us, is at least 2½ trail miles away by either trail we can take, and one wonders why a trail was not built directly to it. If you've not found water so far, take the trail ¼ mile down to always reliable Frog Creek. Rather than ascend back up to the junction, you might ascend first along the west side of the creek, then along the west side of the lake's outlet creek.

From your junction, 5.3 miles beyond your trailhead, follow the often shady trail northeast, dip to cross a bracken-bordered creeklet, then soon hike alongside a linear meadow that in season is profuse with arrow-leaved senecio and Bigelow's sneezeweed, two kinds of sunflowers. The meadow pinches off at a low gap, beyond which we quickly find ourselves in the southwest corner of a triangular meadow. Staying among white firs and lodgepole pines, we parallel the meadow's edge northeast over to its east corner, called Beehive, where there is a trail junction. About 20 yards before it, just within the meadow, is a usually reliable spring. Just beyond the junction, among trees, is a spacious campsite. From the junction the Laurel Lake trail veers northwest, while the Jack Main Canyon trail starts east (see **Hikes 11** and **12**). Beehive was the site

of an 1880s cattlemen's camp, and a log cabin once stood north of the trail junction.

By walking northwest 160 yards on the Laurel Lake trail, we reach another trail junction. Here a path that loops around Laurel Lake's north shore branches north, while a shorter trail to the lake's outlet strikes west. Following this latter route, we drop easily down into a white-fir-shaded gully and then broad Frog Creek, which could be a wet ford in early season. Along its north bank we contour west briefly, then ascend steeply to a heavily forested ridge before gently dropping to good camps near Laurel Lake's outlet. A brief stint brings us to a junction with the north-shore loop trail, branching northwest to the best campsites (and more-secluded ones beyond). At fairly deep 60-acre Laurel Lake, western azalea grows thickly just back of the locally grassy lakeshore, a fragrant accompaniment to huckleberry and thimbleberry. Fishing is fair for rainbow trout.

By continuing north around Laurel Lake, one will encounter a large packer campsite on the northwest shore. There the trail turns east through a bracken-overgrown deadfall, negotiates an easy ridge, and drops to a camp beside Frog Creek, here running through cobbles and past tall American dogwood shrubs. Across that stream, the route turns southeast, ascending easily to a junction with the southern Laurel Lake trail, just north of Beehive.

For an alternate return route, leave Laurel Lake near its outlet, heading southwest on the Frog Creek trail under a dense canopy of white fir. Within ½ mile this walk becomes a gradually steepening descent, down an open nose of fire-damaged conifers. A trail junction is reached midway down the nose, where we must make a choice of return routes. The first contours 1¼ miles east to Frog Creek, then another ¼ mile up it to the trail we came in on, leaving one with 5.3 miles of backtracking to Hetch Hetchy. The second—straight ahead—descends to Miguel Meadow.

Should you choose the longer route via Miguel Meadow, head west from the trail junction and drop steeply on sandy tread, with views west over Lake Eleanor and down on conifer-shaded Frog Creek. Beyond an emergency campsite, we easily hop rocks to the south bank and climb a short switchback. Now a traverse leads southwest through dry forest to a nearby ridge saddle clothed in manzanita, from where the Beehive trail formerly dropped west to Lake Eleanor. We turn south from this saddle, gently descend into the basin of Miguel Creek, and there walk under a pleasant canopy of Jeffrey pines and black oaks where flickers and white-headed woodpeckers dwell. Below 5400 feet our path comes out into the open on a bouldery, sunny hillside. Lower down, we pass north of unseen Gravel Pit Lake, then traverse southwest to a road. You could head just ⅓ mile southwest down it to Miguel Meadow, where there is an NPS ranger station and pleasant camping under large black oaks. However, to return to Hetch Hetchy, turn southeast on the road, cross nearby Miguel Creek, wind east for 3.2 miles up a shallow, open-floored canyon, top a mile-high saddle, drop a few hundred yards to the Laurel Lake trail junction, up which you ascended, and retrace your steps down the switchbacking route to the trailhead.

<hr>

HIKE 10

HETCH HETCHY TO RANCHERIA FALLS

Distance: 12.7 miles round trip

Grade: 3D, moderate day-hike

Trailhead: Same as the Hike 9 trailhead. **B3.**

Introduction: A stately grove of pines and incense-cedars harboring a spacious camping area near Rancheria Falls marks the terminus of this hike. Its cascades and pools are the goals for some, but also rewarding are inspirational vistas of the awesome cliffs and early-summer waterfalls seen along the undulating path on the north wall of Hetch Hetchy Reservoir. The route, being quite open and at a relatively low elevation, is best begun in early morning if you are hiking it on a potentially hot day.

Description: See the first part of **Hike 9**, which starts across the top of O'Shaughnessy Dam and after one mile along a road reaches the junction with the Rancheria Falls trail. On it we descend gently first south and then east across an exfoliating granitic nose, then

switchback once down to a broad, sloping ledge, sparingly shaded by gray-green foothill pines and scrubby mountain mahogany. From April through June you may see an assortment of wildflowers in bloom, along with patches of mosslike selaginella, a relative of ferns. We follow this ledge ½ mile to an unnamed, minor stream which descends, until about early summer, hundreds of feet as Tueeulala Falls. Beyond it we wind down along the north shore of Hetch Hetchy Reservoir to a bridge over a steep ravine, where our views east to the lake's head expand impressively. On the north wall stands multifaceted Hetch Hetchy Dome, guarding split-level Wapama Falls. Opposite this monolith towers the obdurate, warshiplike prow of Kolana Rock, which forces a constriction in the 8-mile-long reservoir's tadpole shape.

A few minutes of easy traverse east from here end at a steep, dynamited descent through a field of huge talus blocks under a tremendous unnamed precipice. Soon, if we're passing this way in early summer, flecks of spray dampen our cobbly path, as we come to the first of several bridges below the base of Wapama Falls. During some high-runoff years, even these high, sturdy bridges are inundated by seasonally tumultuous Falls Creek.

East of Wapama Falls, our rocky path leads up around the base of a steep bulge of glacier-polished and striated granite under a fly-infested canopy of canyon live oak, bay tree, poison oak, and wild-grape vines. Huge flakes of shattered granite also dot this bench, spalled from the walls above. After our terrace tapers off, the frequently dynamited trail undulates along a steep hillside in open chaparral of yerba santa and mountain mahogany, switchbacking on occasion to circumvent some cliffy spots. Eventually our path descends to the oak-and-pine-shaded gorge cut by Tiltill Creek, and we cross two bridges, the second one high above the creek. You can get water just above this bridge by making a cautious traverse over to a pool at the brink of the creek's fall. When the current's not too strong, the pool is great to dip in on a hot day.

Beyond the creek our route climbs the gorge's east slope via a set of tight switchbacks to emerge 250 feet higher on a gentle hillside of sunny, gray-lichened slabs, foothill pines, and whiteleaf manzanitas. Where this ascent eases off, you may see, on your right, the start of an

Tueeulala Falls and lower Wapama Fall above Hetch Hetchy Reservoir

old, abandoned trail, which nevertheless is in very good condition. It follows a descending ridge just south of Tiltill Creek, ending just above Hetch Hetchy Reservoir. Signs down there advise you that no camping is allowed within 200 feet of the shoreline. Camping in this vicinity avoids the crowds that are sometimes found at the Rancheria Falls camping area.

Soon our way levels off, and we spy Rancheria Creek. By walking a few paces right, we have an excellent vantage point of it. The creek here slides invitingly over broad rock slabs, its pools superb for skinny-dipping. Every step of your way has been on granite, but just 0.2 mile past your vantage point you may note a different substrate: a small deposit, essentially granitic, which is a tiny remnant of a much larger deposit that was transported to this spot in a south-directed eruption of latite tuff about 9½ million years ago. More important, the deposit shows that no erosion of the bedrock here has occurred, despite repeated

passage by glaciers up to 4000 feet thick. If you could have hiked here 9½ million years ago, you would have seen that the Hetch Hetchy canyonlands would have been almost as deep and wide back then as it is today.

Just 0.1 mile past the volcanic remnants we reach a junction with a short trail to the spacious Rancheria Falls campsite. Rancheria Creek is a moment's walk away, and you can head up and down it in pursuit of cascades and pools. One nearby cascade is a small fall, about 25 feet high, which in high volume shoots over a ledge of resistant dark intrusive rock. Fishing below the falls might yield pan-size rainbow trout. Be warned that this popular camping area is often shared with marauding black bears, so store your provisions out of their reach. Perhaps after a side hike to Tiltill Valley (**Hike 11**) or to panoramic LeConte Point (**Hike 13**), retrace your steps to O'Shaughnessy Dam.

HIKE 11

HETCH HETCHY TO LAKE VERNON AND TILTILL VALLEY

Distance: 29.8 miles loop trip

Grade: 5E, moderate 4-day hike

Trailhead: Same as the Hike 9 trailhead. **B3.**

Introduction: This relatively low-elevation loop, a good early-summer conditioner, first visits two relatively large lakes—Laurel and Vernon—both good rainbow-trout fisheries. It then visits meadowed Tiltill Valley, an interesting pocket of spring wildflowers and grasses having several isolated creekside campsites. For the finale, the route returns with a traverse from bench to bench above Hetch Hetchy Reservoir, and it offers changing panoramas of Yosemite-like Hetch Hetchy Valley. Be aware that the upper slopes on your descent east into Tiltill Valley can become overgrown with brush. Therefore, first check at the Hetch Hetchy Entrance Station about the trail's condition through the brush. This route offers opportunities for experienced cross-country hikers to explore creekside lands above and below Lake Vernon and along Rancheria Creek east of Tiltill Valley.

Description: Follow **Hike 9** to the Beehive junction—easily your route's greatest ascent—then make a rolling traverse west 1.3 miles to Laurel Lake, and camp there. This lake is too close to your route to bypass. Next day, backtrack to Beehive and take the eastbound trail that winds 1.3 miles easily up to a moraine-crest junction with the Jack Main Canyon trail, just below the slightly higher crest of Moraine Ridge. From the junction we descend to an open, granite bench. Now on bedrock, we follow a well-ducked trail down past excellent examples of glacier-smoothed rock—glacier polish—and glacier-transported boulders—glacier erratics. Scattered Jeffrey pines lend occasional shade along a northeast traverse, their roots seeking out cracks in the granite in which they might take hold and help form a soil. On drier, more inhospitable sites grow rugged western junipers, which manage to survive where the Jeffreys don't because their scalelike leaves lose less water to the atmosphere than do the Jeffrey's long needles.

Along this section we can look across the far wall of Falls Creek canyon until a nearby minor outlier, ½ mile southwest of Lake Vernon, obstructs our view, about 1¼ miles from the last junction. Just after this happens, we angle southeast and follow a winding, ducked route up toward the point, but cross a low ridge just north of it. Now below us lies spreading Lake Vernon, flooding part of a broad, flat-floored canyon. During colder times, glaciers occupied this canyon and buried it under as much as 1800 feet of glacier ice. When the last glacier retreated from the canyon by 14,000 years ago, it left minor depressions in the bedrock floor, which quickly filled to become Lake Vernon and its satellite lakes and ponds.

From this inspirational ridge we descend generally northeast—the trend of this area's master joints—and in ⅓ mile reach a junction with the Lake Vernon trail, about 8½ miles from the Hetch Hetchy trailhead. Leaving a small flat with a few nearby aspens among Jeffrey pines, this trail shoots northeast, at first staying close to the base of a similar-trending wall. After ¼ mile of walking, you'll be close to the shore of the unseen lake, and you can head southeast to it. There you'll find a fairly large campsite among lodgepoles. Others lie along this northwest shore of Lake Vernon.

The trail continues past a snow-gauge marker and adjacent Park cabin, then dies out, about a mile past the lake, by a large camp close to where the creek angles from northeast to north and its gradient increases dramatically. From this vicinity an easy cross-country route climbs north up along the cascading creek to a flat. Above it, the route is steeper, though not dangerously so, if you can discern a proper route up beside the dashing creek. At the top of this ascent, immediately north of the creek's highest cascade, is the Jack Main Canyon trail. This cross-country route to this point takes no more effort than does the trail route up over Moraine Ridge and down to it. The first offers a cascading creek with a refreshing swimming hole or two, the second, sweeping vistas.

Rather than take the Lake Vernon trail, you can take the main trail southeast briefly to a bridge across Falls Creek, then equally briefly northeast around a bedrock slope to Lake Vernon's southwest shore. Additional campsites are found near it. The lake, mostly shallow and lying at about 6450 feet, is one of the warmer Park lakes for swimming. Some people choose to camp below the lake, near Falls Creek below the bridge. There are many opportunities for isolated camping, but the bedrock flats are essentially treeless, so you have to be inventive in protecting your food from hungry bears. An extremely scenic cross-country route goes down Falls Creek to the brink of Wapama Falls, from which a brushy, weedy, viewless route goes west to the shallow gully you ascended past on day one. The first part of the cross-country route is past giant potholes the creek carved, probably as a roaring, boulder-choked river beneath a giant glacier. As usual, I won't describe the route, but will leave it to you to discover. The route takes a lot more effort than you would imagine, is locally brushy and bouldery, has one narrow notch and adjacent, steep, potentially dangerous descent to negotiate. Below it gets into less scenic, hotter lands, where a rattlesnake encounter is more likely than it was above. This is definitely not a route for the inexperienced or inept. Nevertheless, it is extremely rewarding, but you have to work for the rewards.

Most hikers return from Lake Vernon the way they came. Some, along with equestrians, do continue on to Tiltill Valley. From the lake you ascend for about 1000 feet via some three dozen short switchbacks. The view improves with elevation, and the expanding panoramas give us good excuses to take plenty of rests. The views disappear as we enter a minor hanging valley some 700 feet above the lake. Now among firs, we make a short climb up past several lateral moraines until we top the last of them.

With easy hiking ahead, we first dip into a gully, then contour south, passing above two small meadows before crossing another moraine and gently descending to the lower end of a long meadow. The grove of aspens at its upper end may hide a few deer, for aspen leaves are part of their summer diet. Leaving the meadow, we arc southwest up to the crest of a nearby lateral moraine, which from our vantage point is only a low ridge, though it stands a full 4,000 feet above the inundated floor of the Grand Canyon of the Tuolumne River. The glacier that left this moraine was at least that thick. The moraine we stand on once

Lake Vernon

supported red firs, but apparently these were blown down by violent winds along this exposed ridge (see wind-downed firs near Dewey Point, along **Hike 71**). Downed trees exposed the ground to sunlight, shrubs invaded, and this area has become one of the best browsing areas for deer in the entire Park. In addition to snow bush—a favorite food—deer have nearby access to aspen, huckleberry oak, scrubby black oak, gooseberry, and willow.

Our descent along the brushy hillside provides grand views, but the flanking shrubs at times present thorny problems to hikers in shorts. If this stretch of trail is too overgrown, it can become essentially impossible to follow. After an initial brief descent southwest and southeast, the brush abates and the trail traverses east for about a mile, then steepens and on well-built switchbacks descends southeast toward seemingly distant Tiltill Valley.

Our descent ends where thirst-quenching Tiltill Creek spills out onto flat-floored Tiltill Valley. Where the trail crosses the creek you can walk momentarily along its west bank to a small campsite under incense-cedars and pines, which is enjoyable once the mosquitoes abate, usually after mid-July. A cluster of Miwok Indian mortar holes in bedrock lies nearby, under some large black oaks. Also nearby on both sides of the creek are other campsites.

Beyond Tiltill Creek the trail stays close to the base of the valley's towering north wall. At times the trail seems too close to it, for it wanders among large blocks of rockfall-deposited talus; however, a trail built in the meadow would often be waterlogged. After about ½ mile the trail turns south to cross a seasonally boggy meadow, our trail being protected by levees and ditches. Nevertheless, before July you can expect to get wet feet. By the time the meadow dries out, bunchgrasses can grow to thigh-height and harbor abundant rodents as well as their predatory rattlesnakes—be careful here.

In the meadow's center you may find a junction with a rarely used trail that heads northeast to the valley's east end, then switchbacks up a gully, bound for the Pacific Crest Trail. Of more interest is the start of a relatively easy cross-country route to Rancheria Creek. From this point you go about one mile east along the floor of an obvious canyon to where you have a choice of routes. Avoid the deep,

narrow, inviting canyon on the left and continue east about ⅓ mile to an obvious saddle. Some may find a ducked route that ends just north of this saddle, but it is quite exposed and potentially dangerous. From the saddle, Rancheria Creek lies very close below you, and you can find isolated camping near pools and minor cascades for about ¾ mile downstream and for about 1¼ miles upstream, to the base of some major cascades. Only serious mountaineers will want to continue farther. Near the base of these cascades is the lower end of Deep Canyon, whose traverse is a disappointment.

In Tiltill Valley, the trail heads south to the base of some steep bluffs that bound the valley on the south, and it enters a lush stand of aspens, alders, and willows surrounding a small spring. Both the treelike mountain dogwood and the shrubbier, red-barked American dogwood thrive here, shading lady fern, bracken, thimbleberry, raspberry, and currant. A few Douglas-firs hug the hillsides here, sharing the coolness with shrubby mountain maples. Upon reaching the canyon wall, our path immediately begins to climb, taking some well-engineered switchbacks southwest to a large joint-controlled rift. This we follow gently up southwest, past a small, linear pond decked with yellow pond lilies. Overhead, staircased dark cliffs fall from Peak 6595 to the east, overlooking our progress through a forest of white fir and incense-cedar. Seasonally fragrant western azalea is a locally dominant understory shrub, joined in more-open spots by uncommon white-bugled Washington's lily. Straight as an arrow our trail slices through a narrow saddle and then gently descends into another straight-sided canyon, this one also trending southwest.

After ½ mile we angle west out of this canyon onto open slabs, where we have views south over brushy LeConte Point to somber-cliffed Smith Peak. Now the route begins to descend in earnest, high above the forests below. The trail twists itself into numerous sandy, moderate switchbacks, soon dropping to the 5300-foot level, where the slopes can be too warm in summer, and heat-tolerant vegetation exists, including foothill pines and canyon live oaks, which offer meager shade. Here, too, we perceive some slivers of Hetch Hetchy Reservoir, bent around sentinel Kolana Rock to the west. Some 600 feet more of occasionally furnace-hot switchbacking descent follow, depositing us, finally, at a junction with the Rancheria Mountain trail on a manzanita-cloaked sandy hillside. Here we turn right, down some easy switchbacks, and after ½ mile bend briefly south to find the cool haven of a large, thick conifer grove along the north bank of Rancheria Creek—a popular camping area mentioned at the end of **Hike 10**. To complete your route, take this hike in the reverse direction back to O'Shaughnessy Dam.

MORAINE RIDGE-WILMA LAKE-TILTILL VALLEY LOOP

Distance: 40.9 miles loop trip

Grade: 6F, moderate 4-day hike

Trailhead: Same as the Hike 9 trailhead. **B3.**

Introduction: Following a route used around the turn of the 19th century by both illegal sheepherders and their US Army pursuers, the Jack Main Canyon trail (named for one of the early sheepmen) visits a succession of small subalpine meadows along the course of delightful, cascading Falls Creek. Wilma Lake, the gem of Jack Main Canyon, marks the northernmost point in that glacier-scoured trough, and offers pastoral camping with the opportunity to visit over 20 fishing and swimming lakes or climb to more than a dozen viewful summits, each within an easy day's hiking!

Description: Follow **Hike 9** from Hetch Hetchy Reservoir up to Beehive, then west 1.3 miles to Laurel Lake, and camp there the first night. Later, retrace your steps to Beehive and take a trail for a gentle ascent northeast to a forested glade, then moderately above it to a nearby morainal crest, 1.3 miles from Beehive. Here the more popular Lake Vernon trail starts a descent northeast to the lake, from which one could follow Falls Creek, first by trail then cross-country, up to lower Jack Main Canyon (see **Hike 11**).

We, however, veer north on the Jack Main Canyon trail to begin a long, sandy ascent of Moraine Ridge. In a couple of minutes we cross a minor saddle, then in a similar time reach a second one, where we reach the actual crest of Moraine Ridge. In ⅓ mile we make a generally moderate ascent up the crest, then have a nearly level crest traverse for another ⅓ mile. We then resume climbing and over the first ⅓ mile of this 2-mile ascent you can obtain water quite easily by descending north about 200 yards to an unnamed creeklet. Drought-tolerant Jeffrey pines dominate the conifers until supplanted above 7500 feet by red firs and western white pines. Along this ascent one has some views down into the Falls Creek drainage, including glimpses of Lake Vernon, ponds and lakelets beyond it, and the cascading outlet creek of rockbound Branigan Lake. After about 1100 feet of elevation gain, generally at an optimal gradient for backpackers, we top out at about 8110 feet, just below the actual summit of Moraine Ridge.

The entire ridge was completely buried under ice by the last glacier, not just by its predecessors, as previously thought. One sees fresh Tioga-age boulders along the entire ascent, and they are especially numerous on the summit area. From just north of it, another "Moraine Ridge" with similar glacial deposits parallels ours southwest. Between the two is a shallow hanging valley that at first appears unglaciated. Not so. The glacial ice down it was thin, and so flowed slowly, taking with it only sparse sediments. Around the summit area we have panoramas to the north and east, stretching from the broken, water-streaked summits of Richardson, Mahan, and Andrews peaks in the foreground to the distant Saurian Crest, Piute Mountain, Sawtooth Ridge, and Mt. Conness.

Our trail now begins a ⅓-mile descent, aided with short switchbacks, down to a flat with a dogleg in a seasonal creeklet, near which one could camp. For remote camping, you could head cross-country about ⅔ mile north gently up through a broad crest gap to the brink of Frog Creek canyon and then visit one or more of its lakes, which include Miwok and Bearup lakes. By following Frog Creek above Bearup Lake, you eventually would reach the Otter Lakes basin, above our trail's destination, Wilma Lake. From the flat our trail toward Wilma is more demanding—steep, tight switchbacks of riprapped and dynamited granite plunge down along a joint-controlled ravine to a hop across our seasonal creeklet. Immediately beyond it is Falls Creek, which begins a seriously cascading descent toward Lake Vernon. If you took a trail northeast from that lake and then a cross-country route north up the cascades, you would join the trail here.

About 11¾ trail miles into our route, we now begin our ascent of Jack Main Canyon. Our first mile of walking along Falls Creek sets the tone for the rest of our journey: the trail undulates moderately, alternately visiting benches of sunny, glaciated granite dotted with huckleberry-oak thickets and precariously rooted western junipers, and pocket stands of lodgepoles and stately red firs, their canopy shading twinberry, mountain ash, and red elderberry. We pass above a triad of sandbanked pools, then descend slightly to a horseshoe bend in Falls Creek that has a grove of red firs with good camping nearby. East of this bend our still-undulating trail winds among open slabs and up to a piney bench. Here one may choose to leave the trail and strike south across Falls Creek and up through a gap west of striated Andrews Peak to Andrews and Branigan lakes. Our path turns north, drop-

ping to the largest and most beautiful of a number of unnamed lakelets in lower Jack Main Canyon. Shaped somewhat like a horseshoe, this shallow lakelet reflects the broken south face of Mahan Peak while supporting a shoreline garden of Parish's yampah and Bigelow's sneezeweed.

Our route skirts its north shore, then veers south around another pond, following "**T**" blazes back to the north bank of Falls Creek. Here we turn east, on a 30-foot-wide isthmus between the stream and an aspen-bordered pond that lies just north of the trail, fed only by ground water. From the head of this pond, we climb north to a gap, then drop easily to a large meadow known as Paradise Valley. Here our path keeps near the screen of infringing lodgepole pines, leaps the outlet stream of Mahan Lake, and comes to a large complex of streamside campsites surrounding a junction, 3⅓ miles up Jack Main Canyon, with a cutoff east to Tilden Canyon.

This hot, unworthy route is recommended only for those headed for the Branigan Lakes. To take it, wade across sandy Falls Creek just below a wide pool and find the

Along Moraine Ridge

vague trail as it swings east around the south side of a grassy mosquito pond. The little-used route then climbs tortuously southeast through pockets of mat manzanita and open lodgepole pines to a viewful knoll. Next, this route drops momentarily east, then turns southwest up a narrow rock corridor. Near the head of this herbaceously floored ravine, where further progress seems blocked by a talus slide, the path turns abruptly and steeply up to the east. By heading cross-country southwest in a linear, joint-controlled canyon, you would reach Upper Branigan Lake in ½ mile. Ahead, the cutoff trail bends back to the northeast and climbs easily to a tarn-dotted flat. From here you switchback steeply east over gneissic-banded intrusive rocks into a forested canyon. Lodgepoles and hemlocks shade the way as the drainage heads northeast, then south, to 8575 feet, where the route tops out in a narrow gap. From this pass this lateral trail drops southeast to the nearby Tilden Canyon trail.

To finish our hike up Jack Main Canyon to Wilma Lake, 3.3 miles away, we slog through sand beyond the Tilden Canyon cutoff, quickly reaching the lodgepole-shaded shores of a lake that is picturesquely backdropped by a lichen-covered cliff. Beyond it, we're led back through a gap to Falls Creek, now a wide lagoon, and we walk north near its meanders, which are hidden by tall willows. Above us, the ancient Falls Creek glacier enhanced the resistant rock of Peak 8280 with some fantastic fins which today provide excellent multipitch rock climbs. Later, Sybol Lake, a seasonal lily pond in an encroaching meadow, is passed with only a glimpse of it through lodgepoles and aspens.

North of Sybol Lake, Falls Creek, true to its name, tumbles through a narrow gorge of mafic rock and slides over some smooth slabs that are ideal for bathers, and our path takes some rocky, dynamited switchbacks up along it. Above the gorge our streamside way is more gentle as it winds northeast over slabs dotted with erratic boulders, mat manzanita, and hummocks bearing dense stands of lodgepoles. Note that many of the lodgepoles hereabouts have prominent "witches' brooms"— bizarrely twisted branches of too-dense needles—that are caused by a virus which disrupts their growth pattern. Presently, we spy turf-bounded Wilma Lake lying across the stream, in a pleasant mixed-conifer forest. Now our route ascends a final shoulder and drops to a large, dry flat from where the Pacific Crest Trail leads up Jack Main Canyon (see **Hike 42**). You'll see a seasonal rangers' cabin nearby.

On the PCT we turn east to wade broad Falls Creek near some heavily used camps, then striking southeast, we soon reach Wilma Lake, which has rainbow trout. The PCT skirts close along the lake's south shore, past lodgepoles and hemlocks. We then wind moderately up a canyon past two pleasant tarns to a junction with the Tilden Lake trail, which ascends north to its namesake.

At this junction we turn south down the PCT for 110 yards to the Tilden Canyon trail, and take it southwest down along Tilden Canyon Creek under an often mosquitoey lodgepole canopy. This shady walk soon reaches a pear-shaped, grassy tarn rimmed with Labrador tea and bilberry. From its west end, we bend south, following blazes and ducks in open lodgepole stands interspersed with erratics and glaciated slabs. In about a mile we again come close to Tilden Canyon Creek—here a wide lagoon cut deep through meadow turf—where one might disturb a family of mallard ducks. Pressing on, we negotiate a small rise, then ascend once more, this time via steep, eroded, rocky switchbacks, past a junction with the cutoff route west to lower Jack Main Canyon. The grind abates minutes later, when we level off just below a low summit on a glacier-smoothed ridge. It is well worth a minute taken to reach it, for it presents sweeping panoramas of northern Yosemite. You can look all the way up Jack Main canyon to Bond Pass; then, swinging your gaze east, spot Tower Peak, Matterhorn Peak, Piute Mountain, and the Cathedral Range from Fairview Dome to Mt. Lyell.

Resuming our trek, we walk south along a low, broad ridge, then drop on a switchback to an easy traverse that is shaded by red firs, mountain hemlocks, and western white pines. Uncommon bleeding hearts and common dwarf lousewort grow in the shade here. Presently we ascend to a broad, forested saddle, then descend to a diminishing lakelet, our last permanent water source for about 8 miles, in Tiltill Valley. Below the lakelet, we walk for a while beside its meadowed outlet creek, then veer away on a rocky descent around a steep bluff before resuming a creekside route under moderate forest cover. We walk easily for a mile down through an understory of yarrow, meadow rue, aster, senecio, and corn lily to small Tiltill Meadow, in which once stood a cabin built by H. G. Kibbie.

South of Tiltill Meadow, we continue in the same easy manner for ½ mile, then turn southwest down a dry morainal slope to a red-fir grove beside a small meadow drained by a step-across branch of Rancheria Creek. Now begins a 2300-foot descent to Tiltill Valley. Chaparral areas allow views south and east over the bluffs of Smith Peak and Rancheria Mountain. Moderate switchbacks ease our descent to 7300 feet, and then we drop more gently southwest down a sandy canyon and look west to a brush-covered Mt. Gibson. Next we work south along a bouldery, brushy bench, and then begin the final 1300-foot plunge. At first we stay on the north side of a ridge, descending steeply on sand in the relative shade of tall huckleberry-oak brush and scattered Jeffrey pines. But below 6600 feet we swing onto the ridge's south face, which allows our first views of lush Tiltill Valley and, beyond it, Hetch Hetchy Reservoir. But the south face also subjects us to the full heat of the midday sun.

Eventually, at 6330 feet, we reach a gap on the ridge, which affords some shade and a good spot to appreciate the size of the Rancheria Creek and Tuolumne River glaciers. At this elevation, during the height of the last glaciation, we would have been buried under about 1700 feet of ice, since in our vicinity the sea of ice of the Yosemite north country had a surface elevation of about 8000 feet, if not more. Below this instructional rest stop are more steep, rocky, exposed switchbacks, this time leading east through canyon-live-oak scrub. Eventually the trail bends south and lowers us to the long-awaited shade of a grove of incense-cedars, black oaks, and Jeffrey pines at the eastern edge of Tiltill Valley. We turn west onto the flats and emerge into a hummocky, open grassland, then follow its edge to join the main trail. If you need water or want to camp in this valley, take this trail west, along the north edge of the valley, reaching, in about ½ mile, Tiltill Creek and adjacent campsites. This creek is relatively small, but nevertheless is large enough to support a few small trout. To end your journey, follow **Hike 11** to

Rancheria Falls, then the reverse of **Hike 10** out to O'Shaughnessy Dam.

RANCHERIA MOUNTAIN-BEAR VALLEY-TILTILL VALLEY SEMILOOP

Distance: 52.4 miles semiloop trip

Grade: 7G, strenuous 5-day hike

Trailhead: Same as the Hike 9 trailhead. **B3.**

Introduction: The broad, conifer-robed massif of Rancheria Mountain affords a generally snow-free early-summer route into the Yosemite north country. Hikers who don't demand a spectacular, high-level trail will find that the floral gardens and the serene forests on this north rim of the Grand Canyon of the Tuolumne, coupled with secluded hemlock-bower camping beside Bear Valley Lake, compensate for the prolonged climb in.

Description: Follow **Hike 10** from O'Shaughnessy Dam to the Rancheria Falls campsite, about 6¼ miles, and camp there the first night. The next morning, ascend ⅓ mile moderately up to a junction with the Tiltill Valley trail (see **Hike 11**), then 300 yards beyond to a 50-foot-long bridge over Rancheria Creek. This stream bumps and slides frothily below through a series of well-worn potholes and slabs, inviting divers, swimmers, and sunbathers. Tank up on water at this creek, for your next source will be an often-hot 3000 feet higher and 5 miles farther, on the west slope of Rancheria Mountain. Our trail now ascends briefly south past brush and scattered foothill pines, then commences a 1300-foot switchbacking ascent. The slopes are fairly open, though you can stop and rest in the shade of black oaks, which are the dominant tree along this stretch. As we progress higher, vistas west over the reservoir and Kolana Rock improve. About 2 miles past Rancheria Creek, we finally top a 6230-foot nose, littered with gravel and boulder glacial deposits. This lies just east of an obvious saddle, from which many hikers climb a crest to its summit, LeConte Point. Should you wish to

Bear Valley Lake   Ben Schifrin

visit this spectacular viewpoint—a sometimes pilgrimage destination for Sierra Club hikers—leave the trail before the nose, at any point where you feel comfortable heading to the saddle.

Onward, our trail traverses ½ mile east along sandy chaparral slopes to the head of a minor hanging canyon, in which we encounter the first white firs of our journey. The ascent resumes on dusty switchbacks up past some fire-cleared forest openings that now support a thriving population of deer. At 6800 feet we swing onto a south-facing chaparral slope and can look south across the Grand Canyon of the Tuolumne River to the rolling upland region across it. This harbors hidden White Wolf Resort and Campground, a mere 5 air miles away, but some four times that by extremely strenuous trails. From a minor bench our path enters a burned area and first ascends on a comfortable gradient then begins to switchback after ½ mile. We tediously zigzag up them, climbing 300 feet in elevation, then enter forest slopes, mantled with volcanic deposits, as we approach a reliable stream. This we parallel east for ⅓ mile before crossing it at about 7700 feet elevation. Be sure to tank up here. Above its opposite bank is a mostly open, gentle, gravelly slope adequate for camping.

Onward, our trail soon ascends under lodgepoles and red firs to another creek, ½ mile farther. In a pleasant glade on its north bank is the site of a former log cabin, constructed, like the one in Tiltill Meadow, by pioneer fish-propagator H. G. Kibbie. Beyond this site we briefly parallel the creek, then angle

northeast away from it, ascending up over a morainal divide back to the first creek that we met, 1¾ miles beyond where we first crossed it. Standing almost head-high in the height of flowering season are stalks of blue-bonnet larkspur, slender lupine, umbrella-leaved cow parsnip, red elderberry, and four-petalled monument plant. Reaching to between our knees and our waists are lacy meadow rue, purple aster, white yarrow, yellow senecio, aromatic mint, and leather-leaved mule ears. Under all these at times can be a mat of Jacob's ladder, which at times can grow in large numbers. The abundance of these wildflowers is due in part to the streamside environment, but also to volcanic soils, which are more nutrient-rich than are granitic soils. For many hikers, the 7+ mile route from the Rancheria Falls campsite will leave them exhausted, since they'll have ascended some 4000 feet with a heavy pack. You may find yourself camping in this vicinity, to weary to continue.

From this flower garden our path turns east-northeast up a broad, shallow swale and soon leaves lush surroundings behind as it climbs easily along dry volcanic slopes of a broad, low, west-heading ridge from the northeast summit of Rancheria Mountain. This volcanic-mudflow material and the overlying darker layer of harder andesite, which caps three summits, settled here some 9½ million years ago, having come from the Little Walker caldera, about 28 miles to the north. Enough material was transported to deeply bury not only the Park's northern uplands, but also to fill the already deep Tuolumne River canyon sufficiently to spill over its two rims below Hetch Hetchy Valley. Most of the easily erodible material in the Park was removed by thick glaciers, but since our summit was blanketed with only thin, barely flowing ice, much of it still persists.

After a mile past the creek our way becomes a ridgetop amble, bringing us in ½ mile to our high point (8650 feet) on Rancheria Mountain. To reach the 8020-foot saddle north of us, our path makes a moderate descent in deep duff. Five switchbacks spare our knees on the steep hillside, then the trees disperse momentarily, and we look northeast to Sawtooth Ridge and closer Volunteer Peak. A short distance later, some 16 miles from our trailhead, we reach a junction with the Pleasant Valley trail (see **Hike 14**).

The Bear Valley trail crosses the timbered saddle, then climbs up a steep, shaded pitch to a small, grassy pond. This knee-deep lakelet does have a fair campsite just behind the fringe of Labrador tea. We climb gently north from this pond along a sandy ridge to the willowy east bank of an unnamed creek. Then in ½ mile, a big leap takes us across this stream so that we can climb northwest through a grassy meadow to top a lateral moraine and find yet another unnamed creek. After jumping to its west bank we ascend gently north on a sparsely timbered slope. Soon our lightly traveled trail fades to a faint depression in meadow turf. Small cairns and ducks may guide you, but you cannot miss your goal, a saddle flanked by huddled whitebark pines, lying just under 9500 feet. Beyond, 700 feet below, is pastoral Bear Valley, overshadowed by knife-edged Bear Valley peak. Farther north, the Yosemite north country rears its shining ivory summits, and red-volcanic Relief Peak, near Sonora Pass, touches the horizon.

Raucous Clark's nutcrackers may oversee our knee-jarring plummet north down the cirque wall of Bear Valley. At first our path is contorted into short, tight, rocky switchbacks, but later the legs lengthen as we descend a seasonally wet route through a lush thicket of willows, mountain maple, meadow rue, and seasonal forbs. After rapidly losing 500 feet of altitude, the descent becomes gentler and turns northwest down to the south side of meadowed Bear Valley. The path can be lost for some 150 yards north across the hummocky, frequently soggy grassland, but we can pick it up again easily enough at a metal sign. We then climb easily over a forested medial moraine and drop to the east end of a small, hospitable lakelet circled by lodgepoles and western white pines. Just a minute north of this tarn we hop across Breeze Creek, then ascend northeast along it over open, slabby terrain. Soon the trail levels off through a delightful open stand of pines and hemlocks and arrives at the outlet of long-awaited Bear Valley Lake. This shallow gem sits in a washboard-bottomed glacial trough, and numerous outcrops of polished granite break the lake's surface. These picturesque islets, combined with a shoreline of short grasses, red heather, and dwarf bilberry, provide a stunning foreground for soaring, photogenic Bear Valley

peak. Excellent camps lie among conifers back from the north shore.

The next morning we walk a short distance northwest from the lake's outlet to a small gap between two low domes and gird ourselves for a 1200-foot descent north into Kerrick Canyon, involving the better part of 100 moderate-to-steep switchbacks. For the first 400 feet of this direct descent, our way is shaded by hemlocks and western white pines, and we can survey north over intervening ridges to Snow Peak and ragged Tower Peak. Lower down, however, the views are hidden by a rising horizon and a thick growth of hemlocks and lodgepoles. Finally reaching morainal till rearranged by sometimes-raging Rancheria Creek, our descent abates and we turn east through dry lodgepole flats to arrive at a junction with the Pacific Crest Trail where it bends north to cross Rancheria Creek.

From here you take the PCT north and then west as described in **Hike 42**, 7.3 miles to Wilma Lake, and camp there. The following day, retrace your steps 1.5 miles to the Tilden Canyon trail, described in **Hike 12**. Proceed down it about 10 miles to Tiltill Valley, with your best campsites. Walk out to O'Shaughnessy Dam the next day by following **Hike 11** down to Rancheria Falls and then reversing your first day's course.

<hr>

HIKE 14

PLEASANT VALLEY-RODGERS CANYON-WILMA LAKE-MORAINE RIDGE LOOP

Distance: 69.5 miles loop trip

Grade: 7G, strenuous 7-day hike

Trailhead: Same as the Hike 9 trailhead. **B3.**

Introduction: This is this book's longest trip in the Yosemite north country, and it also visits the greatest variety of subalpine settings to be found anywhere in the Park. Our lightly traveled path through Pleasant Valley to subalpine Rodgers Meadow is a more isolated alternative to using the Pacific Crest Trail to reach the Benson Lake region.

Description: Take the trail described in **Hike 10** to Rancheria Falls and camp there the first night. The next day, follow **Hike 13** to the Pleasant Valley trail junction on a broad, red-fir-forested saddle north of Rancheria Mountain, perhaps camping several miles before you reach it. Here we branch southeast, then head more eastward down a shallow draw to the rim of Piute Creek canyon's 1200-foot western scarp. Emerging from a thick stand of aspens, we are treated with superb vistas northeast over sparsely forested Pleasant Valley to a rolling landscape of dark exfoliating domes and slopes above Piute Creek, terminating this side of spiry Sawtooth Ridge. A part of little-visited Irwin Bright Lake, one of several shallow, granite-rimmed lakes arcing around Pleasant Valley, can be seen on a forested bench below.

We switchback moderately-to-steeply downward across slopes of volcanic deposits, which viewed from the opposite side of Piute Creek canyon, appear as a broad **V**. Around the start of the 20th century, Henry W. Turner saw it and inferred that an ancient Tuolumne River once flowed west through a canyon now buried by the volcanic deposits. In the northern Sierra, such **V**-shaped deposits of varying sizes are quite common, for example, a few miles south of Donner Pass, a mammoth one extends from the Sierra crest down to the floor of the North Fork American River Canyon. None of these **V**s have anything to do with buried river channels, even though river gravels may exist at their bases (interestingly, geologists seem unaware that gravels don't exist on the other side of the ridge!). These **V**-shaped deposits are merely uneroded remnants filling **V**-shaped side gullies of canyons. Nevertheless, this ancient idea of a buried river, like other Sierran geomyths, refuses to die.

Below 7500 feet our trail swings northeast past huckleberry oaks, scattered conifers, and black oaks. Soon we reach a hanging-valley aspen grove and walk in the seasonal creekbed that drains it, then descend along the stream in a narrow chute. A few short switchbacks lead us north from this ravine down to the floor of Pleasant Valley, at 6860 feet. Here we find a mixed forest of dominant lodgepole pines plus red and white firs, Jeffrey pines, junipers, and incense-cedars. Not seen are singleleaf pinyon pines. This pine grows almost exclusively east of the Sierra crest, but a few small groves do occur west of it, and one of them is about a mile south and 400 feet below us, on dry slopes west above Piute Creek. Did it get seeded by Piute (Mono) Indians?

A few minutes' amble through the forest brings us to a trail branching northeast 0.2 mile to large packer camps beside a pool on Piute Creek. From this spur trail our main path veers south to momentarily reach shaded Piute Creek, incised deeply in cobbly alluvium. This ford could be a 50-foot-long wade in early summer. On the east bank another spur trail heads upstream to more camps, but we turn downstream to soon begin a moderate, if short, ascent up dark slopes of diorite. From the south shoulder of a low ridge the trail then dips easily to a crossing of Table Lake's outlet stream. The best campsites by Table Lake are reached by ascending north along an open bench just before crossing this stream. Between the main lake, which is ringed with low, broken bluffs and shrubs, and its southern arm, which is shallow and dotted with pond lilies, is a dry peninsula, with sparse Jeffrey pines and the best campsites. Fishing for rainbow

Murdock Lake and imposing Volunteer Peak   Ben Schifrin

trout in Table, Irwin Bright, and Saddle Horse lakes is good due to a scarcity of anglers.

Eastward from the Table Lake environs the main trail passes through an aspen grove, in which an old trail once headed north for Irwin Bright Lake. Near this old junction we hop a stream, and then ascend rapidly onto brushy slopes. Soon we pant up the inevitable rocky switchbacks and are partly consoled by an improving picture of Pleasant Valley. Our zigzag course persists until 7600 feet, where we top a bench to find, in another aspen grove, the stream we crossed lower down. Now our climb moderates, proceeding southeast through alternately well-watered and dry-rocky plant associations, to a ridgetop just under 8000 feet. This open spot lets us look south down Piute Creek's gorge and beyond to 9782-foot Double Rock, and it also marks the start of an undulating traverse south. On it we cross numerous small, steep gullies, usually under shade, above Piute Creek's gaping canyon, and in a mile reach a sloping aspen glade, which has a junction with the southwest-descending Pate Valley trail (see **Hike 22**).

Our route starts initially southeast and quickly climbs south across an open volcanic slope where a small spring trickles across the path. Excellent views and myriad wildflowers recommend this spot for a break. Then we gear down for a short but initially steep ascent east to the crest of a bouldery, conifer-robed moraine. From it we descend east across volcanic slopes and in about a mile reach our low point along the north rim of the Grand Canyon of the Tuolumne River. Here, in a field of glacial erratics, we are face-to-face with cliff-girded Colby Mountain, named for an early president of the Sierra Club who was on its board of directors for 49 years.

Just a few minutes later we enter Rodgers Canyon, then abruptly turn uphill. The trail ascends a series of well-forested glacial steps to come alongside seasonally large Rodgers Canyon creek just under 8000 feet. For the next 1½ miles our gently to moderately climbing trail keeps west of the creek, passing through typical subalpine pockets of lodgepoles that cluster near the cascading stream. After one cobbly pitch we soon emerge on the south edge of lengthy Rodgers Meadow. Here Rodgers Canyon creek cuts a broad, lazy snake through the sedge turf, overshadowed by a small dome near Neall Lake, above the meadow's north end. Staying near the forest that demarcates the west side of Rodgers Meadow, we amble north to find a very good campsite among lodgepoles. A few yards north of this camp we leave the meadow and cross to the east bank of Rodgers Canyon creek, only to cross back moments later. Now we come abruptly to a trail junction, at 8800 feet. By continuing north you can take a shorter route to the PCT, via Murdock Lake, described later.

Most hikers will branch right on the longer, far more scenic trail to Neall and Rodgers lakes. This route heads east to Neall Lake's outlet creek, then climbs pleasantly east along its north bank. Less than a mile past the trail junction, we find a short spur trail going south to Neall Lake, which has fine campsites nestled by its outlet. Cupped by a terminal-moraine arc under the sharp crest of West Peak, small Neall Lake reflects surrounding cliffs, blue sky, fringing conifers, and willowy fell-fields. Secluded campsites lie everywhere but on the talus of the south shore. Fishing for rainbow trout is excellent.

Heading toward Rodgers Lake, the main trail steeply ascends a cobbly ridge under a western outlier of Regulation Peak. Soon we swing north, wind over terraced sedge flats, and come to the south shore of long, subalpine Rodgers Lake, named for the second Yosemite National Park superintendent. This lake is divided into two bodies by a low granitic isthmus, the larger, eastern portion being more open and rockier. Our way rounds the lake to a handsome grove of lodgepoles and hemlocks on the north shore. Here lie some good camps that afford excellent panoramas over the shallow waters to the ruddy north faces of Regulation and West peaks. Farther east we pass another group of camps, then begin to switchback north over metasediments that have been intruded by a netlike swarm of quartz veins.

Presently we arrive atop a grassy saddle at 9790 feet, where the stunning sheer profile of nearby Volunteer Peak completely dominates a horizon of greater summits throughout the north country—Piute Mountain, Price and Tower peaks, and Crown Point. Descending north from this gap via short switchbacks, we soon re-enter forest and wind past huge talus blocks, seasonal willow-fringed tarns, and hummocky meadows to a junction with the

Pacific Crest Trail. Here, under the brooding face of Volunteer Peak, which has been frost-riven into myriad vertically oriented flakes, we may decide to strike northeast one mile on the PCT to Smedberg Lake, or continue west 3.6 miles along the PCT (see **Hike 42**) to spend the night at large Benson Lake. Within ⅓ mile along our way to Benson Lake, we strike the Murdock Lake trail, the shortcut from upper Rodgers Canyon.

If you don't take the scenic longer route, then from the trail junction at 8800 feet in Rodgers Canyon, take the Murdock Lake trail northward moderately up along slopes, quickly leaving behind the canyon-floor forest. Soon you tackle a set of very steep, sandy switchbacks, then angle northeast, passing below a small spring. The remainder of this ascent ends abruptly on a level subalpine meadow at 9530 feet. Shallow Murdock Lake is cupped in a depression in this rolling grass-land. Some adequate camps lie in lodgepoles above its west shore and offer interesting views of Volunteer Peak, Matterhorn Peak, and Sawtooth Ridge. Leaving the ridgetop meadowland, the trail descends back into mixed conifers and soon reaches the PCT.

To complete your hike, follow **Hike 42** west to Wilma Lake, with the best campsites in Jack Main Canyon. Then reverse the steps of **Hike 12** out via Moraine Ridge, take a trail to Laurel Lake, and spend your last evening there. On the last day, reverse the steps of **Hike 9** to Hetch Hetchy Reservoir.

Chapter 6
Trails of Yosemite's West-Central Lands, between the Tuolumne River and Highway 120

Introduction: The land explored in this chapter is one of contrasts. Some of the trails in its low, western section are seldom used, while those in its high, eastern section are extremely popular. The reason for this is obvious: the lower areas tend to be hot in summer and devoid of spectacular scenery. They are best hiked in spring or fall, when the Tioga Road is closed, preventing access to the higher trails. The trails of this chapter cover the great altitude span, 8420 feet from 2430 feet early on the Preston Flat trail to 10,850 feet at Mt. Hoffmann's summit. Between these elevations you'll find all of the Park's seven plant communities, from Foothill Woodland to Alpine Fell-Fields. Only Chapter 11 rivals this altitude span, and that is only if you include all of the Alder Creek trail, most of which is outside the Park.

Supplies and Services: Absolutely everything you'll need for a Yosemite outdoor experience can be purchased in the western-foothills town of Sonora. This includes full backpacking and mountaineering gear, these available at the Sierra Nevada Adventure Company. This town also has several large grocery stores, numerous dining places, and two hospitals.

Groveland, about 24 miles west of the Park's Big Oak Flat Entrance Station, is the last town you'll pass on Highway 120; however, several resorts, gas stations, and campgrounds are found closer to the Park. Gas, meals, and lodging are found at Evergreen Lodge, on Evergreen Road just 0.6 mile before it ends at the Hetch Hetchy Road in Camp Mather (for San Francisco residents).

Once inside the Park you can find virtually anything you'll need—*other than fuel*—down in Yosemite Valley, but this is crowded and is out of your way. Should you need last-minute food or fuel, you can get them at Crane Flat. Fewer supplies are at White Wolf Lodge, the center for Hikes 20-23, though it offers breakfast and dinner.

Wilderness Permits: If you want to reserve a permit, rather than get one in person, see the "Wilderness permits" section on page 59. In person, if you are driving east up Highway 120, get a permit at the Big Oak Flat Information Station, which is immediately past the Park's entrance station. Note that from about early April through late October you can get a permit at the Hetch Hetchy Entrance Station (by the Mather Ranger Station). You cannot get a permit in the White Wolf area. If you are driving up Highway 140 or 41, get your permit at the Visitor Center in Yosemite Valley, and if you are driving west down Highway 120, stop in Tuolumne Meadows (see "Wilderness Permits" at start of Chapter 8).

Campgrounds: For Hikes 15-17, you could spend the night at Dimond O Campground, about 5.6 miles north on Evergreen Road, which begins from Highway 120 just 0.6 mile before the Park's boundary below the Big Oak Flat Entrance Station. Within the Park you can stay at Hodgdon Meadow Campground, reached by turning left immediately after passing through the Big Oak Flat Entrance Station. This is good for Hikes 15-19. Driving east on Highway 120, you'll reach another possibility, Crane Flat Campground, just ¼ mile before Crane Flat. This is ideal for Hikes 18-19. Both these campgrounds are on a reservation system—see Chapter 1. After turning left at the flat's junction, you then drive 14.5 miles up the Tioga Road (Highway 120) to the White Wolf road. Opposite this road's White Wolf Lodge is the entrance to the White Wolf Campground, ideal for Hikes 20-23. Those taking Hikes 24-28 can also stay here or at Porcupine Flat Campground, on the Tioga Road 9.2 miles past the White Wolf road junction. During the summer season all these campsites can be full, so plan to find a campsite early in the day.

HIKE 15

POOPENAUT VALLEY/ PRESTON FLAT TRAILS

Distances: 2.4 miles round trip/8.6 miles round trip

Grades: 1C, strenuous half-day hike/2B, easy day hike

Trailheads: Just 0.6 mile before the Park's boundary below the Big Oak Flat Entrance Station, drive north 7.4 miles on Evergreen Road to its junction with Hetch Hetchy Road 12. For the Poopenaut Valley trail, you head right, east; for the Preston Flat trail, you head left, west. For the former, go 1.3 miles east to the Mather Ranger Station, then an additional 3.9 miles to a clockwise turn in the road. On the road's right side is parking for two vehicles. **B3.** For the latter, go 7.7 miles west on Road 12 to a junction with Road 17, bound for Cherry Lake (this junction is 5.3 miles from the Highway 120/Road 17 junction). Descend Road 17 for 3.1 miles to a bridge across the Tuolumne River, turn right, and ascend a road 0.8 mile to a trailhead parking area at its end. **A3.**

Introduction: You have a choice of two trails in the Yosemite area that provide access to the

Tuolumne River below Hetch Hetchy Reservoir. One, the Poopenaut Valley trail, is quite old, and is the steepest trail described in this book. If it was only slightly steeper, many hikers would take spills. The ascent back to the trailhead, while short in length, is nevertheless exhausting, and all but top-shape athletes will make stops to catch their breath. A more recent, 1980s-vintage alternative, located west of the Park, is the Preston Flat trail, which parallels the Tuolumne River up-canyon. Most of it is easy, although there are steep, but short, sections to surmount minor ridges. The Tuolumne River can flood even in July and possibly later, so don't swim in it if the current is fast. Because the river's gradient is nearly zero in Poopenaut Valley, that stretch has the safest swimming. You can fish and camp along both trails, but few would want to take the Poopenaut Valley trail for these activities, when one can do either quite effortlessly early along the Preston Flat trail. The latter has a spectacular ending, a view of the Tuolumne River plunging over a low escarpment. Be forewarned that *poison oak* grows along both trails, especially along the latter.

Description: The Poopenaut Valley trail starts across an open expanse of granodiorite that supports a drought-tolerant growth of manzanita and incense-cedar. An extensive 1996 fire reached this area, but after 200 yards of descent northeast, we leave severely burned vegetation for a basically intact forest. Here the trail turns north to begin an excessively steep descent for just over 1000 feet. Along it, white fir and sugar pine gradually yield lower down to incense-cedar, black oak, Douglas-fir, and ponderosa pine. The trail approaches a cascading, seasonal creek, eases its gradient, and follows one of its distributaries toward a large, grassy meadow, which is quite wet in spring.

You have two route choices. If you like swimming and diving, traverse west through the meadow (or skirt along its edge, if boggy), aiming for the base of a granitic ridge hosting gray-green foothill pines. Since this resistant ridge constricts the river, it has cut a deep channel, in contrast to the shallower, willow-lined channel above the meadow. The ridge has ledges that permit you to dive from heights of 25 feet or more into the river. Because the river drains from Hetch Hetchy's cold waters, the swimming hole stays cold even on the hottest day. To avoid excessive sweat on your return trip, you could camp down here (wilderness permit required), and start your ascent in the cool of the morning. Should you wish to camp or fish, then from the distributaries start a traverse north along the edge of the meadow, staying near the base of a granitic ridge. There is a good campsite where the ridge meets the river, and by heading up-canyon across low ridges, you can find others, as well as good fishing spots.

The Preston Flat trail starts as an old road which goes ¼ mile to a stream-gaging station. Ahead is a generally very good trail, usually shaded with ponderosa pine, incense-cedar, Douglas-fir, and black and live oaks. In spring, buckeye trees have very showy flowers on stalks, but with summer's heat they soon drop both flowers and leaves. The heat brings out the aroma of a lowly shrub, mountain misery, with sticky, finely divided foliage. About ⅓ mile from the trailhead, you reach a small campsite on a bouldery flat beside the river. The trail ahead rises and falls from the river-bank several times, and each time you reach the river, you can usually find adjacent camping. If you build a fire here or elsewhere, you'll need to get a permit first from the Forest Service office in Groveland.

After about 1¾ miles the trail may appear to end at the base of a sloping, granitic slab. Here, beside the lower end of a short, inner gorge, is a good campsite, as well as mortar holes drilled in the granite by former Native Americans. The route up the slab stays close to the brink of the inner gorge, before climbing just above it. Along a following short traverse are small patches of smooth rock, and if the lighting is right, you may see faint striations cut by glacier-transported rocks. Although this canyon was repeatedly occupied by giant glaciers, it is a classic **V**-shaped canyon, not a **U**-shaped one. The last two glaciers flowing through here were about 2000+-feet thick, which was enough to spill ice across the canyon's south rim. In contrast, the last two glaciers flowing through Yosemite Valley averaged only about 1400 feet in thickness. In both areas, glaciers performed very little erosion; before glaciation, the Tuolumne River canyon

A rock-lined swimming hole at the lower end of Poopenaut Valley

and Yosemite Valley looked very much as they do today. In the former, the last two glaciers ended an estimated 2-3 miles beyond the Tuolumne River's confluence with Cherry Creek, west of our trailhead.

The trail soon descends to the river and continues its generally shady traverse, but around 3½ miles into the route, you reach a meadow, which in spring can have a conspicuous waterfall plunging down toward it. Then, the meadow can be a boggy traverse. About ¾ mile beyond the meadow the trail ends at a campsite beside a low, granitic slab. From the slab you have a view across a 100-yard-diameter pool of Preston Falls, a 15-foot thunderous drop in the Tuolumne River at the lower end of an inner gorge.

HIKE 16

LOOKOUT POINT

Distance: 3.0 miles round trip

Grade: 1B, easy half-day hike

Trailhead: See the previous hike's trailhead directions to the Mather Ranger Station. Since parking is limited, ask a ranger where to park. **B3.**

Introduction: For good views of the lower Tuolumne River canyon, the hike to Lookout Point is an excellent choice. It is particularly enjoyable in springtime, when temperatures are mild, water is present, and wildflowers abound.

Description: This hike is best done in the morning, when temperatures are still fairly cool and shadows are good for photography. Our starting point, Mather Ranger Station, sits on a broad, glaciated granitic bench that has a shady, fairly dense cover of ponderosa pines, incense-cedars, and black oaks. From the station's east side we follow a trail briefly south to a junction with a trail heading right to nearby Camp Mather. We turn left and parallel Hetch Hetchy Road east, quickly entering lands burned by an extensive 1996 fire. Our trail rollercoasters across rocky slopes rich in springtime flowers, then climbs briefly up a gully, which in springtime usually has a flowing creeklet and lush displays of water-loving flowers. Above the gully we level off and parallel its seasonal creeklet northeast to a quick junction with the Lookout Point spur trail.

Branching left on it, we walk north for a minute, skirt around a seasonal pond, then circle counterclockwise up the northeast side of a largely barren, glacier-smoothed knoll. The trail tread dies, and before climbing up bedrock slopes to the close-by, obvious summit, check this spot, since it can be easily

A lone Jeffrey pine and glacial chatter marks atop Lookout Point

missed on your descent. Around the summit grow a few dwarfed Jeffrey pines and clumps of lowly penstemons known as mountain pride, both species sending their roots along cracks, helping to oh-so-slowly disintegrate this summit. Give them a few tens of millions of years to complete the job.

The knoll stands despite repeated glaciation, the last two major glaciers being about 700 feet thick at your summit and about 2500 feet thick at the unseen floor of the Tuolumne River canyon about one mile northwest of you. The last glacier retreated by or before 15,000 years ago. Smoothed rock, faint striations, and chatter (gouge) marks make up the evidence here. Additional evidence is found on the barren knolls southwest and northwest of us, which have large, glacier-transported boulders strewn over their surfaces. Erosion by the last glacier here was so minimal that the very shallow solution potholes, which existed before that glacier existed, remain virtually unchanged.

You have a 360° panorama, although the most interesting scenery is clockwise from west to northeast, that is, down the Tuolumne River canyon and then up to Hetch Hetchy Reservoir. Above the reservoir, Tueeulala Falls adds accent to the springtime landscape while to the right, voluminous Wapama Falls, fed by Falls Creek, which originates at the Sierra crest, flows year round.

HIKE 17

MATHER RANGER STATION TO SMITH PEAK

Distance: 16.0 miles round trip

Grade: 4D, moderate 2-day hike

Trailhead: Same as the Hike 16 trailhead. **B3.**

Introduction: Smith Peak, with its all-encompassing view of the northwest half of Yosemite National Park, can be reached from White Wolf or from the Hetch Hetchy Road. If you are hiking in May, June, October, or November, then take this hike to avoid snow problems. If you are hiking in July, August, or September, then take Hike 21, the White Wolf Route.

Description: The preferred route described here is the one requiring the least effort. You could also begin on another equally long trail starting from the Hetch Hetchy Road beside a prominent gully about 6.0 miles beyond the Mather Ranger Station. This climbs about 1½ miles to a junction with a little-used trail to the ranger station, then about 4 miles more up to Smith Meadow. Its disadvantage is that because it starts lower, you have an additional 500 feet of climbing. On the other hand, Cottonwood and Smith meadows can be quite soggy through spring, and this alternate route avoids both.

The preferred route follows Hike 16 1.2 miles up to a junction with the Lookout Point spur trail. If you hike up to and back from the point—a worthwhile objective while you're fresh—add 0.6 mile to your total distance. From the junction we continue ahead just 0.2 mile to another, and if you would continue straight ahead for a similar distance, you would reach a linear lakelet. This lakelet is along the aforementioned little-used trail, which rambles for a total of 3½ miles to the alternate trail. This offers another route to Smith Meadow, one that is about 2 miles longer and involves about 800 feet of additional elevation gain. Furthermore, where it traverses through meadows, the trail's tread can be obscure. On the other hand, it largely escaped the 1996 fire, whose charred evidence is seen along most of the preferred route. But as you will see along it, while the fire torched virtually every tree in several localities, over most of the route it did relatively minor damage, leaving mature trees virtually unaffected.

At our second junction we turn right to begin a well-graded, winding ascent ½ mile to a broad saddle, from where a trail formerly descended west to Camp Mather. We traverse east just over ½ mile to a junction with the Base Line Camp road, which climbs initially southwest before eventually dropping on a circuitous route to Camp Mather. The elevation here, about 5400 feet, is high enough for sugar pines, with their long cones hanging at the ends of branches. East, we traverse a similar distance to another junction, this one with a winding trail 6½ miles south to Aspen Valley. Before the *new* Big Oak Flat Road opened in 1940, the old Highway 120 was routed along part of Evergreen Road, then east up the old Tioga Road to Aspen Valley, where you

First-year cones hang at the ends of a sugar pine's long branches

entered the Park. Before then, traffic was so light that motorists were requested to sound the horn to get the attendant's attention, who would often be off doing other chores. These days, at the Big Oak Flat Entrance Station, you may hear weekend motorists sounding their horns to protest the long wait to get in, due to sheer numbers of visitors.

From the Aspen Valley trail junction, the Base Line Camp road quickly ends, and from it a trail climbs to a reliable creek with a water tank, the source of water for the Mather area. You undoubtedly will have noticed the pipe line running along the road.

Again we tick off another ½ mile east, this time a moderate climb to the crest of a broad ridge. This is a lateral moraine, 2500 feet above Poopenaut Valley, and it represents the minimum thickness of the last glacier that flowed down the Tuolumne River canyon, retreating from this site perhaps 16,000 years ago. At its maximum, this glacier may have been thick enough to spread laterally eastward across the Cottonwood Creek drainage. In preglacial time Cottonwood Creek may have drained west down to the Tuolumne River in western Poopenaut Valley, but today the moraine forces the creek to drain southwest down to the much smaller Middle Tuolumne River.

Jeffrey pines began to replace ponderosa pines on our ascent, and now in the Cottonwood Creek drainage we find white firs quite common and lodgepole pines bordering nearby lower Cottonwood Meadow. Also bor-

dering it are aspens, which are related to cottonwoods, which, if present, are not conspicuous. Once we leave this meadow the lodgepoles disappear, for conditions are now drier, and about ½ mile beyond it you will notice a trailside slab on your left with over three dozen mortar holes. Sugar pines, known as *hi 'ymachi* by the local Native Americans, grow in this vicinity, and the Native Americans ate the seeds probably after grinding them here. They also made use of the tree's whitish sugar, which they considered a delicacy. About a mile northwest of this mortar site are black oaks, whose acorns were a major part of their diet, in ground form providing them with bread, mush, and even soup.

A mile farther we enter upper Cottonwood Meadow, and in it we cross Cottonwood Creek, which is generally a wet ford before July. Continuing northeast, we soon climb moderately up to a broad ridge, and descend briefly to its opposite side, beside which flows Cottonwood Creek along the southwest edge of Smith Meadow. If the creek is too broad to jump across, look for one or more nearby logs across it. Like the nearby peak, the meadow is named for a sheep rancher who claimed that this part of Yosemite belonged to him. Ignoring the land's Park status, he grazed his sheep in its meadows well into the 1920s. We continue northeast up this sloping meadow on a trail that can be boggy and obscure before July. Immediately above its northeast corner, just within forest cover, we reach an intersection with the westbound trail from White Wolf (**Hike 21**).

If you are backpacking, you won't want to carry a heavy pack up to the summit of Smith Peak. Look for adequate campsites on gentle, forested slopes about 100-200 yards west of the trail intersection. The trail to the summit is direct and steep, so before you start, you might want to get some water at a trickling creeklet only a few yards from the intersection. If conditions are dry, you'll have to get water at Cottonwood Creek, which you crossed about ¼ mile back.

We start our climb in a forest of white firs, sugar pines, and incense-cedars, and by the time we reach the first of three seasonally wet meadows—all of them rich in summer wild-flowers—we have left the incense-cedars behind. If you're hiking this trail before July, you're likely to run into snow patches from here on. Although you may lose the trail beneath them, you won't lose your way as long as you keep heading northeast upslope. A second wet meadow, marking the halfway point, is quickly passed; then we pass a third one midway between it and the Tuolumne River canyon crest. By the time we reach the crest, red firs have become the dominant forest tree, with Jeffrey pines occupying the drier, sunnier spots and white firs in between. If you came up on horses, leave them at the canyon-crest saddle, for the footpaths ahead are steep and narrow.

The final 250-foot elevation gain can be made by any of several brush-lined paths. Perhaps the safest and most frequently used path is the one that climbs the west slope, then traverses along the south slope. To reach the best viewpoint, atop pitted granitic rocks, you'll have to plow through a dense, brushy cover of huckleberry oaks. The solution pockets—some of them filling with water after recent rains—result from extremely slow weathering locally found on gentle-sloped surfaces of granitic rock. Solution pockets rarely form on metamorphic or volcanic rock.

From the pocketed rocks you can gaze down into the deep Grand Canyon of the Tuolumne River and see the Hetch Hetchy Reservoir, about 4000 feet below you. During the last two major glaciations, glaciers filled the canyon below us to a depth of 3500 feet or more, coming to within 500-600 feet of our summit. Being so thick, these glaciers exerted a force of about 100 tons per square foot on the canyon's bottom; nevertheless, the shape and depth of the canyon haven't changed all that much despite repeated glaciation over at least the last 2 million years. Indeed, it hasn't deep-ened much in the last 10 million years, if not considerably longer. As you can see, the canyon is distinctly **V**-shaped in cross profile, as it is below the reservoir. From its dam site, the two glaciers advanced about 17 to 20 miles farther down-canyon. You can also see that much of the Yosemite landscape north, south, and west of the river's canyon is a gentle, rolling uplands topography, which has evolved only very slowly over the last 80 million years.

Scanning the northeast skyline, keen map users should be able to identify, from east to northeast, Mt. Hoffmann plus the prominent crest summits of Mt. Conness, Matterhorn Peak, and Tower Peak. Across the main canyon, Tiltill Creek canyon descends toward us, its floor and slopes stripped bare of soil by glaciers, exposing naked granite. In contrast, Rancheria Mountain, above its east slopes, is

Solution pockets on Smith Peak's summit

Tiltill Creek canyon, left of Tower Peak (center horizon), cascades down to Hetch Hetchy Reservoir

quite forested. Volcanic deposits are rare within the Park, and the bulk of them are on or near this flat-topped mountain, which stood above glaciers.

Unless a storm is approaching, don't be in a hurry to leave this view-packed summit. Scarcity of water prevents tall conifers from overpowering it and blocking our views. The shallow, dry soils, however, are the perfect medium for the densely packed, shrubby huckleberry oaks, whose small, evergreen leaves keep the plant's water loss at a minimum. On the more snowbound slopes of Smith Peak grows the bush chinquapin, a distant cousin of the huckleberry oak. Also found here are a few black oaks, which stand hardly more than knee-high, though in Yosemite Valley they grow up to 80 feet tall. This oak prefers sunny slopes, and in the absence of conifers it has managed to survive. At about 7750 feet in elevation, this patch of black oaks may be the highest one in Yosemite; only in a few other parts of the Park are they seen at the 7500-7600 foot level. This oak together with whitebark pine are the only two Yosemite trees that reduce to shrub height as they approach the upper limit of their ranges. A final bush worth noting is the snow bush, a spiny *Ceanothus* that prefers dry, gravelly granitic soils. We've seen it along drier sections of the Cottonwood Creek drainage.

Descend to Smith Meadow, then retrace your steps to the trailhead. Alternatively, you could start west along the equally long trail, which ends along the Hetch Hetchy Road about 6.0 miles beyond the Mather Ranger Station, as mentioned at the start of this hike's description. Another suggestion is to follow the alternate route about ¾ mile west to where it turns south and parallels Cottonwood Creek, and continue along the joyful, cascading creek for a similar distance. Where the creek starts to drop below the trail, you could soon go cross-country south on slopes about ½ mile or less to the main trail, reaching it just below upper Cottonwood Meadow. By doing this you avoid the creek ford in this meadow.

MERCED GROVE OF BIG TREES

Distance: 3.0 miles round trip

Grade: 1B, moderate 2-hour hike

Trailhead: This is located along the Big Oak Flat Road where it crosses a divide about 4¼ miles east of the Big Oak Flat Entrance Station and about 3¾ miles west of the Tioga Road junction in Crane Flat. **B4.**

Introduction: Having only a few parking spaces, the trailhead parking area limits the number of visitors to this smallest of the Park's three groves. So if you want to see giant sequoias but want to avoid crowds, this hike is for you. Both the Merced Grove and the nearby Tuolumne Grove (next hike) have over a dozen trees at least 10 feet in diameter near the base, which pale in comparison with the much larger Mariposa Grove's (Hike 93) approximately 200 trees of similar or larger size. In each of the two small groves, a few trees reach about 15 feet in diameter, the largest being about 10 feet short of the diameter of the Mariposa Grove's Grizzly Giant. Although you are likely to see a few more of the larger specimens in the Tuolumne Grove than in the Merced Grove, you will almost certainly see more tourists, since its trailhead parking area is quite large and is often quite full.

Description: In the area covered by this book's map, there are three sequoia groves, Merced, Tuolumne, and Mariposa. However, about 5 miles due south of the Mariposa Grove (just off the map) lies the Nelder Grove. Perhaps before 15 million years ago, when the summers were wetter, the Merced and Tuolumne groves probably were one large grove, as probably were the Mariposa and Nelder groves. What all four have in common today are similar elevations, between 5000 and 6000 feet, and perhaps more importantly, some underlying metamorphic bedrock. Indeed, the Merced and Tuolumne groves grow entirely on metamorphic bedrock. There are many suitable alcoves at

the proper altitude in our area, but almost all lie in granitic bedrock. Metamorphic bedrock weathers to produce soils with more nutrients and more ground-water capacity than soils derived from granitic bedrock, and in times of warmer, drier climates, such as a few thousand years ago, metamorphic soils may have enabled our sequoias to survive.

Unlike on the next hike, mountain bikes are allowed along this one. The first half of our hike is along a nearly level, gated, limited-access road, shaded by white firs and, to a lesser extent, incense-cedars and ponderosa pines. A fire almost razed the grove, but fortunately it stopped just above part of the road, and shrubs have taken over in the burned area. After about 0.7 mile we reach a junction with a closed road and branch left on it. This makes a counterclockwise, moderate descent through a gully shaded by Douglas-firs, white firs, and sugar pines—typical sequoia associates at this latitude. In late spring and early summer you're also likely to see mountain dogwood in bloom, the tree's large, white bracts making up "petals" around the cluster of small, green, actual flowers in the center of the bracts.

The road next makes a clockwise, moderate descent out of the gully, briefly paralleling audible Moss Creek before curving into a dry gully, about 1.4 miles from the trailhead. Here grow a half-dozen sequoias ranging, at breast height (the standard, if arbitrary height for measurement) between 5 and 8 feet in diameter. As a generality, for the first 800 years, the sequoia adds one foot in diameter per century,

Hikers admire the giant sequoias

making these about 500-800 years old. To reach 12 feet takes about 1500 years, and 15 feet, about 2000 years. Although the sequoias in this gully are relatively young, they nevertheless are close to a maximum average height of about 250 feet, being an estimated 200+ feet in height. Water should flow down this gully during the wet season, but there is no sign of a creek bed. Sequoias are thirsty individuals, like their cousins the coast redwoods, and soak up a lot of ground water.

We pass several more giants midway to several more, these opposite a cabin some 1.5 miles from the trailhead. Above the cabin are two outhouses, should you need one. In this vicinity you'll see a number of sequoias, from about 14 feet in diameter and up to 270 feet high, down to saplings. Large trees are few in number, and the last large one you'll see is about 200 yards down the road. Superficially, one gets the impression that the trees are not regenerating. However, small trees are easily missed and also they may be confused with incense-cedars, which have similar bark, but different leaves and cones. As many as 200 saplings grow within the grove, the great bulk of them in the lower part of the grove.

HIKE 19

TUOLUMNE GROVE OF BIG TREES

Distance: 2.4 miles round trip

Grade: 1B, moderate 2-hour hike

Trailhead: Drive to the junction of the Big Oak Flat Road with the Tioga Road, at Crane Flat, then drive ½ mile up the Tioga Road to a large parking area on your left. **B4.**

Introduction: See the previous hike's introduction.

Description: First read the first two paragraphs of the previous hike's description, which mentions the elevations and soils the giant sequoias inhabit, and the trees' approximate growth rates. The route is obvious, an old, now-closed road for hikers only. It first curves ¼ mile over to a gully below the back side of the Yosemite Institute, which provides week-long outdoor education to groups of students and to other groups. The road then descends to a switchback west, then to one north, and just past it, about 0.9 mile into your hike, you enter the Tuolumne Grove. About 0.2 mile farther down the road, you come to a junction beside an impressive sequoia about 15 feet in diameter. You could continue down the main road, but the alternate road is more desirable. About 130 yards along it you pass through the Tunnel Tree, a dead, charred hulk with a diameter of about 20 feet. In its glory, it must have been one of Yosemite's tallest specimens. A tunnel was carved in it back in 1878, before two were carved in the Mariposa Grove.

From the Tunnel Tree the alternate road goes 160 yards down to a reunion with the main road. Here you will find a picnic area plus two trails. One bridges a creek to head over to a group of sequoias, and should you take it, you might think the first trees on your left are young sequoias. These are incense-cedars, which have similar bark. Compare the leaves and cones (only several scales for the incense-cedar) with those of nearby sequoias. The second trail first heads down the creek before veering from it. Most folks turn around at the picnic area, but you can descend the main road ¼ mile to the lower, northern edge of the grove. If you look to your left you'll see a lone giant sequoia at the far edge of a gently sloping flat, among mature sugar pines and white firs. What sets it apart, besides its isolation, is that it is growing along the brink of North Crane Creek's gully. Should this tree live long enough, it may be undercut by erosion. Beyond the grove's northern edge the road descends about 4½ miles to Hodgdon Meadow Campground, which lies just east of the Big Oak Flat Entrance Station.

HIKE 20

WHITE WOLF TO HARDEN LAKE

Distance: 5.6 miles round trip

Grade: 2B, easy half-day hike; no camping allowed

Trailhead: From Crane Flat drive northeast 14½ miles up Highway 120 to the White Wolf turnoff and follow that road down to where it is closed to motor vehicles, about ¼ mile beyond White Wolf Campground. **C4.**

Introduction: Only an hour's hike from White Wolf Campground, this lake attracts quite a number of summer visitors. In late July the water level usually begins to fall and the relatively warm lake becomes ideal for swimming.

Description: Our route, a closed fire road, immediately bridges the infant Middle Tuolumne River, then parallels its sometimes splashing course down unglaciated granitic terrain that sustains a healthy stand of lodgepole pines. After a mile of easy descent, we come to a closed spur road that goes to a sewage-treatment pond, constructed in the mid-1970s as part of a Park-wide program to upgrade treatment plants to tougher environmental standards. Beyond this road, ours climbs over a low ridge of glacial deposits before dipping into a shady alcove of lodgepole pines and red firs. In days past, the Park had far more camping than it unfortunately has at present, and a primitive campground once lay

here, done in by tougher environmental standards. Today, only a trail junction exists.

We take the trail, which traverses the slope of a large glacial moraine. The well-drained sediments of this moraine support a different plant community than our generally rocky-road descent, and on this moraine grows a forest of Jeffrey pines together with some white firs and aspens. Thousands of bracken ferns seek the forest shade together with chinquapins, the bushes with spiny, seed-bearing spheres. Seeking the sun are snow bushes, which have spine-tipped branches. In ⅔ mile our trail ends at the Harden Lake road. This road leaves the main road about ½ mile west of our trail junction. The main road parallels the Middle Tuolumne River almost the whole distance of 8 miles to Aspen Valley, which is a private inholding that once was the west entrance to Yosemite National Park. Today, the gently graded road is a pleasant stroll for those looking for a lightly used creekside excursion. Meanwhile, those on the last part of the Harden Lake road walk across relatively flat glacial sediments. After a few minutes you reach a gravelly junction with a trail to Pate Valley (the return route of **Hike 22**), but

Harden Lake, before its shoreline drops

Before the new *Big Oak Flat Road opened in 1940, you entered Yosemite via Aspen Valley*

adhere to the road as it bends left and goes almost to the southwest corner of Harden Lake. Here, at road's end, **Hike 21** continues northwest on a trail.

Harden Lake has a rather uncommon origin, for it occupies a small depression that formed between two lateral moraines. This shallow, 9-acre lake has no surface inlet or outlet, and not long after adjacent snow patches melt, the lake's level begins to drop. In the drought year of 1977 this lake dwindled to barely a pond by summer's end, and its stocked rainbow trout died, and have *not* been replanted. The lake's diminishing size not only reduced food and oxygen available to these trout, but it also raised the water temperature into the mid-70s—great for swimming but fatal for trout. Swimmers, if they are careless, could scrape their feet on the lake's many submerged glacier-transported boulders. Since glaciers retreated from the Park, permanent lakes have filled with 5-30 feet of sediments, mostly derived from pollen and windblown dust. However, this does not occur with lakes, such as Harden, that dry up. It has only a veneer of sediments, too thin and too contaminated with lake-bottom vegetation to permit an accurate carbon-14 date of its basal sedi-

ments, which would tell us when the lake first came into existence. Most Sierran lakes have existed for only 13-16,000 years, but Harden *could* have originated earlier.

HIKE 21

WHITE WOLF TO SMITH PEAK

Distance: 20.0 miles round trip

Grade: 5D, moderate 2-day hike

Trailhead: Same as the Hike 20 trailhead. **C4.**

Introduction: Looking for a nice weekend hike without the summer crowds? Then take this hike. Its elevation range is perfect for summer hiking—not too cold, hot, windy, or exposed. Near the end of your hike you can enjoy a refreshing swim at Harden Lake—that is, before it drops substantially in late summer.

Description: For the first 2.8 miles follow the route description of **Hike 20**, which directs you to a road end near the southwest shore of Harden Lake. From it a trail starts northwest,

Life-size photo of western dwarf mistletoe, a joint-stemmed parasite growing, in this case, on a red-fir branch

hemmed in by a meadow on the left and a bouldery moraine on the right. Soon we cross the crest of the moraine, which sits almost 4000 feet above the unseen east end of Hetch Hetchy Reservoir. The glacier that left it was at least this thick. On slopes we now traverse west through a red-fir forest, crossing two small meadows before briefly descending to a larger one atop a broad saddle. Meadows, being often damp, support all too many mosquitoes, but usually by late July most of them have died as the meadow's soils have dried out, and then this meadow is particularly enjoyable for botanizing. Here you may find a rainbow of colors in the flower blossoms: white-flowered cow parsnip and Richardson's geranium, creamy corn lily and bistort, yellow senecio and monkey flow, orange alpine lily, red columbine, maroon shooting star, blue-violet lupine, and blue Leichtlin's camas. On the nearby drab forest floor bits of color may be seen in the whitish-yellow-stemmed coralroot and the all-red snow plant. Both plants are

saprophytes—they derive their food from soil fungi rather than by photosynthesizing scarce sunlight.

Beyond the lodgepole-fringed meadow and the low crest just north of it, red firs yield to white firs and Jeffrey pines as we make a diagonal descent across south-facing slopes. Bracken ferns and snow bushes also thrive on the forest slopes, and scrubby black oaks make a showing just before we reach the crest of a glacial moraine. As we traverse west down this crest we can see Smith Peak, to the northwest, through the trees. Eventually we abandon the crest, and by descending shady slopes we exchange the company of Jeffrey pines for that of red firs, then white firs, and by the time we reach a creeklet, incense-cedars join us. Soon we cross the creeklet, which is lined with alders, azaleas, thimbleberries, bracken ferns, and water-loving wildflowers, and we follow it down to a seasonally wet meadow. Just beyond the meadow you'll cross Cottonwood Creek and arrive at eastern Smith Meadow. At times your trail through it can be hard to follow, but it generally goes northwest, re-entering forest cover near the meadow's north edge. Then to avoid damp soil, the trail stays close to the base of Smith Peak as it traverses northwest to western Smith Meadow, by which you'll find a junction with the Smith Peak trail. Just northwest ahead are suitable camping spots between the traversing trail and Cottonwood Creek.

A detailed description of the Smith Peak trail and the summit environs is given in **Hike 17**. After climbing the peak, return the way you came, perhaps stopping at Harden Lake for a refreshing swim, when the lake is full or nearly so. If someone is willing to drive to Mather Ranger Station, you can follow **Hike 17** down to it, which is easier than climbing back up to White Wolf.

<hr />

HIKE 22

WHITE WOLF TO PATE VALLEY

Distance: 21.3 miles semiloop trip

Grade: 5E, strenuous 2-day hike

Trailhead: From Crane Flat drive northeast 14½ miles up Highway 120 to the White Wolf turnoff and follow that road one mile down to the trailhead opposite White Wolf Lodge. **C4.**

Introduction: Pate Valley is sort of a miniature Yosemite Valley without the automobiles and tourists. It therefore attracts quite a number of backpackers, who in turn attract a few bears. Nevertheless, if you want to have a warm, spacious camp along the Tuolumne River, Pate Valley proper or its outlying areas may be just for you.

Description: This hike is described as a semi-loop trip since I feel that both trails leading to the Pate Valley trail are worth taking. However, if mosquitoes in the White Wolf area are intolerable, often until mid-July, you should first follow **Hike 20** to Harden Lake, then take the Pate Valley trail northeast. Our described route, however, first skirts the south edge of White Wolf Campground and then traverses about ¾ mile through a shady lodge-pole-pine forest to a crossing of the Middle Tuolumne River—maybe a ford in early season—about ¼ mile before reaching a junction with a trail right to Lukens Lake (**Hike 23**). We go left and continue a traverse across the flat, forested floor. A short climb soon follows, which ends on a broad, shallow gap.

Leaving the crest we descend northwest down a gully to the east edge of a meadow, beyond which we enter level terrain strewn with glacial sediments. Only one significant creek drains this terrain, seasonally rich in ground water, and by late summer it can be dry. Just beyond the creek we climb to the crest of a lateral moraine. Amid red firs we now start the long descent to Pate Valley, hiking over or past the crests of four more moraines, these left by a Tioga-age glacier which retreated from this area by 15,000 years ago. By the time our 1⅓-mile descent with its dozen-plus switchbacks ends at a junction with the Pate Valley trail, the forest cover has changed from red firs and western white pines to white

Black bears, adept at climbing trees, are common in Pate Valley

firs, Jeffrey pines, and incense-cedars. Bushy black oaks are also found near the junction.

Our return route goes west to Harden Lake, but we strike east on a sympathetic trail that drops only very gently, thus giving our knees a chance to recover from our first switchbacking descent. In ½ mile you'll cross a spring-fed creeklet whose banks are hidden among a luxuriant growth of water-loving vegetation—alders, aspen, American dogwoods, bracken ferns, thinbleberries, and currants. In late summer this is your last reliable source of water until you reach the floor of the Grand Canyon of the Tuolumne River. In a few minutes we cut through a flat-floored notch high on this canyon's south wall, then after a few more minutes of gentle descent reach seasonal Morrison Creek. After paralleling it for ¼ mile we come to a low, rocky knoll, on our left. Here you may be scolded by Steller's jays—avian indicators of a warmer plant community. Onward we start our second set of short switchbacks—about four dozen of them—which lead us on a descent to a crossing of Morrison Creek.

Along this descent through a white-fir forest, note that sugar pines appear, incense-cedars grow in numbers, and black oaks now have tree stature. On the dry, rocky ridge paralleling our descent grow scraggly western junipers and pervasive huckleberry oaks. Finally we come to a crossing of Morrison Creek, which in late summer can be bone-dry, and then flies can be a special nuisance. During this season they can become almost unbearable on the canyon floor, way below you, if you are covered with sweat.

Our last set of switchbacks—about 55 of them—down to the river—begins just past Morrison Creek. Along this descent you'll get numerous views of the Grand Canyon of the Tuolumne River, whose distant floor gradually draws nearer. Black oaks tend to be the dominant shade tree at first, but halfway down, after we cross a dramatic water-polished gully that descends the canyon's south wall, the vegetation soon changes. Canyon live oaks and bay trees slowly put in an appearance. Afternoon temperatures are hot, even under the trees, by the time we cross a granite gap. Greenleaf manzanitas, seen higher up, are now replaced by whiteleaf manzanitas.

Beyond the gap is a grassy pond, which can dry up in late season but before then

makes a warm swimming hole. At the pond's east end we cross the crest of a low moraine, then negotiate the few remaining switchbacks down to the flat floor of this great river canyon. Here the forest composition is nearly identical to that of Yosemite Valley, dominated by ponderosa pines, black oaks, and incense-cedars. Over the next 2 miles of fairly level hiking you'll pass several near-river campsites, and isolated camps could be set up in a number of places. Only several hundred yards before two crossings of the Tuolumne River, you'll enter Pate Valley proper and pass through a very large riverside camping area popular with equestrians. In the past its popularity could be judged by the over-abundance of toilet paper to be found under almost any moveable log or rock—the price paid when a popular area lacks a pit toilet.

Backpackers can find more isolated sites by crossing the two bridges over the chilly Tuolumne River, then climbing through a narrow bedrock notch and arriving at the north bank of the river's main branch. To keep your food safe from bears, you might place it in a rodent-proof stuff sack, then perch it on an inaccessible rock ledge, for bears are poor rock climbers. About a minute's walk beyond the north-bank camps you'll come to a trail junction. For most, the dry 4.7-mile climb to the Pleasant Valley trail—**Hike 14**, 3500 feet higher—is not worth the toil and sweat. Furthermore, when this steep trail is not maintained, it can become seriously overgrown with brush. However, some may want to do the first ¾ mile, with about 500 feet of ascent, to where the trail levels off, then in the next ½ mile—before serious climbing starts—leave it for good-to-excellent camping near either bank of Piute Creek.

To return to your trailhead, retrace your steps 6 miles southwest back up to the trail junction one mile west of Morrison Creek. On this ascent, start early, while it is still cool, take it easy, resting often, and carry *at least* one quart of water. When you reach the mentioned junction, head for Harden Lake on a trail whose first mile is a comfortable contour. Many aspens are passed along the second half of this contour, which fill their thirsty appetites by tapping the large "reservoir" of water stored within the morainal sediments we traverse across. One source of this "reservoir" is our immediate goal, Harden Lake, which has no surface outlet, but rather loses some of its water via percolation through the morainal sediments.

To reach Harden Lake we climb moderately to steeply up about 20 switchbacks, entering a forest of lodgepole pines, then of red firs and western white pines. When you arrive at Harden Lake you'll need a rest and probably a refreshing swim. From the lake your trail quickly ends at a road which you follow southeast for ¼ mile, then take a short trail over to the old Tioga Road, which heads up to White Wolf. This hike from Harden Lake is described in detail (in the reverse direction) in **Hike 19**.

WHITE WOLF TO LUKENS LAKE

Distance: 4.6 miles round trip

Grade: 1A, easy half-day hike; no camping allowed

Trailhead: Same as the Hike 22 trailhead. **C4.**

Introduction: This is the longer, yet more popular route to Lukens Lake. The second route, Hike 24, would be more popular if its trailhead were better signed. Since Lukens Lake is already heavily visited, however, it is perhaps best that the shorter route's trailhead is not that conspicuous. Lukens Lake is very similar to Harden Lake (Hike 19), and if you enjoy one, you'll enjoy the other.

Description: If you stay at White Wolf Campground and rise early in the morning, you just might be fortunate enough to see a great gray owl perched on the trailhead sign or on a small lodgepole that has invaded White Wolf meadow. With keen, alert senses, this largest species of the North American owls waits for one of the meadow's many rodents to make a move. In this mid-elevation meadow, the likely prey would be a shrew, deer mouse, meadow mouse, western jumping mouse, Belding ground squirrel, or perhaps even a pocket gopher. Also preying on these rodents is the more-abundant coyote, a predator that is found in all of Yosemite's plant communities except the alpine one. Coyotes and great gray owls may also be seen in another similar habitat, Crane Flat meadow.

Our trail to Lukens Lake skirts the south edge of White Wolf Campground and traverses about ¾ mile through a shady lodgepole-pine forest to a crossing of the Middle Tuolumne River—maybe a ford in early season—about ¼ mile before reaching a junction with a trail

A peaceful afternoon spent fishing at Lukens Lake

north to Pate Valley (**Hike 22**). Until mid July the mosquitoes can be particularly abundant along this level stretch, for the ground is nearly saturated with water. During this time horses' hooves can turn the trail into a mire, but in late season, hikers will find little evidence of this, for once the trail dries out, the multitude of ensuing hikers plow it smooth again.

From the junction we hike east upstream for a nearly level, shady, short mile and come to a second junction. The trail east toward Ten Lakes first climbs and then descends, for a total of 3.8 miles, to the shorter, more popular Ten Lakes trail (**Hike 25**). Leaving the junction, we head south a few steps, jump across the infant Middle Tuolumne River, then begin a continuous, generally moderate, ½-mile ascent to Lukens Lake. Climbing this trail segment, we cross at least four glacial moraines, the final one forming a rim along the north shore of Lukens Lake. Along this shore we now find a well-mixed conifer forest, with red firs, western white pines, and mountain hemlocks, joining the lodgepole pines, which have dominated so much of our route.

Like Harden Lake, Lukens Lake is a 9-acre, shallow, warm lake, and it lacks views of stunning peaks. Unlike Harden, Lukens has trout—rainbow, brook, and brown—and it tends to have a grassy bottom, not a bouldery one. Since it is illegal to camp at this lake, try White Wolf Campground or more-secluded Yosemite Creek Campground. The latter is reached by driving on Highway 120 just ⅓ mile east past the White Wolf turnoff to a junction with the old Tioga Road, on your right. Follow it 4¾ miles to Yosemite Creek.

HIKE 24

TIOGA ROAD TO LUKENS LAKE

Distance: 2.2 miles round trip

Grade: 1A, easy half-day hike; no camping allowed

Trailhead: From Crane Flat drive northeast 14½ miles up Highway 120 to the White Wolf turnoff, then continue an additional 1.9 miles

to a paved turnout on the highway's south side. **D4.**

Introduction: This is the shorter approach to Lukens Lake (see Hike 23).

Description: From the Highway 120 turnout, located in a shady gully near a curve in the highway, look for a signed trailhead on the north side of the road. Among red firs and western white pines, make an easy ⅓-mile climb to a viewless saddle. As is often the case, chinquapin bushes are found associated with the firs. Leaving the saddle, you make an equally easy descent to the southeast end of a sedge-dominated meadow that also contains conspicuous corn lilies and, as usual, willows. From this meadow's corner the main trail strikes northwest toward the lake's north shore and a lesser trail—one of use—strikes west toward its south shore. For more information of this lake see the last part of **Hike 23**.

HIKE 25

TEN LAKES BASIN VIA YOSEMITE CREEK

Distance: 12.6 miles round trip distance to first lake; side trips to other lakes extra

Grade: 3D, moderate 2-day hike

Trailhead: From Crane Flat drive northeast 19⅔ miles up Highway 120 to the trailhead parking area, on *both* sides of the highway, immediately before the highway bridges signed Yosemite Creek. **D4.**

Introduction: The Ten Lakes Basin is extremely popular with weekend backpackers, for with only a few hours' hiking effort you can attain any of its seven major lakes.

Description: From the west end of the highway's north parking lot a spur trail goes 90 yards northwest to the main trail, the Ten Lakes trail. On it we hike up-canyon, first through a lodgepole-pine flat, then soon climb away from unseen Yosemite Creek and encounter Jeffrey pines and huckleberry oaks. Shaggy-barked western junipers are next met as we climb, seemingly too much, up to drier

Hikers resting at pass above Ten Lakes Basin; Sierra crest on skyline

granitic slopes. This ascent, however, takes us above most of the lodgepoles, which tend to harbor mosquitoes. The climb also gives us views of Yosemite Creek canyon, Mt. Hoffmann, and the county-line crest north of it. Soon after we get these views the trail levels, enters a forest of red firs and lodgepoles, and then, about 2¼ miles into our hike, reaches a creekside junction with a trail from White Wolf.

From the junction we boulder-hop the creek and leave a nearby campsite to begin a moderate climb up a well-forested moraine left after the retreat of a large glacier by 15,000 years ago. Our climbing ends momentarily and we descend to and cross three seasonal creeklets. Then we climb, steeply at times, in a forest of red fir and western white pine to the top of a moraine. Behind it lies crescentic, wet Half Moon Meadow, which probably exists because the moraine impedes the meadow's drainage. The trail cuts across the meadow's relatively dry north edge, which nevertheless contains enough water to support a healthy crop of corn lilies. By its northeast corner, about 4½ miles from the trailhead, is a campsite, nestled under lodgepoles and close to a creek. The next stretch of ascent is steep and dry, so rest here and perhaps get a drink.

Roughly three dozen short, steep switchbacks guide us about ¾ mile up almost to the Tuolumne/Mariposa county-line crest, from

Lower Grant Lake

Ten Lakes Basin's large western lake

which we veer away to a trail junction. From it a poorly designed trail drops hundreds of feet in its 1.2-mile length to lower Grant Lake. A far better route, at least for cross-country hikers, is to start from the south corner of Half Moon Meadow and climb southeast cross-country up to this lake. There is no maintained trail to upper Grant Lake, but rather just a faint, discontinuous use trail. The more popular lower lake has better campsites than the upper lake, though fishing for rainbow trout may be better at the less visited upper lake.

Leaving the Grant Lakes trail junction, the Ten Lakes trail climbs gently across a gravelly slope that is covered in midsummer with large, deliciously scented lupines. These taper off just before we cross the county-line crest, which here is a broad, level, unglaciated surface that has weathered very little over many millions of years. Here at the pass are two kinds of granitic rock, gray bedrock at our feet and cream-to-white bedrock on the low knolls to the east and west. Just north of the pass we cross two long dikes that have intruded the gray bedrock. Since these dikes are younger than the rock they intrude, their source, the lighter bedrock, is also younger than the darker bedrock.

Leaving Merced River drainage, we enter Tuolumne River drainage as we descend briefly north to a shallow saddle. Just beyond it is a small summit and to the left of it is flat-topped Colby Mountain, which crowns the west rim of the Ten Lakes Basin. This undistinguished summit is named for a very distinguished man, William Colby, the third president of the Sierra Club—just after John Muir and Professor Joseph LeConte. Colby served the club for nearly half a century and was truly one of the greatest conservationists in the early days of Yosemite National Park.

As we start a descent from the shallow saddle, a panorama of steep-sided, glaciated Ten Lakes Basin opens all around us, and three of the western lakes are clearly evident. Our descent, which started close to some wind-blown whitebark pines growing on the county-line crest, ends near the largest of the western Ten Lakes, in a forest of mountain hemlocks and lodgepole and western white pines. The presence of hemlock and lodgepole together with lakeside red heather and Labrador tea indicates prime mosquito country—at least before August—and until then

use a tent to escape their bloodthirsty attacks. However, camping is quite enjoyable by early August, when the lakes are at their warmest temperatures, and also during September, after most hikers have left. It is then that a common, easily missed plant, the dwarf bilberry, makes its thumb-size presence known by turning to a blazing crimson color. Around the largest of the western lakes you'll find at least a half dozen campsites, most of them along its western shore. Swimming is best at the lake's sunnier, shallower, island-dotted north end, and just beyond its nearby outlet are first-rate examples of glacier polish. From the north end you can hike cross-country ¼ mile northeast over a low ridge to one of the basin's more isolated lakes.

Other lakes can be reached by starting at the large lake's southwest corner and following its inlet creek upstream. A path goes up each of its banks to the first lake, which has a large north-shore campsite with a view of towering cliffs. Beyond this popular lake only the east-bank path continues, and it climbs ½ mile to a campsite at the outlet of the next lake, then ends at a campsite at its inlet. Few hikers climb cross-country to the steep-sided uppermost large lake.

To get to a large eastern lake, you start from the large western lake's south shore. Draining into the lake's south end is a creeklet, and on its east bank you'll find a maintained trail climbing southeast up to a sedge-filled meadow, then northeast from it up a bedrock ridge. The trail is steep in places, but the view improves with height, urging you on. Nearing the top of the crest, the trail enters a shady forest of hemlocks and lodgepoles, then soon makes a ½-mile traverse southeast to the outlet of the large eastern lake. Although it lacks the dramatic esthetics of its western counterpart, it has almost as many campsites but not as many campers. The best sites are along the west and north shores. If you want secluded camping, then start a cross-country hike down from the north shore, soon following a creek that goes ½ mile down to the basin's northeastern lake.

After visiting one or more of the basin's sparkling gems, hike back out the way you came—or from the large eastern lake follow the long trail out to May Lake (the reverse of **Hike 28**).

HIKE 26

OLD TIOGA ROAD TO MAY LAKE

Distance: 2.4 miles round trip

Grade: 1B, easy half-day hike

Trailhead: From Crane Flat drive northeast 27 miles up Highway 120 to the old Tioga Road, this junction being 3.7 miles west of the trailhead parking area by the southwest shore of Tenaya Lake. Take the old Tioga Road, signed for May Lake, 1¾ miles northeast up to an obvious trailhead parking area. **E4.**

Introduction: May Lake is a very popular destination because it is a short hike, and its shores provide good base-camp sites for an ascent of Mt. Hoffmann.

Description: Although this walk is treated here as a day hike, there is no reason that one should not stay overnight at the May Lake High Sierra Camp. Its cabins, however, usually are reserved months in advance, leaving the majority of overnighters to stay in a hikers' camp just above the lake's south shore.

The trail begins by the southwest side of a small pond on Snow Flat in a moderately dense stand of hemlock, red fir, and western white and lodgepole pines. To the northwest is the peak which is at the geographic center of the Park, Mt. Hoffmann. In a little vale to the east of the trail, water lies late in the season, permitting corn lilies to bloom into August. Our sandy trail ascends gently through forest cover, where we recognize the western white pine by its long, narrow cones and checkerboard bark pattern, and we notice how the red-fir cones, near the tops of these trees, stand upright on the branches, unlike the hanging cones of pines and hemlocks.

The initial ascent leads up open granite slabs dotted with lodgepoles. Then, as we switchback west up a short, steep slope, we have fine views of Cathedral Peak in the east, Mt. Clark in the southeast, and Clouds Rest and Half Dome in the south. Near the top of the slope, the forest cover thickens and the western white pines become larger and more handsome. Just beyond the crest, we find ourselves in a flat beneath a half-dozen superb, large hemlocks by deep, chilly May Lake. Swimming is not allowed, but you may try your luck at catching the lake's brook or rainbow trout while contemplating the lake's beautiful backdrop of the east slopes of massive Mt. Hoffmann, whose summit ascent is described in the next hike.

A summit view east: May Lake, Tenaya Lake, and the Sierra crest from Tioga Pass to Mt. Lyell complex

HIKE 27

MT. HOFFMANN VIA MAY LAKE

Distance: 6.0 miles round trip

Grade: 2D, strenuous day hike

Trailhead: Same as the Hike 26 trailhead. **E4.**

Introduction: Mt. Hoffmann, centrally located in Yosemite National Park, provides the best all-around views of this Park's varied landscapes. Perhaps more hikers ascend it than any other 10,000+ peak in the Park, with only Mts. Lyell and Dana challenging its popularity. As with any high-peak ascent, wear dark glasses and lots of sunscreen, for there's ⅓ less air on the summit, and the ultraviolet rays come on strong. Also, avoid altitude sickness, which is brought on by overexerting yourself, particularly after a large meal. If you are not in shape, camp overnight at May Lake to get partly acclimatized, then climb the peak the next day. Take it easy, for the route is short. However, abandon your attempt if a thunderstorm is approaching.

Description: Follow **Hike 26** to May Lake, above whose southeast corner you'll see a trail striking west. On it you immediately pass a backpackers' camp, which extends west, and in that direction you traverse across metasedimentary rocks cropping out above the lake's southwest shore. You now follow it south, first through a small gap, then through a boulder-strewn wildflower garden. You might lose the trail here, but the route south—up a shallow gully to a small, linear meadow—is quite obvious. From the meadow's south end, near a saddle, the trail goes 100 yards southwest and then climbs northwest up to the lower end of the broad, sloping, lupine-decked summit area. Numerous summits exist, but the western summit is the highest, and you have an easy, safe scramble to its top. If you have a picnic here, you'll almost certainly attract marmots, but please don't feed them. Using this guidebook's topo map of the Park, you can identify almost every major peak in it, since most are visible from here. Note how Mt. Hoffmann's nearly flat summit plateau contrasts with the mountain's steep sides. Mass wasting, accelerated by the presence of past glacial climates, has caused retreat through rockfall on all sides of this mountain, diminishing the size of the plateau. The same has occurred on summit areas of Mt. Conness, Dana Plateau, Dore Pass, and a few other spots that once were part of an extensive, rolling landscape back in the late days of the dinosaurs some 80-65 million years ago. When you return, take the path you ascended. Other routes are steeper, have loose rock, and are potentially dangerous.

HIKE 28

TEN LAKES BASIN VIA MAY LAKE

Distance: 22.2 miles one way

Grade: 5E, moderate 3-day hike

Trailhead: Same as the Hike 26 trailhead. **E4.**

Introduction: At 14.6 miles to the easternmost lake in the Ten Lakes Basin, this hike is the "back door" entrance to the basin. Since it is about twice as long as the regular route to the basin, Hike 25, few hikers take it. Therefore, it is a route on which you escape the crowds. However, when you're ready to leave, you'll probably want to exit via the regular route. Should you return the way you came, you'll hike a total of 29.2 miles if you go only to the easternmost lake and don't take any side trips.

Description: Follow Hike 26 to May Lake, then continue along its east shore to its north shore. Camping is not permitted along these shores. Leaving the lake on the High Sierra Camps loop trail, you climb to a quickly reached shallow pass that seasonally is painted bluish purple with a field of aromatic, waist-high lupines. From the pass the trail soon begins a switchbacking descent that provides views of Cathedral Peak, standing high above Polly Dome. After about a dozen switchbacks, our descending trail's gradient eases, and in forest shade we wind southeast, crossing four seasonal creeklets before sighting Raisin Lake, located just off the trail and about 3 miles from our trailhead. Being shallow and having no icy creeks to feed it, this can be one of the warmest swimming holes in the Park.

Beyond the lake our trail goes briefly east toward a low knoll, then heads north beside it up to a nearby, second shallow pass. At it, a panorama of the High Sierra unfolds, with Mt. Conness dominating the Sierra crest. Note that Polly Dome is very *un*-domelike and rather is basically rectangular. You'll see long, straight fractures—*joints*—which govern the dome's shape and along which rows of conifers grow. Leaving the pass and its southward view of Clouds Rest, we descend some rocky switchbacks, then traverse north for ¾ mile, staying high on the slopes above Murphy Creek and its largely hidden trail (**Hike 37**). At the end of the traverse, we cross our third shallow pass in a stand of lodgepoles that obstruct a backward view of Tenaya Lake. As our trail descends north-facing slopes for ¼ mile to a junction, the forest cover becomes increasingly dominated by mountain hemlocks, which do well in areas of long-lasting snow cover.

At the trail junction, 4¾ miles from our trailhead, we leave the popular High Sierra Camps loop trail (**Hike 40**), and start southwest on the lightly used eastern part of the Ten Lakes trail. After ¼ mile the trail veers north, and as we hike in that direction, lodgepole pines, red firs, and western white pines increase in numbers but then soon diminish as we gain altitude, giving us fair views east toward the Cathedral Range. Moderately graded switchbacks take us up to a crest saddle—a good breather stop—and then we continue almost ½ mile farther, first up to a higher crest, and then across to a nearby pond. This is a good rest spot, although at 7¾ miles from the trailhead, on might look for isolated campsites in this vicinity, first obtaining drinking water

from the pond. From sites about here, one can experience beautiful sunrises. Also from here, one can head about ½ mile southwest up a ridge to steeper slopes of Tuolumne Peak proper, which can be scrambled up—cautiously—without a rope.

From the pond our trail climbs, drops, and winds westward to a good overlook point high above the South Fork Cathedral Creek canyon. Short, rocky switchbacks carry you down toward the canyon floor, and then you veer south on a long contour just below a low-angle cliff, only to resume more switchbacks. You reach the South Fork in minutes, and hiking down along it can find suitable campsites on either side of this creek. After 2 miles of near-creek winding trail, you cross this creek—a ford in early season—go briefly downstream, then prepare for a two-dozen-switchback climb of a generally open, juniper-dotted slope. Your last chance for secluded camping is in this vicinity, below the crossing.

As you labor up the switchbacks, stop and rest and take in the ever-expanding views of northern Yosemite, from Mt. Gibbs westward, with the north wall of the mighty gorge of the Tuolumne River dominating the foreground. As the switchbacks abate, the trail enters forest shade and then climbs a mile to a seasonal pond. Beyond it, about 150 feet below, is the large eastern lake of the Ten Lakes Basin—an area with abundant potential for camping and exploration. See **Hike 25** for a description of this basin and the trail west out from it.

Chapter 7

Trails of Yosemite's West-Central Lands, between the Tioga Road and Yosemite Valley

Introduction: Of all this guide's sections, this is the only one that lacks a prominent, nearby peak. It is chiefly a heavily forested uplands landscape of rolling, gentle topography. However, along this land's southern perimeter, the slopes end in steep-walled cliffs that make up the north wall of Yosemite Valley. Lacking alpine scenery, the trails in this section get only light-to-moderate use except for the stretch of trail that descends from the brink of Upper Yosemite Fall to the Valley floor. Compensating for the alpine deficiencies are five spectacular viewpoints along the Valley's north rim: El Capitan, Eagle Peak, the Upper Yosemite Fall brink, Yosemite Point, and North Dome. Furthermore, you can study the ever-changing perspective of Half Dome along your descent into Tenaya Canyon (Hikes 34 and 35).

Supplies and Services: See "Supplies and Services" in Chapter 6.

Wilderness Permits: See "Wilderness Permits" in Chapter 6.

Campgrounds: All the campgrounds mentioned in the "Campgrounds" of Chapter 6 can be used plus the two following ones. After driving east 3¾ miles up the Tioga Road from Crane Flat, branch right immediately before Gin Flat and follow the old Big Oak Flat Road 3 winding miles to Tamarack Flat Campground. This camp is best for hikes 30 and 31. The second campground is also off the highway. Just ⅓ mile past the White Wolf road junction is a junction with the old Tioga Road, on your right. Follow it 4¾ miles to the Yosemite Creek Campground, best for Hike 32. At all campgrounds look for a site early in the day.

HIKE 29

NEW BIG OAK FLAT ROAD TO CASCADE CREEK

Distance: 8.0 miles round trip

Grade: 2C, moderate day hike

Trailhead: From Crane Flat drive east 5 ¾ miles toward Yosemite Valley down the new Big Oak Flat Road to a small trailhead parking area on the south. The trail begins opposite the parking area, from the north side of the road. If you continue ¼ mile farther, you will reach the Foresta road junction. **C5.**

Introduction: During late spring, when most of Yosemite's trails are under snow, this trail is at its best. Views are few and lakes are nonexistent, so it will appeal only to those who want an invigorating yet not exhausting walk and to those who appreciate the finer details of mid-Sierran ecology.

Description: The trail initially makes an ascent east across open slopes, and during spring, one might find harlequin lupines in bloom, these identified by their pink-and-yellow flowers. Later on the flowers will be replaced by pea pods, and nearby whiteleaf manzanitas, with their gray-green leaves, will have produced berries. The first third of our route was burned in a 1990 lightning-caused fire, which left charred snags, but it also allowed much more light to reach the ground—hence the profusion of shrubs and wildflowers. Particularly on an initial 400-foot, ½-mile climb to a ridge—which has views of El Capitan and Half Dome—dense herbs and shrubs can crowd the trail, and since this vegetation abounds in rodents, it is a prime habitat for rattlesnakes, so watch your step.

In the next ½ mile our trail briefly climbs the ridge, then traverses north to a moist area with a seasonal spring. Over the next ½ mile we enter unburned forest and then descend to usually flowing Wildcat Creek. Soon we begin to climb again, and do so for almost a mile until we start a short, steep descent along a ridge, which offers a view, across the Merced River canyon, of the Wawona Road traversing the flanks of Turtleback Dome. The steep descent continues down to nearby Tamarack Creek, which in summer flourishes with giant-leaved umbrella plants growing from its stream bed. At times this creek is a wet ford.

Again we make a mile-long climb, then make a momentary drop to a Cascade Creek tributary, which we boulder-hop only yards before reaching the old Big Oak Flat Road. At this creek crossing, serviceberries hug the bank of a small pool fed by a photogenic cascade. Once on the road we have a brief walk down to the Cascade Creek bridge—a good spot for a lunch break (camping prohibited). In late summer the flow of Cascade Creek is slow and warm enough for safe and enjoyable splashing around in the small pools immediately downstream. During summer, when the road to Tamarack Flat Campground is open, you'll want to take the much shorter **Hike 30** down to Cascade Creek.

HIKE 30

TAMARACK FLAT C. G. TO CASCADE CREEK

Distance: 4.4 miles round trip

Grade: 1B, easy half-day hike

Trailhead: From Crane Flat drive northeast 3¾ miles up the Tioga Road to the Tamarack Flat Campground turnoff, immediately before the Gin Flat scenic turnout. Drive southeast down the old Big Oak Flat Road to the east end of Tamarack Flat Campground, 3¼ miles from the Tioga Road. **C4**

Introduction: Around mid-morning, Tamarack Flat Campground becomes temporarily abandoned, only to receive another flood of motorized campers in late afternoon. Take the time to enjoy the campground during the tranquil part of day, and while you're in the vicinity, you might take a few hours to make this pleasant, easy hike.

Description: Until the mid-1970s you could drive from Tamarack Flat Campground down to Cascade Creek, but now that the road is closed to motor vehicles, this stretch is a relaxing hike, one that is ideal for appreciating the peaceful forest and for reflecting on your role in nature. *Homo sapiens* is an integral part of the total biosphere, planet Earth, yet too often he tries to isolate himself from it and to dominate or destroy it. Early visitors traveling to Yosemite Valley by this road from 1874 onward thought little about man's role in nature, at least not while in their stagecoaches, which were crowded and uncomfortable. They had already traveled about 100 miles or more just to reach Tamarack Flat and still had a few more anxious miles to go.

Tamarack Flat derives its name from its extreme predominance of tamaracks, known today as lodgepole pines. However, as you leave the flats and hike across slopes on the old Big Oak Flat Road, white firs become dominant. Along both sides of the road you'll see

Cascade Creek's northwest tributary

large, partly buried granitic boulders. These were not carried here by glaciers, as John Muir once supposed, for this local terrain was never glaciated. Instead, they developed right where you see them, being resistant enough to subsurface weathering that they finally emerged at the surface quite intact, while the adjacent, less resistant, more fractured bedrock was chemically broken down and slowly stripped away by erosion. Thus these boulders did not "grow" out of the ground, but rather, the ground around them was slowly removed—a process that took millions of years.

Just before you reach a prominent cluster of rocks—ideal for rock-climbing practice—your road begins a steady descent to Cascade Creek. At a road switchback just 240 yards before the bridge across this creek, you'll see a junction with a trail to the new Big Oak Flat Road, **Hike 29**. Down at this lower, warmer, drier elevation you'll find Jeffrey and sugar pines intermingled with the firs. Along the first 200 yards below its bridge, Cascade Creek splashes down low cascades into small pools, and in late season these make nice "swimming

holes." Before then the creek is likely to be too swift for safe frolicking, particularly since the water-polished rock can be quite slippery. Rooted in this creek are large-leaved umbrella plants, and growing just beside the water's edge are creek dogwoods, willows, western azaleas and serviceberries. Huckleberry oaks crowd the dry rocks above the banks. Your day hike can be rounded out with a creekside picnic, under shady, spacious conifers, before you return to the campground.

HIKE 31

TAMARACK FLAT C. G. TO EL CAPITAN

Distance: 15.4 miles round trip

Grade: 4D, strenuous day hike

Trailhead: Same as the Hike 30 trailhead. **C4**

Introduction: The vertical walls of 3000-foot-high El Capitan attract rock climbers from all over the world, and more than five dozen extremely difficult routes ascend it. For non-climbers this hike provides a much easier, safer way to attain El Capitan's summit, which stands only 15 feet above the north-side approach.

Description: Descend to Cascade Creek, as directed in **Hike 30**, then continue ½ mile down the old Big Oak Flat Road—now more like a trail—to a junction with Yosemite Valley's north rim trail. Or, continue *only* 200 yards below Cascade Creek to a well-graded, abandoned road, on the left, and follow it ¼ mile up to the El Capitan trail. Since the Big Oak Flat Road down to the valley floor is quite abandoned, the Park Service ought to also abandon the current trail junction and place it at the junction with the abandoned road. This change would save hikers almost ½ mile. From either junction a major climb of almost 2,000 feet confronts us. Along the lands between here and El Capitan, USGS geologist François Matthes mapped seven glacial moraines, extensive, scattered glacial deposits, and 20 glacial erratics. None of the moraines or deposits exist, and all of the erratics are merely

Panorama from El Capitan: Clouds Rest and Quarter Domes on rim of Tenaya Canyon; Half Dome; twin summits of Mts. Maclure and Lyell above Bunnell Point cliff and Little Yosemite Valley; Glacier Point ridge in foreground; finlike Mt. Clark above rounded Sentinel Dome, which is above and right of the top of Sentinel Rock; Gray Peak above Mt. Starr King, which is just right of Sentinel Dome; Red and Merced peaks on the far right skyline.

locally derived boulders. None of your route ahead was ever glaciated.

Starting in a summer-warm forest of incense-cedar, ponderosa and sugar pines, and white fir, we climb hundreds of feet—steeply at times—up to drier slopes with clusters of greenleaf manzanita and huckleberry oak. Also growing in the gravelly soils are some common drought-tolerant wildflowers—streptanthus, spreading phlox, pussy paws, and mat lupine. When we do re-enter forest, it is one of white firs and Jeffrey pines. Occasionally we see black oaks, but these diminish to shrub height as we climb higher, disappearing altogether by the time we reach a small drop on a ridge. In this vicinity chinquapins compete with huckleberry oaks, and they herald the imminent encounter with red firs, which we find growing near the top of the crest. Three miles from the trailhead, lodgepoles join in the ranks as we make a short descent from it down to a sedge-filled damp meadow that sprouts short-blooming shooting stars, marsh marigolds and other water-loving wildflowers. The meadow guides us to a crossing of a Ribbon Creek tributary—a wide bog in early summer—and then we parallel it east one mile down to Ribbon Creek. Ribbon Meadow, which we traverse on the first part of this descent, is more forest than meadow, and on the bark of lodgepoles you'll see blazes to guide you where the route becomes a little vague. Along the banks of Ribbon Creek are the trail's only acceptable campsites—but waterless when the creek dries up about midsummer. Now only 1¼ miles from our goal, we make a brief climb, an equally brief descent, and then an ascending traverse east to the top of El Capitan Gully. One Yosemite Valley's mountaineering tragedies occurred in the upper part of this gully when on June 5, 1905, Charles Bailey fell to his death. His partner, J. L. Staats, became the first known person to ascend the gully successfully. Every year a few climbers are killed on the walls of Yosemite Valley. This shouldn't happen, for rock climbing has the potential to be a very safe sport. All too often, however, it attracts reckless individuals who spurn safety precautions.

Your first views of El Capitan and the south wall of Yosemite Valley appear on this traverse to El Capitan Gully, and views continue through the sparse stand of Jeffrey pines as you climb south from the gully past dense shrubbery to a junction with the El Capitan spur trail. If you are hiking this trail in late summer, after Ribbon Creek has dried up, you may want to continue on the main trail ½ mile northeast to two trickling springs. The trail beyond them is not all that interesting, but it does get you to Eagle Peak (see **Hikes 32** and **69**).

Along the spur trail south to El Capitan's broad, rounded summit, you can gaze up-canyon and identify unmistakable Half Dome, at the Valley's end, barely protruding Sentinel Dome, above the Valley's south wall, and fin-shaped Mt. Clark, on the skyline above the dome. Take your time exploring El Capitan's large, domed summit area, but don't stray too far from it. The first 200 yards below it are safe, but then the summit's slopes gradually get steeper and you could slip on loose, weathered crystals, giving you a one-way trip to the bottom. Remember that many climbing deaths occur after the triumphant party has reached the summit.

HIKE 32

TIOGA ROAD TO YOSEMITE VALLEY VIA YOSEMITE CREEK

Distance: 12.8 miles one way

Grade: 3C, moderate day hike

Trailhead: Same as Hike 25 trailhead. **D4.**

Introduction: This is perhaps the best hike along which to observe the differences between two distinct landforms: steep-walled Yosemite Valley and the rolling uplands of Yosemite Creek. This route also takes you to the dramatic viewpoint at the brink of Upper Yosemite Fall with only one-third the climbing effort of Hike 68, which starts from the floor of the Valley. unfortunately, when the waterfall is at its best—before late June—snow patches and mosquitoes are prevalent along the Yosemite Creek trail.

Description: You begin by walking on the Tioga Road 120 yards west from the parking area to the signed trailhead. Except perhaps for snow patches your route ahead is quite clear. Being a mid-elevation, near-creek hike,

the route is dominated by lodgepoles, though red firs and western white pines thrive on shady slopes and junipers and Jeffrey pines on dry, rocky ones. After a mile of rambling trail we reach and boulder-hop wide Yosemite Creek. An additional mile of walking, this one close to the creek's east bank, gets us to the north end of Yosemite Creek Campground.

Along the campground's east sites we follow a dirt road south several minutes to a junction with the old Tioga Road, and then tread its rutted surface southwest down-canyon ½ mile to a recrossing of the creek. Beyond it we soon enter the campground proper, with a telephone booth, then cross an often-sluggish tributary and in 25 yards come to a resumption of our trail. You could drive to this point and start here, saving 2¾ miles of walking. To get to it by car, start from Crane Flat and drive northeast 14½ miles up the Tioga Road to the White Wolf turnoff, then an additional ⅓ mile on the highway to a junction with the old Tioga Road. Turn right and follow its rambling course 5 miles to this Yosemite Creek Campground trailhead.

From the campground we hike south through a fairly open forest on a trail that stays a short distance from the creek, then, after 1½ miles, climbs up a ridge away from it. Glaciers advancing from Mt. Hoffman scoured this countryside, but our route up across the barren bedrock is adequately marked. Large boulders resting atop polished slabs constitutes evidence of glaciation. From the ridge we can look across the canyon and see a low dome that is exfoliating—shedding slabs of granite as a giant onion might peel its layers.

Short switchbacks guide us down from the ridge, and then the trail shoots west over to three closely spaced creeks of a tributary canyon. Between the first and second is a junction with a northbound, lightly used trail. About ½ mile southeast from this junction we join the west bank of Yosemite Creek at a spot where the creek's course has migrated laterally west to abut against granitic bedrock. Small pools soon appear in the creekbed as we descend south; then, farther downstream, the pools are interspersed with water-polished slabs. None of the pools is large enough for a swim, though many are suitable for a refreshing dip. Along this section of creek you may see a small campsite; then, just past it, the trail makes a short, winding drop down a low

View down mildly glaciated Yosemite Creek canyon; the gentle topography gives no hint of the dropoff to come

ridge, touches the creek, ducks into a small cluster of aspens, and in ¼ mile becomes almost level. The trail now hugs the creek for ⅔ mile before temporarily veering away from it to skirt around a large gravel bar. Beyond it the trail winds southeast for ⅔ mile, then comes to seasonal Eagle Peak Creek. A moderate-sized campsite lies between it and Yosemite Creek—worth considering since camping is illegal within ½ mile of the Valley's brink.

Climbing from the shady campsite, we hike south up a gully to a divide and on it meet the Eagle Peak trail, **Hike 69,** striking west. If you've got the time, you might make the 7-mile round trip to Eagle Peak and back. It involves only about 1000 feet of climbing, and the peak's panoramic views are certainly worth the effort. Beyond this trail junction we descend into a second gully, climb out of a third and descend to another trail junction in the fourth. All four lie in a straight line, which probably represents a major fracture in the bedrock. From this last junction, among mature Jeffrey pines, we follow the description of **Hike 68** in reverse, first climbing east, then descending south to the fenced-in viewpoint near the brink of Upper Yosemite Fall, then retracing our steps to this junction and finally

descending 3 miles to the floor of Yosemite Valley.

HIKE 33

TIOGA ROAD TO NORTH DOME

Distance: 9.6 miles round trip

Grade: 2D, moderate day hike

Trailhead: From Crane Flat drive northeast 23.7 miles up the Tioga Road to the Porcupine Flat Campground, then an additional 1.1 miles to a closed road, on your right. If you're westbound, the trailhead is 2.1 miles west of the May Lake turnoff. **D4.**

Introduction: North Dome, which looks so inaccessible from the Yosemite Valley floor, can be reached in a couple of hours by this route. From the dome you get perhaps the best views of the expansive faces of Half Dome and Clouds Rest, as well as excellent views of Yosemite Valley. Along this hike you can also visit one of Yosemite's few known natural arches. Another one is, surprisingly, underwater, near Tuolumne Meadows Lodge (Hike 55).

Description: Through 1976 you could drive to Porcupine Creek Campground, a primitive campground with rutted roads and overused sites, and down this former road we walk. Just ¼ mile from the Tioga Road you'll notice the faint, abandoned old Tioga Road crossing your route. To the east this road goes 1.0 mile to a highway turnout that is 1.1 miles short of the May Lake spur road, a continuation of this historic road. To the west it goes 1.2 miles to the Tioga Road and the entrance to Porcupine Flat Campground, continues west through the campground and recrosses the highway in 1.0 mile, then descends 2.6 miles to the east campsites in Yosemite Creek Campground. Armed with this knowledge you can plan hiking routes that link up with May Lake and Yosemite Creek. Our obvious route descends to the former site of Porcupine Creek Campground, and in the westernmost part of this site, a trail begins at Porcupine Creek.

Porcupine Creek and Porcupine Flat are well named, for they are located in a nearly pure stand of lodgepole pines—the favorite food of the Park's porcupines. They seem to prefer lodgepoles among all conifers because of this tree's thin bark, and they usually attack the tree's upper section, where the bark is especially thin. What they relish is the tree's

Delicate arch on Indian Ridge

soft growing tissues immediately beneath the bark. The porcupine's chief enemy is the fisher, a minklike carnivore only one fourth its size, which can swiftly attack its vulnerable, unprotected belly. Coyotes, mountain lions and bobcats are less adept at killing porcupines, and they often receive a good share of quills in their attempts. The porcupine population also may be controlled by diseases and internal parasites.

From the west bank of Porcupine Creek our trail contours for a little over a mile to a junction atop a shady saddle dominated by red firs. From here a trail leads east, then south, descending 2¾ miles to a junction with the Tenaya Lake and Tuolumne Meadows trail (**Hike 35**). Just 20 yards beyond the crest of

Bald, exfoliating North Dome, from Indian Ridge

our saddle, we reach a second junction, and here a trail forking right descends 1.6 miles down along Lehamite Creek to the North Dome trail (**Hike 70**). We fork left and traverse ⅓ mile to a spur ridge with a large boulder on it, from whose top you can see Sentinel Dome. Past it we contour an equal distance, then drop to a gully before climbing steeply to a junction located only yards short of a second red-fir saddle. Veering left on a trail signed for Indian Rock, we steeply ascend it ¼ mile up brushy slopes to a delicate arch. Just over a foot thick at the thinnest part of its span, this 20-foot arch came into existence when the highly fractured rock beneath it broke away.

After investigating this curious feature, which is quite easily climbed from the west, return to the near-saddle junction, top the saddle, and head south a mile along Indian Ridge. Red firs and western white pines yield to Jeffrey pines; then, about ¼ mile from a trail junction, these pines give way to huckleberry oaks and other shrubs, and you have superb views of nearby North Dome and more distant Half Dome. Just before your descending trail comes to a junction, you'll note a large dike, composed of resistant *aplite*, standing several feet above its adjacent bedrock. At the junction with **Hike 70**, from the west, we turn left and take the ½-mile spur trail out to the bald, rounded summit of North Dome. Be careful on the first part of this trail, for a slip on loose gravel could send you sliding down a dangerously steep slope.

From the North Dome summit area, you can probably see more of Yosemite Valley and its adjacent uplands than can be seen from any other summit except Half Dome. Note that severely glaciated Tenaya Canyon, to the east, is distinctly **V**-shaped in cross section, not **U**-shaped as glaciated canyons are said to be. The enormous 4000-foot-high face of Clouds Rest dominates the canyon's east side, and to the south and west of it stands mighty Half Dome, perhaps Yosemite's best-remembered feature. Continuing our clockwise scan, we next recognize Mt. Starr King, a steep-sided dome above Little Yosemite Valley. West of this unseen valley is joint-controlled Panorama Cliff, which bears the scar of a large rockfall near Panorama Point, close to Illilouette Fall. Extremely popular Glacier Point stands west of the fall's gorge, and above and right of the point, Sentinel Dome bulges up into the sky.

Looking down Yosemite Valley we see Sentinel Rock, with its near-vertical north face, which is due to the unloading of slabs along the rock's near-vertical joint planes. Opposite the rock stand the Three Brothers, also shaped by joint planes, and beyond them protrudes the brow of El Capitan opposite the Cathedral Rocks. Note the broad, gentle surface north of El Capitan, a surface that has changed but little in at least the last 30 million years. But neither has Yosemite Valley changed that much, which was about as deep back then as it is today. However, it has widened by hundreds of feet. Before leaving North Dome, investigate some of its exfoliating slabs—features common to all of Yosemite's domes.

HIKE 34

TIOGA ROAD TO MIRROR MEADOW VIA SNOW CREEK

Distance: 8.2 miles one-way

Grade: 2A, moderate day hike

Trailhead: At a Tioga Road parking area immediately east of a roadcut through a signed glacial moraine, 0.6 mile east of the May Lake turnoff and 3.1 miles west of the Tenaya Lake trailhead parking area. **D4.**

Introduction: Three trails converge in Snow Creek canyon before uniting to descend to Mirror Meadow: one comes from Porcupine Creek and North Dome (Hikes 33 and 70), another from Tenaya Lake (Hike 35), and this one, which is the shortest, from the Tioga Road. Hikers who want to descend from Tuolumne Meadows to Yosemite Valley via May Lake and Mirror Meadow can follow Hike 40 past Glen Aulin to May Lake, then follow Hike 26 in reverse to the May Lake trailhead. Opposite this trailhead a little-used trail descends southwest for 2¼ miles to the Tioga Road, from where you follow this route, Hike 34, down to Mirror Meadow (total length: 25.6 miles).

Description: You can't ask for a better glacial moraine to examine than the one immediately east of our trailhead, where the Tioga Road

A large erratic; clipboard indicates size

TENAYA LAKE TO MIRROR MEADOW VIA SNOW CREEK

Distance: 11.3 miles one way

Grade: 3B, moderate day hike

Trailhead: On the Tioga Road at the Tenaya Lake trailhead parking area, at a highway bend near the lake's southwest shore, located 30½ miles northeast of Crane Flat and 8½ miles southwest of the Tuolumne Meadows Campground. **E4.**

Introduction: When linked with a trail that parallels the Tioga Road (see Hike 50, first paragraph of "Description"), this hike provides the shortest route from Tuolumne Meadows to Yosemite Valley, only 19.8 miles. Though not nearly as scenic as Hike 49, Hike 35 is shorter and considerably easier, making it best for an unacclimated hiker.

Description: From the Tenaya Lake trailhead parking area you may spy a spur trail that heads south through lodgepoles to the edge of a nearby meadow. Along its edge is the main trail, which goes east to the Sunrise Lakes and Sunrise High Sierra Camp, and connects with other trails to Clouds Rest, Happy Isles, Tuolumne Meadows, and other destinations. On this main trail we make a traverse southwest across the sometimes boggy meadow for ½ mile before reaching a junction with a little-used spur trail that goes ¼ mile north to the Tioga Road. Along this meadow traverse we get backward glances at Polly Dome, rising above the dense lodgepoles that ring our meadow. Few wildflowers are seen in this typical Sierran meadow; rather, it is dominated by sedges and dwarf bilberries. The latter aren't obvious until late August, when they turn a blazing crimson color.

cuts through the crest of a lateral moraine. Note its characteristic composition, a gravelly, unsorted matrix containing boulders of all sizes. Were these combined sediments stream-laid, then we should see sorting, or layering, of gravels and boulders. Note that all the boulders are fresh, a characteristic of the most recent, or Tioga, glaciation. If this moraine had been left in the earlier Tahoe glaciation, many of the boulders would be weathered.

With a rating of only 2A you might expect this hike to be an easy one, but it is rated moderate because of its 4000+ foot descent. The trail, a continuation of one from May Lake, starts from the Tioga Road just by the west side of a nearby closed road that goes 250 yards south to a heliport. From this dirt road our trail climbs west to the crest of the lateral moraine, turns south on it, and goes past red firs and western white pines "blazed" with old license plates. After about a ½ mile crest traverse we come to a giant trailside boulder—an *erratic*—which was dropped here by a glacier. The glacier, descending the canyon immediately east of us, must have been at least 700 feet thick, and we can appreciate its power by marveling at the size of this particular erratic, which weighs at least 100 tons. (Elsewhere in the range I've seen an erratic, left by a similar-size glacier, which I estimated at 1100 tons!) Before leaving the boulder you might note unmistakable Cathedral Peak, to the east, and the Echo Peaks, just south of it. After hiking a couple of minutes past the boulder, our route begins a wandering, 2-mile, 1000-foot drop to a junction with a trail from Tenaya Lake. The remaining 5.4 miles (8.6 km) coincide with **Hike 35** and are described in it.

From the spur-trail junction we walk south ¼ mile along the west edge of a meadow; then, after another ¼ mile past lodgepoles, we cross a head-high glacial moraine and momentarily spy a knee-deep pond, lying just 60 yards east. Beyond it our trail begins to climb, and in a small clearing we can look back and see distant Mt. Conness between Polly Dome and Medlicott Dome, each a ridge, not a dome.

Clouds Rest in late afternoon

Beyond this clearing we enter forest, now containing numerous mountain hemlocks, and climb, ultimately by short switchbacks, up to a gap that lies immediately below perhaps the most popular scenic turnout along the Tioga Road. The turnout, Olmsted Point, is 130 yards north of us, and it provides a view northeast toward stirring Tenaya Lake, and a view south toward Clouds Rest and Half Dome. At the turnout Clark's nutcrackers—oversized jays— are often seen begging tourists for handouts. South from our gap a little-used nature trail goes 170 yards to the top of a low, glaciated knoll that offers a better view of Clouds Rest and Half Dome than that obtained from the scenic turnout. Atop this low knoll, partly clothed with scattered lodgepole, western white and Jeffrey pines, are erratic boulders left behind as a glacier retreated up-canyon 14,000 years ago.

The next ½ mile of trail west from the gap is an incredibly winding one, for the trail avoids many bedrock protuberances and one overhanging cliff. Beyond these our erratic-strewn course tops a low crest, then begins to veer away from the nearby Tioga Road as we switchback down into a forested, damp-floored canyon with plenty of corn lilies, arrow-leaved senecios, lupines, and other moisture-loving wildflowers. Our westbound trail crosses two ephemeral creeks, then angles southwest and descends this glaciated canyon—rich in mosquitoes before August— for a mile before climbing 300 feet up to a crest. Erratic boulders atop it testify to the presence

of a past glacier, and the huge, ice-smoothed southeast wall of Tenaya Canyon, opposite us, adds further evidence, Following our trail's painted metal markers—nailed high on conifers for snowbound travelers—we switch-back down into a forested side canyon, tra-versing below two smooth-sloped domes before arriving at a junction with a trail from May Lake (**Hike 34**). Around this junction white firs begin to compete with red firs for space, and Jeffrey pines, with us for some time now, become more numerous.

Switchbacks drop us well into Snow Creek canyon and then we head south for a mile, dropping 500 feet to campsites under white firs along the banks of Snow Creek. While chickarees (Douglas squirrels) live in red firs higher up, down here western gray squirrels are more likely, living in white firs. About 1987, a fire raged through the creek's drainage basin. However, most firs survived even though many trunks were blackened. From the several campsites the trail bridges the reliable creek, starts down-canyon, and in 140 yards comes to a junction with a trail. This trail first follows the west bank of Snow Creek before veering west to meet the Porcupine Creek-North Dome trail (**Hike 33**). From the junction our southbound trail traverses for ⅓ mile through a forest of white firs, Jeffrey pines, and—surprisingly—ponderosa pines before emerging on more-open slopes to begin a nine-dozen switchback descent to the floor of Tenaya Canyon, ½ mile below us. Our first views of course include the massive northwest face of Half Dome plus short-lived views of Watkins Pinnacles, to the east, and the top of Mt. Clark, behind Half Dome.

About a dozen switchbacks down, we enter a gully and encounter a small commu-nity of trees that include—surprisingly again—Douglas-firs, which usually aren't found up at this elevation (6300 feet). Our trail continues down this gully for another 40 switchbacks, many of them obliterated in an April 1987 rockslide, then rebuilt. We then strike across a dry slope that provides ground for whiteleaf manzanitas and seasonally blooming wildflowers such as the brilliantly colored wavy-leaved paintbrush and the equally colorful showy penstemon. Among rocks here is bird's foot fern, specially adapted—unlike most ferns—to this hot, dry environment.

Clouds Rest and Half Dome continue to dominate the views as we switchback down even lower, and we also take note of Tenaya Creek plunging over a long vertical wall. Near the canyon's bottom our trail passes a cliff that has a blocky, fractured aplite dike running along it. Similar dikes are all-important to climbers ascending certain routes on Half Dome and Pywiack Dome. Beneath this cliff our trail enters a forest dominated by canyon live oaks. Also in it are bay trees, easily identified by the aroma given off from the crushed leaves. On the floor of Tenaya Canyon, near the wide, bouldery bed of Tenaya Creek, our trail meets the Tenaya Canyon trail (**Hike 67**), and on it we walk a fairly level 1.1 miles west to our trail's end, beside a former parking area of a now-closed road, just above the west edge of Mirror Meadow (formerly it existed as Mirror Lake—see **Hike 66**). Be aware that there is no trailhead parking here; the closest is a large lot at Camp Curry, about 1½ miles away.

HIKE 36

TENAYA LAKE LOOP

Distance: 3.1 miles loop trip

Grade: 1A, easy 2-hour hike

Trailhead: Same as the Hike 35 trailhead. **E4.**

Introduction: This is an easy hike around Yosemite's most popular glacial lake, scenic Tenaya Lake. Here you'll find sunbathing, fishing, non-motorized boating, and brisk swimming.

Description: A road heads east from the Tenaya Lake trailhead parking area, and walking along it we soon cross the usually flowing outlet of Tenaya Lake. Immediately beyond this crossing a trail forks right, heading to a nearby trail junction (**Hike 47**), but you may want to walk over to the lake's bouldery southwest shore, spend some time there, then walk briefly east along it to relocate your trail. The boulders were left in this vicinity by a Tioga-age glacier that retreated up-canyon about 14,000 years ago. Along with preceding

glaciers, it helped carve the bedrock basin now occupied by the lake. The surrounding landscape has acquired its soils and vegetative cover only since the last glacier left the area. It used to be thought that since that time, incoming sediments had filled in up to ¼ of the lake's original surface area, creating the gently sloping lands just northeast of the lake. However, as one can observe, the rate of sediment influx is very minor and so the lake's size has diminished very little in the last 14,000 years. Not only has its area not decreased substantially, neither has its depth; there are less than 10 feet of sediments on its floor.

If you plan to go swimming in chilly Tenaya Lake, do so at the bouldery southwest shore. The sandy beach of the northeast shore is lacking here, but so too are the strong up-canyon winds that were needed to form it. Besides, here you'll find a few small boulder islands worth swimming or wading to—something lacking near the northeast shore.

From the lake's southeast corner head a few yards upslope to a trail and walk northeast one mile on it to the sandy beach at the north shore. On this stretch of trail you may see some protruding tree stumps. There is a myth that during a lengthy, past drought this lake dried up, and a forest grew on its floor, then, centuries later, when the rains returned, the forest was submerged beneath the lake's water. Actually, rockfalls carry trees into this 180-foot-deep lake, and their heavier ends can become lodged in the lake's sediments. You don't see stumps at other lakes because they lack one or more of the three necessary ingredients: steep cliffs, forested slopes, and deep water.

Also on this stretch of trail you'll have, as at the south shore, great views of massive Polly Dome and small Pywiack Dome, and you'll also have several opportunities to descend to Tenaya Lake's little-used east shore. Climbers have divided what is commonly called Polly Dome into four domes, from south to north: Stately Pleasure, Harlequin, Mountaineer's and Polly domes. None of these four is a true dome, and only from certain angles do any appear dome-like. Skirting the bases of these domes is the rather new Tioga Road, which was opened to the public in June 1961.

If you were to continue north on the trail rather than cut across the beach toward Stately

Mammoth Polly Dome, seen from Tenaya Lake's outlet, looms over the lake and dwarfs Pywiack Dome, just right of it. From near the lake's north shore, Pywiack Dome (below) seems quite large.

Pleasure Dome, you would reach a junction with the John Muir Trail (**Hike 50**) in about 6.9 miles. This stretch of generally viewless, lodgepole-shaded trail is little used, but when it is combined with **Hike 35**, it provides the shortest route from Tuolumne Meadows to Yosemite Valley, only 19.8 miles. The Mirror Meadow-Tenaya Lake trail section approximates the route taken by Captain Bowling and his 35 men in search of Chief Teneiya's band. In early June 1852 they surprised this band at Py-wi-ack—"Lake of the Glistening (glacier-polished) Rocks." This lake was named by Lafayette Bunnell in memory of the old chief, and before departing for an Indian reservation, both Indians and troops spent the night in what is now the west side of today's trailhead parking area.

Whereas the south shore is best for swimming, the north shore, with its broad, sandy beach, is best for sunbathing. On a hot summer afternoon it is crowded with people, and the parking lot, picnic tables, and restrooms just north of it can be full. Leaving the beach we walk southwest along the Tioga Road, which cuts across the base of glacier-polished Stately Pleasure Dome. On this dome you're likely to see climbers inching upward hundreds of feet above you. The highway curves west to Murphy Creek, which has a trail ascending beside it (**Hike 37**). Then we continue southwest, passing a day-use picnic sites before reaching the spot where we began.

Chapter 8

Trails of the
Tuolumne Meadows Area,
north of the Tioga Road

Introduction: Although this section generally describes trails lying north and west of Tuolumne Meadows, it also describes two that extend beyond this regional area. Hike 40, the High Sierra Camps Loop trail, wanders more than half of its length in the country south of the Tioga Road, and Hike 42, the northbound Pacific Crest Trail, goes through the Park and then winds over to Sonora Pass. Hike 42, at 72 miles, is the longest one described in this guide; Hike 38, at about ½ mile, is the shortest. Between these two extremes you'll find a hiking length ideal for you as you explore this subalpine wonderland. This section's highlights are too numerous to mention. Of all its hikes, only Hike 37 would not receive a spectacular rating. Ragged peaks, crystal-clear lakes, glaciated domes, long canyons and roaring cascades await the High Sierra hiker here.

Supplies and Services: Information, guide books, natural-history books and topographic maps are available at the Tuolumne Meadows Information Center, which is 7½ miles northeast up the Tioga Road from the Tenaya Lake trailhead-parking area and an even 8 miles southwest down the road from Tioga Pass. Just under one mile east of the center are useful facilities, which west-to-east are: a dump station for RVs, a service station, a mountaineering school and sports shop, and a store, cafe, and post office. Just beyond the last of these is the Tuolumne Meadows Campground entrance, and just beyond it is a bridge across the Tuolumne River. Immediately past it is a road branching left (west) to the Tuolumne Meadows Stable, which offers horseback rides ranging from several hours to several days.

Those wanting to stay in the Tuolumne Meadows area in a rustic style should stay at Tuolumne Meadows Lodge. To reach it, drive 0.6 mile northeast on the Tioga Road from the campground entrance, then turn right on the lodge's spur road and follow it to its end. Accommodations at the lodge consist of canvas tents on wooden platforms. Breakfast and dinner are served here, and you can get them without being a guest. On weekends, however, reserve your spot at the dinner table early in the day. Showers are also available; inquire at the office.

Just 2 miles outside the park, you'll find the Tioga Pass Resort, with some supplies, meals and lodging—an alternative to the crowded Tuolumne Meadows area.

This resort is usually open to travelers from late May until mid-October. Most of the Tuolumne Meadows facilities are open for a shorter duration, usually from mid-June until mid-September. The Tuolumne Meadows Campground and the Information Center stay open a few weeks longer. All-year services are available in Lee Vining, just north of the Tioga Road's (Highway 120's) junction with Highway 395. This town is about 19½ miles from the Tuolumne Meadows Campground.

Wilderness Permits: If you want to reserve a permit in advance, rather than get one in person, see the "Wilderness permits" section on page 59. In person, get your permit at a booth in the parking lot a short way down the Tuolumne Meadows Lodge spur road. From late June through the Labor Day weekend this booth is open on Friday nights, and it opens as early as 6 a.m. on Saturdays. After the Labor Day weekend, get your permits at the Information Center.

Campgrounds: For Hike 37, camp at Porcupine Flat Campground (see Hike 33 trailhead directions), west of Tenaya Lake. This campground is also ideal for Chapter 9's Hikes 47-49. For the remaining hikes, camp at large Tuolumne Meadows Campground, whose entrance is just southwest of the Tuolumne River bridge. You may also want to try equally full Tioga Lake and Junction campgrounds, just outside the Park below Tioga Pass.

HIKE 37

POLLY DOME LAKES VIA MURPHY CREEK

Distance: 6.2 miles round trip to the largest lake

Grade: 2B, easy day hike

Trailhead: Across from a picnic area midway along Tenaya Lake. Driving northeast on the Tioga Road you come to this trailhead just 0.6 mile northeast of the lake's walk-in campground. E4.

Introduction: This hike is for those who want to visit a readily accessible lake that isn't being visited by everyone else. A small amount of cross-country hiking is required, but you don't have to be an expert to do it. As long as you don't cross over any divide, you really can't get lost, for if you can't find the Polly Dome Lakes, you can always head back down-

Mt. Hoffmann, right, pokes above lodgepoles encircling the largest of the Polly Dome Lakes

canyon—toward Tenaya Lake—and find your trail again.

Description: Our trail, along seasonally flowing Murphy Creek, climbs 3 miles north to a junction with the High Sierra Camps Loop Trail (**Hike 40**). We begin our uneventful trail by passing a trail branching west across adjacent Murphy Creek early on our hike. This trail descends south to a main trailhead parking area near the southwest corner of Tenaya Lake.

Midway along your hike is ample evidence of glacier action: glacier-transported boulders and glacier-polished bedrock slabs. Across these slabs the trail can disappear, so watch for ducks (man-made stone piles). Near the divide at the head of Murphy Creek you'll reach a trailside pond, on your right. Leave the trail here and progress cross-country ½ mile southeast to the north shore of the largest of the Polly Dome Lakes. Any cross-country route you might take will tend to get a little damp and/or brushy, but the distance is short and the lake is almost impossible to miss, particularly since it lies at the base of Polly Dome. The best campsites are along the west shore of this warm, shallow, boulder-dotted lake. The small lakes northeast of it aren't worth your effort unless you happen to like mosquitoes.

HIKE 38

POTHOLE DOME AND THE TUOLUMNE RIVER

Distance: Approximately 1 mile round trip.

Grade: 1A, easy one-hour hike

Trailhead: Turnout at west end of Tuolumne Meadows, 1½ miles west from the Tuolumne Meadows Information Center **E3**.

Introduction: Pothole Dome is Yosemite's most accessible dome, and its upper slopes provide outstanding views of Tuolumne Meadows and the surrounding peaks and domes. You may see many vehicles parked at the trailhead, but not all visitors climb the dome. Many instead take a use trail to granite slabs along a very scenic stretch of the Tuolumne River.

Description: More people climb this dome than any other in the Park except perhaps Lembert Dome (**Hike 45**), Sentinel Dome (**Hike 74**), or Half Dome (**Hike 80**). From the trailhead, take a trail that starts northwest along an often boggy meadow, then from its tip, heads east along the base of the dome, and you can climb up to its summit wherever you feel it is safe. After 0.3 mile from the start, your

From Pothole Dome: Clouds build over Tuolumne Meadows and the Sierra crest

Author in large pothole on Pothole Dome   Ken Ng

trail curves from east to northeast, and the ascent from this spot is only a walk-up.

Like other glaciated Yosemite domes, Pothole Dome has gentle up-canyon slopes and steep down-canyon slopes, as do most *unglaciated* domes of the Sierra Nevada. Glaciers did not transform any of them from symmetrical to asymmetrical. Glacial evidence includes slopes of highly polished bedrock plus anomalous boulders—*erratics*—resting on them, which could have reached their present locations only by glacier transport. Pothole Dome differs from other domes in the great number of potholes it has, particularly on its south slopes. Potholes are usually found in streams, where boulders swirl around in a bedrock depression and gradually drill out a hole. Obviously, streams did not flow up over Pothole Dome, but glaciers did. Richard Balogh, studying these potholes in 1975, concluded that the potholes were formed by flowing watercourses trapped beneath a glacier, and these courses did flow uphill over the dome.

Another interesting geologic feature is the presence of large, blocky crystals of potassium feldspar that are so characteristic of this hiking section's landscape. About 85 million years ago these crystals solidified just before the molten matrix surrounding them solidified. The resulting large-scale granite body that formed is known as the Cathedral Peak pluton, and it covers much of the Yosemite landscape in Sections 4 and 5.

To reach the Tuolumne River, stay on the trail beyond its curve northeast, traversing along the dome's base. In 0.4 mile the trail heads northwest, and in ¼ mile crosses a very minor divide. Ahead, this use trail may be ill-defined, so if you can't follow it, curve north

over to the often-audible river. This stretch has pools and rapids, and when the water is low, the pools may be safe for swimming. The water is never warm, but summer days often are, and allow you to warm up on glacier-smoothed slabs after a brisk swim.

HIKE 39

TUOLUMNE MEADOWS TO GLEN AULIN

Distance: 11.4 miles round trip

Grade: 3C, easy 2-day hike

Trailhead: At the base of Lembert Dome, at the east end of Tuolumne Meadows, leave the Tioga Road and drive ⅓ mile west on a dirt road to a gate that bars it. If no space is available here, park at the base of Lembert Dome. Mileage is measured from the start of the closed road. **F3.**

Introduction: Scenically, this popular hike is noted for the many beautiful cascades it passes. Because the hike is virtually all down hill, it is ideal for hikers unaccustomed to high elevations. Spending a night at Glen Aulin gets you partly acclimated, preparing you for the hike back up to your trailhead. This trail comprises the easiest section of the High Sierra Camps loop trail (**Hike 40**). It is also a section of the Pacific Crest and Tahoe-Yosemite trails.

Description: From the locked gate we continue west along the lodgepole-dotted flank of Tuolumne Meadows, with fine views south across them toward Unicorn Peak, Cathedral Peak, and some of the knobby Echo Peaks. Approaching a boulder-rimmed old parking loop, we veer right and climb slightly past the old Soda Springs Campground, which once surrounded the still-bubbling natural soda springs. A nature trail goes to them and then on to the conspicuous Parsons Memorial Lodge. From this general area, the signed main trail on gravelly underfooting undulates through a forest of sparse, small lodgepole pines, and in just under one mile descends to a boulder ford or log crossing of Delaney Creek. Just before it, a stock trail from the stables back in the meadows comes in on the right. Immediately beyond the creek we hop a branch of Delaney Creek; in ⅙ mile, hop another, and in ⅙ mile more, pass the Young Lakes trail (**Hike 44**).

At this junction your route goes left, and after more winding through scattered lodgepoles, it descends some bare granite slabs and enters a flat-floored forest. A mile's pleasant walking since the last junction brings one to the bank of the Tuolumne River, just before three branches of Dingley Creek, near the west end of the huge meadows. From here, the nearly level trail often runs along the river, and in these stretches by the stream, there are numerous glacier-smoothed granite slabs on which to take a break—or dip, if the river's current is slow.

After a mile-long winding traverse, the trail leaves the last slabs to climb briefly up a granite outcrop to get around the river's gorge. You can leave the trail and walk toward a brink, from where you'll see, on the south side of the gorge below you, Little Devils Postpile. This is a 9.4-million-year-old lava remnant that has been interpreted by the US Geological Survey as a conduit of a former volcano. Not so. Conduits have nearly vertical columnar lava, but as you can see, the columns beside the river are nearly horizontal, indicating that they formed on the surface in contact with adjacent granitic bedrock. Despite repeated attacks by likely dozens of glaciers, this basalt flow remains, standing as mute testimony to the impotence of glaciers' ability to erode.

Back on the trail you wind down eventually toward a sturdy bridge over the river, and from the far bank one can hike upriver to Little Devils Postpile. Immediately beyond the bridge you can look north up long Cold Canyon to Matterhorn Peak and Whorl Mountain, and, to their right, Mt. Conness. As the river soon approaches nearby Tuolumne Falls, it flows down a series of sparkling rapids separated by large pools and wide sheets of water spread out across slightly inclined granite slopes. Beyond this beautiful stretch of river the trail descends, steeply at times, past Tuolumne Falls and White Cascade to a junction with the trail to May Lake (**Hike 40**). From here it is only a few minutes' walk to Glen Aulin Camp, reached by crossing the river on a bridge below roaring White Cascade. During high runoff, you may have to wade just to

White Cascade plunges into a churning pool

reach this bridge! From the camp is a short trail to sites in the heavily used Glen Aulin backpackers' camp, complete with a "bearproof goalpost" from which to suspend your food bags. Only 15 yards beyond the spur trail across Conness Creek to Glen Aulin High Sierra Camp is the Tuolumne Canyon trail, going left, and ⅓ mile down it are less-used campsites. **Hike 41** continues westward.

HIKE 40

HIGH SIERRA CAMPS LOOP

Distance: 50.4 miles loop trip

Grade: 7F, moderate 6-day hike

Trailhead: Several possibilities. I recommend the large parking lot just beyond the start of the Tuolumne Meadows Lodge spur road. This road is reached by driving 0.6 mile northeast from the Tuolumne Meadows Campground entrance. During most of the summer this large lot, immediately west of the spur road, has a small booth that dispenses wilderness permits. **F3.**

Introduction: Along this loop are six High Sierra Camps, each spaced a convenient day's hike from the next. Many visitors make this loop on horseback. Others hike the trail carrying little more than a day pack, for by making advanced reservations—do this in the fall (see page 3)—they can get all their meals and sleep at the camps.This hike became very popular years ago, and a quota to limit the number of hikers using it is often filled. Therefore, if you plan to hike it, make reservations well in advance or do it out of season, such as after the Labor Day weekend. However, if you are hiking it then, don't expect to find the High Sierra Camps open, and do plan for the possibility of sudden snow storms and know what to do if you're caught in one. You could hike this loop trail either clockwise or counterclockwise from either the Tuolumne Meadows or the Tenaya Lake environs. I prefer counterclockwise from the former, since this way on your first day, when your pack is heaviest and you are perhaps are not in the best of shape, your route is mostly level and downhill.

Description: From your parking lot, take a trail which heads west to the Tioga Road and its westside Lembert Dome parking lot. Now follow **Hike 39** west 6 miles down the Tuolumne River to the backpackers' camp at Glen Aulin, the place most hikers spend their first night.

The second day's hike will be from the Glen Aulin High Sierra Camp to the May Lake High Sierra Camp, about 8½ miles. From the junction immediately south of and above Glen Aulin's bridge across the Tuolumne River, you briefly curve northwest through a notch and then your duff trail ascends gently southwest, soon crossing and recrossing McGee Lake's *northeast*-flowing outlet, which dries up by late summer. Where the trail levels off, McGee

Mt. Conness reflected in McGee Lake

Lake, long and narrow and bordered on the southwest by a granite cliff, comes into view through the lodgepole trees. The dead snags along the shallow margin, and the fallen limbs and downed trees make fishing difficult, and in late summer the lake may dwindle to a stale pond. Adept campers can find isolated, level spots, some with views, on slopes north of the lake, beneath the east end of Falls Ridge.

Beyond the lake your trail descends along its *southwest*-flowing outlet for ¾ mile, and then you cross it. Soon you have a view northwest through the shallow Cathedral Creek canyon to hulking Falls Ridge, which Cathedral Creek has to detour around in order to join the Tuolumne River. After several minutes we reach 20-foot-wide Cathedral Creek, which can be a ford in early season, a boulder-hop later on. Starting a moderate ascent beyond the creek, we soon reach a stand of tall, healthy red firs, and the contrast with the small, over-crowded lodgepole pines earlier on the trail is inescapable.

Higher on the trail, there are good views, and after 3 miles of walking through moderate and dense forest, the panorama seems especially welcome. In the distant northeast stand Sheep Peak, North Peak, and Mt. Conness, encircling the basin of Roosevelt Lake. In the near north, Falls Ridge is a mountain of pinkish granite that contrasts with the white and gray granite of the other peaks. When we look back toward McGee Lake, the route appears to be entirely carpeted with lodgepole pines.

The trail continues up a moderate slope on gravel and granite shelves, through a forest cover of hemlock, red fir, and lodgepole. After arriving at a branch of Cathedral Creek, you cross it, then more or less parallel it for almost a mile to a junction shaded under some tall hemlocks. A trail departs from this junction to go down Murphy Creek to Tenaya Lake (**Hike 37**). Down this trail, a short ½ mile before the lake, a lateral trail departs southwest, parallels the Tioga Road, and ends at a bend in the highway by a trailhead parking area. We'll reach this spot by a longer route.

A half mile from the hemlock-shaded junction, you pass a trail (**Hike 28**) to Ten Lakes that climbs slopes beneath the very steep east face of Tuolumne Peak. Here you branch left and ascend briefly to a long, narrow, shallow, forested saddle beyond which large Tenaya Lake is visible in the south. After

Polly Dome and Tenaya Peak cradle Tenaya Lake

traversing somewhat open slopes of sagebrush, huckleberry oak, and lupine, you reach a spring, then momentarily come to a series of switchbacks. Progress up the long, gentle gradient of these zigzags is distinguished by the striking views of Mt. Conness, Mt. Dana, and the other giants on the Sierra crest/Yosemite border. The trail then passes through a little saddle just north of a glacier-smoothed peak, and ahead, suddenly, is another Yosemite landmark, Clouds Rest, rising grandly in the south: one sees a part of this largest expanse of bare granite in the Park.

Now the trail descends gradually over fairly open granite to a forested flat and bends west above the north shore of Raisin Lake, which is one of the warmest "swimming holes" in this section. It also has campsites, including waterless, isolated ones with views, located about ¼ mile south of the lake. From the lake's vicinity, the trail continues beside a flower-lined runoff stream bed under a sparse forest cover of mountain hemlock and western white and lodgepole pines, and then swings west to cross three unnamed, seasonal streams.

Finally the trail makes a ½-mile-long ascent steeply up to May Lake across a slope sparsely dotted with red firs, western white pines, and other conifers. Views improve constantly, and presently you have a panorama of the peaks on the Sierra crest from North Peak south to Mt. Gibbs. The Tioga Pass notch is clearly visible. At the top of this climb is a gentle upland where several small meadows are strung along the trail, with corn lilies growing at an almost perceptible rate in early season, while aromatic lupine commands one's attention later on. In the west, Mt. Hoffman dominates. Now you swing south at the northeast corner of May Lake and parallel its east shore

to the High Sierra Camp, where you meet the trail of **Hike 26**.

From the lake you follow **Hike 26**, described in the opposite direction, south to the May Lake trailhead. From here you follow the road northeast for two minutes to where it is blocked off, then descend the closed stretch of road southeast to a fairly large trailhead parking area near the southwest corner of Tenaya Lake. During the summer season, shuttle buses ply the road between here and Tuolumne Meadows, offering you a free ride back to your trailhead, should you want or need to cut your trip short.

Now follow **Hike 47** up to Sunrise High Sierra Camp, where you spend your third night. This leg of the loop is about 9 miles long. Leaving the camp, tread the John Muir Trail a short mile, first east and then north to the Echo Creek trail, described in **Hike 52**. Take this lateral trail 6½ miles down Echo Creek to a trail junction, from which you descend ¾ mile to the Merced Lake trail, in Echo Valley. Now you first pass through a formerly burned, boggy area, then climb east past pools to the Merced River's largely unseen but enjoyable pools to Merced Lake's west shore. Don't camp here, but rather continue past the north shore to Merced Lake High Sierra Camp and the adjacent riverside campground, a little less than 10 miles from Sunrise High Sierra Camp. The bear population here is high, but there are bearproof boxes in which you can store your food.

Begin day five by hiking a level mile east to the Merced Lake Ranger Station and an adjacent trail junction. From it you struggle 1½ miles in a 1000-foot climb northeast up to another trail junction, from where you follow the second half of **Hike 56** back to your trailhead. If at the end of day five you plan to camp at or near Vogelsang High Sierra Camp rather than near Boothe Lake, turn right at the scissors junction near Emeric Lake and hike 2⅓ miles northeast up to the camp. Emeric Lake also makes a good last night's stay.

TUOLUMNE MEADOWS TO PATE VALLEY VIA WATERWHEEL FALLS

Distance: 40.4 miles round trip

Grade: 6F, moderate 4-day hike

Trailhead: Same as the Hike 39 trailhead. **F3.**

Introduction: Rather than take Hike 22 to Pate Valley, you can take this route, which is longer but more spectacular. On it a lot of hikers go no farther than Waterwheel Falls, which at 3½ trail miles from Glen Aulin is the westernmost of the Tuolumne River's five major cascades. Go before mid-July to see the "waterwheels" at their best. Horseback riders should check with rangers if they intend to travel beyond Waterwheel Falls; there may be an early-season high-water problem.

Description: Follow **Hike 39** to Glen Aulin, which is the usual first-night's camp even though it is only ⅓ the distance to Pate Valley. From Glen Aulin High Sierra Camp, you see the White Cascade, which tumultuously splashes into a swirling pool. The camp's sandy beach bordering the pool is periodically built up with fresh sand and gravel at times of very high runoff. Just 15 yards past the entrance to the camp, your lateral trail leaves the northbound Cold Canyon trail (**Hike 42**) and climbs over a low knoll that sports rust-stained metamorphic rocks. From it is an excellent view west down the flat-floored, steep-walled canyon. It looks like a glaciated canyon should look: U-shaped in cross section. However, the flat, broad Tuolumne Meadows vicinity upstream and the V-shaped Grand Canyon of the Tuolumne River downstream were also glaciated and are certainly not U-shaped. In Yosemite it is the joint (fracture) pattern of the resistant granitic bedrock that

determines a canyon's shape, not the process of glaciation, which in weaker rocks determines the shape.

Leaving the low knoll, we switchback quickly down into Glen Aulin proper. Paralleling the Tuolumne River through a lodgepole-pine forest, we soon reach a backpackers' camp that has a cable on which you can hang your food. Between here and Waterwheel Falls are several dwarfish, generally cryptic near-trail camps. Also, between here and Pate Valley is abundant evidence of a former, major fire. We tread the gravelly flat floor of the glen for more than a mile, and then, on bedrock, quickly arrive at the brink of cascading California Falls, perched at the base of a towering cliff. Keep your distance from these falls and from any part of the falls you'll see downstream. Even the lower part of a cascade is dangerous, and just because the adjacent bedrock is dry, that doesn't mean it is safe—the bedrock is polished to a very high degree.

Switchbacking down beside the cascade, you leave behind the glen's thick forest of predominantly lodgepole pines with associated red firs and descend past scattered Jeffrey pines and junipers and through lots of brush. At the base of the cascade, lodgepoles, western white pines, and red firs return once more as you make a gentle descent north. Near the end of this short stretch you parallel a long pool, which is a good spot to break for lunch or perhaps take a swim. However, stay away from the pool's outlet, where the Tuolumne River plunges over a brink.

The trail parallels this second cascade as it generally descends through brush and open forest. On this descent, notice that red firs have yielded to white firs. Sugar pines also put in their first appearance as you reach the brink of broad Le Conte Falls, which cascades down fairly open granite slabs. On a flat-floored section of canyon, incense-cedar joins the ranks of white fir, Jeffrey pine and sugar pine, with few if any, lodgepoles to be found. In this forest we reach our fifth and final cascade, extensive Waterwheel Falls. This cascade gets its name from the curving sprays of water tossed into the air, which occur when the river is flowing with sufficient force. It is worth the trip in early season to see the white water turning to rainbow as it sprays the canyon full of light and color. The cascade's classic views are not

Waterwheel Falls reaches its full glory in early summer

National Park Service

from its brink but rather from near its base, about 300 feet lower.

Starting on a trail segment recommended by John Muir and completed in 1925, you follow switchbacks down to the cascade's base, then continue to descend past a smaller set of cascades, beyond which you reach a small campsite beside a Tuolumne River pool. About 200 yards past it a larger campsite is reached, this one located by the east bank of Return Creek. On the map Return Creek up Virginia Canyon looks like a good cross-country tour, but in reality it is overgrown with huckleberry oak and other shrubs, making an ascent up it a sweaty, dusty experience.

Just past Return Creek you'll note a swimming hole between two low cascades—one of many possible swimming holes you'll see before reaching Pate Valley. Unfortunately, these pools are best in August, but if you go then, the river's flow has diminished sufficiently to make Waterwheel Falls just an ordinary cascade. Upon descending to lower elevations—now characterized largely by incense-cedars, black oaks, and canyon live oaks—hikers may face pesky hordes of flies. Continuing down-canyon, you pass a massive south-wall cliff before coming to a fair campsite, and then in ½ mile cross a low ridge. During most of the summer the afternoon temperatures at our now-lower elevations are distinctly warm, if not hot, but most of the route

is shaded and the Tuolumne River is usually close by for dipping. At these elevations ground squirrels and other rodents abound, so rattlesnakes are likely too. At first the route is along a shady, flat-floored valley into which only a minimal amount of talus has fallen in about the last 15,000 years, the time when the last glacier—about 4,000 feet thick at its maximum—retreated up this canyon. After a mile, you begin a curve north around the base of a half-mile-high buttress of Colby Mountain, standing on the west rim of the Ten Lakes Basin. Experienced climbers have successfully descended from that basin to our trail, but others have been less fortunate.

Beyond this buttress the Tuolumne River trail begins a climb up and around the Muir Gorge. Under shade it climbs 400 feet to a viewless subsidiary ridge, arcs counterclockwise across fairly open slabs to a larger ridge, and then encounters a low, joint-controlled trough, which obstructs views, although immediately east, west and south of it are excellent ones. You can now look south straight up the glaciated, plunging Ten Lakes canyon. Your struggle down-canyon is not yet over, for after you descend two dozen switchbacks—a 500-foot drop—you climb again. This, however, is short-lived, and you very quickly pass through a notch, which has been cleft straight as an arrow. It, like so many other geomorphic features, lies along a straight frac-

A glacier-polished wall, east of Muir Gorge

ture in the granitic bedrock. Now you switchback down to a bridge over Register Creek, near its 60-foot plunge into a walled-in pool, and immediately bridge smaller Rodgers Canyon creek. Both may be dry after Labor Day. Just beyond them you can peer through the canyon live oaks and black oaks and look straight "down the throat" of linear Muir Gorge—a product of the Tuolumne River's cutting down along a major fracture. John Muir was probably the first white man to descend the gorge, and in 1931 two Sierra Club parties became the first successful groups to duplicate this feat. Even in times of low water, this hike/swim feat can be dangerous, and yet each year hikers attempt it—at great peril to their lives.

After a few descending switchbacks the trail leaves the mouth of the Muir Gorge behind and traverses a very level mile before presenting one with views of an incredible section of the canyon's north wall. Above you towers a giant wall, with fresh polish and striations, which is dark gray and pale orange, it presents an opportunity for good early-morning color photography. The gray color is not the color of the bedrock, but rather of the lichens growing on it.

Continuing your descent west down the Grand Canyon of the Tuolumne River, you might see wild grapes growing along the trail. The river is forced south by a "mountain"—a

large, glacier-defying bedrock mass within the canyon—and across its lower slopes your trail parallels the river to shadier, easier terrain. The last mile of trail to the Pate Valley junction is nearly flat, and along it you'll see burned snags and flood-strewn logs. From the Pate Valley junction, head for riverside campsites, about 100-200 yards west, or continue beyond the two Tuolumne River bridges to even more campsites.

HIKE 42

TUOLUMNE MEADOWS TO SONORA PASS VIA PACIFIC CREST TRAIL

Distance: 77.2 miles one way

Grade: 7G, strenuous 7-day hike

Trailhead: Same as the Hike 39 trailhead. **F3.**

Introduction: Deep, spectacular glaciated canyons, crossed one after another, characterize this hike. The backpacker here sometimes feels he or she is doing more vertical climbing than horizontal walking. Nearing the north end of this hike, you leave the expansive granitic domain behind and enter Vulcan's realm—thick floods of volcanic flows and sediments that buried most of the northern Sierra Nevada. By hiking these 77 miles you will have completed almost 3% of the entire Pacific Crest Trail, which extends from the Mexican border north. The popularity of this hike is attested to by bears, who have become attracted to most of the good Yosemite campsites along this trail.

Description: Follow **Hike 39** to Glen Aulin, a good place to spend the night if you're taking seven or more days to do this hike. Leaving Glen Aulin, your trail—the Pacific Crest Trail, or PCT—climbs north, sometimes along Cold Canyon creek, 3 miles to a forested gap, then descends ½ mile to the south edge of a large, usually soggy meadow. Midway across it you'll notice a huge boulder, just west. Its overhanging sides have been used as an emergency shelter, but in a lightning storm it is a prime-strike target. Beyond it your route continues north, first for a mile through meadow, then on a gradual ascent through forest to a crest junction with the McCabe Lakes trail. A long-half-mile walk northeast up it would get you to a small campsite just above McCabe Creek; an hour's walk up it would get you to larger, better campsites at scenic Lower McCabe Lake. If you took **Hike 7's** mountaineering route to the McCabe Lakes and you are caught in a snow storm, exit via this route, *not* by the route you came in on, for the Secret Lake pass is far too treacherous when snowbound. If you're trying to do this hike in six days, your first night's goal should be campsites along Return Creek or lower McCabe Creek, both down in Virginia Canyon—a *long* 14 miles from the trailhead if you're carrying a heavy pack. You switchback down to this canyon's floor, cross McCabe Creek—a wet ford before July—and look for nearby campsites or advance briefly to a junction with a spur trail heading briefly up-canyon past additional campsites.

The next morning, ford powerful Return Creek, which usually is a wet ford and in early season can be a dangerous one, especially in the afternoon, when snow is melting rapidly. At times of high water, look up to ½ mile up-canyon for slower-flowing water rather than attempting to cross here. Don't rope up, since hikers have been known to drown before they could untie their rope after they slipped. On the west bank you walk but a few steps southwest before your trail veers right and meets the Virginia Canyon trail (**Hike 6**). On the PCT you start down-canyon, climb west up into Spiller Creek canyon, and then, halfway to a pass, cross the canyon's high-volume creek. A favorite route among mountaineers is to hike from Twin Lakes up Horse Creek canyon to the Park's boundary—a *de facto* trail most of the way—then descend Spiller Creek canyon to this PCT crossing.

Beyond Spiller Creek we soon start up two dozen switchbacks that transport us 2 miles up to a forested pass, which offers fair camps when there is enough snow to provide water. But even up here, bears roam the land. Most hikers continue 1½ miles southwest down to shallow Miller Lake, with good campsites along its forested west shore. From the lake you parallel a meadow north up to a low gap, then execute over two dozen often steep switchbacks down to a canyon floor and a

Sunrise over Lower McCabe Lake

junction with the northbound Matterhorn Canyon trail. **Hike 4** goes north up-canyon, but the PCT descends southwest, reaching this majestic canyon's broad creek in 80 yards. Immediately beyond the often-wet ford lies a large, lodgepole-shaded campsite with ample space to stretch out and dry your feet.

Heading down-canyon for a mile, you pass less obvious and more secluded campsites, then soon leave the glaciated canyon to begin the usual two dozen, short steep switchbacks—this time west up into Wilson Creek canyon, a typical glaciated side canyon that hangs above the main canyon, but not—as is widely believed—because its smaller glacier couldn't erode the landscape as rapidly as the trunk-canyon glacier could. River drainages in the Sierra Nevada have numerous *unglaciated*, hanging, tributary canyons.

We twice ford switchbacking climb up to windy, gravelly Benson Pass, registering a breath-taking height of 10,140 feet. As the passes have become deeper, so too have the canyons become deeper, and our multistage descent to and then ascent up from Benson Lake is exhausting. We begin uneventfully with an easy descent to a large meadow, reaching its peaceful creeklet just before a dropoff. Veering away from the creeklet, we soon begin a switchbacking descent that in 2 miles ends at a south-shore peninsula on Smedberg Lake. Most of the campsites, however, lie along the lake's west and north shores.

From the lake's south-shore peninsula—below the steep-walled sentinel, Volunteer Peak—you continue west, passing a spur trail to the west-shore campsites before winding southwest up a slab-rock trail to a close-by gap. From it the trail switchbacks down joint-controlled granite slabs, only to climb south high up to a meadowy junction with a trail to Rodgers Lake. **Hike 43**, which has coincided with the PCT to this junction now leaves your route, departing in that direction and eventually descending to Pate Valley before climbing east back up to the Tuolumne Meadows trailhead.

At this junction **Hike 14** joins the PCT as it starts southwest, crosses a low moraine and briefly descends northwest to a junction with a trail climbing southwest to a broad saddle that harbors shallow, mosquito-haunted Murdock Lake, and then down Rodgers Canyon. The next step down to Benson Lake is a typical two-dozen-short-switchbacks descent to a ford of Smedberg Lake's outlet creek. The PCT from that lake to here will be virtually impossible to follow in the snowbound early season. Hikers then will want to make a steep cross-country descent west down to this spot on an almost level canyon floor.

Now on the creek's north bank, you pass a small pond before commencing a steady, moderate creekside descent to a second ford—a slight problem in early season. Back on the south bank, you make a winding, switchbacking descent over metamorphic rock down to the last, sometimes tricky ford of the creek. The next ⅓ mile of trail climbs up to a brushy saddle just east of a conspicuous knoll, then descends into a shady forest of giant firs before crossing wide Piute Creek. To keep your feet dry, look for one or more large, fallen logs. No sane person makes this long descent from Benson Pass without visiting the "Benson Rivera"—the long, sandy beach along the north shore of Benson Lake. The spur trail to it winds southwest along the shady, often damp forest floor a short ½ mile to a section of beach near Piute Creek's inlet. *Remember this spot,* for otherwise this route back can be hard to locate. Many campsites just within the forest's edge testify to the popularity of this broad, sandy beach. And if you've brought in a portable folding boat or raft, you'll probably have the whole lake to yourself. Swimming in this large, deep lake is brisk at best, but sunning on the beach can be superb—in late summer, after the water line drops. However, strong, up-canyon afternoon winds can quell both activities. Anglers can anticipate a meal of rainbow or brook trout.

After your stay, return to the PCT and prepare for a grueling climb north to Seavey Pass. At first brushy, the ascent northwest provides views of pointed Volunteer Peak and closer, two-crowned Peak 10060. You cross a

Evening calm comes to Smedberg Lake

Bond Pass, Dorothy Lake Pass, and Forsyth Peak, from Grace Meadow

creek, continue switchbacking northwest along the base of spectacular Peak 10368, then climb north briefly, only to be confronted with a steep 400-foot climb east. On it you are eventually funneled through a narrow, steep-walled, minor gap which rewards your climbing efforts with the sight of a relatively wind-free, sparkling pond. Just past its outlet you'll find a trailside rock from which you can dive into its reasonably warm waters. The PCT parallels the pond's shore, curves east around a miniscule pond, then climbs northeast through wet meadows before switchbacking up to a second gap. At its north base lies a shallow, rockbound pond, immediately beyond which is a third gap, Seavey Pass. A small meadow separates it from a fourth gap, beyond which you reach a more noteworthy—and the highest—gap. Now you bend northwest, travel past the head of a linear lake to a sixth gap, and switchback quickly down into a southwest-trending trough, spying a shallow pond 200 yards off in that direction. Turn right and immediately top your last gap, from which you descend northeast ¼ mile to a junction in Kerrick Canyon. **Hike 4,** descending south to this junction, follows the PCT east to Matterhorn Canyon before turning to climb back north.

A cursory glance at the map suggests that it is an easy 3-mile down-canyon walk to the Bear Valley trail junction, but closer scrutiny reveals a longer, winding, too-often-ascending route. A short northward jog of your Kerrick

Canyon trail segment ends at the Bear Valley trail junction. From it **Hike 13** climbs south to Bear Valley before starting its long descent to Hetch Hetchy Reservoir. Immediately beyond this junction we cross voluminous Kerrick Canyon's bouldery Rancheria Creek. Major joints cut across this area's canyons and this creek has eroded along some of them, so that now it has an angular, joint-controlled course. After crossing this creek, which can be a rough ford through mid-July, locate a north-bank spur trail striking east up to campsites that are popular with both backpackers and bears.

The PCT climbs west, affording dramatic cross-canyon views of Bear Valley peak and Piute Mountain. The trail eventually climbs north to a shallow gap, and just east of it you'll find a campsite near the west end of a small lakelet. Proceeding north from the gap, we have the usual knee-shocking descent on a multitude of short, steep switchbacks down to the mouth of Thompson Canyon. Here we make a shady, short descent west to a large camp beside Stubblefield Canyon creek. The main trail meets the creek just below the camp, and across from it a spur trail up the opposite bank quickly meets the main trail. (If you hike this route in reverse, you probably won't see this large creekside camp. From it you can rock-hop—in late season only—to the north end of *our* large camp.) Cross where you will, locate the main trail near the opposite bank, and start down-canyon. In ¼ mile you leave the shady floor for slabs and slopes, in an hour

Last view of Tower Peak (left), from a crest notch above Latopie Lake

arriving at a false pass. A short, steep descent west leads to a corn-lily meadow, from which you wind ¼ mile northwest up to the true Macomb Ridge pass.

With the deep canyons at last behind, the 500-foot descent northwest into Tilden Canyon seems like child's play. Just beyond the west bank of Tilden Canyon Creek, you meet the Tilden Canyon trail, on which **Hike 12**, from Wilma Lake, heads south. **Hikes 13** and **14,** coming west on our trail, also turn south here. From this junction we hike up-canyon north on the Tilden Lake trail just 110 yards to a second junction. From here the PCT heads west to Wilma Lake and then goes up Jack Main Canyon. A slightly longer alternate route continues north gently up to huge, linear Tilden Lake, which has many near-shore campsites and a healthy population of rainbow trout. From the lake's outlet this route then descends west to Falls Creek and the adjacent PCT.

Our main route, however, adheres to the PCT, which goes left at this junction and winds northwest past several ponds, nestled on a broad gap, before descending west to large, shallow Wilma Lake, which, like so many of Yosemite's High Sierra lakes, contains rainbow trout. Good campsites are found just beyond it, along broad, tantalizing Falls Creek. A few minutes' walk northwest up-canyon takes one to a shallow, broad ford of the creek, then past spacious campsites to a junction with the Jack Main Canyon trail. **Hike 12** comes north up this canyon to our junction, while **Hike 14** descends from it, and those looking for an isolated spot to spend a layover day can follow the trail several miles southwest, then go cross country to one or more of the dozen or so easily reached lakes of the Andrews Peak-Mahan Peak area.

From our junction, which is near a seasonal ranger's cabin, the PCT first winds northward up-canyon, touching the east bank of Falls Creek only several times before reaching a junction with a trail east to Tilden Lake. Chittenden Peak and its north satellite serve as impressive reference points as you progress northward, passing two substantial meadows before arriving at the south end of even larger Grace Meadow. Here the upper canyon opens into plain view, with—east to west—Forsyth Peak, Dorothy Lake Pass, and Bond Pass being the guiding landmarks. Under lodgepole cover along the meadow's edge you can set up camp.

Leaving Grace Meadow, you soon pass through a small meadow before the ever-increasing gradient becomes noticeable. People have camped at small sites along this stretch, perhaps hoping to avoid bears, which are usually found lower down, but alas, no such luck. Our upward climb meets the first of two trails that quickly unite to climb to nearby Bond Pass, on the Park's boundary, the route of the Tahoe-Yosemite Trail. Just beyond these junctions volcanic sediments and exposures are noticed in ever-increasing amounts—a taste of what's to come—before you reach large, exposed Dorothy Lake. Clumps of lodgepoles here provide minimal campsite protection from the winds that often rush up-canyon. A short climb above the lake's east end takes one up to Dorothy Lake Pass with the last good view of the lasting snowfields that grace the north slopes of Forsyth Peak.

Leaving Yosemite National Park, we enter Toiyabe National Forest, pass rocky Stella Lake, approach tempting Bonnie Lake, and then switchback east down to campsites along the west shore of Lake Harriet. Larger, more-isolated camps are on the east shore. The PCT crosses Cascade Creek just below the lake, and then it makes short switchbacks down confining terrain, reaching a large campsite in about ½ mile. Just 50 yards beyond it, we cross the creek on a footbridge. Ahead, the way is still winding, but it is nearly level, and we soon reach—just past a pair of ponds—a junction with a trail that descends 1.5 miles to the West Walker River trail. Onward, we start north, then bend west and pass three ponds before winding down to a creek that has a junction just past it. West, the original, more desirable PCT route contorts 1.0 mile over to Cinko Lake, with adequate campsites. The former PCT route then descends 0.5 mile to the West Fork West Walker River trail and follows the river, making fords, 1.5 miles down to a junction with the newer route.

On this official, lackluster segment, we first parallel the creek we've just crossed, and soon pass several gray outcrops of marble, which differ significantly in color and texture from the other metamorphic rocks you've been passing. Beyond them you curve left into a small bowl, then make a short, steep climb through a granitic notch before dropping west to a seasonal creeklet. After winding briefly northwest from it, the PCT turns northward, taking almost ½ mile to descend to the West Fork West Walker River trail. On it you descend just ¼ mile downriver to a nearby junction by paltry, sedge-choked Lower Long Lake. Here we take a steel bridge across a small gorge that confines the river, and find a large, lodgepole-shaded campsite immediately past it—the best one this side of Sonora Pass. If you're lucky, you've left Yosemite's bears behind by now, though bear-bagging might not be a bad idea here.

A few mountain hemlocks are seen as you wind westward ¼ mile in and out of small gullies, then lodgepoles take over for another ¼ mile to the west edge of the southernmost Walker Meadow. Between meadow and granite the PCT passes through a lodgepole corridor to a crossing of a wide but ephemeral creek, whose water flows mostly underground through the porous volcanic sediments. About ½ mile north from this ephemeral creek is another one, which splashes in a two-stage drop into a volcanic alcove—an ideal lunch stop. Your traverse north continues for another ½ mile, and you can leave the trail at any point

to descend to the flat-floored forest just below and make camp.

By the time the trail turns northwest up Kennedy Canyon, granitic bedrock has reappeared, but ½ mile up-canyon, not far beyond a potential campsite, it disappears for good. Continuing up this brown-walled, volcanic canyon, you have an easy uphill hike for a mile, cross the canyon's creek, then labor up an increasingly steeper trail segment to a junction with a jeep road not far north of a broad saddle. We have now left behind all reasonable campsites; none lie between here and Sonora Pass, almost 10 miles away. Ahead, water in frozen form is usually too plentiful, but if snowfall has been scarce, then late-season hikers should fill up before climbing to this jeep road, for they may have to hike almost to Sonora Pass to encounter a permanent creek.

Switchbacking northward up the usually closed jeep road, one has ever-improving views of Kennedy Canyon and the adjacent volcanic landscape. Whitebark pines, which have been with us since upper Kennedy Canyon, are now wind-cropped down to stunted forms. Trees disappear altogether by the time you reach a high crest that presents views westward. Leaving the crest and its expansive views over the northwest Yosemite boundary area, our jeep road climbs quickly up to a tight switchback, and here we leave the road to follow in reverse **Hike 1**, partly in Emigrant Wilderness, 8 miles to Sonora Pass.

HIKE 43

TUOLUMNE MEADOWS TO PATE VALLEY VIA RODGERS CANYON

Distance: 54.9 miles semiloop trip

Grade: 7G, strenuous 5-day hike

Trailhead: Same as the Hike 39 trailhead. **F3.**

Introduction: This rugged hike is for canyon lovers. Heading west on the Pacific Crest Trail, you cross one scenic canyon after another. Then, returning on the Tuolumne River trail, you hike up through Yosemite's largest

Rodgers Lake   Ben Schifrin

canyon, passing many gorgeous pools and cascades.

Description: Follow **Hike 42's** description, backpacking 26 miles, to Smedberg Lake. One mile beyond it leave the Pacific Crest Trail, climb over a nearby ridge, and descend to Rodgers Lake. The route from the PCT past this lake down to the Pate Valley lateral is described in reverse direction in part of **Hike 14.** Essentially your route goes from Rodgers Lake 1 mile south down to Neall Lake—both lakes having rainbow trout—then drops west into Rodgers Canyon proper. This you descend for several miles before veering west 2 miles to a junction with the Pate Valley lateral. Before leaving Rodgers Canyon, fill up on water, for the rest of the hike down to Pate Valley can be dry in late season.

The Pate Valley lateral starts at a small patch of volcanic-mudflow deposits, which represents a remnant of what was once a part of extensive deposits burying the Tuolumne River canyon and most of the northern Yosemite landscape. The age of these deposits is about 10 million years, and since that time most of them have been removed by stream and glacier action.

Our 3¾-mile-long lateral starts among aspens, junipers, Jeffrey pines, and white firs and descends nine dozen switchbacks before reaching spacious Pate Valley, shaded mostly by ponderosa pines, black oaks, and incense-cedars. Bears frequent this area, so hang your food sacks properly or place them on hard-to-reach rock ledges. (Bears are excellent tree climbers but poor rock climbers.) From the valley's trail junction you go west 100-200 yards to find riverside campsites. Additional campsites can be found across the Tuolumne River. From Pate Valley you follow the Tuolumne River trail east 20 miles back up to your trailhead. This route is described in the opposite direction in **Hike 41** (from Glen Aulin to Pate Valley) and in **Hike 39** (from Tuolumne Meadows to Glen Aulin).

HIKE 44

TUOLUMNE MEADOWS TO YOUNG LAKES

Distance: 14.5 miles semiloop to and from the lowest lake's outlet

Grade: 3D, moderate 2-day hike

Trailhead: Same as the Hike 39 trailhead. **F3.**

Introduction: The Young Lakes are the only reasonably accessible lakes north of Tuolumne Meadows at which camping is allowed. This isolated cluster of lakes, backdropped by the scenic Ragged Peak crest, is quite popular, though not overcrowded like the Cathedral Lakes and the lakes near Vogelsang High Sierra Camp.

Description: The first part of this trip follows the Glen Aulin "highway," a heavily traveled path from Tuolumne Meadows to the High Sierra Camp down the Tuolumne River. From the Lembert Dome parking area west of the Tioga Road we stroll down a dirt road, pass a locked gate that bars vehicles, and continue west along the lodgepole-dotted flank of Tuolumne Meadows, with fine views south across the meadows of Unicorn Peak, Cathedral Peak, and some of the Echo Peaks. Approaching a boulder-rimmed old parking loop, we veer right and climb slightly to the former Soda Springs Campground. Once this campground was the private holding of John Lembert, namesake of Lembert Dome. His brothers, who survived him, sold it to the Sierra Club in 1912, and for 60 years Club

Cathedral Range summits, from Unicorn Peak to Fairview Dome, rise high above Tuolumne Meadows

members enjoyed a private campground in this marvelous subalpine meadow. In 1972 the Club deeded the property to the National Park Service so that everyone could use it, but in 1976 the Service closed the campground.

From the effervescent Soda Springs, the sandy trail undulates through a forest of sparse, small lodgepole pines, and then descends to a ford of multibranched Delaney Creek. Beyond the creek, your trail almost touches the northwest arm of Tuolumne Meadows before ascending to the signed Young Lakes trail. Turning right, you ascend slightly and cross a broad expanse of boulder-strewn, grass-pocketed glaciated sheet granite. An open spot affords a look south across broad Tuolumne Meadows to the line of peaks from Fairview Dome to the steeplelike spires of the Cathedral Range. After crossing the open, glacier-polished granite, your trail climbs a tree-clothed slope to a ridge and turns up the ridge for several hundred yards before veering down into the bouldery, shallow valley of Dingley Creek, an easy ford except in early season. The reason for the creek's boulders and our trail's gravels is that this ascent route we are following was glacier-covered before about 15,000 years ago; then this area's glaciers retreated and dropped their loads of boulders, gravel, and sand. About ¼ mile beyond this small creek, we jump across its west fork and then wind moderately upward in shady pine forest carpeted with a flower display even into late season. Senecios, daisies, lupines, and gooseberries all are colorful, but one may admire more the delicate cream flower cups of Mariposa lily, with one rich-brown spot in the

throat of each petal. Near the ridgetop, breaks in the lodgepole forest permit glimpses of the whole Cathedral Range, a foretaste of the magnificent panorama we will see on the return route.

On the other side of the ridge a new panoply of peaks appears in the north—majestic Tower Peak, Doghead and Quarry peaks, the Finger Peaks, Matterhorn Peak, Sheep Peak, Mt. Conness, and the Shepherd Crest. From this high viewpoint a moderate descent leads to a ford of a tributary of Conness Creek, where more varieties of flowers decorate the green banks of this icy, dashing stream. Immediately beyond it the Dog Lake trail meets ours, and we start a rollercoaster traverse northeast through a forest of hemlock and pine. On a level stretch of trail we cross a diminutive branch of Conness Creek, and then switchback ¼ mile up to a plateau from where the view is fine of the steep northwest face of Ragged Peak. After rounding the edge of a meadow, we descend to the west shore of lower Young Lake, whose north shore has campsites. At the lake's northwest corner you can hop its outlet creek—a wet ford in early season—and climb ¼ mile east to a junction. Here a short lateral veers right to the only good campsite at small middle Young Lake. If you keep left, you'll climb ⅓ mile up to a broad, open crest, from where you can start cross country to Mt. Conness or Roosevelt Lake. Most likely, however, you'll want to make an easy, nearly level, open traverse southeast to upper Young Lake.

After exploring this area, retrace your steps about 2 miles to the Dog Lake trail junction. Turn left and ascend a boulder-dotted slope under a lodgepole-and-hemlock forest cover. As the trail ascends, the trees diminish in density and change in species, to a predominance of whitebark pine, the highest-dwelling of Yosemite's trees. From the southwest shoulder of Ragged Peak the trail descends through a very large, gently sloping meadow. This broad, well-watered expanse is a wildflower garden in season, laced with meandering brooks. Species of paintbrush, lupine, and monkey flower in the foreground set off the marvelous views of the entire Cathedral Range, strung out on the southern horizon.

Near the lower edge of the meadow you cross the headwaters of Dingley Creek and then descend, steeply at times, some 300 feet past exfoliating Peak 10410 through a moderately dense forest of lodgepoles and a few hemlocks to a seasonal creek. Another seasonal creek is crossed in ⅓ mile, and then we make a short but noticeable climb up to the crest of a large, bouldery lateral moraine. Down its gravelly slopes we descend to a very large, level meadow above which the reddish peaks of Mt. Dana and Mt. Gibbs loom in the east. Here Delaney Creek meanders lazily through the sedges and grasses, and Belding ground squirrels pipe away. The Delaney Creek ford is difficult in early season, but shallower fords may be found upstream from the main ford.

After climbing over the crest of a second moraine, your route drops once more toward Tuolumne Meadows. Lembert Dome, the "first ascent" of so many visitors to Tuolumne Meadows, can be glimpsed through the trees along this stretch of trail. The trail levels off slightly before it meets the ¼-mile lateral to Dog Lake (**Hike 45**), a worthwhile side trip. In about 230 yards your route passes a junction with a trail that leads east along the north side of Dog Dome, the lower adjunct of Lembert Dome. We keep southwest, parallel a creek from Dog Lake, and begin a 450-foot switchbacking descent that is terribly dusty due to the braking efforts of descending hikers on this overly steep section. At the bottom of the deep dust, the trail splits into two paths. The right one leads to the stables, the left one to the Lembert Dome parking area. About 130 yards along the latter is a junction with a redundant, overly steep trail, from the south side of Dog Dome, paralleling our descent route.

LEMBERT DOME-DOG LAKE LOOP

Distance: 4.8 miles semiloop trip; 2.8 miles round trip to Dog Lake only; 2.8 miles round trip to Lembert Dome only

Grade: 1B, moderate half-day hike

Trailhead: Large parking lot ⅓ mile west of the Tuolumne Meadows Lodge parking lot. To reach this lot from Tuolumne Meadows Campground, drive 0.6 mile northeast on the Tioga Road, turn right on the Tuolumne Lodge spur road and follow it 0.4 mile to the lot, on your left. **F3.**

Introduction: This is perhaps the finest day hike you can take in the Tuolumne Meadows area. It you have only a few hours to spare, then hike only to the top of Lembert Dome. However, don't overexert yourself, for at this area's elevation you can easily get altitude sickness.

Description: From the parking lot, walk briefly east toward the lodge, finding the trailhead immediately before a dirt road forks left from the lodge's paved road. A brief climb northwest on the trail gets one to a crossing of the Tioga Road, beyond which you climb more steeply up to a junction, about ⅔ mile into your route and just 80 yards shy of a broad, lodgepole-forested saddle. To climb Lembert Dome, branch left and ascend westward on a trail that at first stays just below the crest. In about ⅓ mile it reaches a minor gap, from which you can make a brief, safe ascent north to the adjacent summit of Dog Dome, with its precipitous north face. Like all domes in the Tuolumne Meadows area, this one is domelike in appearance only from a certain angle, and generally un-domelike from most other angles. On this dome you'll see several large boulders left behind by a former glacier. Like the bedrock of Dog Dome, they are granitic, but unlike it, they lack the large, blocky feldspar crystals. They originally came from an eastern pluton (a body of granitic rock).

Glaciers also left other evidence of their presence. In some places the bedrock has been polished by the fine layer of transported basal sediment. These striations mark the direction the glacier traveled—generally westward. Another feature you might note is the presence of chatter marks. These may be due to erratic gouges made by large boulders or may be due solely to the enormous force of thick, moving glaciers acting against irregularities in the bedrock. Whereas a glacier smooths and polishes the stoss, or up-canyon, side of a dome, it may quarry the lee, or down-canyon, side. In the Sierra Nevada, quarrying has been minimal. Lembert Dome is not really a dome but rather it is, like most of Yosemite's domes, a *roche moutonnée*. Other prominent examples of roches moutonnées are Fairview Dome and Pywiack Dome, both seen along the Tioga Road. In Yosemite Valley, Liberty Cap and Mt. Broderick are examples. However, Sentinel Dome and Mt. Starr King, both unglaciated, are true domes.

To reach the summit of Lembert Dome from the minor gap, you head about 0.2 mile up the bedrock slopes to its summit. While one can tackle it head-on up a steep slope, most hikers first veer to the left and then arc right up to it. Both routes are somewhat intimidating, so if you feel unsure, don't do it; descending is always worse than ascending. Your view from 150-foot-higher Lembert Dome is nearly identical to that from Dog Dome.

After exploring the Lembert Dome summit, first return to the trail at the minor gap. This descends first briefly west and then too steeply southwest—not a desirable route for those descending to the Tioga Road. Rather, retrace your steps. To reach Dog Lake, from the minor gap you retrace your steps to a junction,

and then turn sharply left and in 80 yards reach the aforementioned broad, lodgepole-forested saddle. Beyond it you drop briefly west-northwest, then traverse in the same direction, having a view of the north cliffs of Dog Dome and skirting past a pond that seasonally has wild onions growing in wet ground near its shore. Just 100 yards beyond it you cross the outlet creek of an unseen, sedge-filled pond, then in 150 yards reach a trail junction. An alternate, less-desirable, longer return route to your trailhead would be to descend this overly steep trail southwest to a parking lot at the foot of Lembert Dome, then cross the Tioga Road and follow a trail—mostly an abandoned road—back to your starting point.

To reach Dog Lake, first head about 230 yards northwest up this trail, to a junction from where a trail continues about 5 miles to the first of three Young Lakes (**Hike 44**). Veer right and make an easy ascent ¼ mile to the outlet of Dog Lake, at its western end. The official trail ends here, but you could go either right, along the lake's south shore, or left, along its north shore. Encircling the lake is difficult, due to boggy ground by its eastern end.

From the lake's west shore just north of the outlet creek, you obtain sometimes-reflected views of Mt. Dana, Mt. Gibbs, and also Mt. Lewis. A long peninsula extends east into the lake from your shoreline, and on it you can walk—usually in knee-deep water—well out into the middle of this large but shallow lake. Because it is shallow, it is one of the high country's warmest lakes, suitable for swimming and for just plain relaxing. Camping,

Dog Dome presents hikers with a panoramic view of the Tuolumne Meadows area

Mts. Dana, Gibbs, and Lewis, together with Mono Pass, backdrop placid Dog Lake

however, is prohibited. Like many High Sierra lakes, this one is visited in the summer by spotted sandpipers, who usually nest close to the lake's shore. Among the shore boulders you may find metamorphic ones—rocks that could have got here via glacier transport from their source area, the Gaylor Peak/Tioga Hill area. Today no stream connects this area with Dog Lake, which lies in a purely granitic watershed. Leaving Dog Lake, retrace your steps back to your trailhead.

HIKE 46

TIOGA PASS TO GAYLOR AND GRANITE LAKES

Distance: 5.7 miles or longer—mileage variable; semiloop trip

Grade: 2C, easy day hike

Trailhead: Beside the Tioga Pass Entrance Station. **F3.**

Introduction: Five subalpine lakes await those who take this hike, part of which is easy cross-country. You can also reach these glistening gems from Tuolumne Meadows Lodge by first taking a trail 2 miles east from it up the Dana Fork to the Tioga Road, crossing it, and going 2½ miles up to Lower Gaylor Lake (see start of Hike 56). However, the route description that follows is about 8 miles shorter, round trip. Camping is *not* allowed in the Gaylor Lakes area, which includes the Granite Lakes.

Description: From the restrooms by the Tioga Pass Entrance Station, your rocky trail ascends steeply through lodgepole forest, and in sea-

son you pass a profusion of wildflowers, including single-stemmed senecio, Sierra penstemon, Gray's lovage, daisy, pussytoes, baby elephant heads, lupine, monkey flower, and Sierra wallflower. You may see a lone whitebark pine, a conifer that in maturity can range from a 50-foot-high tree down to a knee-high bush. The bark of lodgepole and whitebark pines looks similar; however, the former tree has two needles per bunch while the latter has five. Your steep trail begins to level off near the top of the ridge, and on this stretch the flower "collector" may add spreading phlox, red mountain heather, buckwheat, and coyote mint to the day's journal. Atop the ridge, the well-earned view includes, clockwise from north, Gaylor Peak, Tioga Peak, Mt. Dana, Mt. Gibbs, the canyon of the Dana Fork, Kuna Peak, Mammoth Peak, Lyell Canyon, and the peaks of the Cathedral Range. From the vantage point you can see where red metamorphic rocks to the northeast are in contact with gray granites to the southwest. This division extends north to our locale.

As you move west on the ridgetop, the rocks underfoot become quite purplish, a hue shared by the flowers of penstemon and lupine that obtain their mineral requirements from these rocks. Now the trail descends steeply past clumps of whitebark pine to Middle Gaylor Lake, and skirts the lake's north shore. Across the lake, the peaks of the Cathedral Range seem to be sinking into the lake, for their summits barely poke above the water.

Taking the trail up the inlet stream, we begin a short, gradual ascent to Upper Gaylor Lake. Surveying the Gaylor Lakes basin, we can see that campsites are so few and wood so scarce that only a few summers of camping, were it allowed, would finish off the environment here. From the upper lake we can see a

Gaylor Peak and Gaylor Lakes, from Great Sierra Mine

rock cabin, which bespeaks the activities of a mining company that sought to tap the silver veins that run somewhere under Tioga Hill, directly north of the lake. Should you go to the cabin, you can admire the skill of the dryrock mason who built this long-lasting house near the Sierra crest. Farther up the hill are other works—including one dangerous hole—left by the miners, in various states of return to nature. This was once the "city" of Dana. Atop Tioga Hill you have all the earlier views plus a view down into Lee Vining Canyon. A scant mile northeast of us another "city," Bennettville, sprang up near the mouth of a tunnel being dug to exploit the silver lodes. Its founder projected a population of 50,000! The white and lavender columbines and other living things around the summit may owe their lives to the absence of these hordes.

From this general area, make your way west cross country across a ridge and down to the easily found Granite Lakes, liquid gems backed by steep granite heights. Like the upper lake with its near-shore island, lower Granite Lake is coldly swimmable in mid-to-late season. In any event, its grassy eastern shore is a fine place to sun oneself. Finally you curve southwest, down toward Lower Gaylor Lake. In this meadowy upland you are likely to see many marmots and Belding ground squirrels. At this lake you may also see a few California gulls on the spit. Spotted sandpipers, identified by their bobbing walk, are also common summer visitors to High Sierra lakes. After a pleasant rest, make an easy, generally open, cross-country climb northeast back to Middle Gaylor Lake, then follow the trail back to Tioga Pass.

Chapter 9

Trails of the Tuolumne Meadows Area, south and east of the Tioga Road

Introduction: Except for Little Yosemite Valley, an outlier of Yosemite Valley, no other area in the Park receives such intensive backpacker use. Consequently, it is very desirable that you get a wilderness permit long before you start your *overnight* hike. The extreme popularity of this area is due in part to its supreme scenery, which is dominated by the Cathedral Range and the Sierra crest. In part its popularity is also due to its accessibility, for in a few hours' hiking time you can easily reach crest passes and subalpine lakes. How can one forget the alpenglow on the metamorphic Sierra crest? the form of twin-towered Cathedral Peak? the expansive panorama from Mt. Dana? the beauty of an alpine wildflower garden? the enormous granite wall below Clouds Rest? These and many other sights continue to lure backpackers and dayhikers to this area year after year.

Supplies and Services: See "Supplies and Services" in Chapter 8.
Wilderness Permits: See "Wilderness Permits" in Chapter 8.
Campgrounds: See "Campgrounds" in Chapter 8.

HIKE 47

TENAYA LAKE TO SUNRISE HIGH SIERRA CAMP VIA SUNRISE LAKES

Distance: 11.4 miles round trip

Grade: 3D, easy 2-day hike

Trailhead: Same as the Hike 35 trailhead. **E4.**

Introduction: Considerable climbing at fairly high elevations would normally make this hike a moderate one, but its distance is so short for a backpack trip that we've rated it easy. Some hikers go only as far as upper Sunrise Lake, only an 8-mile round trip and a good, moderate day hike. However, if you camp near Sunrise High Sierra Camp you are rewarded with a beautiful sunrise—the reason for the camp's being situated where it is.

Description: A road heads east from the Tenaya Lake trailhead parking area, and walking along it you soon cross the usually flowing outlet of Tenaya Lake. Immediately beyond this crossing a trail forks right, and you take it to a nearby trail junction. **Hike 36** goes left, northeast, to start a loop around the lake. Consult that hike for a brief description of this locale's glacial history and of a myth about the origin of the lake's protruding tree stumps. You veer right, on a trail that heads south for ¼ mile along Tenaya Creek. Then over the next ½ mile it ascends southeast in sparse forest

Left: *Telephoto of Cathedral Peak, from upper Cathedral Lake*

163

Above: *Matthes Crest, from Sunrise High Sierra Camp*
Below: *Exfoliation slabs and talus slope above lower Sunrise Lake*

through a thinning cover of lodgepole pine and occasional red fir, western white pine, and mountain hemlock. As your trail rises above Tenaya Canyon, you pass several vantage points from which you can look back upon its polished granite walls, though you never see Tenaya Lake. To the east the canyon is bounded by Tenaya Peak; in the northwest are the cliffs of Mt. Hoffman and Tuolumne Peak.

Now on switchbacks, one sees the Tioga Road across the canyon and can even hear vehicles, but these annoyances are infinitesimal compared to the pleasures of polished granite expanses all around. These switchbacks are mercifully shaded, and where they become steepest, requiring a great output of energy, they give back the beauty of the finest flower displays on this trail, including lupine, penstemon, paintbrush, larkspur, buttercup, and sunflowers such as aster and senecio. Finally the switchbacks end and the trail levels as it arrives at a junction on a shallow, forested saddle.

Here we turn left (**Hikes 48** and **49** go straight ahead), contour east, cross a low gap and descend north to lower Sunrise lake, above whose east shore you'll see excellent examples of exfoliating granite slabs. The large talus slope beneath them testifies to the slabs' instability. Climbing from this lake and its small campsites, we reach a crest in several minutes, and from it one could descend an

over a little rise and drops to a ford of Mildred Lake's outlet, which, like the other streams between Tenaya Lake and the Sunrise trail junction, can dry up in late season.

Beyond the Mildred Lake stream the trail undulates and winds generally south, passing several pocket meadows browsed by mule deer. The trail then begins to climb in earnest, equally short distance north to more isolated, island-dotted middle Sunrise Lake. The trail, however, veers east and gains a very noticeable 150 feet in elevation as it climbs to upper Sunrise Lake, the largest and most popular lake of the trio. Campsites are plentiful along its north shore, away from the trail.

Leaving this lake, the trail climbs south up a gully, crosses it, then soon climbs up a second gully to the east side of a broad gap, from which you see the Clark Range head-on, piercing the southern sky. From the gap, which is sparsely clothed with mountain hemlocks, whitebark pines, and western white pines, you descend south into denser cover, veer east, and then veer north to make a steep descent to Sunrise High Sierra Camp. This has an adjacent backpackers' camp perhaps complete with metal poles on which to bearbag your food. An overnight stay here gives you an inspiring sunrise over Matthes Crest and the Cathedral Range.

HIKE 48

TENAYA LAKE TO CLOUDS REST

Distance: 14.0 miles round trip

Grade: 3D, strenuous day hike

Trailhead: Same as the Hike 35 trailhead. **E4.**

Introduction: Although Clouds Rest is higher than Half Dome, it is easier and safer to climb, and it provides far better views of the Park than does popular, often overcrowded Half Dome. Except for its last 300 yards, the Clouds Rest trail lacks the terrifying, potentially lethal drop-offs found along Half Dome's shoulder and back side, thereby making it a good trail for acrophobic photographers. If you're an avid photographer, you'll want to start this trek at the crack of dawn in order to reach this summit before shadows become poor for photography. All hikers should strive to reach this summit by noon or thereabouts, for lightning storms are a real possibility in the mid-to-late afternoon.

Description: Follow **Hike 47** 3 miles up to the Sunrise Lakes trail junction. Then, with all the hard climbing behind you, descend south along the Forsyth trail. This switchbacks down to a shady, sometimes damp flat, then climbs up to a block-strewn ridge that sprouts dense clumps of chinquapin and aspen. Beyond it the trail descends briefly to a tree-fringed pond—adequate for nearby camping—then wanders south for ½ mile before veering west to cross three creeklets, which will be your last reliable sources of water. After you cross the first creeklet, follow the trail briefly downstream, then veer left to cross the second creeklet before climbing up to the third. Beyond it the trail rapidly eases its gradient and soon

From Clouds Rest, both Half Dome and Yosemite Valley captivate your attention

reaches the Clouds Rest trail junction, about 5.2 miles from the trailhead.

The Forsyth trail—not worth taking— forks left, but you keep right and for about a mile ascend the Clouds Rest trail west to a forested, gravelly crest and then follow it down to a shallow saddle. The final ascent begins here. After a moderate ascent of ¼ mile, you emerge from the forest cover to get your first excellent views of Tenaya Canyon and the country west and north of it. After another ¼ mile along the crest you come to a junction with a horse trail. If you're riding a horse from Tenaya Lake to Yosemite Valley via the Clouds Rest trail—the most scenic of the possible routes to the Valley—you'll want to take this trail after first walking to the summit. The Clouds Rest foot trail essentially dies out here, so scramble a few feet up to the narrow crest. Acrophobics may not want to continue, but they can get some spectacular views of Tenaya Canyon, Half Dome, and Yosemite Valley which are nearly identical with those seen from the summit. Spreading below is the expansive 4500-foot-high face of Clouds Rest—the largest granite face in the Park.

Those who follow the now steeper, narrow, almost trailless crest 300 yards to the summit are further rewarded with views of the Clark Range and the Merced River Canyon. Growing on the rocky summit are a few knee-high Jeffrey pines and whitebark pines plus assorted bushes and wildflowers. Some hikers like to spend a waterless night on the summit in order to experience an incredible sunrise. If you do this, pack out your litter and make your latrine off the summit—it is too small to withstand pollution.

On Half Dome's cables

Introduction: Yosemite Valley's two loftiest, most scenic viewpoints—Clouds Rest and Half Dome—are visited along this hike. The energy expended attaining the two summits is equivalent to that of Hike 81, which starts at the valley floor and climbs only to Half Dome. Good judgment is required for this hike, for both summit routes have potentially fatal drop-offs. Strong hikers can make this hike in one day, but many will want to take two. If you do, then plan to make a dry camp in the Clouds Rest environs or down along Sunrise Creek, so that you will reach the start of the Half Dome climb early on, avoiding both the hordes of people who start it later and the potential for an afternoon lightning storm.

Description: Hike 48 describes the 7-mile trek up to Clouds Rest and the views seen from it. Leaving Clouds Rest—an exfoliating high crest on the Tenaya Canyon rim—you first negotiate short switchbacks south down through a dense growth of chinquapin bushes, then descend longer ones past western white pines and a few Jeffrey pines to a junction with the Clouds Rest horse trail, which starts east. Red firs join the pines as you descend southwest from the junction, and chinquapins compete with pinemat manzanita, snow bush, and even sagebrush. The trail descends past the back sides of the two Clouds Rest "pinnacles," both broken with an abundance of horizontal fractures. Just beyond these you reach a spur ridge with several bedrock knobs that are similarly fractured. Most geologists interpret these fractures as the result of pressure release. These granitic rocks, which are a part of the 86-million-year-old Half Dome granodiorite pluton, solidified several miles beneath the earth's

HIKE 49

TENAYA LAKE TO HAPPY ISLES VIA CLOUDS REST AND HALF DOME

Distance: 21.2 miles one way, including side trip

Grade: 5E, strenuous 2-day hike

Trailhead: Same as the Hike 35 trailhead. **E4.**

surface at pressures a *few thousand times* the atmospheric pressure they are exposed to today. Hence the granitic rock tends to expand, cracking in the process, and eventually it unloads slabs.

From the low knobs and their adjacent western junipers, an initially steep descent yields to a more moderate one as you pass beneath the overhanging south wall of the southern Clouds Rest pinnacle. More dome-like from our trail's vantage points, the two Clouds Rest pinnacles were certainly named by someone who viewed them from the north-west. Your west-descending trail almost touches the rim of Tenaya Canyon before it begins about one dozen switchbacks, which drop into a vegetation zone that now includes huckleberry oaks and white firs. On this descent you pass a trickling spring, flowing near Labrador tea, a water-loving bush that is easily identified by the turpentine smell of its crushed leaves. Don't be misled by its name; it leaves will not produce a suitable tea. Instead, they produce convulsions and paralysis.

Another set of switchbacks drops you into sufficient forest cover to obstruct your recently plentiful views of towering Half Dome. It is about here, at the end of a 400-yard-long switchback west—easily the longest—that adventurous hikers can start a cross-country traverse west for ⅓ mile to the Quarter Domes, the upper one providing an exceptional view of the face of Clouds Rest. They can then make a somewhat brushy cross-country descent southwest to the broad saddle midway between these domes and Half Dome. This alternate route saves you some 500 feet of climbing you will have to do to approach that saddle via trail.

On the Clouds Rest trail, your moderate-to-steep descent soon leaves red firs behind, and through a forest of white firs and Jeffrey pines you drop eventually to a junction with the John Muir Trail (**Hike 51**). Here, close to a tributary of Sunrise Creek, you'll find camp-sites. Just east on the John Muir Trail, between this tributary and Sunrise Creek, is a larger campsite. There are no more flat, desirable, near-water sites between here and the summit of Half Dome, about 2⅔ miles farther.

From the campsite junction we descend ½ mile west along the John Muir Trail to a junction with the Half Dome trail. Now follow the last part of **Hike 80** up to that dome's summit.

Rather than carry your backpack all the way to the summit, hide it in some bushes and carry only a day pack up this strenuous section. After your exploration of the dome's expansive summit, descend to Happy Isles on the floor of Yosemite Valley, following the description of **Hike 80** in reverse.

HIKE 50

TUOLUMNE MEADOWS TO LOWER CATHEDRAL LAKE VIA JOHN MUIR TRAIL

Distance: 7.8 miles round trip

Grade: 2C, moderate half-day hike

Trailhead: In Tuolumne Meadows, 1.5 miles west on the Tioga Road from the Tuolumne Meadows Campground entrance. **E4.**

Introduction: Justifiably popular Lower Cathedral Lake receives so much backpacker use that those who can visit this scenic lake in only one day—an easy task—should do so. The popularity of this lake is confirmed by the presence of black bears, lured there by the tempting prospect of backpackers' food sup-plies. Since free shuttle buses operate between Tuolumne Meadows and Tenaya Lake, strong day hikers have another option: after visiting Lower Cathedral Lake, follow the John Muir Trail to Sunrise High Sierra Camp (Hike 51), then head out and down to Tenaya Lake (Hike 47 in reverse), for a grand total of about 15 miles. Then take the shuttle bus back to your trailhead.

Description: From a trailhead beside Budd Creek, walk southwest 120 yards to a junction with the Tuolumne Meadows-Tenaya Lake trail. Starting from the east side of Tuolumne Meadows Campground, this trail traverses west to our junction, then continues for a gen-erally viewless 8.1 miles down to the trailhead near the southwest shore of Tenaya Lake. By continuing on **Hike 35**, you can descend to Mirror Meadow, a hike that is the shortest route from Tuolumne Meadows to Yosemite Valley—about 19¾ miles.

Bedrock-lined lower Cathedral Lake

Now on the John Muir Trail, we climb moderately up a stretch that can at times be objectionably dusty due to humus mixing with the abundance of glacial deposits. Lodgepoles dominate your ¾-mile ascent to the crest of a lateral moraine, from which the trail briefly descends west before turning southwest. From this spot you can hike cross-country ½ mile northwest to the lower slopes of Fairview Dome. During glacial periods the Tuolumne Meadows glacier was so thick that it buried this dome under as much as 700 feet of glacier ice, which then overflowed the river basin to descend into Yosemite Valley via Tenaya Canyon. Non-climbers should not attempt to climb to its summit.

The John Muir Trail traverses southwest ½ mile to a creeklet, which you cross, and then ascend short, moderate-to-steep switchbacks beneath the shady cover of lodgepole pines and mountain hemlocks. After 300 feet of climbing, your trail's gradient eases and you traverse along the base of largely unseen Cathedral Peak, a mass of granodiorite towering 1400 feet above you. Repeated attacks by glaciers have chiseled away on all of the peak's sides to create a steep-walled monolith that is the realm of the mountain climber.

Your traverse leaves the Tuolumne River drainage for that of the Merced River and soon, after a brief descent, you come to a junction with the lower Cathedral Lake trail. This spur trail descends ⅔ mile to the lake's bedrock east shore. A rust-stained waterline on the meadow side of the bedrock marks the high-water level when the meadow floods in early season. The iron from the rust is derived from the meadow's soil, not from the iron-deficient granitic bedrock. Bear-frequented campsites abound on both the north and south shores, the northern ones being roomier. Campfires are not allowed. Due to high angler use, fishing for brook trout is likely to be poor. Because of the relative shallowness of this fairly large lake, swimming in it is tolerable despite its 9300+ foot altitude.

From the lake's outlet you can look across to Polly Dome, standing high above Pywiack Dome. Also seen are Mt. Hoffman and a bit of Tenaya Lake, nestled between Tenaya Peak and Polly Dome. By hiking cross country ¾ mile north from your lake's outlet, you can follow the rim of Tenaya Canyon to a seldom seen lakelet near the summit of Medlicott Dome. Seen from this lakelet, the dome in no way resembles a dome, but Mariuolumne Dome, ½ mile northeast of it, bears a striking resemblance to Lembert Dome (**Hike 45**). Mariuolumne Dome gets its name from the nearby drainage divide, which separates *Mari*posa county from T*uolumne* county.

HIKE 51

TUOLUMNE MEADOWS TO HAPPY ISLES VIA JOHN MUIR TRAIL

Distance: 21.7 miles one way

Grade: 5D, moderate 2-day hike

Trailhead: Same as the Hike 50 trailhead. E4.

Introduction: This section of the John Muir Trail is perhaps the most popular route from Tuolumne Meadow to Yosemite Valley. For those who have done the first 190 miles of this famous trail, which originates at the summit of Mt. Whitney, these final scenic miles—most of them downhill—make a perfect ending.

Description: Follow **Hike 50** about 3 miles up to the junction with the lower Cathedral Lake spur trail. Visiting this lake adds about 1½ miles to your hike's length. From this junction make an easy mile-long climb to the southeast corner of very shallow upper Cathedral Lake. Although camping is discouraged here, you may enjoy a rest on the south-shore peninsula, which offers a fine view of two-towered Cathedral Peak. The trail then climbs ¼ mile to broad Cathedral Pass, where the excellent views include Tresidder Peak, Cathedral Peak, Echo Peaks, and Matterhorn Peak far to the north.

Beyond the pass is a long, beautiful swale, the flowery headwaters of Echo Creek. Your path traverses up the east flank of Tresidder Peak on a gentle climb to the actual high point of this trail, at a marvelous viewpoint overlooking most of southern part of the Park. The inspiring panorama here includes the peaks around Vogelsang High Sierra Camp in the southeast, the whole Clark Range in the south, and, farther away, the peaks on the Park's border. Your high trail soon traverses under steep-walled Columbia Finger, then switchbacks quickly down to the head of the upper lobe of Long Meadow. Here it levels off and leads down to a gradually sloping valley dotted with lodgepole pines to the head of the second, lower lobe of l-o-n-g Long Meadow. After passing a junction with a trail down Echo Creek (**Hike 52**), the route heads south ½ mile before bending west ¼ mile to pass below Sunrise High Sierra Camp, perched on a granite bench just above the trail. South of the camp are some backpacker campsites from where you can take in the next morning's glorious sunrise.

For variation you could head west over to the Sunrise Lakes, then down to a junction with the Forsyth trail (the reverse of the second half of **Hike 47**), then follow **Hikes 48** and **49** to Clouds Rest and Half Dome. By taking this scenic route you'd be taking perhaps the most scenic route of a dozen or so that go from Tuolumne Meadows to Yosemite Valley.

From the camp the John Muir Trail continues through the south arm of Long Meadow, then soon starts to climb up the east slopes of Sunrise Mountain. You top a broad southeast-trending ridge, and then, paralleling the headwaters of Sunrise Creek, descend steeply by switchbacks down a rocky canyon.

At the foot of this descent you cross a trickling creek, then climb a low moraine to another creek, and in a short ½ mile top the linear crest of a giant lateral moraine. This moraine is the largest of a series of ridgelike glacial deposits in this area, and the gigantic granite boulders along its sides testify to the transporting power of the glacier that once overflowed Little Yosemite Valley. At its maximum, it had a surface higher than this Tioga-age moraine. Lower down, additional morainal crests appear on both sides of the trail, and you see Half Dome through the trees before your route reaches a junction with the Forsyth trail. The steep hike up it to the Clouds Rest trail is not worth taking. Look for fair campsites along Sunrise Creek about 150 yards north of this junction.

Here we turn south and in a moment reach the High trail (**Hike 81**) coming in on the

Cathedral Peak and upper Cathedral Lake

Tresidder Peak and pointed Columbia Finger

left. Turn right and descend southwest, your path being bounded first on the north by the south buttress of the Clouds Rest eminence and then on the south by the northeast end of a ridge, Moraine Dome. For admirable views and interesting geology, I strongly recommend you ascend south some 200 feet in elevation to attain the broad ridgecrest, then walk southwest along it to the obvious summit of Moraine Dome. This is named for a lateral moraine that descends southwest from just below the dome's summit. This moraine, hanging on the south side of Moraine Dome about 1750 feet above the floor of Little Yosemite Valley, does not represent the approximate thickness of the last glacier, geological experts to the contrary. It and earlier glaciers topped it by hundreds of feet. Atop Moraine Dome you'll see—besides an utterly fantastic panorama—two geologically interesting features. One is an 8-foot-high dike of resistant aplite, which stands above the rest of the dome's surface because it weathers more slowly. Nearby just downslope is a large erratic boulder which, unlike the rock of Moraine Dome, is composed of Cathedral Peak granodiorite, easily identified by its large feldspar crystals. Ongoing exfoliation of adjacent bedrock, aided by a lengthy root from a nearby Jeffrey pine, has left the erratic perched precariously atop a 3-foot-high pedestal.

Meanwhile, along the John Muir Trail a mile from the last junction, you ford Sunrise Creek in a red-fir forest, then in ¾ mile see a good campsite on a large, shady creekside flat. You then curve northeast to quickly cross the creek's tributary, which has two west-bank campsites. Immediately past these is a trail to Clouds Rest (**Hike 48**), and ½ mile west from this junction you meet the trail to Half Dome (**Hike 80**—about 4 miles round trip—an incredible hike that shouldn't be missed). From this junction your shady path switchbacks down through a changing forest cover that includes some stately incense-cedars, with their burnt-orange, fibrous bark. At the foot of this descent we reach the floor of Little Yosemite Valley. Due to the area's popularity, the Park Service now directs camping activity hereabouts. A seasonal ranger stationed here answers questions, such as where to camp and where to find bearproof food-storage boxes. The route down to Yosemite Valley is described in the reverse direction in **Hike 79**.

TUOLUMNE MEADOWS TO HAPPY ISLES VIA ECHO CREEK AND MERCED LAKE

Distance: 32.2 miles one way

Grade: 6D, easy 4-day hike

Trailhead: Same as the Hike 50 trailhead. **E4.**

Introduction: In the first 2 miles of hiking you'll complete half of this hike's climbing, and this accomplishment leaves you with a remaining 30 miles of easy hiking. This route is an excellent one for novice backpackers who want to try a multiday wilderness experience. In the environs of Sunrise High Sierra Camp, Merced Lake, and Little Yosemite Valley, there are bearproof food-storage facilities.

Description: Follow **Hike 51** to Sunrise High Sierra Camp, spend the night, experience the glorious sunrise, and then backtrack a short mile up Long Meadow to a junction with the Echo Creek trail, on which you will immediately ford the meadow's creek on boulders. The trail quickly switchbacks up to the top of a

Echo Peaks, from John Muir Trail

forested ridge and then descends through dense hemlock-and-lodgepole forest to a tributary of Echo Creek. Cross this, descend along it for ⅓ mile, recross, then momentarily reach the west bank of Echo Creek's Cathedral Fork. From Cathedral Pass, above and south of the Cathedral Lakes, experienced backpackers can hike easily cross country down-canyon to this fork. By contouring south from Echo Lake they can also meet Matthes ("Mat'-tees") Lake's outlet creek, trace it up to that lake and explore fascinating, serrated Matthes Crest—a mountaineer's paradise.

From the trail beside the Cathedral Fork we have fine views of the creek's water gliding down a series of granite slabs, and then the trail veers away from the creek and descends gently above it for more than a mile. Even in late season these shaded slopes are watered by numerous rills that are bordered by still-blooming flowers. On this downgrade the trail crosses the Long Meadow creek, which has found an escape from that meadow through a gap between two domes high above our trail.

The route then levels out in a mile-long flat section of this valley where the wet ground yields a plus of wildflowers all summer but a minus of many mosquitoes in early season. Beyond this flat "park" the trail descends more-open slopes, and eventually you can see across the valley the steep course of Echo Creek plunging down to its rendezvous with its western Cathedral Fork. A fine cross-country route starting at Nelson Lake (**Hike 54**) descends 4 miles along Echo Creek to this confluence.

In this area your trail levels off and passes good campsites immediately before you take a bridge over Echo Creek. Beyond it, your trail leads down the forested valley and easily fords a tributary stream, staying well above the main creek. This pleasant, shaded descent soon

becomes more open and steep, and it encounters fibrous-barked juniper trees and butterscotch-scented Jeffrey pines as it drops to another bridge 1⅓ miles from the first one. Beyond it, the trail rises slightly and the creek drops precipitously, so that you are soon far above it. Then the sandy tread swings west away from Echo Creek and diagonals down a brushy slope. There the views are excellent of Echo Valley, which is a wide place in the great Merced River canyon below. On this slope you arrive at a junction with the High trail, which goes 3 miles west to a junction with the John Muir Trail. Leaving the dense growth of huckleberry oak, chinquapin, greenleaf manzanita, and snow bush behind, we start southeast and make a drop 450 feet into Echo Valley. In it we quickly arrive at another junction, this one near an adequate camping area. Here is the Merced Lake trail, described in **Hike 81**. On it you go east, immediately bridging Echo Creek, pass through a burned-but-boggy area, then climb east past the Merced River's largely unseen, but enjoyable, pools to Merced Lake's west shore. Don't camp here, but rather continue past the north shore to Merced Lake High Sierra Camp and the adjacent riverside campground, a little under 10 miles from the Sunrise High Sierra Camp. You can count on seeing bears here, so be sure to safely store your food.

On your third day you hike almost 14 miles to the floor of Yosemite Valley, which isn't that hard because it is mostly down hill and you've gotten sufficient exercise and acclimation to handle it. First retrace your steps to Echo Valley, then continue on the Merced Lake trail as it descends to Little Yosemite Valley, referring to the first part of **Hike 81**, which describes this stretch in the opposite direction. **Hike 79** describes Little Yosemite Valley (a possible layover day here) and **Hike 78** describes your possible routes down to Happy Isles.

HIKE 53

TUOLUMNE MEADOWS TO BUDD LAKE

Distance: 5.4 miles round trip

Grade: 2C, moderate half-day hike

Trailhead: Same as the Hike 50 trailhead. **E4.**

Introduction: Mountaineers take the unmaintained, *de facto* trail to Budd Lake, for it provides the fastest access to climbing routes on Cathedral Peak, Echo Peaks, the Cockscomb and Unicorn Peak—all encircling the lake—and on Matthes Crest, south of the Cockscomb. I would not describe this unmaintained trail were it not for significant geological features round around chilly Budd Lake, which are worth investigation.

Description: The unsigned trail up to Budd Creek can be hard to find. From the Hike 50 trailhead walk 120 yards southwest to a junction with the John Muir Trail, then start southwest up it toward the Cathedral Lakes. After a long ¼ mile, a use trail starts south from a point where the John Muir Trail curves northwest—the only place it does so on the lower part of its ascent. The use trail quickly becomes more obvious and its first mile is easy to follow. However, it then levels off and forks. One branch makes a brief, gentle descent, but you should stay on the right branch, which first climbs up to a granitic bench and then heads south along its brink. In about ⅓ mile this branch rejoins the lower one; then the path can become vague just before crossing Budd Creek. Once on the east bank of Budd Creek, you may see a third branch, one that had split from the lower one. From the crossing a single tread climbs a short mile up Budd Creek, crossing it again just before reaching Budd Lake.

Along your ascent of this trail you'll note that Unicorn Peak, to the east, has three summits, not one, as you might assume from the name. Although the peak is mentioned in *The Climber's Guide to the High Sierra,* no mention is made of the better climbing on the long cliff below and northwest of the peak. At Budd Lake camping is not allowed, but perhaps you will find an overly friendly marmot waiting to empty your pack while you're off exploring the area. Budd Lake is perhaps unique in Yosemite in that it contains two geologically recent moraines. The older moraine, perhaps formed only a few hundred years ago, rests along the north shore of 10,050-foot-high Budd Lake. The younger one, perhaps almost as old, arcs across the lake's south end.

While you're admiring Cathedral Peak, the Echo Peaks, and the Cockscomb basin, you might take a close look at the granitic rock that composes them. Dated about 85 million years old, it was originally classified as a true granite, then briefly as a quartz monzonite, and now—by international standards—as granodiorite. The mineral and chemical composition of this Cathedral Peak pluton varies from place to place, but it generally becomes richer in feldspar and quartz toward the center, and this variation complicated the classification. Regardless of its classification, this pluton is easy to identify in Yosemite, for it contains large, blocky, protruding crystals of potassium feldspar. Climbers new to the Tuolumne Meadows area quickly discover that these make good holds. In addition to the mountaineers, fishermen visit Budd Lake, for it contains brook trout.

A young moraine arcs across Budd Lake; Cathedral Peak in background

TUOLUMNE MEADOWS TO ELIZABETH AND NELSON LAKES

Distance: 4.8 miles round trip to Elizabeth Lake, 12.0 miles round trip to Nelson Lake

Grade: 1C, moderate half-day hike

Trailhead: Near the horse camp loop of the Tuolumne Meadows Campground. Walk through the campground and find the trailhead just past campsite 49. **F4.**

Introduction: Due to its accessibility Elizabeth Lake ranks with Dog Lake (Hike 45) in popularity. Dog Lake is certainly better for swimming, Elizabeth Lake for scenery. Fairly isolated Nelson Lake can be reached by a *de facto* trail from Elizabeth Lake.

Description: The signed Elizabeth Lake trail in the campground goes only 50 yards to a crossing of a trail that heads east to Lyell Canyon and west to Tenaya Lake. You continue straight ahead for a steady southward ascent. Along this lodgepole-pine-shaded climb the trail crosses several runoff streams that dry up by late summer. Before then, expect lots of mosquitoes. More than a mile out, the trail veers near Unicorn Creek, and the music of this dashing, gurgling, cold-water stream makes the climbing easier. After rising 800 feet, the trail levels off, and lodgepoles now are both stunted and farther spaced. You emerge at the foot of a long meadow, and part way through it take a short spur trail southwest to Elizabeth Lake. Few places in Yosemite give so much for so little effort as this lovely subalpine lake. Backdropped by Unicorn Peak, the lake faces the snow-topped peaks of the Sierra crest north of Tuolumne Meadows. From the east and north sides of the lake, the views across the waters to Unicorn Peak are classic. The glacier-carved lake basin is indeed one of the most beautiful in the Tuolumne Meadows area.

From the lake's spur trail junction a *de facto* trail climbs one mile to a notch in the Cathedral Range, then descends 2 miles past the spectacular Cockscomb crest before veering ½ mile east up to Nelson Lake. Because this trail is unofficial, I'm not describing it in detail, but rather am leaving it for competent back-

packers to explore. From Nelson Lake and its population of brook trout, these backpackers can head cross-country down Echo Creek for 4 relatively easy miles to the creek's confluence with its Cathedral Fork (see **Hike 52**).

TUOLUMNE MEADOWS LOOP

Distance: 5.7 miles for the complete loop

Grade: 2A, easy half-day hike

Trailhead: At or just west of Lembert Dome; essentially the same as the Hike 39 trailhead. **F3.**

Introduction: A good way to get acclimatized to this area's high elevation is to take this almost level loop trip through and around Tuolumne Meadows. Parts of this trail are favorite spots for anglers and photographers.

Description: You can start the loop at any of a number of points, but I'll start at the parking lot at the foot of the meadow's prominent landmark, Lembert Dome. Walk west to where the road turns north up to the Tuolumne Meadows Stable, then continue west on a closed dirt road. After a pleasant walk with views south to the western Cathedral Range peaks, you go through a low gap and the road forks. Keep right, then in a few paces leave the road and take a short trail to the rust-stained, iron-rich Soda Springs. Being effervescent, they act like tonic water and can be added to any powdered drink you may have brought along.

From the springs and the adjacent Parsons Memorial Lodge—once the property of the Sierra Club—head south to the large bridge across the Tuolumne River. Lembert Dome, a ridge that looks more like a half dome, is plainly seen from the bridge. The dome's northwest face, being laced with vertical fractures, was only minimally quarried by repeated glaciation. During the last glaciation the top of the dome was buried under about 2000 feet of glacier ice. When the glacier retreated up-canyon by about 15,000 years ago, primeval Tuolumne Meadows came into existence. At first it was nearly lifeless—just a large accumulation of recently deposited sands, gravels and boulders. Quite likely a braided stream—one with several dividing and reuniting channels—flowed through it. Small, shallow ponds may also have existed, but never a large lake, such as Tenaya. Sedges eventually encroached upon the sediments; then they were followed by willows and finally by lodgepoles. Until about 2500 years ago a lodgepole forest may have dominated; then laker came a minor ice age. (The feeble Sierran glaciers we see today are remnants of it.) It was during these wetter times that Tuolumne Meadows and many other High Sierra meadows formed—due to rises in groundwater tables which drowned the trees. We can be thankful for this event, for without Tuolumne Meadows the rugged peaks surrounding it would be largely unnoticed by most Park visitors and certainly they would be less photogenic.

Leaving the bridge, your trail crosses the open meadow, aiming first at Unicorn Peak, with only its northernmost summit showing, then aiming gradually westward at the Cockscomb, the Echo Peaks, and finally, near the Tioga Road, at Cathedral Peak. We cross the road and, starting by the east end of an RV-sewage disposal site built in 1976, walk a few minutes south up into a lodgepole forest to meet an east-west trail. The John Muir Trail goes west but we go east, skirt the south border of large Tuolumne Meadows Campground, and at its east end reach a trail junction above the south bank of the Lyell Fork of the Tuolumne River. Now we parallel the Lyell Fork east ¾ mile to a junction, turn left and cross a small meadow to reach two bridges over the Lyell Fork. Note the north-south fracture pattern of the granite here and how it forces the river, when low, to take a tortuous path. When free of such fractures, or joints, granite is almost immune to erosion and even massive glaciers can at best shave away only a few yards. Try visiting this spot in the evening, as the day's cumulonimbus clouds start breaking up and then turn a fiery red to match the aspenglow on Mt. Dana and Mt. Gibbs.

A short, winding climb north, followed by an equal descent, brings one to the Dana Fork of the Tuolumne River, only 150 yards past a junction with an east-climbing trail to the Gaylor Lakes. Immediately beyond the bridge we meet a short spur trail to the Tuolumne Meadows Lodge. Beyond it you hear the Dana Fork as it makes a small drop into a clear pool, almost cut in two by a protruding granite finger. At the base of this finger, about 8-10 feet down, is an underwater arch—an extremely rare feature in any kind of rock. If the water is slack and you feel like braving the cold water, 50° F at best, you can dive under and swim through it.

Just beyond the pool we approach the Lodge's road, where a short path climbs a few yards up to it and takes one to the entrance of

Glacier-smoothed Lembert Dome and the placid Tuolumne River

a large parking lot for backpackers. Now you parallel the paved camp road westward, passing the Tuolumne Meadows Ranger Station and quickly reaching a junction. The main road curves north to the Tioga Road, but you follow the spur road west, to where it curves into a second large parking lot for backpackers. Your road past the lot becomes a closed dirt road and diminishes to a trail by the time we arrive at our loop's end, back at Lembert Dome.

HIKE 56

TUOLUMNE MEADOWS-MERCED LAKE SEMILOOP

Distance: 33.0 miles without any side trips; semiloop

Grade: 5E, moderate 4-day hike

Trailhead: Same as the Hike 45 trailhead. **F3.**

Introduction: Although this hike can be made in two days, four are recommended because it is too scenic to hurry through. At this leisurely pace you have time for most if not all of the side trips.

Description: Start on the John Muir Trail, which runs beside the Dana Fork of the Tuolumne River just yards south of the Tuolumne Meadows Lodge road. On the trail you hike ⅓ mile up the Dana Fork to a junction with a spur trail that goes to the west end of the lodge's parking lot. From this junction you bridge the Dana Fork and after a brief walk upstream reach a junction with a trail to the Gaylor lakes. Unless you are riding a horse, you'll want to reach these lakes from Tioga Pass, via a much shorter route (**Hike 46**).

Veering right, the John Muir Trail leads over a slight rise and descends to the Lyell Fork, where there are two bridges. The meadows above these bridges are among the most delightful in the Sierra; anytime you happen to be staying all night at the lodge or nearby, the bridges are a wonderful place to spend the last hour before dinner, something to consider for your hike out to the Tuolumne Meadows trailhead. Mts. Dana and Gibbs glow on the east-

ern horizon, catching the late sun, while trout dart along the wide Lyell Fork.

About 70 yards past the bridges we meet a trail that comes up the river from the east end of the Tuolumne Meadows Campground (**Hike 55**), turn left (east) onto it, and skirt around a long, lovely section of the meadow. Going through a dense forest cover of lodgepole pine, our route reaches a junction on the west bank of Rafferty Creek. The John Muir Trail (**Hike 58**) continues east, crossing the creek's two major branches, but our route turns right and immediately begins one of the toughest climbs of this entire trip. Even so, the grade is moderate as often as it is steep, the trail is fairly well shaded by lodgepole pines, and the length of the climb is well under a mile. Then, as the ascent decreases to a gentle grade, we pass through high, boulder-strewn meadows that offer good views eastward to reddish-brown Mt. Dana and Mt. Gibbs, and gray-white Mammoth Peak. Soon the trail dips close to Rafferty Creek, and after 2 miles of near-creek hiking, the gently climbing trail passes near the edge of a large meadow and continues its long, gentle ascent through a sparse forest of lodgepole pines.

In the next mile you cross several seasonal creeks, and, about 3.4 miles up the Rafferty Creek trail, reach an even larger meadow. Through this you ascend an easy 1.6 miles to Tuolumne Pass, having backward views north to the Sierra crest between Tioga Pass and Mt. Conness and views ahead to cliffbound, dark-banded Fletcher Peak and Vogelsang Peak to the right of it. At Tuolumne Pass, lodgepole pines and a few whitebark pines diminish the force of winds that often sweep through it. Then your path leaves the green-floored forest and enters an area of granitic outcrops speckled with a few trees. Around this bedrock and past these trees you meander down to the west side of saucer-shaped Tuolumne Pass, a major gap in the Cathedral Range. Taking the signed trail to Vogelsang from the junction here, you follow a rocky, dusty path along a moderately steep slope below which Boothe Lake and its surrounding meadows—part of your return route—lie serene in the west.

Finally the trail makes a short climb, and tents of Vogelsang High Sierra Camp spread out before us at the foot of Fletcher Peak's rock glacier. This rock glacier likely has a complex origin. The author believes that during the

Little Ice Age, a large snowfield rather than a glacier built up at the base of Fletcher Peak and large granite blocks, falling from the peak's very fractured face, slid down the snowfield to its base. The accumulated blocks thus formed a crescentic ring. Later, when conditions warmed and the snowfields melted back, additional blocks fell, and these came to rest behind the crescentic "dam" of earlier blocks, gradually filling in the void once occupied by the Little Ice Age snowfield.

At Vogelsang High Sierra Camp a few snacks may be bought, or dinner or breakfast if you have a reservation. Dispersed camping is not allowed. Rather, use a designated camping area just to the northeast at Upper Fletcher Lake. Here you can find cables on which to bearbag your food. If you camp in this area you might also take the time to explore Townsley and Hanging Basket lakes, above Upper Fletcher Lake.

Taking the Vogelsang Pass trail from the camp, you descend slightly to ford Fletcher Creek on boulders and then begin a 600-foot ascent to the pass. The panting hiker is rewarded with increasingly good views. Fletcher Peak, with its dozens of good climbing routes, rises grandly on the left, far north is Mt. Conness, and Clouds Rest and then Half

Dome come into view in the west-southwest. The trail skirts above the west shore of Vogelsang Lake as we look down on the turfy margins and the large rock island of this treeline lake. Nearer the pass, views to the north are occluded somewhat, but expansive new views appear in the south: from left to right are Parsons Peak, Simmons Peak, Mt. Maclure, the tip of Mt. Lyell behind Maclure, Mt. Florence, and, in the south, the entire Clark Range, from Triple Divide Peak on the left to Mt. Clark on the right.

From Vogelsang Pass, which has clumps of windswept whitebark pines, the trail rises briefly northeast before it switchbacks steeply down into sparse lodgepole forest. Many small streams provide moisture for thousands of lupines, with their light blue, pea-family flowers. The singing of the unnamed outlet stream from bleak Gallison Lake becomes clear as the trail begins to level off, and then you reach a flat meadow, through which the stream slowly meanders. There is a fine campsite beside this meadow, though wood fires are illegal here. After proceeding down a rutted, grassy trail for several hundred yards, you cross the Gallison outlet, top a low ridge, and make a brief, steep, rocky descent that swoops down to the meadowed valley of multibraided Lewis

Rafferty and Johnson peaks backdrop Vogelsang Lake while Fletcher Peak rises from its shore

Boothe Lake and Tuolumne Pass

Creek. In this little valley in quick succession we boulder-hop the Gallison outlet and then cross Lewis Creek on a log. In a few minutes we reach a lateral trail that makes a steep ½-mile climb to Bernice Lake. At that lake, among dwarf bilberry, red mountain heather, and stunted lodgepole and whitebark pines, you can find small, marginal campsites. Perhaps the lake's best use is as a treeline base camp for those who want to explore the snow-fields and alpine lakes between here and Simmons Peak. The lake is also well-located for enjoying the sight of alpenglow on the Sierra crest.

In a short ½ mile from the Bernice Lake trail junction, you cross a little stream, then descend to another equally small one as you wind ¼ mile through dense hemlock forest to a good campsite beside Florence Creek. This year-round creek cascades spectacularly down to the camping area over steep granite sheets, and the water sounds are a fine sleeping potion if you should choose to camp here.

Leaving the densely shaded hemlock forest floor, the trail descends a series of lodge-pole-dotted granite slabs, and Lewis Creek makes pleasant music in a string of chutes not far away on the right. Then, where the creek's channel narrows, the traveler will find on the left a lesson in exfoliation: granite layers peeling like an onion. One is more used to seeing this kind of peeling on Yosemite's domes, but this fine example is located on a canyon slope. As the bed of Lewis Creek steepens to deliver the stream's water to the Merced River far below, so does the trail steepen, and your

descent to middle altitudes reaches the zone of red firs and western white pines. After dipping beside the creek, the trail climbs away from it to a junction with the High trail (**Hike 88**), which climbs south up to the east rim of the Merced River canyon. From here the Lewis Creek trail, now out of earshot of the creek, switchbacks down moderately, sometimes steeply, under a sparse cover of fir, juniper and pine for one mile to a junction with the Fletcher Creek trail. We'll be returning on this trail.

First, however, we'll hike to Merced Lake, which is visible on part of our descent toward it. Because cascading Lewis Creek is entrenched in a small gorge, our switchbacking trail keeps a short distance away from it, reaching a small flat with large Jeffrey pines before passing a small point with an excellent lake view. Half Dome stands on the distant down-canyon skyline. Open switchbacks lined with brush give way to ones with junipers and Jeffrey pines, and then, near the valley floor, to ones with white firs. Among lodgepoles on the valley floor we come to a junction that is just 40 yards north of the Merced Lake Ranger Station. You could hike 2¼ miles up-canyon to Washburn Lake (**Hike 88**), which is more scenic than Merced Lake, but our Hike 56 takes us to the Merced Lake High Sierra Camp. A level, viewless mile walk west gets one to this camp and its adjacent riverside backpackers' campground. Here you will find bearproof boxes in which to store your food. Merced Lake, which is quite photogenic in late evening or in early morning, lies ¼ mile west of the High Sierra

Camp. Some hikers prefer to continue from here down to Happy Isles (**Hike 81**), about 14 miles farther and a total distance of about 31 miles from your trailhead.

After your stay return to the Lewis Creek trail and ascend it to the Fletcher Creek trail junction. Here you turn left onto this path and descend on short switchbacks to a bridge over Lewis Creek. Just 50 yards past it is a good campsite, and then the trail enters more open slopes as it climbs moderately on a cobbled path bordered with proliferating bushes of snow bush and huckleberry oak. Just past a tributary ½ mile from Lewis Creek, you have fine views of Fletcher Creek chuting and cascading down from the notch at the base of the granite dome before it leaps off a ledge in free fall. The few solitary pine trees on this otherwise blank dome testify to nature's extraordinary persistence.

At the notch your trail levels off and reaches the side trail to Babcock Lake. This optional ½-mile trail arcs west to nearby Fletcher Creek, then northwest up to a low ridge. From it the trail goes southwest, crosses a second low ridge, then reaches the lake's northeast end. Among fair lodgepole-shaded campsites by the southeast shore, the trail dies out short of the lake's tiny island. Better campsites are on the opposite shore. Suitable diving slabs are along both shores of this fairly warm lake.

From the Babcock Lake junction, the sandy Fletcher Creek trail ascends steadily through a moderate forest cover, staying just east of Fletcher Creek. After ¾ mile this route breaks out into the open and begins to rise more steeply via rocky switchbacks. From these one can see nearby in the north the outlet stream of Emeric Lake—though not the lake itself, which is behind a dome just to the right of the outlet's notch. If you wish to camp at Emeric Lake—and it's a fine place—leave the trail here, cross Fletcher Creek at a safe spot, climb along the outlet creek's west side and then camp above the northwest shore of Emeric Lake. The next morning circle the head of the lake and find a trail at the base of the low granite ridge at the northeast corner of the lake. Follow this trail ½ mile northeast to a scissors junction in Fletcher Creek valley.

If you choose not to camp at Emeric Lake, continue up the trail into a long meadow guarded in the west by a highly polished knoll

and presided over in the east by huge Vogelsang Peak. When you come to the scissors junction, take the left-hand fork up the valley and follow this rocky-dusty trail through the forest fringe of the long meadow that straddles Fletcher Creek. This trail climbs farther from the meadow and passes northwest of a bald prominence that sits in the center of the upper valley of Fletcher and Emeric creeks, separating the two. You might look for isolated camping sites in this vicinity, particularly above the far bank of Emeric Creek. Camping is not allowed at Boothe Lake. After topping a minor summit, your trail descends slightly and then winds almost level past several lovely ponds that are interconnected in early season. Next is a lakelet, 100 yards in diameter, which would offer good swimming in some years. Just beyond it, the trail traverses northeast to a little swale with another possible swimming pond before reaching an overlook above Boothe Lake. Your trail then contours along meadowy slopes just east of and above the lake, passing a junction with a rutted use trail down to the lake. About ¼ mile farther you pass another trail descending to this lake. Just ahead is Tuolumne Pass, and the junction with the trail to Vogelsang, from where we retrace our steps north back to Tuolumne Meadows.

HIKE 57

TUOLUMNE MEADOWS-VOGELSANG-LYELL CANYON SEMILOOP

Distance: 20.5 miles semiloop

Grade: 5D, moderate 2-day hike

Trailhead: Same as the Hike 45 trailhead. **F3.**

Introduction: This is a popular weekend hike because you can reach the Vogelsang area in only a morning's walk, which gives you a whole afternoon to explore its half-dozen nearby lakes or more distant Emeric Lake. The second day's walk is mostly open, giving the hiker many interesting, diverse views.

The Sierra crest from Mt. Dana to Mt. Conness, seen from the Evelyn Lake bench

Description: Follow **Hike 56** 7 miles up to Tuolumne Pass. From it you can hike southwest to nearby Boothe Lake or 3.7 miles to Emeric Lake, or you can traverse south 0.8 mile to Vogelsang High Sierra Camp. At the camp you can branch off to explore Vogelsang, Upper Fletcher, Townsley and Hanging Basket lakes plus the alpine lake one mile above Townsley Lake. A good exercise in fairly easy cross-country hiking is to go to Ireland Lake from Upper Fletcher Lake. First follow its inlet creek up to Townsley Lake, then climb northeast from it to a large, broad plateau. Strike east across this, then climb up to a long ridge north of Peak 11440+, a high point on the Cathedral Range. From this ridge the descent southeast to Ireland Lake is obvious.

The trail, however, leaves Upper Fletcher Lake, climbs steadily up to an indeterminable drainage divide, eases its gradient and passes through a flat-floored gully whose walls contain large, blocky feldspar crystals so typical of Cathedral Peak granodiorite. Beyond the gully a far-ranging view opens, and on a large flat below us lies spreading, shallow, windswept Evelyn Lake, to whose outlet we now descend. The momentary ascent to the lake is worth it for the geologically inclined. In the process of solifluction, rising subsurface ice has lifted blocks on both sides of this unique lake's outlet to form a low, natural dam, slightly raising the lake's level.

Hikers who would like to try a slightly adventurous alternative to the Lyell Canyon trail as a route back to Tuolumne Meadows can descend the outlet creek along the west slope of its canyon. You pass through a beautiful, large, secluded meadow and walk beside delightful stretches of creek. Eventually, on the west side of the stream, you see a cliff which gradually diminishes in height. When the height has diminished to about 10 feet, find a place to scramble up the cliff and then walk a few hundred feet west to find the Rafferty Creek trail.

Leaving desolate Evelyn Lake and its population of Belding ground squirrels, the trail heads east, then climbs through an open forest of stunted whitebark pines before dropping to a smaller, unnamed lake. Though higher than Evelyn Lake, it has some whitebark pines nearby, providing protection from the wind for those who camp here. About a ½-mile climb northeast from this shallow lake takes one up to a low point on a long north-south crest. You have now left the Cathedral Peak pluton (a large, granitic body) behind and tread upon another pluton—one that lacks the conspicuous feldspar crystals.

Descending from this viewful crest and its brushy whitebark pines, follow a trail segment that contorts down slab after bedrock slab, soon bringing you to a junction with the 1½-mile-long Ireland Lake trail. Lying beneath both granitic and metamorphic peaks, this large alpine lake is unsuited for camping unless you've brought along a tent to protect you from the wind.

Starting east from the trail junction, we soon descend gently south for ½ mile, then angle northeast to make a long 2-mile descent that usually stays within earshot of Ireland Creek. We begin this descent first along its tributary creek, and are in a dense forest of lodgepole and whitebark pines, but the latter give way before we reach the flat floor of Lyell Canyon. This descent could be more enjoyable if the trail were not so steep. On the floor of Lyell Canyon the trail ends at **Hike 58**, which has many trailside campsites in this part of the canyon. The walk back to Tuolumne Meadows through this nearly level canyon is very easy—good therapy for the shocked knees incurred on the descent you've just completed.

HIKE 58

TUOLUMNE MEADOWS TO SILVER LAKE VIA JOHN MUIR TRAIL

Distance: 26.2 miles one way

Grade: 5D, moderate 3-day hike

Trailhead: Same as the Hike 45 trailhead. If you are starting at Silver Lake, go 60 yards west on the spur road that is opposite the entrance to the Silver Lake Campground. This entrance is on the June Lake Loop road (State Route 158). From Highway 395, northbound drivers reach this spot by driving on the loop road (past June Lake) for 8.5 miles while southbound drivers reach it by driving (past Grant Lake) 7.1 miles. **F3, G4.**

Introduction: This section of the John Muir Trail is described in its easiest direction—southbound—to the Park's border. Then, the description goes out to the first trailhead, although most hikers go no farther than upper Lyell Canyon. If you plan to hike Yosemite's *entire* section of the John Muir Trail (JMT), you'll want to start from Silver Lake, which is easier than starting from Yosemite Valley. You could start at Agnew Meadows or Reds Meadow, but the road to them is restricted and, being deeply buried by winter snow, is one of the last roads to open in the Yosemite region. Doing the whole walk from Silver Lake to Yosemite Valley, you cover 50.9 miles. Following this hike's description in reverse, you can get to eastern Tuolumne Meadows, then you walk west past the base of Lembert Dome to the iron-stained Soda Springs. From there, walk south across the western meadows, cross the Tioga Road, then in a few minutes traverse west to the start of **Hike 51** to Yosemite Valley.

Description: Follow **Hike 56** 1⅔ miles to the Rafferty Creek trail junction. Here you branch left and cross two branches of Rafferty Creek.

The first ford may be difficult in early season. East of the creek the trail traverses alternating wet-meadow and forest sections—with clouds of mosquitoes before August—then veers southward, climbing between two resistant granite outcrops. The silent walker may come upon grazing deer in the meadows and an occasional marmot that has ventured from the rocky outcrops. Fields of wildflowers color the grasslands from early to late season, but the best time of the year for seeing this color is usually July. From the more open parts of the trail, one has excellent views of the Kuna Crest as it slopes up to the southeast, and the river itself has delighted generations of mountain photographers. In the meadows of Lyell Canyon you can see Ragged Peak and its crest, to the northwest.

About 4.4 miles past the last junction, your nearly level route passes a trail branching southwest to Evelyn Lake and Vogelsang High Sierra Camp (**Hike 57**), with campsites near the junction. Look for bear-proof cables. Beyond, the trail fords multibranched Ireland Creek, passes below Potter Point, and ascends gently for 3 miles to the fair campsites at Lyell Base Camp, just beyond cascading Kuna Creek. This camp, surrounded on three sides by steep canyon walls, marks the end of the meadowed sections of Lyell Canyon, and is the traditional first-night stopping place for those touring the Muir Trail south from Tuolumne Meadows.

From Lyell Base Camp the lodgepole-shaded trail ascends the steep southern terminal wall of Lyell Canyon, leaving an understory of sagebrush behind before reaching a granite bench. On it you pass a few campsites just before the Maclure Creek-Lyell Fork confluence. Then the route crosses a bridge to the east side and switchbacks up to some popular campsites among clumps of whitebark pines just before recrossing the fork at the north edge of a subalpine meadow. The rocky underfooting beyond the crossing takes you up past the foot of superb alpine meadows, from where views of the glaciers on the north faces of Mt. Maclure and Mt. Lyell are superlative. Hikers who wish to obtain a more intimate view or to ascend to these ice fields via the lake-dotted basin at their feet should take the ducked route that leaves our trail where we turn east and recross the infant Lyell Fork at the north end of a boulder-dotted pond.

From this ford the John Muir Trail winds steeply up rocky going and eventually veers southeast up a long, straight fracture to Donohue Pass (11056′) at the crest of the Sierra and on the Park's border. Just before and just after the pass—not at it—one has great views of the Sierra crest, the Cathedral Range to the northwest, and the Ritter Range to the southeast. At the broad pass we enter Ansel Adams Wilderness. On a sometimes obscure trail we descend northeast away from a prominent peak and go past blocks and over slabs before turning east for a wet slog across the tundra- and stone floor of an alpine basin. West of this basin is a conspicuous saddle, which northwestbound early-season hikers too often mistake for Donohue Pass. When the JMT is largely snowbound, these hikers will have to remember to hike southwest up toward the prominent peak until the real Donohue Pass becomes obvious.

Beyond the alpine basin, whitebark pines rapidly increase in size and numbers as we drop farther. Generally heading southeast, the JMT winds excessively in an oft-futile attempt to avoid the boulders and bogs of the near-treeline environment. Three miles from Donohue Pass you arrive at the Marie Lakes' outlet creek, which can be crossed at a jump-across spot slightly downstream. Immediately beyond the creek we meet a trail that climbs southwest up to the lower, large alpine lake, and then we parallel these lakes' outlet ⅓ mile down-canyon to a low ridge. On it you get your last good views of—east to west—Banner Peak, Mt. Ritter, and Mt. Davis, then you descend via short, steep switchbacks to a junction with the Rush Creek trail. This junction is in the Rush Creek Forks area, where campsites must be at least 100 feet from any creek or trail. Although you have left Yosemite, you have not left its black bears, for they have spilled beyond the Park's boundaries in search of humans' food. If you camp here, expect to have these night-time prowlers.

Among lodgepoles you leave the John Muir Trail to follow the Rush Creek trail 9½ miles down to Silver Lake. Immediately you ford two of the creek's many forks, then descend ⅔ mile to a small campsite on the west shore of Waugh Lake. Your trail hugs this lake, then in about 10 minutes you pass your second lodgepole-shaded, lakeshore campsite. After an easy mile hike beyond it, some of the dis-

Potter Point reflected in Lyell Fork

tance being past sagebrush, you leave the lake, switchback down below the base of its dam and immediately meet a trail that climbs south to Weber and Sullivan lakes.

Paralleling Rush Creek, we continue down-canyon—now on a lodgepole-lined, closed service road of the Southern California Edison Company—and in a few minutes reach a large campsite. Another campsite is passed just where the road leaves Rush Creek to climb through a 30-foot-high, glacier-polished granite gap. Beyond it you hike down toward Rush Creek, curve northeast and in ¼ mile reach a short spur trail that goes south to a large creek-side campsite. On the road you quickly meet a junction with a trail to Agnew Pass. At this junction turn left, then climb north past a pond and a closer, larger one, Billy Lake, and in ¼ mile top a low notch in a ridge that is composed of metavolcanic rocks. A short, steep descent east follows, then a gentle one north. The road quickly descends to the west shore of Gem Lake, but before it does so, you leave it and traverse north ¼ mile on trail to Crest Creek. Here, among an abundance of small-lodgepole-shaded campsites, you meet the Alger Lakes trail. By following **Hike 60** in

From near Donohue Pass: Amelia Earhart Peak, Lyell Canyon, and Kuna Crest

reverse you can take this extremely scenic trail back into Yosemite National Park and then descend the Tioga Road 4.6 miles to the Dog Lake trail, on which you quickly drop to your trailhead parking lot. This high-altitude loop is 41½ miles long and is for those who want to escape the crowds at the expense of some strenuous climbing.

In late season we can rock-hop Crest Creek, but normally one must cross it on a log. Aspens—brilliant in early fall—join ranks with lodgepoles in shading a creekside campsite. Farther east aspens give way to sagebrush, junipers, and Jeffrey pines and even to an occasional whitebark pine. Your trail generally stays above Gem Lake's steep shoreline, then climbs to one ridge before descending and climbing to a second one, this one above the lake's dam. This ridge and the bedrock north and south of it are composed mostly of Paleozoic-age sediments that have been metamorphosed, usually to hornfels. These ancient rocks are roughly 100 times older than the dark andesite flows we see above Gem Lake's forested south slopes. These thick, horizontal flows originated in conjunction with faulting, which began about 3 million years ago, and which caused lands east of the Sierra crest to subside.

We leave Gem Lake behind and, for a spell, Ansel Adams Wilderness, as we descend to the Agnew Lake dam. On this descent, mountain mahogany dominates the dry, south-facing slopes, in contrast to the forested, north-facing ones just below Agnew Pass. In

the dam's vicinity grow giant blazing stars, whose oversized yellow flowers will be blooming for late-season hikers.

Beyond the dam, switchbacks lead you north down alongside a tramway, which you cross twice, and then descend slopes toward Silver Lake. At first these slopes have mountain mahogany, juniper, and even pinyon pine, but then, not far beyond a small waterfall, they are gradually replaced with waist-high vegetation. Draining west into Silver Lake is Reversed Creek, which has an interesting history. Glaciers originating near the Sierra crest descended to the large canyon we're in, then split into two lobes, each lobe going on one side of Reversed Peak. Each glacial lobe built up a considerable terminal moraine at its snout, and when these lobes finally retreated, a lake formed behind each moraine. Before the waters backing up behind the June Lake moraine were able to breach it, they overflowed southwest into the Grant Lake drainage, and today these waters continue to flow in that direction—directly opposite that of the glacier's flow—as *Reversed Creek*. It is also reversed in the sense that it is the flows toward the range's crest rather than away from it.

Near Silver Lake's west corner our trail almost touches the June Lake Loop road, which has very limited parking here, then arcs behind Silver Lake Resort and fords several branches of Alger Creek. It finally traverses behind Silver Lake Trailer Court to quickly end at a trailhead parking area amid sagebrush, mule ears, rabbitbrush, and bitterbrush.

HIKE 59

DANA MEADOWS TO MONO PASS

Distance: 8.0 miles round trip

Grade: 2C, moderate day hike

Trailhead: Mono Pass trailhead, which is 5.6 miles east of the Tuolumne Meadows Campground, or 1.4 miles south of Tioga Pass. F3.

Introduction: This day hike to a historic pass on the Sierra crest is great for alpine scenery, for the views improve constantly and culminate at the pass, from where one can gaze down the great gash of Bloody Canyon to the vast, high desert east of the Sierra.

Description: Starting under a dense canopy of lodgepole pines, you leave the trailhead, descending on a wide trail, once a dirt road. In a meadow ¼ mile from the trailhead, lodgepoles, as elsewhere, ceaselessly attempt to invade this meadow, but wet years raise the water table and this may directly or indirectly kill them. These young trees' needles are also susceptible to brown-felt fungus and to icy winter winds.

About ½ mile from the trailhead you cross Dana Meadows creek and Dana Fork just above their confluence. Beyond these two crossings your trail climbs to the crest of a low moraine, crosses two more, and then near Parker Pass Creek comes to the ruins of a pioneer log cabin. Sagebrush intermingles with lodgepoles as you pass creekside meadows that in early morning hours often have browsing deer in them. A little more than 2 miles from our trailhead you come to a junction, and from it a trail climbs 1.9 miles gently up along Parker Pass Creek to shallow, meadow-bordered Spillway Lake (camping prohibited). This and other lakes of the Mono Pass-Tioga Pass area have California gulls as frequent visitors, these birds nesting on islands in large, alkaline Mono Lake (**Hike 61**). From Spillway Lake you could hike cross-country east up to alpine Parker Pass, then head back on a trail to the Mono Pass area.

Our trail up to the Spillway Lake trail junction has been easy, but now it climbs nearly 700 feet, passing the ruins of a second pioneer cabin, on the right, just ¼ mile before the Parker Pass trail junction. From that junction, near a large whitebark pine, **Hike 60** describes that trail all the way to Gem Lake. After ¼ mile of nearly level hiking our trail passes a lakelet situated between two ponds. From the east shore of the lakelet a trail starts south toward five old cabins but dies out in 300 yards. From that point, however, the cabins just south above you are easily reached. These cabins, constructed from local whitebark pines, once housed workers on the nearby Golden Crown and Ella Bloss gold mines, both long defunct. If you visit these cabins, you'll get a good view north at Mt. Gibbs' south shoulder. Note the difference between its lower slopes and steeper higher ones. Whitebark pines are able to grow on the lower slopes, but not on the unstable upper ones. You'll also note that the upper slopes have patterned ground, which indicates slope movement. In Yosemite's alpine areas, mass movement takes place only on slopes of metamorphic rocks, not those of granite, because ice wedging breaks metamorphic bedrock into many small, unstable rocks, whereas it heaps granite into large, relatively immobile blocks.

Just east of the cabins' spur trail you encounter Summit Lake, straddling often breezy Mono Pass. The lake appears to lie immediately east of the pass—the Park's boundary—but careful scouting among the lake's west-end willows will reveal that the lake does indeed have a west-flowing outlet as well as a more obvious east-flowing one. Nesting beneath the willows are white-crowned sparrows, which are usually seen with Brewer's blackbirds. The blackbirds nest at lower elevations during the spring but usually migrate up to these heights by the time the Mono trail is snow-free.

Our hike has followed only a small portion of the Mono trail, which is an old Indian trail that started near Cascade Creek, high above westernmost Yosemite Valley. This trail started like today's eastbound El Capitan trail, but continued northeast along Bluejay Creek to Yosemite Creek, then up to Porcupine Flat, from where it took a route similar to that of the later Old Tioga Road. From Mono Pass the Mono trail continued down Bloody Canyon, which may have been named for the reddish colored bedrock of metamorphosed sediments, but more likely was named for the

A lakelet straddles Mono Pass, backdropped by the Kuna Crest and Mammoth Peak

treachery of this canyon. In 1864 William Brewer and Charles Hoffmann—two younger members of Josiah Whitney's State Geological Survey—descended Bloody Canyon. Brewer later said of it:

> You would all pronounce it utterly inaccessible to horses, yet pack trains come down, but the bones of several horses or mules and the stench of another told that all had not passed safely. The trail comes down three thousand feet in less than four miles, over rocks and loose stones, in narrow canyons and along precipices. It was a bold man who first took a horse up there. The horses were so cut by sharp rocks that they named it "Bloody Canyon," and it has held the name—and it is appropriate—part of the way the rocks are literally sprinkled with blood from the animals.

Today this trail is still a steep descent over rocks and loose stones, but it is considerably safer. Upper Sardine Lake, only ¾ mile distant by this trail, is worth the effort, but beyond it a big drop to cold, deep Lower Sardine Lake makes for an exhausting return hike.

HIKE 60

DANA MEADOWS TO SILVER LAKE VIA PARKER PASS

Distance: 20.0 miles one way

Grade: 5D, moderate 2-day hike

Trailhead: Same as the Hike 59 trailhead. If you're starting from Silver Lake, consult the Hike 58 trailhead information. **F3.**

Introduction: Knowledgeable backpackers prefer this route to the popular, nearby section of the John Muir Trail (Hike 58). Being mostly along metamorphic terrain, this route is certainly more colorful, and by staying high—often at or above treeline—it has a wild aspect about it. At these elevations dark glasses and sunscreen are a must. This route is no place to be caught in a lightning storm or a snowstorm, so only weather-wise backpackers should attempt it. However, the 10.5 miles to Parker Pass and back make a fine high-altitude day hike for anyone in good health.

Description: Follow **Hike 59** 3½ miles up to a junction just ½ mile short of broad, deep Mono Pass. From a large whitebark pine near the junction, strike south-southwest 300 yards across a meadow, following ducks that guide you to a resumption of obvious tread. Continuing in the same direction, climb to the crest of a broad moraine that here and there has rusty exposures of Triassic-period metavolcanics (metamorphosed volcanic rocks). On this ascent you pass many whitebark pines that are reduced to shrub height, and so get largely unobstructed views that include shallow Spillway Lake, lying at the base of the Kuna Crest. Note how the granitic upper slopes of this crest differ not only in color but in shape and texture from the lower metamorphic slopes.

Up at treeline, we see the deep cleft of Parker Pass more than a mile before we attain it. Stunted whitebarks and yellow-blossomed bush cinquefoils yield to mats of alpine willow—a favorite summer haunt of white-crowned sparrows—then these bushes yield to sedges and finally, at the broad, signed pass, to coarse gravel. A low, broad moraine south of you hides barren Parker Pass Lake and it also provides a suitable habitat for marmots. Briefly during midsummer, a marmot's sole food source may be Sierra wallflowers and

Brewer's lupines. The first species can turn the moraine's slopes bright yellow and mask the presence of the equally prevalent lupine. Other plant species appear both before and after these two, and all provide the marmot with a diverse selection, which it readily consumes before going into hibernation in October.

From Parker Pass, day hikers can wander northeast up to a crest that leads to the top of windswept Mt. Lewis. However, don't attempt this technically easy but thin-air climb if the weather looks threatening. At Parker Pass backpackers enter Ansel Adams Wilderness and leave all vestiges of the granitic Yosemite landscape behind. Descending on Paleozoic-era metasediments, they first cross an outlet creek from two nearby ponds, recross it at a third, and then traverse southeast toward a series of ominous looking switchbacks that climb the northwest slope of Parker Peak. About ¾ mile beyond the pass you cross a seasonally churning tributary that gets its vigor from a permanent snowfield lodged high on the slopes between Kuna and Koip peaks. Just past this tributary the deep canyon cleft between Mt. Lewis and Parker Peak begins to open, and through it we see the Mono Craters and the distant White Mountains.

One-half mile closer to trail's end, you reach an alpine tarn and from it can gaze straight down the enormous Parker Creek cleft. Parker Lake is almost hidden, but larger Grant Lake, with its giant lateral moraines, is easily seen, This stupendous view may divert one's interest from the seemingly ordinary tarn. This pond is, however, very un-Sierran, for near its outlet the shallow rocky bottom is patterned with a network of polygon stone rings. Repeated freezing and melting of ice over hundreds of years have separated the coarse rocks from the finer particles. If you step in the middle of one of these polygons—usually a hexagon—you'll sink into clay. This phenomenon is not seen at many High Sierra ponds because they typically exist in granitic terrain. This pond, however, is in metamorphic terrain, and at high elevations like here, metamorphic rock is shattered by ice wedging, which breaks it into many small, unstable blocks.

Beyond this tarn we are confronted with a ¼-mile net vertical climb to Koip Peak Pass. First we climb to our second snowfield-fed Parker Creek tributary. Panting up to the first

of many switchbacks, take a breather, scan the ever-improving panorama and now see most of large, alkaline Mono Lake and the summits of Mts. Gibbs and Conness, the latter rising above Parker Pass. During July you may see the unmistakable sky pilot, a blue-petaled polemonium that thrives in the bleakest alpine environments. Around Yosemite you'll rarely find it growing below 11,000 feet. Sharing this harsh habitat are members of the *Draba* genus, which has a dozen hard-to-key species that exist above treeline in the Sierra Nevada. You'll note that its yellow flowers are virtually identical to those of the Sierra wallflower, often seen west of Parker Pass, for both are mustards.

Finally, switchbacks yield to a gradually easing ascent southwest to shallow Koip Peak Pass, which at 12,280 feet is one of the Sierra's highest trail passes. Before early August, snowfields may cover parts of the trail to the pass, and they could present a problem since

A marmot surveys its domain in an alpine fell-field near Parker Pass

you have 600 feet of steep, potentially fatal slopes below you. On your ascent to the pass you may have noticed the gentle summits of Parker Peak, Mt. Wood, and even Mt. Lewis. If you have the time, you might scramble up the scree slopes to either Koip or Parker Peak.

Leaving the pass, you exchange views of Mts. Conness, Gibbs, Dana, and Lewis for ones of the Alger Lakes, the June Lake ski area, volcanic Mammoth Mountain, distant Lake Crowley and the distant central Sierra Nevada crest. While topographic constraints made a string of short switchbacks necessary for your ascent, they are lacking for your descent, which is a pleasant, occasionally switchbacking drop deep into the Alger Lakes basin. As the trail's gradient eases, you cross Alger Creek, and then, with a low, fresh-looking moraine on your right, parallel the creek for ¾ mile before crossing a multicrested moraine and descending past cairns for ¼ mile to a point between the two fairly large Alger Lakes. Only 50 yards and a 2-foot drop separate the two treeline lakes, and on the bedrock landmass that separates them you can set up camp among its windblown whitebark pines. These will be the first partly sheltered sites you'll encounter on this hike, for no camping is allowed in Yosemite's Dana Fork drainage and all possible sites this side of Parker Pass are above treeline. Immediately beyond lower Alger Lake's outlet you'll also find a trailside campsite.

From the outlet we climb up our moraine's low crest, glancing back across the open terrain at the dramatic setting of this glaciated, somber-toned rock basin, which has metasediments composing the northeast canyon wall and metavolcanics composing the southwest one. Now 6 miles from Parker Pass and 4 from Gem Lake, you follow the generally open moraine's crest south past a nearby lakelet, then descend steeply about 300 feet to a second one, along whose fragile shore one should not camp. Along this morainal route you'll probably note a flat-topped mass standing immediately east of Gem Pass. Your route ends near its base.

Despite the high altitude, your second lakelet provides an acceptable habitat for dozens of yellow-legged frogs. Large rocks forming small islands testify to the instability of a nearby cliff. Just 250 yards beyond this tarn, you enter your first stand of lodgepoles.

Among its protective confines is a campsite, on the left, which is certainly the place you'll want to stay if you have to wait out a lightning storm. In only a minute's walk toward Gem Lake, you'll come to a shallow pond—the camp's closest water source. Beyond this pond you climb for ½ mile to forested Gem Pass while Alger Creek, hundreds of feet below you, drops out of sight to your final goal, Silver Lake. Shortly before Gem Pass the trail forks. The left branch descends, only to climb again, but it may be the better of the two in early season, when the snow is piled deep. From 10,500-foot Gem Pass we have our first views of the famous Ritter Range, dominated by Mt. Ritter and Banner Peak. Now under a continual canopy of protective forest, we descend first through whitebark pines and then lodgepoles, cross Crest Creek after ¾ mile, and switchback down alongside it, reaching well-used campsites above Gem Lake after a 2-mile, 1,400-foot drop. Among these campsites you'll meet the Rush Creek trail, on which you hike almost 5 miles east to trail's end, near the Silver Lake Campground. This stretch is described in the last part of **Hike 58**.

HIKE 61

DANA PLATEAU AND MT. DANA

Distance: 5.8 miles round trip

Grade: 2D, strenuous half-day hike

Trailhead: On Highway 120 at Tioga Pass—the Park's east entrance. **F3**.

Introduction: Dark glasses and good health are both necessary for this climb to the second highest summit in Yosemite. Only Mt. Lyell exceeds it—by only 61 feet—but the Lyell summit requires mountaineering skills. Because Dana vies with Mt. Hoffman as Yosemite's most accessible peak, it is very popular, and on weekends you may find dozens of persons walking up it. Its summit views are among the Sierra's best, but turn back if the weather looks threatening.

Description: The trail up Mt. Dana, like the one up Mt. Hoffmann (**Hike 27**), is one of use and not an officially maintained trail. Dana's trail, however, is not random, but rather was established by Dr. Carl Sharsmith, Yosemite's eminent botanist, who in probably the 1930s chose a route that would minimize damage to this area's fragile subalpine and alpine environments.

From Tioga Pass the footpath starts due east, then meanders southeast past the south shores of two ponds that are among two dozen that developed when the last major glacier retreated. Cirque glaciers originating on the Kuna Crest, about 6 miles south of us, coalesced to form a trunk glacier that mainly descended the Dana Fork to unite with the Lyell Fork glacier and create the Tuolumne glacier. Being strengthened by dozens of feeder glaciers, this mammoth glacier was able to descend tens of miles down-canyon, to about Cherry Creek, down at 2150 feet elevation (see **Hike 15**). Before 20,000 years ago, at the height of the Tioga glaciation, the Dana Fork branch was about 1000 feet thick where it overflowed *north* across Tioga Pass to join the Lee Vining glacier. This originated in the nearby Hall Natural Area, and together they descended to spall icebergs into Lake Russell, a high-water predecessor of Mono Lake. However, it appears that by about 16,000 years ago the Lyell Fork glacier had retreated sufficiently so that now the Lee Vining glacier briefly overflowed *south* into the Tuolumne drainage.

About 200 yards beyond the second pond your path starts a moderate ascent, then ⅓ mile later it becomes a steep one and generally stays that way for almost 1500 feet of elevation gain. About midway up this steep stretch you can rest in an *alp*—a miniature alpine pasture. The end of the steep section is noted by a cairn atop a south-descending spur ridge. Here, well above treeline, the path ends, about 1.1 miles from and still 1400 feet below the summit. Several use paths, one more prominent than the others, head up the rubbly, ancient slopes to the windblown summit. Most people climb east to a shallow saddle, at about 12,150 feet in elevation and immediately east of a crest high point, then hike southeast up the ridge to the top. Early in the hike the views west are great, but the panorama continually expands with elevation, saturating the optic nerves with overpowering vistas. When you hike southeast up the ridge, your views take on another dimension, adding to your elation. However,

Members of an alpine-botany course at Dana Plateau's Cape Royal

take this ridge ascent slowly, for the atmosphere is thin and in your euphoria you can easily overexert yourself. Being above the 12,000-foot elevation, July hikers can expect to see the sky pilot blooming with its dense head of blue flowers.

At the summit your exhausting efforts are rewarded by a stupendous 360° panorama. The Sierra's east escarpment can be viewed as far as the Wheeler Crest, about 40 miles to the southeast. East of it extends a long north-south mountain chain, the White Mountains, which were a part of the Sierra Nevada until downfaulting created a proto Owens Valley, perhaps about 80 million years ago. Faulting began much more recently, about 3-4 million years ago, and for decades geologists have assumed—very incorrectly, as the abundant field evidence demonstrates—that Owens Valley began to form around then.

At the north end of the White Mountains stand the pale, isolated twin summits of Montgomery and Boundary peaks, both over 13,000 feet high. Gambling is legal on the Boundary Peak summit for it is ¼ mile in from the Nevada border. Below these twin summits rises Crater Mountain, the highest of Mono Domes (formerly "Mono Craters") many volcanic summits, and, like most of them, less than 10,000 years old.

The youthfulness of Mono Domes strongly contrasts with the ancient age of giant, orbicular Mono Lake, directly north of them. Lakes are generally short-lived features, but this one may be over 1 million years old. Sediments beneath the lake are up to almost 4000 feet thick. This lake's longevity was threatened by humans, water-hungry Los Angeles residents in particular, who have diverted inflowing creeks, thereby causing the lake to drop some 40 feet in historic times. This drop increased the lake's alkalinity almost to a pH of 10, which causes its water to feel like clothes-detergent water. In addition, when the lake reached a low during the summer of 1977, a land bridge emerged, linking 1000-year old Negit Island to the Black Point shoreline. This island, a major nesting ground for thousands of California gulls and other birds, thus became accessible to predators. With diminishing nesting sites and increasing alkalinity, the populations of gulls and other migrant birds have unfortunately decreased. Fortunately, in a landmark 1994 decision, the State Water Resources Control Board mandated that diversions from the lake be reduced until it reaches a healthy water level of about 6,392 feet, about

15 feet higher than its lower elevations in the 1970s and '80s. Additionally, streams gone dry due to diversions now have flowing water to support both trout and riparian vegetation.

During glacial times, Mono Lake was much larger than today. At its maximum size, Lake Russell—glacial Mono Lake—was about 345 square miles in area and up to 950 feet deep, versus about 86 square miles and 186 feet deep in historic time before Los Angeles started diverting water away from it. In the 1980s, the lake had shrunk to about 60 square miles and 150 feet deep. The volume of the lake at these three times respectively was about 120, 4, and 2 million acre feet. Instead of being an alkaline desert lake, Lake Russell was a freshwater lake that at its maximum had icebergs, which were spalled from the snouts of the Lundy Creek, Lee Vining Creek, Walker Creek, and Rush Creek glaciers. In all of the 48 states, only two other large lakes are known to have had glaciers encroach upon them: Lake Tahoe and Lake Bonneville, now existing in dwarfed form as Utah's not-so-Great Salt Lake.

Below our summit is deep Glacier Canyon, which holds only the few-hundred-year-old Dana "glacier," which is more a permanent snowfield than a flowing glacier. Being only a two-hour hike up-canyon from Tioga Lake, this "glacier" is frequented by mountaineers who practice their skills up it. Another feature worth visiting is the broad, gently sloping Dana Plateau, with its rare, ankle-high snow willows. Like Peak 12568, which is 1½ miles southeast of our summit, this is a relict of an old, unglaciated or lightly

Summit view of Dana Plateau and Mono Basin. Circle indicates plateau's Cape Royal

glaciated landscape. For that matter, Mt. Dana and Mt. Gibbs are left over from that landscape, as are many of this area's gentle-sloped peaks. By scanning the horizon you can see a number of them and then you can mentally reconstruct the ancient eastern-Yosemite landscape. A nearly universal belief, unfortunately promulgated by the author in previous editions and in other Sierran books, is that this gentle landscape existed until glaciers, starting in earnest some 2 million years ago, deeply eroded existing drainages. Not so. The gentle landscape is very ancient, having originated some 80 million years ago, and glaciers, despite their enormity, performed only minor deepening and widening of canyons.

Continuing your counterclockwise scan west, you see deep-blue Saddlebag Lake and above it, the serrated Shepherd Crest. Next comes pointed North Peak, with its south-facing ancient surface, then a true "Matterhorn," Mt. Conness. Beyond a sea of dark-green lodgepoles lies Tuolumne Meadows and its sentinel, Lembert Dome, whose bald summit is barely visible. On the skyline above them stand Tuolumne Peak and Mt. Hoffmann, while south of these stand the craggy summits of the Cathedral Range. Examining it counterclockwise, you can identify blocky Cathedral Peak, north-pointing Unicorn Peak, clustered

Echo Peaks, and the adjacent Cockscomb plus the fin-like Matthes Crest, extending south from it. A bit farther are sedate Johnson Peak, more profound Rafferty Peak, and broad Tuolumne Pass, through which former Tuolumne glaciers overflowed into the Merced drainage.

To the south-southwest stands the Park's highest peak, Mt. Lyell (13,114'), which also harbors the Park's largest glacier, today cleft in two by a northwest-dropping ridge. When members of the Whitney Survey first climbed our summit in 1863, they saw a Lyell glacier twice today's size, and it partly buried the ridge as well as extended north beyond it. Flanking Lyell is Mt. Maclure and its glacier to the west, and pointed Rodgers Peak to the southeast. Mt. Ritter and Banner Peak barely poke their summits above the temporarily stagnant Kuna Peak-Koip Peak glacier to the south. Finally, Parker Peak and Mt. Wood stand above closer Mt. Gibbs, while Mt. Lewis, of intermediate distance, projects just east of them. Once a part of a low continental borderland, all the red or dark metamorphic summits (including Mt. Dana's) are made of rocks with an extremely long history. See the first part of Chapter 2 for details of the area's early geologic history.

Chapter 10
Trails of the Yosemite Valley Area

Introduction: Rightly called "The Incomparable Valley," Yosemite Valley is a magnet that attracts visitors from all over the world. As John Muir noted long ago, the Sierra Nevada has several "Yosemites," though none of them matches Yosemite Valley in grandeur. Hetch Hetchy, to the north, is the foremost example of such a Yosemite. Though some of these "Yosemites" rival or exceed Yosemite Valley in the depth of their canyons and the steepness of their walls, none has the prize-winning combination of its wide, spacious floor, its world-famous waterfalls, and its unforgettable monoliths—El Capitan and Half Dome.

This section is actually composed of four parts. Hikes 62-67 acquaint you with the views and natural history seen along the Valley floor. Hikes 68-70 guide you up to and along the Valley's north rim, while Hikes 71-76 guide you along its south rim. Finally, Hikes 77-81 direct you up a multi-stepped climb east from the Valley to thundering Vernal and Nevada falls, forested Little Yosemite Valley, intimidating Half Dome, and popular Merced Lake.

Supplies and Services: Yosemite Village is a small-scale urban center—and like one, it is all too crowded. Parking space is at a premium, so I recommend you reach it by taking a free shuttle bus or by walking or bicycling. At the "Village" are the Visitor Center and Museum plus a general store, eating establishments, medical clinic, post office, and other services. The services are expected to undergo some changes in the early 2000s. The only service you'll find lacking at the Village is lodging, which is available—along with meals—at Yosemite Lodge to the west, the Ahwahnee Hotel to the east, and Curry Village to the southeast. West of Curry Village is its Housekeeping Camp, which currently has a laundromat next to its showers. Showers are also available at Camp Curry proper and at Yosemite Lodge. These two operations each have a swimming pool, a bike rental, and a post office. The prestigious Ahwahnee Hotel formerly had tennis courts and a 9-hole golf course, but now offers only (besides elegant ambiance) a guest-only swimming pool. At Glacier Point, high above the Valley's southeast end, you can buy snacks, film and a few other items. The same is true at the foot of the Glacier Point cliff—Happy Isles.

Wilderness Permits: Most of the hikes in this section are day hikes. For multiday hikes, get your permit at the Wilderness Center, located in Yosemite Village. If you want to *reserve* a permit in advance, which I recommend you do for Hikes 79-81, see the "Wilderness permits" section on page 59.

Left: Tall trees are dwarfed by the lower part of Middle Cathedral Rock's northeast face

Campgrounds: Back in the early days, when visitation was light by today's standards, there were up to 14 campgrounds in the Valley. Today there are only three regular campgrounds—North, Upper, and Lower Pines—plus two smaller, walk-in campgrounds—Sunnyside and Backpackers. The former is heavily dominated by rock climbers, and the latter is for backpackers who have a wilderness permit and need a place to stay the night before they start their hike. For most visitors, camping in the Valley will remain an unfulfilled dream. For south-rim trails, you should stay at Bridalveil Creek Campground, south of the Valley, whose entrance is midway along the Glacier Point Road.

HIKE 62

VALLEY FLOOR, BRIDALVEIL FALL LOOP

Distance: 6.9 miles loop trip

Grade: 2B, easy half-day hike

Trailhead: Bridalveil Fall parking lot, 120 yards before the descending Wawona Road reaches a junction on the floor of Yosemite Valley. **C5.**

Introduction: This is the first of six Yosemite Valley floor hikes in this book, which are arranged from west to east. Because the Valley contains so much history, natural history and spectacular scenery, the hike descriptions are long even though the hikes are short. On this first loop hike you'll see Bridalveil Fall, the Cathedral Rocks and El Capitan all at close range.

Description: You could start this loop from any of several pullouts along the Valley's roads, but we're starting from the Bridalveil Fall Parking lot, since it has the most parking space. From the lot's east end you hike just two minutes on a paved trail to a junction, veer right and parallel a Bridalveil Creek tributary as you climb an equally short trail up to its end. During May and June, when Bridalveil Fall is at its best, your trail's-end viewpoint will be drenched in spray, making the last part of the trail very slippery and making photography from this vantage point nearly impossible. Early settlers named this fall for its filmy, veil-like aspect, which it has in summer after its flow has greatly diminished. However, their predecessors, the Miwok Indians, named it *Pohono,* the "fall of the puffing winds," for at

low volume its water is pushed around by gusts of wind.

Of Yosemite's other falls, only Vernal Fall leaps free over a dead-vertical cliff, but its flow—the Merced River—is too strong to be greatly affected by the wind. The other major falls drop over cliffs that are less than vertical, and hence the falls partly glide down them. Bridalveil's cliff owes its verticality to vertical joints along which the cliff's granite flakes off. The cliff and waterfall are very old, having changed little in the last 30 million years. Glaciers did very little to steepen or backwaste this cliff. For some 50 million years before then, under warm, wet climates Yosemite Valley widened principally through weathering and through rockfalls; glaciers played only a minor role in widening it. Along most of our easy hike, we'll be treading across sediments, some deposited since the glaciers left. Locally, they are as much as 1000 feet deep—2000 feet deep in the eastern part of the Valley—however, the bulk of this material likely is decomposed, subsurface bedrock that long ago had weathered in place.

After descending back to the trail junction and turning right, you quickly encounter several branches of Bridalveil Creek, each churning along a course that cuts through old rockfall debris. From a junction with a short trail to the Valley's eastbound Southside Drive, you continue ahead on our broad trail—the old Wawona Road until 1933—and almost to the present road, then quickly veer right to climb up to the crest of Bridalveil Moraine. From it you get a good view of the loose west wall of Lower Cathedral Rock and also the overhanging west wall of Leaning Tower.

Just past the moraine's crest we enter a gully lined with big-leafed maples, and here we have an excellent head-on view of mammoth El Capitan. Then, only yards away from the base of the forbidding north wall of Lower Cathedral Rock, we can stretch our necks and look up at its large ledge, covered with canyon live oaks, that almost cuts the face in two. While violet-green swallows perform aerial acrobatics high overhead, we continue east through a conifer forest, soon crossing a narrow, open talus field. At its base stands a second moraine, similar to Bridalveil, and like all the Valley's moraines it is recessional—that is, it was left where a glacier temporarily halted its retreat. It's been widely believed by the public as well as by some prominent geologists that diminutive, essentially unseen El Capitan Meadow moraine, left by the Tioga-age glacier about 16,000 years ago, dammed the Merced River to create mammoth (though mythical) Lake Yosemite. After the last glaciation and ones before it, the Valley often may have been quite swampy due to temporary dams created behind recessional moraines or dams created by periodic rockfalls that originated on Lower Cathedral Rock's loose north wall, above us. Indeed, the first visitors found the Valley too swampy and mosquito-ridden, so in 1879 the large rockfall blocks clogging the nearby Merced River channel were blasted apart, which deepened the channel some 4½ feet and thereby, lowered the Valley's water table. The river, rather than meandering widely and changeably across the Valley became entrenched, and ponderosa pines and incense-cedars invaded at the expense of wet-meadow vegetation and black oaks. The blasting was also expected to reduce all flooding, but major floods occurred about every 15-20 years. Two exceptionally large ones, which covered about two thirds of the Valley's floor, occurred in 1955 and 1997.

Walking among white firs, incense-cedars, ponderosa pines, Douglas-firs, and black oaks, you continue on a generally view-impaired route to a brief climb almost to the base of overwhelming Middle Cathedral Rock, and here you'll find it worth your effort to scramble 50 yards up to the actual base. From it you'll see most of El Capitan plus Middle and Lower Brother, North Dome, Sentinel Rock and Taft Point. But greater than this panorama is a sense of communion with nature one gets just by touching the base of this rock's overpowering, 2,000-foot-high, monolithic face. It can be a humbling experience.

Beyond the massive northeast face and its two pinnacles, you gradually descend to a level area, from which you could walk northwest a bit to a turnout on the eastbound road. From that turnout you can plainly see the two Cathedral Spires. These spires, and the 500-foot-high buttress they stand on, resemble a two-towered Gothic cathedral—hence the name. Despite their apparent inaccessibility, both were first climbed way back in 1934, during the early days of Yosemite Valley rock climbing. Until the 1960s both were popular climbs, but since rockfall altered the original

Bridalveil Fall

ascent routes, they are somewhat dangerous and undesirable.

After about a ⅓-mile traverse across a forested flat, you arrive at a signed trail, veer left, northwest, on it, and descend to a point on the eastbound road only 20 yards west of the Cathedral Picnic Area entrance. The few people who head north to the picnic area will be rewarded with two classic views, one of El Capitan and the other of the Three Brothers. Our route, however, continues northwest almost to a bend in the Merced River, from which you are bound to see—at least on summer days—sunbathers basking on the long, sandy "beach" of the far shore. Since our route eventually goes over to that vicinity, hikers with swimsuits on can shortcut (from about July through September) across the chest-deep Merced to that beach. Others follow the trail briefly west to the El Capitan Bridge. Here, by the eastern edge of El Capitan Meadow, the hiker gets a noteworthy view of the Cathedral Rocks, and one can see why the Miwok Indians visualized the lower monolith as a giant acorn. Across the meadow are some trees that in spring 1979 were subjected to prescribed burning. Such intentional burning began in 1971, when the Park Service decided that fires were necessary in order to return Yosemite Valley's vegetation to its former character—a more-open, mixed stand of oaks and conifers. The many years of fire suppression had seen the growth of a dense, view-obstructing conifer forest.

From the El Capitan Bridge you walk north either along the road or its adjacent riverbank trail to a sharp bend. By continuing east about 250 yards you can reach the site of Devils Elbow Picnic Area, closed in 1993 due to riverbank erosion from heavy use. However, above a second river bend there is access to the sandy beach and its nearby mid-river boulder, which originated from a rockfall high on El Capitan's massive face. The rock's obstruction of the Merced's channel forces the river to flow more swiftly past it, and the water scours the channel and makes it deep enough for safe diving.

At the river bend you cross the main road and start west along an old road that in ⅓ mile comes to a small hollow from whose north end a climbers' trail heads up to the nose of El Capitan. For the visitor new to Yosemite Valley, the size of El Capitan, like the

Cathedral Rocks and other Valley landmarks, is too large to really comprehend, and many visitors who first try to estimate its size swear it is only 1000 or so feet high. If you take the climbers' trail up the left (southwest-facing) side of El Cap's "Nose," you'll probably see rock climbers, who hundreds of feet up the monolith's 3000-foot-high walls are reduced to antlike stature. The 3,000-foot route from the foot up its "Nose" takes only one day for world-class climbers, and the first to ascend it without direct-aid slings was Lynn Hill. Rock climbing is a sport where women indeed are on par with men. The base left of El Cap's "Nose" has several dozen relatively short routes that go nowhere near the top. If you've ever wondered how it is possible to climb "unclimbable" cliffs, walk up the trail and observe climbers for yourself. The trailside vegetation of whiteleaf manzanita and canyon live oaks, growing on talus deposits, is ideal for California ground squirrels and other animals, who in turn make suitable prey for rattlesnakes. You probably won't see these snakes, but they nevertheless are here, as are loose boulders, so please be safe.

Beyond the small hollow your road rolls gently west and then southwest to a trail branching west. You could take this, and so avoid traffic, but you would also miss some views. Therefore, I suggest that you stay on the closed road and quickly reach the Valley's westbound Northside Drive at the west end of El Capitan Meadow. By building a parking strip along this road's meadowy stretch, the Park Service eliminated the parking jams that used to result in the '60s and early '70s when visitors parked their cars in the road as they searched for climbers—just specks—ascending one or more of the major routes up El Capitan. Today one can park and leisurely set up a telescope without impairing traffic. During midsummer, sensible climbers stay off El Capitan's multiday routes, for then the rocks temperature often exceeds 100°F, requiring many gallons of extra water (and perhaps an ample supply of six-packs).

After Yosemite became a national park in 1890 El Capitan Meadow became the Valley's first free public campground and Bridalveil Meadow soon became the second, though its use was mostly by US Army troops sent to patrol the Park. Three other campgrounds—all in meadows—were soon operating, in contrast to the forested ones we have today. Back then, horse pasturage was a prime concern—hence the need for meadow sites. In 1906, however, all five were closed, because sanitation—or lack thereof—had become a problem.

Leaving the meadow's edge you walk briefly west along the paved road and cross two usually dry branches of Ribbon Creek. (In pioneer days it was known as Virgin Tears Creek—a name in harmony with Bridalveil Creek, across the Valley floor). In ¼ mile you come to a dirt road, and by walking just a few paces up it reach a little-used westbound trail. (If you had taken the trail branching west, mentioned above, you would end up here.) After walking about five minutes west on it we cross a low recessional moraine, then drop almost to the paved road's edge. Here a turnout provides an unobstructed view Bridalveil Fall. From this turnout, you might note that the Merced River's south-bank, water-laid deposits contrast with the angular north-bank rockfall deposits. We are now at the foot of deposits derived from an unstable band of highly fractured cliffs called the Rockslides. Continual rockfalls from the Rockslides eventually led to the closing of the old Big Oak Flat Road and its replacement with today's tunneled road in June 1940. Under the pleasant shade of ponderosa pines and incense-cedars we continue west, passing some cabin-size rockfall blocks immediately before skirting the north end of the Bridalveil Meadow recessional moraine. There is no terminal moraine, since the last glacier ended lower down, in the Merced Gorge, which was too narrow to have one form and survive.

Soon we enter a swampy area with cattails and at its west end cross trickling Black Spring. Here, pioneers got an oak-and-conifer-framed view of Bridalveil Fall and the Cathedral Rocks, but due to the Park's old fire-suppression policy, incense-cedars and other conifers invaded the area, totally obstructing the view. Past the spring the trail more or less parallels the westbound road, shortly arriving at the back side of the Valley View scenic turnout. The view from the riverside turnout is one of the Valley's most famous, and it is a shame that the one-way road system prevents visitors from seeing this awe-inspiring view until they are ready to leave the Valley. Here we see El Capitan, Bridalveil Fall, and the Cathedral Rocks magnificently standing high

Climbers above the base of El Capitan

above the stately conifers that line Bridalveil Meadow. Barely rising above the trees are the distant landmarks of Clouds Rest, Half Dome and Sentinel Rock.

From the Valley View area we reach our trail's westernmost point at the Pohono Bridge, which is the current ending point of the north-valley one-way traffic. From a stream-gaging station across the bridge our feet tread a riverside path past roadside Fern Spring, then past trailside Moss Spring. Pacific dogwoods add springtime beauty to this forest as sunlight filters down to light up their translucent leaves and their large, petal-like, creamy-white bracts. Douglas-firs locally dominate the forest as we hike through it to Bridalveil Meadow, which is a shallow bowl that attracts enough ground water to generally prevent trees from invading it, From its edge we see a panorama from Ribbon Fall clockwise past El Capitan, the Cathedral Rocks and the Leaning Tower up to often-ignored points in the Valley's south rim. Avid map readers will identify Dewey, Crocker, Stanford and Old Inspiration points, all of them located along the Pohono Trail (**Hike 71**).

Now you walk northeast along the road's side, staying above seasonally boggy Bridalveil Meadow. By the meadow's edge, the trail resumes, and it goes north to a bend, where you cross the Bridalveil Meadow moraine. From here one can walk 40 yards north to a large rock by the Merced River's bank and see a plaque dedicated to Dr. Lafayette Bunnell, who was in the first-known party of white men—the "Mariposa Battalion"—to set foot in Yosemite Valley. Camping in the meadow on March 27, 1851, they held an evening campfire, at which Bunnell suggested the name "Yo-sem-i-ty," which he had incorrectly inferred was the name of the Indian tribe that inhabited this valley.

From the moraine you parallel the Merced River southeast almost to the eastbound road, which you can take 0.2 mile east back to the Wawona Road, then go briefly up it to the Bridalveil Fall parking lot. Doing so in springtime avoids the possibility of getting your feet wet in the nearby fords of multibranched Bridalveil Creek. After the last ford the trail parallels the creek's northern branch east about 300 yards to long turnouts on both sides of the eastbound road. Here you can head southwest on the road to the parking lot, or from the turnout on the far side of the road find a short trail going southeast to the trail you originally started on. On it retrace your steps 0.3 mile to the lot.

HIKE 63

VALLEY FLOOR, YOSEMITE LODGE LOOP

Distance: 7.0 miles loop trip

Grade: 2A, easy half-day hike

Trailhead: Yosemite Falls parking lot, which is immediately west of the Yosemite Creek

bridge and immediately north of the Yosemite Lodge complex. **D5.**

Introduction: Most of this loop is relatively quiet and lightly traveled. On it you'll get a classic view of the Three Brothers plus other less famous but equally dramatic views.

Description: Behind the restrooms at the west end of the Yosemite Falls parking lot you'll find a trail heading southwest. On it you almost touch the main road, then curve right to the base of Swan Slab, which is a low cliff that attracts many rock climbers. Before 1956, when the new lodge opened, the main buildings of Yosemite Lodge were located here, while south of them hundreds of tent cabins lay scattered around the forest floor. During the 1960s the new lodge was shifting its orientation away from tent cabins to fairly luxurious motel units. Some people cried "profiteering," but in fact the vacationing public had changed: America had come to expect less spartan accommodations. Perhaps we can define an "old timer" as one who longs for the lodge's primitive, woodsy tent cabins.

A little less than a ½ mile from the falls' lot we intersect the Yosemite Falls trail (**Hike 68**), then pass behind Sunnyside Campground. This was converted to a walk-in campground in 1976, the last of the Valley's old campgrounds to be converted to camp-only-in-designated-sites status. Before then, campers used to jam into this camp, transforming it into a noisy "tent city." In the late '60s this was true for all the campgrounds, and on 3-day weekends crowds of 50,000 or more would park their cars bumper to bumper, finding less peace and quiet here than in the noisy cities they had fled. Today all the Valley campgrounds are more pleasant, for they hold only a fraction of this number, but the crunch of the population explosion, coupled with increased mobility, is certainly felt daily by thousands of summer visitors who are forced to camp outside the Valley or even outside the Park. Back in the '60s Camp 4—the old Sunnyside Campground—was specifically designated for dogs and climbers—the two being nearly indistinguishable in the eyes of many. Climbers, as evidenced by the many brightly colored climbing ropes seen around the camp, still make up most of the camp's patronage.

Just west of Sunnyside Campground our trail once skirted along the Valley's paved,

Leidig Meadow view of North Dome, Royal Arches, Washington Column below Clouds Rest, and Half Dome

one-way road to a flat, gravel turnout. Today this is littered with debris from a March 1987 rockfall. If you look above the turnout you'll see a huge water-streaked wall, whose black streaks of moss mark the paths of the most persistent—though still ephemeral—streams of water. This wall has the Valley's best examples of glacier polish—in the form of small patches high on the wall and also near the base of Rixon's Pinnacle. Not a real pinnacle, this giant slab is recognized by canyon live oaks growing on its summit as well as by one prominent specimen growing on a ledge halfway up it. Note also the large, curving bend of granite—a dike—cutting across the face of the wall. The wall's rock, solidifying beneath the earth's surface about 90 million years ago, was fractured and injected with this dike material, which came from another, slightly younger molten mass of magma that was intruding it.

You get more views of these features after you cross the paved, one-way road, Northside Drive, and on a trail parallel it southwest. In about a minute you may see a trail, branching southeast. This unofficial path goes across the west edge of grassy Leidig Meadow to a sandy beach beside the Merced River, and then parallels it about ½ mile upstream to a long, sturdy bridge that spans this river. From the west edge of the meadow you can see a sandy beach on the opposite bank of the Merced River. This is only lightly visited by users of Sentinel

Creek Picnic Area, reached from the Valley's eastbound, one-way road.

In Leidig Meadow you get one of the Valley's best views of North Dome, Royal Arches, Washington Column, Clouds Rest and Half Dome. Partly obscuring Half Dome is a large descending ridge on whose dry slopes the Four Mile Trail (**Hike 76**) zigzags down from Glacier Point. Leidig Meadow—the original Camp 4 site—is named for George F. Leidig, an early resident who ran a hotel (popular because of his wife's cooking!) near the base of Sentinel Rock. As late as 1924 dairy cattle grazed in this and other Valley meadows. Looking west from this meadow, you get a clear view of the Three Brothers, named for three sons of Chief Teneiya taken prisoner here in May 1851 by the Mariposa Battalion. The vertical east face of the Middle Brother was the origin of the March 1987 rockfall and later rockfalls that left most of the rocky debris you are about to cross. Shrubs and young trees are invading the debris slopes—talus—but a future rockfall could eradicate them.

Returning to the main trail, we find that it is now confined to a narrow strip of vegetation between the busy, paved road above us and the quiet river at our feet. Soon we leave the river's side and parallel the road at a short distance, hiking through a forest of ponderosa pine, incense-cedar, and black oak. After a mile of pleasant walking along the trail, part of it with fair views, we arrive at the El Capitan Picnic

Mortar holes

Area site, closed due to riverbank erosion from overuse (now no river access). A trail north-northeast goes to Northside Drive and the new picnic area. In ⅓ mile we enter a meadow and have good views of many of the Valley's prominent features, particularly looming El Capitan, the angular Three Brothers, and the domed Cathedral Rocks. In the past our path split in the meadow, the two branches then rejoining in about 0.1 mile at the roadside site of the Devils Elbow Picnic Area, also closed due to overuse. However, there still is access to its sandy beach and a nearby mid-river rockfall boulder that is perfect for diving.

From the picnic area site your trail quickly curves south, hugging both road and river for ¼ mile to the El Capitan Bridge—one of the Valley's most scenic spots (see **Hike 62**), where again there is river access. At the north side of the bridge's east end the trail resumes, heads east to a bank opposite the south end of the Devils Elbow beach, then angles southeast to eastbound Southside Drive. Just 20 yards east lies the entrance to the Cathedral Picnic Area and on its road we walk north down to the riverbank for two famous and instructive views. Look northeast and note the amazing

similarity among the Three Brothers. They present a classic case of joint-controlled topography. Each is bounded on the east and south by nearly vertical joint planes and on the west by an oblique-angle joint plane. These three planes govern the shape of each brother, and when a rockfall does occur, the rock breaks off parallel to one of these planes, thus maintaining the triangular shape.

Now look northwest and see the massive south face of El Capitan and on the east part of it identify the dark-gray "North America map," which is a band of diorite that intruded and then solidified within the slightly older El Capitan granite. About five dozen extremely difficult climbing routes have been pushed up El Capitan. Perhaps the most famous route is the "Nose," which goes from the monolith's foot up to its brow, and the most infamous one is the "Wall of the Early Morning Light," which ascends the blank wall just right of it. The former, first climbed continuously in 6½ days back in 1960, was climbed in a grueling 17-hour ascent in the mid-1970s. Later, faster ascents were done, and now to do it in one day is nothing special for first-rate climbers. The latter route, first climbed in 1970, took 26½ days—an unheard of time—and the ascent upset many climbers, angered Park officials and received national press coverage.

Leaving the willow-lined Merced, return to your trail, cross the road, and walk 250 yards southeast to a junction with the Valley's south-side trail. On it we start east and immediately cross a creek bed that is densely lined with ponderosa pines. These pines probably sprouted after the usually dry creek became a swollen torrent during a flood and, like other creeks, created fresh soil exposures that became ripe for seed germination. Looking upstream you see overhanging Taft Point, then get other views of it as you progress east. After ½ mile of shady, south-side walking, you come to a huge, trailside slab, on whose flat summit you'll find about 20 mortar holes used by the Indians to grind acorns to flour. Not a glacier-transported rock, this 1000-ton slab broke off a steep wall of this side canyon above us. After perhaps sliding down a layer of ice and snow, this slab came to rest at this spot centuries ago. As you continue on, Douglas-firs and white firs mingle with the more dominant ponderosa pines, incense-cedars, and black oaks. Gray squirrels scamper about, and in earlier days they vied with Indians for acorns. However, they in fact benefited the Indians, for they buried many acorns and forgot about some, and these sprouted to produce the Indians' most cherished food source, the black oak.

Scattered views are obtained over the next mile from the big slab, and near its end you cross Sentinel Creek—barely a trickle by the first day of summer. After summer solstice you're lucky if multistage Sentinel Fall, seen high above the creek, is a even a gossamer mist. Voluminous only in flood stage, this fall is best seen in the warming days of late May, when runoff is about maximum and when winter's dormant seeds have awakened to dot the forest floor with a multitude of wildflowers.

After crossing the creek you come to an old spur road—the end of the Four Mile Trail from Glacier Point (**Hike 76**). In this vicinity Leidig's Hotel, the westernmost of several pioneer hotels, once stood. Beyond here your trail soon draws close to the Valley's eastbound road, and where you see a large roadside parking area, about ¼ mile beyond the old spur road, leave the trail, cross the busy road, and enter a picnic area. Black's Hotel once stood in this area, together with Clark's cabin. Galen Clark was one of the Valley's first tourists, being one of about 30 visitors to see it in the summer of 1855. Later, discovering he had a serious respiratory condition, he returned to the mountains, perhaps to die, but Yosemite's environment acted like an elixir, restoring his health. He first established a small lodge at Wawona, then became a Yosemite's first guardian, later saw it made into a National Park, and in 1910—during the Hetch Hetchy controversy—died at a ripe old age of 96.

Descending through the picnic area, you reach a long, sturdy bridge that replaces an earlier suspension bridge across the Merced River. From it you have good views of Yosemite Falls, Royal Arches, Washington Column, North Dome, Clouds Rest, Sentinel Rock, the Cathedral Rocks, and the Three Brothers. From its far end we take a broad, paved foot-and-bike path north to a bend in the road on the grounds of Yosemite Lodge. The path next winds northeast, then heads north, finally crossing the Valley's Northside Drive on the east side of the entrance to the lodge's grounds. This spot is also the west entrance to the Yosemite Falls parking lot, your starting point.

HIKE 64

VALLEY FLOOR, YOSEMITE VILLAGE LOOP

Distance: 3.3 miles loop trip

Grade: 1A, easy 2-hour hike

Trailhead: Same as the Hike 63 trailhead. **D5.**

Introduction: Famous views of Yosemite Falls, Half Dome and Royal Arches are seen along this short hike.

Description: While a steady stream of visitors make a short pilgrimage north to the base of Yosemite Falls, you start from the parking lot's east end and walk southeast, quickly bridge Yosemite Creek, then cross the main road, Northside Drive, to start east on a trail along its south side. Your trail quickly branches, and you angle right, away from the road to immediately cross a short spur road that heads south. Near its end a water well was drilled in the early 1970s, and it went 1000 feet down before hitting either a large boulder or bedrock. Yosemite Valley is in reality a 4000-foot-deep canyon, for on average its bedrock floor is buried under 1000 feet of sediments and decomposed bedrock. Beneath the grounds of the Ahwahnee Hotel, one mile east of us, these reach 2000 feet in thickness.

Beyond the spur-road your paved trail enters a beautiful, view-blessed meadow, through which you start southeast but have the option to branch right, bridge the Merced River and head toward the Yosemite chapel. Ironically the chapel stands close to the site of the Valley's first murder, which occurred in May 1851 during the so-called "Indian Wars." Two braves tied to a tree were allowed to free themselves so they could be shot down. The villainous soldier who planned this foul deed succeeded in killing only one of the Indians, but unfortunately it was Chief Teneiya's favorite son, and this certainly increased the old chief's mistrust of the intentions of the Mariposa Battalion. However, in all fairness it must be stated that the battalion behaved with remarkable restraint when rounding up the chief's band, especially considering that some of its volunteers had suffered personal losses at the hands of the Indians.

Half Dome in winter, from Sentinel Bridge

By not branching right in the meadow, you end at a parking area with picnic tables, just north of a 1994-vintage Sentinel Bridge, built immediately upstream from the site of its predecessor. Particularly during August, when Upper Yosemite Fall is only a vestige of its springtime self, rafters with life vests slowly float down the river, adding a human element to the famous tree-framed view of stately Half Dome. By strategically locating their hotel in the area between this bridge and the chapel, Buck Beardsley and G. Hite in 1859 provided guests with the best of all possible views. Business, however, was poor, and in 1864 James Hutchings—one of the Valley's first tourists—bought the hotel. Hutchings earlier had begun to attract tourists to the Valley by exposing this great California wonder to them in his magazine, "Hutchings' Illustrated California Magazine," a monthly that existed from 1856 to 1860. As he closed his magazine, he replaced it with a book called *Scenes of Wonder and Curiosity in California*, a popular guide that had a long section on Yosemite.

Hutchings also encouraged the development of this Valley area, both through words and investments, and there gradually arose what is now referred to as the "Old Village," which contained, among 21 structures, the National Park Headquarters. Today the Yosemite chapel is the only significant structure remaining. Originally built between Black's and Leidig's hotels in 1879, it was later moved ½ mile northeast up the road to its present site, and today it stands as the Valley's oldest building. A final point about Hutchings is that because he resided in the Valley for quite a few years, he became aware of almost all of the past geologic processes that created it. Nevertheless, because he was not a geologist, he was totally ignored by the geological establishment, which, due to a fatally flawed view on how mountain landscapes form, never did correctly determine how the Valley originated. For over a century, visitors to the Valley have been treated to geomythology.

From the south end of Sentinel Bridge you walk east on a riverbank trail, then cross the adjacent one-way road. Onward, you continue east beside the road, pass the bustling Housekeeping Camp, and soon arrive at a granite structure, the LeConte Memorial Lodge. A student of the world-famous Louis Agassiz, Joseph LeConte was invited to become the first professor of geology at Berkeley's then-infant University of California. During the summer of 1870 he visited Yosemite Valley, met John Muir, and was profoundly impressed by both. As a pioneering geologist he would later trek through much of the High Sierra, much as the Whitney Survey had done in Civil War days. However, like Muir, LeConte was not interested in topographic mapping and potential mining sites but rather in the beauty and origin of this "range of light." Appropriately, LeConte died in one of his most loved sites, Yosemite Valley, in 1901. During 1902-03 the commemorative lodge was built, erected near the youthful Camp Curry. The camp, however, prospered and expanded, so in 1919 the lodge was dismantled and then rebuilt, stone by stone, at its present location. This site was selected by Yosemite's foremost photographer, Ansel Adams, who chose it for its clear view up the Valley. As you can see, tall incense-cedars and ponderosa pines obstruct most of the view today. This lodge was once the terminal point

A black-oak-shaded view of Royal Arches, Washington Column, Half Dome and Ahwahnee Meadow

of the John Muir Trail (**Hikes 51 and 58**), but today it ends at Happy Isles.

Leaving the LeConte Memorial and its trailside Indian mortar holes, and its large boulders chalked white by climbers, we cross the road and follow a short path north along the east side of the Housekeeping Camp, reaching a sturdy bridge to the site of flooded, closed Lower Riverside Campground. Heading toward Yosemite Falls, we turn our backs on views of Glacier Point, the sweeping Glacier Point Apron, and Grizzly Peak as we follow a path downstream alongside alders and willows. On this short stretch large blocks were laid along the bank to prevent the river from meandering into either camp. All told, the river was once lined with about 14,500 feet of rip-rap revetment. Ponderosa pines, incense-cedars, and black oaks provide shade until a small stretch of Ahwahnee Meadow, just before the Valley's central road. In this small stretch our foot-and-bike path momentarily heads straight toward Upper Yosemite Fall and, looking right, you have unobstructed views of North Dome, Royal Arches, Washington Column, and Half Dome. Below these towering landmarks stands one of

America's grandest hotels, the Ahwahnee. Opened to the public in 1927, this magnificent granite-and-timber architectural treasure replaced Kenneyville, which like the Old Village and Camp Curry was a site of active tourism. Before that there had been the nearby Harris Camp Grounds, established in 1878, in which, for a fee, you could camp. However, with the establishment of Yosemite National Park in 1890, free public campgrounds were opened and this privately run camp folded.

After you cross the Valley's central road, you walk north, shaded by large black oaks growing along the edge of Ahwahnee Meadow. In ¼ mile you reach the west end of the Church Bowl, which has a paved roadside path and a dirt one, just behind the first, which you'll ascend northwest into the canyon live oaks. But first note that the Valley crossing you've just completed contains a sufficient diversity of plant species to allow selective feeding by all seven of the Valley's common summertime warblers. In the shady, moist confines immediately behind the LeConte Memorial, you might find MacGillivray's warblers foraging among the thimbleberries and bracken ferns. Just north, in the ponderosa pines and incense-cedars, you might stretch your neck and see yellow-rumped and hermit warblers. The larger, more common yellow-rumped warbler hunts for insects in the outer foliage of the trees' lower and middle branches while the misnamed hermit warbler hunts among the upper branches. Along the Merced River you might observe yellow and Wilson's warblers, the former searching among the alders and cottonwoods, the latter searching lower down among the willows and adjacent shrubs. Along the northbound traverse of the edge of Ahwahnee Meadow, the Nashville warbler would be expected in the black oaks overhead, and, upon climbing into the canyon live oaks above the Church Bowl, you'd expect to see the black-throated gray warbler. Thus you may see seven different warblers all hunting insects in Yosemite Valley. Yet none is in direct competition with any other, for each has found its own niche. Competition is mainly among individuals of the same species.

Climbing from the Church Bowl up past the medical clinic, you quickly reach Indian

Lower Yosemite Fall

Canyon Creek. Its canyon was a principal Valley exit used by Indians heading up to the north rim, and early pioneers built a trail of sorts up it, then west to a Yosemite Falls overlook. In early season you may note one of the Valley's lesser-known falls, Lehamite Falls, which plunges down a branch of Indian Canyon. "Lehamite" is actually the name Chief Teneiya's people gave to Indian Canyon.

Beyond the canyon's creek and its huge rockfall boulders, you climb northwest to avoid a mosaic of Park buildings and residences of the "New Village," then contour west beneath sky-piercing Arrowhead Spire and the highly fractured Castle Cliffs. Approaching a spur trail down to the nearby government stables, we spy Lost Arrow—a giant pinnacle high on the wall of Upper Yosemite Fall. Heading west ¼ mile toward Lower Yosemite Fall, you pass above the Park's family-residence tract and its associated elementary school, then come to a junction. The trail left descends along Yosemite Creek to your trailhead, but you keep right in order to visit Yosemite Falls, whose base it just to the west. Along this ¼-mile stretch a sawmill once stood. It was located here because fast-flowing Yosemite Creek provided the water power necessary to turn the sawmill's large blade. John Muir built this sawmill for James Hutchings "to cut lumber for cottages…from the fallen pines which had been blown down in a violent wind-storm [winter of 1867-68] a year of two before my arrival." When not off on his treks Muir sometimes worked at this mill, for at it he could enjoy "the piney fragrance of the fresh-sawn boards and be in constant view of the grandest of all the falls." His love of wilderness had grown so great that he preferred to spend the night perched on a ledge above the Valley floor, lulled to sleep by a splashing lullaby from nearby Lower Yosemite Fall.

From the bridge of Lower Yosemite Fall early-summer visitors are treated to the thunderous roar of the fall, a sound that reverberates in the alcove cut in this rock. During this season the visitor is further treated to the fall's spray as well. By late August, however, the fall, like its upper counterpart, is usually reduced to a mist, and even this can be gone by the Labor Day weekend. Dry or not, the fall should not be examined at close range, for even if boulder-choked Yosemite Creek is bone-dry, its rocks are water-polished to an icelike finish. You may see climbers ascending the nearly vertical walls surrounding the fall, and being roped, they are in a safer environment than you are if you clamber around on the creek's rocks.

The scenic bridge is occasionally swept away. It has been dislodged by winter's intense, flood-causing storms, which periodically occur, but it has also been dislodged by unseasonably warm springtime weather that causes rapid snowmelt. This in turn causes the huge snow cone at the base of the upper fall to swell with water and rapidly descend, avalanche-style, carrying the winter's rockfall debris with it as it plunges over the lower fall and slams into the bridge.

Before leaving the bridge, note how the lower fall has indirectly cut its alcove. Stream action has barely cut into the granitic bedrock since glaciers last left the Valley, but in winter the fall's spray freezes in the surrounding rocks, expands, and pries loose lower slabs that in turn remove support from upper ones—hence the blocky nature of Yosemite Creek's bed in this area. Walking back to your parking-lot trailhead, make stops for additional views of both falls. Long ago a swath of trees was logged just to provide these views.

these fruit trees are still seen in the area today. This orchard stands at the south end of Stoneman Meadow, whose grasses were nightly trampled by summer spectators watching the Firefall being pushed off Glacier Point—until the show was ended in January 1968. That meadow got its name from Governor George Stoneman, who was the State's chief executive when a large, state-financed hotel, the Stoneman House, was completed in 1887. Part of a political scandal, this pretentious but shoddy hotel began to fall apart almost as soon as it was finished, and fortunately it burned to the ground in 1896, thus ridding the Valley of one of its trues eyesores. Today, Camp Curry's west-end shuttle-bus stop occupies the approximate site of that hotel. Three years after the fire, Camp Curry made a very modest start, and as a company it eventually outgrew all its competitors to become the Park's largest concessionaire.

From the lot's southeast corner start on a paved path east along the south edge of a paved road. Both soon bend southeast and equally soon reach a junction with a shuttle-bus road to Happy Isles. Seventy yards beyond the junction your path crosses a short spur road to a trailhead parking lot for *wilderness-permit holders only* (e.g., **Hike 79**). This lot was a former garbage dump, which attracted

---

HIKE 65

VALLEY FLOOR, CAMP CURRY LOOP

Distance: 2.8 miles loop trip

Grade: 1A, easy 2-hour hike

Trailhead: Camp Curry parking lot, in eastern Yosemite Valley. **D5.**

Introduction: More like a stroll, this is one of the easiest hikes described in this guide. It is recommended for those who enjoy a leisurely pace, and want to take the time to commune with the squirrels, birds, and wildflowers and to reflect on the Valley's natural and human history.

Description: Back in the 1860s, long before any car entered Yosemite Valley, the Camp Curry parking lot was an apple orchard, and rows of

Staircase Falls, above Camp Curry

Glacier Point Apron

bears, which were fed by rangers until 1941—the start of the bear problem. As backpackers became far more numerous in the 1960s, "delinquent" Yosemite bears who were trucked out of the Valley pursued them into new territory and eventually over much of the High Sierra. From this lot you can also hike up to the base of broad, curving Glacier Point Apron, a good place to view climbers. "Sticky soled" shoes, developed in the 1980s, allowed climbers to waltz up new routes that would have been unthinkable in the '70s. Hence, new routes proliferated and now over 100 exist.

You could take the paved, roadside path to Happy Isles, but a quieter one begins from the southeast edge of the trailhead parking lot. This rolls southeast, staying about 100–150 yards from the unseen shuttle-bus road. In ⅓ mile it intersects a southbound stock trail that links the Valley stables to the John Muir Trail. Beyond this intersection you head east on planks across a boggy area, and although mosquitoes may be bothersome in late spring and early summer, the bog then produces its best wildflowers. At a huge, lone boulder by the bog's east side, your trail angles southeast toward the hub of the Happy Isles area.

You'll probably see dozens if not hundreds of visitors in this area, and here you'll find, besides restrooms near the shuttle-bus road, an informative nature center. A July 1996 rockfall from the top of a cliff to the southwest stopped just short of the center, as you can see

from the debris. While here, visit two adjacent Happy Isles. Immediately below the lower isle you'll see a stream-gaging station by the east end of a wide bridge. Records show that late in the summer, just before autumn rains, the river's discharge can fall to less than 5 cubic feet per second, while during a rampaging flood it can rise to a staggering 10,000 cubic feet per second! Most of the river's sediment is transported during times of high water, and since the Merced River's volume is considerably greater than that of Tenaya and Yosemite creeks, it brings a disproportionately large amount of sediment into the Valley. Overall, the historic rate of sediment is quite insignificant, being—according to my detailed calculations—about 2500 tons per year for the Merced River and 330 tons for all the Valley's remaining creeks that lie east of Lower Cathedral Rock (that is, within the Valley proper). An undying myth is that a large Lake Yosemite, averaging about 200 feet in depth, occupied a basin covering most of the Valley floor, after the last glaciers left the Valley about 16,000 years ago. However, at best, the incoming sediments could have filled in only about 13 feet. Windblown silt plus rockfalls and mudflows could have added as much as 7 more feet, so today there should be a lake averaging 190 feet in depth. At best, Lake Yosemites that formed after each major glaciation were shallow; more likely, most were Yosemite Swamps.

Departing north from the Happy Isles bridge, you have a choice of three pleasant routes: the Merced's west-bank trail, its east-bank trail, and the shuttle-bus road's east-side trail. The east-side trail begins about 100 yards north of the stream-gaging station, where it branches right, away from the east-bank trail. On the east-side trail you pass some cabin-size, moss-and-lichen-covered rockfall blocks, and then, where the trail climbs to cross the "Medial Moraine," you descend momentarily west to cross the road to the west-bending river. Both riverbank trails are relaxing strolls along the azalea-lined river, but perhaps the east-bank trail is more interesting since it traverses along the base of the west-trending moraine. François Matthes, who produced a monumental report on Yosemite glaciation in 1930, concluded that this moraine was probably left at the lower end of a glacier extending down Tenaya Canyon. Eliot Blackwelder, his contemporary, disagreed, saying it was a medial moraine, that is, one left between two glaciers, which in this case would be glaciers from Tenaya and from the upper Merced Canyon. After examining all the glacial evidence here and much in other Sierran canyons, I believe this west-trending ridge is a recessional moraine left by the retreating Merced Canyon glacier. In addition to local evidence, supporting evidence for this interpretation lies in the Stanislaus River drainage. The evidence is too lengthy and complex to be provided here, but it is in chapters 16 and 18 of my treatise, *The Geomorphic Evolution of the Yosemite Valley and Sierra Nevada Landscapes* (see "Recommended Reading and Source Materials").

Skirting the south base of this moraine, the east-bank trail goes northwest almost to the Valley stables. Here, at the moraine's end, turn left and immediately cross Clarks Bridge, named for Galen Clark, the Park's first guardian. From its west side, west-bank-trail hikers now join us for a brief walk past the entrances to the Upper and Lower Pines campgrounds. Beyond them we soon meet the southeast-heading shuttle-bus road, cross it, and walk west along a roadside trail leading past the north edge of our parking-lot trailhead.

Mirror Lake as it appeared in 1976

HIKE 66

VALLEY STABLES TO MIRROR MEADOW

Distance: 3.3 miles loop trip

Grade: 1A, easy 2-hour hike

Trailhead: Walk or take the shuttle bus through the Pines campgrounds to a shuttle-bus stop just across Clarks Bridge, and near a parking lot for patrons of the Yosemite stables. **D5.**

Introduction: First cars and then shuttle buses once went to Mirror Lake and Indian Caves, but now the road is used by bicyclists. Most hikers also use it, though paths offer quieter route to these sites.

Description: The low ridge you see just behind the shuttle-bus stop is the Valley's "Medial Moraine," a glacial deposit whose origin is mentioned near the end of **Hike 65**. A trail goes east along each side of the moraine, the south-side, riverbank trail being more scenic since it also goes along the Merced River. It is also quieter, for there aren't any trailside bicyclists. Take this riverside trail, walking east along the base of the smooth moraine to a junction and veer left to the adjacent shuttle-bus road. Immediately before this junction is a large white rock derived from the upper Merced River drainage, indicating that *its* receding glacier left this end moraine.

We cross the road and ascend a spur trail about 40 yards east to a main trail. Starting north on it we immediately top the moraine's crest, then descend northwest toward a road junction. The shuttle-bus road goes west to our starting point while bicyclists bound for Mirror Lake take the road north. Still on our trail, we meander north, skirting an area of giant rockfall boulders that testify to the instability of Half Dome's west flank. Beyond them

Washington Column's east face

we come to a trail intersection beside Tenaya Bridge. West, the trail parallels Tenaya Creek to the back side of the stables. East, it dies out, for its upper part was not repaired after the January 1997 flood damage.

From the north side of the bridge a trail climbs briefly north to the Indian Caves area, which we'll visit later. First, we take the paved bike path northeast up to a junction with a bike path west to the caves, then we start east and momentarily spy a broad footpath branching left. Choose either route northeast, both reuniting about 0.4 mile later near a shallow pond. Formerly it was deeper and until the mid-1990s was a popular summertime

swimming hole. But it is paralleling the evolution of adjacent Mirror Lake, reverting to just a broad stretch of Tenaya Creek. From the north side of the former swimming hole a nature trail loops over to the southwest edge of former Mirror Lake, as does the main trail, a former road, which no longer is paved (no bikes here). From the road's end, a former parking area, is a horse trail that you can take southwest to Indian Caves or northeast up lower Tenaya Creek canyon (see **Hike 67**). In this vicinity you'll see that Mirror Lake exists no more. The lake used to dry up by late September, and at that time in past years the Park Service would excavate the lake, sometimes removing thousands of tons of sand and gravel. This material was later spread on snow-covered winter roads to make them more drivable. It was an efficient system. Environmentalists, however, thought otherwise, so the procedure was stopped, and after 1971 Mirror Lake began to silt up. Today, sand (and many Park employees) are transported to the Valley, expending wasteful amounts of fuel that add unnecessary carbon dioxide to an already overladen atmosphere.

There will be many disheartened tourists to Mirror Meadow, but perhaps as with the Firefall (see the start of **Hike 65**), the public was led to expect the unnatural to be natural. Mirror Lake was not a deep, reflective gem when it was discovered, but rather was a shallow, rockfall-dammed pond. However, with the addition of a manmade dam about 1890, the lake assumed its reflective qualities, which were then maintained from 1914 to 1971 by yearly excavation. Today visitors must console themselves with Mirror Meadow, with broad, gravel-floored Tenaya Creek flowing through it. Ultimately the meadow may disappear, replaced by invasive trees. Without the fortuitous rockfall, Mirror Lake would not have been created and hence would not be missed.

Another nearby feature, remembered perhaps only by historians, is also gone: Iron Spring. Located by Tenaya Creek just 500 yards down the road from Mirror Lake's former satellite pond, the spring was the focal point of Camp 10, whose popularity exceeded available resources.

To resume your hike, look for a trail that starts near the back end of the former parking area. (Since this is a heavily used, often smelly, horse trail, you might want to take the previously mentioned foot trail.) Starting south on the horse trail, you see, high above, North Dome and Half Dome. Next, your trail passes myriad oversize boulders that originated from the vertical east wall of Washington Column. Soon your trail switchbacks briefly down to the paved bike path, then goes 100 yards west to enter the Indian Caves area. In the past this area was a favorite, with its several caves located among dozens of house-size boulders. However, apparently there were too many climbing accidents and too much liability for the Park, so in the early '90s the area officially ceased to exist. If you bring children here, use the utmost caution. In this area, inspect a large, low slab that lies along the trail's north side. On its flat top are mortar holes made by the Yosemite Indians and used by them to pulverize acorns.

Continuing west you have a choice: either stay on the trail or take the paved bike path, just south of the caves. The two diverge, and then, near the northeast corner of the former, flood-eradicated Group Camp (old Camp 9), they come together. On this stretch you pass under the forbidding south face of Washington Column and you may think you hear faint voices coming from high up on it. You actually might, for there are several popular crack systems on it that rock climbers ascend to the top. Where the trail and the bike path come together, you can look up a deep cleft—eroded along a vertical fracture—which separates Washington Column from that giant lithic rainbow, Royal Arches.

After 150 yards of westward traverse the two parallel paths cross a very low deposit, mapped as a moraine. Actually, it is an old rockfall deposit similar to one immediately west of the Backpackers Walk-In Campground. Note that all the rocks are entirely covered with crustose lichens, a growth process that takes centuries. On the basis of their age, together with age estimates of the tall surrounding ponderosa pines and incense-cedars, one can see that a major rockfall has not occurred here for hundreds of years. Perhaps the source of the last major rockfall was the greatly thinned skyline arch, which is just a fraction of its former self. The large skyline arch just west of Royal Arches proper could fall any day, but then it might stand for millennia.

About a two-minute walk past the low moraine we come to a trail junction, where, by cutting south through the campground, one can save ⅓ mile. However, by continuing west for a few minutes along the bike path (the trail goes to the Ahwahnee Hotel), we reach the Sugarpine Bridge, named for a huge sugar pine growing by the northeast corner of the bridge. Like a royal arch, this stately giant could fall any day. From the bridge you take a trail first southeast up the Merced River, then briefly northeast up Tenaya Creek. Where you meet the southbound shortcut trail you take it, immediately bridge Tenaya Creek, and walk southeast past the back side of North Pines Campground to the bus stop.

Under the old system of campground nomenclature Upper, North, and Lower Pines campgrounds used to be, respectively, Camps 11, 12 and 14. Camp 13 never existed, for superstitious reasons. The camps' names were changed when they were modified to a fixed-site system. This system limited the number of vehicles per campground and greatly reduced the number of campers, who previously used to pack the camps till they overflowed. This dramatic campsite reduction resulted in a significant reduction in Valley sewage sent down to the Bridalveil Moraine sewage plant. In May 1976 this plant was replaced by a new sewage plant opened in El Portal, thus removing one more undesirable, manmade feature from the Valley.

The campgrounds may seem about as perfect as one could realistically desire—for the lucky minority who can get a site. However, there has developed relatively recently, so to speak, a crucial underlying problem: root rot. In prehistoric times the Valley's vegetation was in part dynamically governed by periodic fires. After fire-suppression policies were introduced, the Valley's oak woodlands were invaded by conifers, resulting in the campground cover you see today. The conifer concentration, lacking periodic burns, invited attack by a root-rot fungus, *Fomes annosus*. The aging conifers are bound to fall, but the fungal invasion hastens their doom, and some people worry about the risk of camping in these forest groves. The lesson to be learned: man's changes in Nature, even when well-intentioned, often lead to unwanted or unforeseen results.

HIKE 67

VALLEY STABLES TO LOWER TENAYA CANYON

Distance: 6.6 miles loop trip

Grade: 2A, easy half-day hike

Trailhead: Same as the Hike 66 trailhead. **D5.**

Introduction: In addition to visiting the site of former Mirror Lake, you get ever-changing views of Half Dome and other features of deep Tenaya Canyon.

Description: First follow **Hike 66** to the vicinity of former Mirror Lake. If you hike to and return from the lake via the paved bike path—the most popular route—you will hike 4.6 miles. But if you follow all of Hike 67, you will hike 5.3 miles. Before continuing onward, you'll want to descend a few steps to what was once Mirror Lake's most famous viewpoint. Visitors who have seen beautiful photographs of Mt. Watkins reflected in the lake's calm morning waters are due for a rude surprise. As

Glacial polish on cliff above Mirror Meadow

elaborated in **Hike 66,** Mirror Lake, originally formed behind a rockfall and then was artificially raised by a manmade dam, is now just a broad stream through a meadow.

Now from the former parking area you take a broad trail that quickly comes to the northwest arm of the former lake. About 100 yards beyond it, where the trail bends right, you will come to a 1990s rockfall at the base of a cliff, which has conspicuous polish on it, imparted by a glacier before it retreated up-canyon about 14,500 years ago. In contrast to this glacier, the upper Merced Canyon glacier, which flowed through Little Yosemite Valley, lingered at the east end of Yosemite Valley for perhaps a few hundred years before it retreated up its canyon.

Your trail leads up-canyon under a shady forest cover, and soon you approach Tenaya Creek—a good picnic spot. Beyond it your trail rolls northeast toward the south spur of Mt. Watkins, which is occasionally seen through the forest canopy. About 1.1 miles from the former parking area you come to a junction with a trail that switchbacks over 100 times in its 2,600-foot climb out of Tenaya Canyon and into its hanging tributary of Snow Creek (the descent route of **Hike 35**). Many believe that such canyons became hanging because trunk glaciers eroded their canyons far deeper than tributary glaciers did theirs. However, a hike up *treacherous* Tenaya Canyon would show that in its steepest parts, where glaciers flowed fastest and should have eroded most, the canyon retains its preglacial **V**-shaped cross section. So in this vicinity, where the floor is flat and glaciers flowed more slowly, erosion would have been less, and hence the **U**-shaped cross section is preglacial. And indeed, *unglaciated*, **U**-shaped Sierran canyons—both trunk and hanging tributary—do exist.

From the trail junction a loop trail used to go 0.3 mile to a bridge over Tenaya Creek. However, the January 1997 flood damaged the bridge and parts of the trail below it, and the trail now is abandoned. If you want to continue ahead, treat it as cross-country. Unless you find a fallen log across Tenaya Creek, you may have to ford it through most of the summer. From the bridge site a use trail heads about 0.3 mile up along the south bank to the creek's falls, whose brim is a worthy goal for safety-minded hikers.

Return to Mirror Meadow the way you came, and from the back end of the former parking area, mentioned in **Hike 66,** take the horse trail, foot trail, or paved bike path over to Indian Caves, and then follow that hike back to your trailhead.

A large roof by brink of upper fall

HIKE 68

SUNNYSIDE CAMPGROUND TO YOSEMITE FALLS

Distance: 6.6 miles round trip

Grade: 2D, strenuous half-day hike

Trailhead: Park in the westernmost part of the Yosemite Lodge parking lot. **D5.**

Introduction: Most Park visitors walk to the base of Lower Yosemite Fall. This popular trail gets you to the other end—the brink of Upper Yosemite Fall. Like other early trails of Yosemite Valley, the Yosemite Falls trail was privately built and then was operated as a toll trail. From 1873 to 1877 John Conway labored intermittently to produce a route to the Upper Fall's brink—a route to replace the defunct Indian path that once climbed Indian Canyon. After reaching the fall's brink he extended the trail up to airy Eagle Peak.

Description: From the northwest corner of the parking lot for Sunnyside Walk-In Campground, take a trail 120 yards northwest up to the north-side Valley floor trail (**Hike 63**). By walking west on it about 25 yards, you reach the start of the Yosemite Falls trail. We leave conifers behind as we start up nearly four dozen switchbacks. Characteristic of old trails, each switchback leg is short. Under the shade of canyon live oaks, which dominate talus slopes like the one we're on, our so-far viewless ascent finally reaches a usually dry wash that provides us with framed views of Leidig Meadow and the Valley's central features.

With more than one fourth of the elevation gain below you, you pass more oaks and an occasional bay tree as you now switchback east to a panoramic viewpoint, Columbia Rock, which is a worthy goal in itself. At its safety railing you can study the Valley's geom-etry from Half Dome and the Quarter Domes west to the Cathedral Spires. A few gravelly switchbacks climb from the viewpoint, and then the trail traverses northeast, drops slightly, passes an enormous Douglas-fir and bends north for a sudden dramatic view of Upper Yosemite Fall. Hiking toward it you can see that some of its spray is caught behind the top of a large, notched flake, and this water then flows from the notch as a minor fall. West of Upper Yosemite Fall's lower section is a large white scar, over 200 feet high, from which a 1000-ton rock slab fell, after being struck by lightning in June 1976. In clear weather in November 1980, a 4000-ton slab, probably weakened by the May 1980 Mammoth Lakes earthquakes, fell from the site where you see a conspicuous scar on the cliffs west of and above the trail, killing three hikers. Smaller rockfalls have occurred, and over tens of millions of years countless rockfalls—not glacial erosion—widened the Valley.

Sentinel Rock, from Yosemite Falls trail

and tumble over the brink. Beside the lip of Upper Yosemite Fall you see and hear it plunge all the way down its 1430-foot drop to the rocks below. Just beyond the fall is a large roof—one that indicates the size of a slab that broke loose from this cliff in the not too distant past. On the skyline beyond the roof stands the pride of the Clark Range, finlike Mt. Clark.

After returning to the crest campsites you can descend east to a bridge over Yosemite Creek and obtain water. However, be careful! Every year one or more persons, wading in the creek's icy water, slip on the glass-smooth creek bottom and are swiftly carried over the fall's brink. From the creek's bridge you could continue eastward ⅓ mile up a trail to Yosemite Point, a highly scenic goal.

HIKE 69

SUNNYSIDE CAMPGROUND TO EAGLE PEAK VIA YOSEMITE FALLS TRAIL

Distance: 12.4 miles round trip

Grade: 3E, strenuous day hike

Trailhead: Same as the Hike 68 trailhead. **D5.**

Introduction: Strategically located Eagle Peak, highest of the Three Brothers, provides commanding views both up and down Yosemite Valley. The hike to it also provides exciting views, including some close-range ones of Upper Yosemite Fall.

Description: Follow **Hike 68** up to the Upper Yosemite Fall fenced-in viewpoint, then return to the trail junction in the gully west of the fall. Here at the junction you're bound to see chartreuse-colored staghorn lichens growing on the white firs They thrive on the firs but do poorly on the sappy pines. However, lichens, being capable of photosynthesis, do not require nourishment from a host to thrive. Indeed, most of Yosemite's lichens grow on bare rock, and their organic secretions may be the first agents to initiate chemical decomposition of the rock. Lichens, which in the past were incorrectly classified as plants, are composed of a fungus and an alga. In a symbiotic

Your climb up a long, steep trough ends among white firs and Jeffery pines, about 135 switchbacks above the Valley floor. Here, in a gully beside a seasonal creeklet, your trail turns right while the Eagle Peak trail, **Hike 69,** continues ahead. Your trail makes a brief climb east out of the gully and reaches a broad crest with several overused campsites. Their heavy use puts a strain on this area's vegetation, and it is best not to camp here. Along the crest you follow a trail south almost to the Valley's rim; then at a juniper you veer east and descend more steps to a fenced-in viewpoint. If you're acrophobic you should not attempt the last part of this descent, for it is possible, though unlikely, that you could slip on loose gravel

Summit view east toward Half Dome

relationship the fungus provides structure and protection from the elements while the photosynthetic alga produces nourishment for both.

You now commence a shady trek north, climbing out of the gully, descending into a second, and climbing out of a third to a trail junction. These gullies plus the one north of the junction are all in line and they probably owe their existence to relatively easy erosion along a straight, major fracture in the granitic bedrock. Leaving the Yosemite Creek environs, whose northbound trail is described in **Hike 21,** you climb more than 300 feet, at first steeply, before leveling off in a bouldery area— part of a terminal moraine which was left by a glacier that descended from the west slopes of Mt. Hoffmann. Now you turn south, generally leaving Jeffrey pines and white firs for lodgepole pines and red firs as you climb to Eagle Peak Meadows, whose north edge is blocked

by an older moraine. It is this moraine that diverts Eagle Peak Creek northeast, and it also dams up the meadow's ground water, thereby keeping conifers out of it.

Beyond the sometimes boggy meadow we cross the headwaters of Eagle Peak Creek and in a few minutes reach a hillside junction. From it an old trail climbs and drops along a 1¾-mile course to the El Capitan spur trail. To reach the summit of that monolith, it is easier to start from Tamarack Flat Campground (**Hike 31**). From the junction we branch left for a moderate ⅔-mile ascent to the diminutive summit of Eagle Peak. Like El Capitan, this summit has a register. From the weather-pitted, brushy summit you have far-ranging views that extend all the way to the Sierra crest along the Park's east boundary. Below, central Yosemite Valley spreads out like a map, and if you've brought along a detailed map of this Valley, you should be able to identify most of its major landmarks plus dozens of minor features.

At 3200 feet above the Valley floor one can appreciate the Valley's magnitude. About two million years ago, when glaciers may have first entered the Valley on a regular basis (some may have entered occasionally considerably earlier), it already was deep and quite wide, typical of some tropical granitic canyons. The Valley, you see, more than anything else is the result of weathering and erosion under a warm, wet climate that lasted for about 50 million years, until about 33 million years ago. In tropical lands, subsurface chemical weathering is very intense, disintegrating highly jointed bedrock as much as 2000 feet below the surface. Coincidentally, the thickest "sediments" in the Valley are about 2000 feet and below your summit, in Leidig Meadow, are about 1000 feet. These have been called glacial deposits because early geologists were unaware of subsurface chemical weathering. Glaciers certainly have left some deposits, perhaps the upper 200-400 feet, so ironically the Valley has lost some of its depth because of this infilling. Glaciers, which performed very little erosion, were mammoth, but the largest never overtopped the Valley's rim except perhaps at Royal Arches and Washington Column. The last glacier, where it passed below your summit, was about 1400 feet thick.

HIKE 70

YOSEMITE FALLS, YOSEMITE POINT, AND NORTH DOME VIA NORTH RIM TRAILS

Distance: 19.2 miles one way

Grade: 4E, strenuous day hike

Trailhead: Same as the Hike 68 trailhead. **D5.**

Introduction: Since good campsites are off-route, do this as a day hike. Only those in good condition should attempt it, for it has a total elevation gain of about 6300 feet. This may seem too strenuous to be a day hike, but it represents a typical daily effort I, back in my mid-30s, expended while originally researching for this book. Turn back if you're exhausted when you reach Yosemite Point.

Description: As in **Hike 68** climb to the Upper Yosemite Fall viewpoint, backtrack to the main trail, and then descend briefly east to the Yosemite Creek bridge. Here, bilingual signs warn of the very real danger of waders being swept off their feet for a one-way trip over Upper Yosemite Fall. From the bridge our climb to Yosemite Point first goes north, then east up short switchbacks on brushy slopes, and finally south to the rim of Yosemite Valley. Here at Yosemite Point the view is even more spectacular than that from the Yosemite Fall viewpoint. The dramatic panorama extends from Clouds Rest south past Half Dome and Glacier Point, then west to the Cathedral Rocks. Near you a massive shaft of rock, Lost Arrow, rises almost to the Valley's rim, and beyond it you view most of the switchbacking Yosemite Falls trail. A better view of Lost Arrow would certainly be desirable but to obtain it you have to get *dangerously* close to this spire.

Leaving Yosemite Point, you start up a crest and in a few minutes pass a quartz vein, the source of crystals you may have noticed on the slope just before you reached the point. About 120 yards farther you encounter pitted boulders, which are not glacial erratics but merely local boulders that have been weathering more or less in place for hundreds of thousands of years, if not one million years. Just higher on the crest you pass a low, pitted knob of very weathered bedrock, then climb moder-

Lost Arrow spire

ately for 300 feet before crossing a forest-clad crest.

With no more major climbing between here and North Dome we start a welcome, shady, gentle descent north. White firs and Jeffrey pines dominate the terrain, though by a trailside knoll you'll see at least one mature sugar pine, recognized by large cones growing at the tips of the tree's long branches. At about 7300 feet elevation these trees are close to the upper extent of their elevation range. Beyond the knoll we dip into a shallow bowl, pass three more trailside knolls and make a ⅓-mile descent through a red-fir-shaded gully. Indian Canyon Creek heralds the end of our descent and provides a well-deserved drink. An Indian trail once descended Indian Canyon, hence the name, and careful hikers can still find their way down to the Valley's medical clinic at the foot of the canyon. Careless hikers will find themselves in it. With minor but time-consuming obstacles in it, this canyon is definitely not a shortcut to the Valley floor.

Beyond a low ridge east of the Indian Canyon Creek ford you encounter Lehamite Creek, which lies a minute's walk past a trail junction. From it a trail climbs 1.6 miles northeast up to a saddle, then 1.8 miles beyond to the Tioga Road. We'll climb to that saddle after first visiting North Dome. Beyond generally flowing Lehamite Creek, which gives rise ½ mile down to Lehamite Falls, you climb over a slightly higher ridge, then drop to seasonal Royal Arch Creek, shaded by white firs, Jeffrey pines, and sugar pines. These give way to brush, particularly huckleberry oak, as you climb to lower Indian Ridge. Ascending it, you quickly encounter a spur trail that drops south to the summit of North Dome. This summit and its views are described in the last part of **Hike 33**, a route which you now follow in reverse up Indian Ridge to the aforementioned saddle. If you don't take the side trip up to delicate Indian Ridge arch, you'll cut ½ mile off your hike. From the saddle a shady trail lined with red firs and western white pines descends east to cascades along Porcupine Creek and then, in the realm of white firs, descends south to a junction near a bridge across Snow Creek. From it you follow the last part of **Hike 35** down to the floor of Tenaya Canyon—a spectacular descent—then walk southwest 1.1 miles, following the first part of **Hike 67** in reverse to trail's end above Mirror Meadow. Since you're bound to be tired, end your hike by taking the shortest route—the 1.2-mile-long paved bike path—down to the shuttle-bus stop just east of Clarks Bridge.

Precipitous Crocker Point

Trailhead: Discovery View, at the east end of Wawona Tunnel, on the Wawona Road 1.5 miles west of the Bridalveil Fall parking lot entrance. **C5.**

Introduction: Five viewpoints are visited: Inspiration, Old Inspiration, Stanford, Crocker, and Dewey. The first two, however, are somewhat blocked by vegetation. By hiking only to Stanford Point, you cut about 2½ miles and 900 feet of climbing from your hike. The creeks found along this route typically dry up by early summer, so make sure you bring enough water.

Description: Your signed trail starts at the west end of the south-side parking lot and makes a switchbacking, generally viewless 500-foot ascent for 0.6 mile up to an intersection of the old Wawona Road. Constructed in 1875, this old stage route got a lot of use before it was closed with the opening of the newer Wawona Road in 1933. Today it provides a quiet descent 1.6 miles down to the newer road, meeting it just ⅓ mile above the entrance to the Bridalveil Fall parking lot.

Beyond the intersection your oak-and-conifer shade continues all the way up another 500-foot ascent, keeping you relatively cool but also hiding most of the scenery. At Inspiration Point we meet a bend in old Wawona Road, a point where early travelers got their first commanding view of El Capitan, Bridalveil Fall, and the Cathedral Rocks. Today the passage of time has taken its toll, and incense-cedars,

---

HIKE 71

WAWONA TUNNEL TO STANFORD, CROCKER, AND DEWEY POINTS

Distance: 10.9 miles round trip

Grade: 3D, moderate day hike

black oaks, and ponderosa pines obstruct the view.

With most of the climb still ahead, pace yourself while winding up 1200 vertical feet of the Pohono Trail to arrive at springtime-active Artist Creek. Sugar pines and white firs now replace the lower conifer species, though Douglas-firs make sporadic appearances all the way to Stanford Point. Now at an elevation with cool rather than warm afternoon temperatures, make a steep 300-foot climb to Old Inspiration Point, whose view is in part blocked by a large sugar pine.

Red firs now add shade to the forest canopy as we briefly ascend before dropping to a welcome spring and nearby Meadow Brook. If any water remains along this trail through mid-summer, it will be found here. Beyond the creek and its large grove of alders, head north and soon descend to your first significant viewpoint, at the end of a short spur trail—Stanford Point. From it you see the gaping chasm of western Yosemite Valley and identify its prominent landmarks: Leaning Tower, Bridalveil Fall, the Cathedral Rocks, El Capitan and, seasonally, Ribbon Fall. This stunning panorama should motivate you to climb ½ mile farther to reach Crocker Point after more than 400 feet of elevation gain. Crocker Point, at the brink of an overhanging cliff, provides a heart-pounding view similar to the last one, through better. Now most of the Valley's famed landmarks stand boldly before us and we look over all the Cathedral Rocks to see the Three Brothers. To the left of Clouds Rest are twin-towered Cathedral Peak and broad-topped Mt. Hoffmann, with distant Mt. Conness between them, marking the Sierra crest along the Park's northeast boundary.

After the Crocker Point revelation, can you expect anything better? You'll have to judge for yourself after continuing ⅔ mile to Dewey Point. Now closer to the Cathedral Rocks, your perspective is different and you look straight down the massive face that supports Leaning Tower. Also intriguing is the back side of Middle Cathedral Rock, whose iron-rich, rust-stained surface stands out among the rest of the Valley's gray, somber colors. Finally you see the Cathedral Spires head-on so they appear as one. After scanning the Valley and the horizon, leave the point and descend the way you came.

BRIDALVEIL CREEK CAMP-GROUND TO DEWEY POINT

Distance: 10.0 miles round trip

Grade: 3C, moderate day hike

Trailhead: From a signed junction along the Wawona Road, drive 7.6 miles up the Glacier Point Road to the Bridalveil Creek Campground spur road. Turn right and drive 0.5 mile to the campground's entrance. **C5-D5.**

Introduction: This is the easier of two routes to scenic Dewey Point, and it requires less than half the climbing effort of the previous hike, but then it doesn't visit Stanford and Crocker points.

Description: At Bridalveil Creek Campground's entrance, take a closed road that departs southwest away from the camp's Loop A. On it you cross in ¼ mile a creek that drains Westfall Meadows, then immediately meet a trail. South, this undesirable trail passes through these meadows, then makes a brush-choked descent to an old logging area—a 1920s "battleground" between environmentalists and the Yosemite Lumber Company. The environmentalists won, but the scars remain.

We take the trail north, which climbs gently over weathered terrain to the Glacier Point Road. By starting here—¼ mile west of the campground's spur road—you could knock 1¾ miles off your total distance. From the road your lodgepole-shaded route gently descends almost to the north tip of largely hidden Peregoy Meadow before topping a low divide. Next it drops moderately and reaches the south edge of sedge-filled McGurk Meadow, in which we cross its creek. At times, the meadow may have an abundance of wildflowers such as shooting star, paintbrush, cinquefoil, and corn lily. Looking east from the meadow, note the low, unglaciated summits of the Ostrander Rocks, whose west slopes, at least one past geologist claimed, supported a small glacier that joined a Bridalveil Creek glacier. Actually, there is no evidence whatsoever of glaciation in the Bridalveil Creek drainage north of the Glacier Point Road.

At Peregoy Meadow's north end you first re-enter a lodgepole forest, soon crest a shallow, viewless saddle, and then descend at a reasonable gradient to a low-crest trail fork. The fork right quickly joins the Pohono Trail and drops to Bridalveil Creek. We fork left, quickly join that trail, and start west on it. Nearing a broad, low divide, we traverse a dry, gravelly slope dotted with streptanthus, pussy paws, and mat lupine.

The forest cover now becomes dominated by firs—both red and white—and on the damp shady floor beneath them you may find wintergreen, snow plant, and spotted coralroot, the last two living off soil fungi. Two Bridalveil Creek tributaries are crossed, then a smaller third one before we start up a fourth that drains a curving gully. On the gully's upper slopes Jeffrey pine, huckleberry oak, and greenleaf manzanita replace the fir cover and in a few minutes we reach highly scenic Dewey Point, described at the end of **Hike 71**. If you can get someone to meet you at the Wawona Tunnel, then descend to it along this highly scenic portion of the Pohono Trail.

crop that is almost entirely composed of glistening whitish-gray quartz. It also has small amounts of pink potassium feldspar. Lacking the surrounding bedrock's dark minerals, which are more prone to weathering, this outcrop is eroding more slowly than the adjacent landscape, so it protrudes. In a minute we come to seasonal Sentinel Creek, whose limited drainage area keeps Sentinel Fall downstream from being one of Yosemite Valley's prime attractions. After boulder-hopping the creek, follow an undulating trail west past pines, firs, and brush to a crest junction with the Pohono Trail (**Hike 75**). Just north of it are some large boulders. Not left by glaciers, these have weathered in place and will continue to become "taller" as the surrounding bedrock is stripped away.

From the junction we descend to a seeping creeklet that drains through a small field of corn lilies. In this and two other nearby damp areas you may also find bracken fern, lupine, paintbrush, bluebells (lungwort), mountain monkey flower, arrow-leaved senecio, Richardson's geranium, green gentian (monument plant), and alpine lily. The last two, like corn lily, can grow to head height. Descending

HIKE 73

GLACIER POINT ROAD TO FISSURES AT TAFT POINT

Distance: 2.6 miles round trip

Grade: 1A, easy 2-hour hike

Trailhead: From a signed junction along the Wawona Road, drive 13.2 miles up to the Glacier Point Road to a scenic turn out, on your left, which is 2.3 miles before the Glacier Point parking-lot entrance. **D5.**

Introduction: The views from Taft Point rival those from Glacier Point. However, since Taft Point is reached by trail, it is sparsely visited compared to Glacier Point. Generally lacking protective railings, Taft Point and the Fissures are potentially dangerous, so don't bring along children unless you can *really* keep them under strict control.

Description: From the road-cut parking area you descend about 50 yards to a trail, turn left, and start southwest on it. After about 150 yards of easy descent you pass a trailside out-

Overhanging, exposed Taft Point

One of the five Fissures

ing Profile Cliff, beneath you. For the best views of Yosemite Valley and the High Sierra walk west to *exposed* Taft Point, from where you see the Cathedral spires and rocks, El Capitan, the Three Brothers, Yosemite Falls, and Sentinel Rock. Broad Mt. Hoffmann stands on the skyline just east of Indian Canyon and east of this peak stands distant Mr. Conness, on the Sierra crest. Taft Point was named to commemorate President William Howard Taft's October 1909 visit to Yosemite Valley. On it he met John Muir, who hoped to convince the President to prevent construction of a dam in Hetch Hetchy. The President, tiring of Muir's arguments, jokingly suggested that Yosemite Valley also be dammed. Muir, not seeing the humor, was offended. To his credit, Taft did oppose the dam, but it was built later. From Taft Point the Pohono Trail is described westward in **Hike 75.**

HIKE 74

GLACIER POINT ROAD TO SENTINEL DOME

Distance: 2.4 miles round trip

Grade: 1B, moderate 2-hour hike

Trailhead: Same as for the Hike 73 trailhead. **D5.**

Introduction: Sentinel Dome rivals Half Dome as the most-climbed dome in the Park. Tuolumne Meadows' Lembert and Pothole domes rival them, but neither is a true dome; each is a *roche moutonnée*—an asymmetrical, glacier-smoothed ridge. Indeed, most of the Sierra's domes, glaciated or unglaciated, are asymmetrical ridges.

toward the Fissures, you cross drier slopes that are generally covered with brush. Here you may find two wildflowers belonging to the same wildflower tribe: the single-stemmed senecio and the soft arnica. The first has alternate leaves; the second, opposite. Two other yellow wildflowers seen are the sulfur flower, a buckwheat, and the Sierra wallflower, a mustard. Soon you arrive at the Fissures—five vertical, parallel fractures that cut through overhanging Profile Cliff, beneath your feet. Because the Fissures area is unglaciated, it is well weathered, and a careless step could result in an easy slip on the loose gravel—dangerous in this area.

Beyond the Fissures, walk up to a small railing at the brink of a conspicuous point and get an acrophobia-inducing view of overhang-

Description: From the road-cut parking area you descend about 50 yards to a trail, turn right and make a curving, generally ascending traverse ¾ mile north almost to the south base of Sentinel Dome. Here we meet and briefly hike north on a road, which has several large boulders along it. These, and ones between this dome and Glacier Point, are widely thought to have been left by ancient glaciers. They were not; the boulders are locally derived. No glacier ever filled Yosemite Valley

Sentinel Dome's lone Jeffrey pine, as it appeared in 1976

to its rim, except perhaps along the tops of Royal Arches and Washington Column. On the road we soon come to a fork, where we veer left, and in 30 yards, at another fork, we veer left again. In a few minutes we arrive at the dome's north end, where we meet a path from Glacier Point. We now climb southwest up quite safe, unexposed bedrock slopes to the summit.

At an elevation of 8,122 feet, Sentinel Dome is the second highest viewpoint above Yosemite Valley. Only Half Dome—a strenuous hike—is higher. Seen from the summit, El Capitan, Yosemite Falls, and Half Dome stand out as the three most prominent Valley landmarks. West of Half Dome are two bald features, North and Basket domes. On the skyline above North Dome stands blocky Mt. Hoffmann, the Park's geographic center, while to the east, above Mt. Starr King (an unglaciated, true dome), stands the rugged crest of the Clark Range. In years past almost everyone who climbed Sentinel Dome expected to photograph its windswept, soli-

tary Jeffrey pine, made famous by Ansel Adams. That tree, unfortunately, finally succumbed to vandalism in 1984.

HIKE 75

GLACIER POINT TO TAFT, DEWEY, CROCKER, AND STANFORD POINTS

Distance: 13.5 miles one way

Grade: 3D, moderate day hike

Trailhead: From a signed junction along the Wawona Road, drive 15.5 miles up the Glacier Point Road to its end. If possible, take a Park bus up to crowded Glacier Point, since at times the parking lot can be full. **D5.**

Introduction: This hike, the Pohono Trail, takes you past several excellent viewpoints, each showing a different part of Yosemite Valley in a unique perspective. After early June carry enough water (usually one quart) to last you until midpoint, Bridalveil Creek, which is the hike's only permanent source of water.

Description: On the low crest just east of the entrance to the Glacier Point parking lot, start south up a signed trail that quickly forks. **Hike 87** branches left but you branch right and under white-fir cover momentarily cross the Glacier Point Road. Beyond it you immediately branch right again since the path ahead climbs to a ranger's residence. Your still-climbing trail curves west up to a switchback, then south to a road. This you cross and then continue up the relentless grade to a north-descending crest, which you cross before climbing briefly south to a gully. In it, almost a mile from Glacier Point, you face a choice. Our route, the Pohono Trail, goes west to the brink of Sentinel Fall—usually dry by midsummer—while the alternate route, which starts north before climbing south, goes to scenic Sentinel Dome. Should you take the dome route, you can return to the Pohono Trail or you can take a more level route that adds ⅔ mile to your total distance. From the dome this route follows **Hike 74** in reverse, then the first half of **Hike 73**, which takes you back to the Pohono Trail.

Our main route, the Pohono Trail, leaves the gully, traverses southwest across a lower face of Sentinel Dome, then drops to a gravelly gully with north-side boulders. The gravel and boulders here, like all between Glacier Point and Sentinel Dome, are locally derived, not lingering deposits left by an ancient glacier. Your route stays gravelly on a short, sometimes steep descent to seasonal Sentinel Creek. Here you can follow its bank 90 yards out to a point to get a good Valley view. Before mid-June hikers will see upper Sentinel Fall splashing down a chute immediately west of the point.

Beyond the seasonal creek, climb past lodgepole pines and white firs, and then, before a broad-saddle junction, past Jeffrey pines and red firs. At the junction you rejoin the alternate route and, as in the second half of **Hike 73**, descend a trail to the Fissures and Taft Point. Be careful when exploring this scenic though precipitous area. From the westernmost fissure the Pohono Trail descends south, then contours west to a low ridge. By following the ridge about 250 yards out to its end you'll reach an unnamed point that pro-

vides a view down upon the Cathedral Rocks, lined up in a row. Descending from the low ridge, the shady Pohono Trail drops 700 feet to a bridge over Bridalveil Creek. Level ground is limited, so if you plan to camp, you can get water here, and perhaps camp in isolated spots on lands north and west of two nearby trail junctions.

From the creek, which is your hike's approximate midpoint, climb shortly west to these two connectors to a lateral trail. This lateral climbs 2 miles south to the Glacier Point Road, then a short mile beyond it to Bridalveil Creek Campground. This lateral trail constitutes the first half of **Hike 72** (described in the northward direction), and turning to the second half of that hike's description, let it guide you over to Dewey Point. West from that point, follow **Hike 71**, described in the reverse direction, down to Discovery View, at the east end of Wawona Tunnel.

HIKE 76

GLACIER POINT TO YOSEMITE VALLEY VIA FOUR MILE TRAIL

Distance: 4.6 miles one way

Grade: 1A, easy 2-hour hike

Trailhead: Same as the Hike 75 trailhead. **D5.**

Introduction: This trail provides a very scenic descent to Yosemite Valley—a descent that will acquaint you with the Valley's main features. This knee-knocking descent also gives you a feel for the Valley's 3000-foot depth.

Description: Before building the Yosemite Falls trail (**Hike 68**) John Conway first worked on this trail, completing it in 1872. Originally about 4 miles long, it was rebuilt and lengthened in 1929 but the trail's name stuck. Our trail starts west from the north side of a concessionaire's shop, which along with other minor structures replaced the grand Glacier Point Hotel. This three-story hotel, together with the adjacent historic Mountain House—built in 1878—burned to the ground in August 1969. Descending west from the concessionaire's shop, you enter a shady bowl whose

white firs and sugar pines usually harbor
snow patches well into June. You then contour
northwest, eventually emerge from forest
shade and, looking east, see *unglaciated* Glacier
Point's two overhanging rocks capping a vertical wall. (One of Yosemite's popular geologic
myths is that it at least once lay under as much
700 feet of glacier ice.) Soon you curve west,
veer in and out of a cool gully, then reach a
descending ridge. On it you generally
exchange views of Royal Arches, Washington
Column, and North Dome for those of
Yosemite Falls, the Three Brothers, El Capitan
and, foremost, Sentinel Rock, which provides a
good gauge to mark our downward progress.

Switchbacks begin, and where gravel lies
on hard tread, one can easily take a minor spill
if not careful. Chinquapin, greenleaf manzanita, and huckleberry oak are shrubs that
dominate the first dozen switchback legs,
thereby giving us unobstructed panoramas,
though making the hike a hot one for anyone
ascending from the Valley floor on a summer
afternoon. However, as you duck east into a
gully, shady conifers appear, though they
somewhat censor your views. If you had been
on this trail on some early morning through
the 1970s until June 1990, when hang gliders
were banned, you could have seen pilots land
in meadows below you, taking sky trails from
Glacier Point to the Valley floor.

About midway down the series of switchbacks, canyon live oaks begin to compete with
white firs and Douglas-firs, and your view is
obstructed even more. After descending two
thirds of the vertical distance to the Valley
floor, the switchbacks temporarily end. A long,
steady descent now ensues, mostly past
canyon live oaks, whose curved-upward
trunks are their response to creeping talus.
(The talus has been erroneously mapped by
the US Geological Survey as glacial deposits.)
Black oaks and incense-cedars also appear, and
after ¼ mile you cross a creeklet that usually
flows until early July. Down it you have an
excellent view of Leidig Meadow. Your steady
descent again enters oak cover and you skirt
below the base of imposing but largely hidden
Sentinel Rock. At last a final group of switchbacks guide you down to a former parking
loop, closed about 1975, and you proceed
briefly north, intersecting the Valley floor's
southside trail, **Hike 63**, just before your end
point, Southside Drive.

*By today's climbing standards, the north face of
Sentinel Rock is a relatively easy climb*

HIKE 77

HAPPY ISLES TO VERNAL FALL BRIDGE

Distance: 1.6 miles round trip

Grade: 1A, moderate 2-hour hike

Trailhead: Happy Isles shuttle-bus stop in eastern Yosemite Valley. **D5.**

Introduction: Popular, paved paths go to near the bases of Yosemite and Bridalveil falls, and a paved one goes to this bridge. If you have only one day here, take all three. The trail to the bridge, however, is steep—intimidating for out-of-shape flatlanders.

Description: From the shuttle-bus stop you walk briefly east across an adjacent bridge and head south, soon reaching a stream-gaging station. See the middle of **Hike 65** for a discussion of the Merced River's varying discharge, its sediment-transport capacity, and the implications of this capacity. From this station the famous John Muir Trail heads about 210 miles southward to the summit of Mt. Whitney. Bay trees, Douglas-firs, and canyon live oaks dominate the forest canopy as we start up it, and after a few minutes we meet a trail on the right that descends to the nearby Merced River. In a few more yards we reach a small spring-fed cistern with questionably pure water.

Beyond it the climb south steepens, and before bending east you get a glance back at Upper Yosemite Fall, partly blocked by the Glacier Point Apron. This smooth, curving apron contrasts with the generally angular nature of Yosemite's topography. Note the canyon wall south of the apron, which has a series of oblique-angle cliffs—all of them remarkably similar in orientation since they've fractured along the same series of joint planes. At the canyon's end Illilouette Fall plunges 370 feet over a vertical, joint-controlled cliff. Just east of the fall is a large, light-colored scar that marks the site of a major rockfall that broke loose during the winter of 1968–69.

Climbing east, head up a canyon whose floor in times past was buried by as much as 2,000 feet of glacier ice. Hiking beneath the unstable, highly fractured south wall of Sierra Point, you cross a talus slope—an accumulation of rockfall boulders. The May 1980

Mammoth Lakes earthquakes perhaps set up three rockfalls here, which finally occurred in conjunction with heavy rains in late spring 1986. More may occur. Entering forest shade once more, you ascend a steep stretch of trail before making a quick drop to your destination, the Vernal Fall bridge. From it you see Vernal Fall, a broad curtain of water plunging 320 feet over a vertical cliff before cascading toward us. Looming above the fall are two glacier-resistant masses, Mt. Broderick (left) and Liberty Cap (right). Just beyond the bridge are restrooms and an emergency telephone (heart attacks, slips on dangerous rocks). **Hike 78** continues onward from here.

HIKE 78

VERNAL-NEVADA FALLS SEMILOOP

Distance: 5.9 miles semiloop trip

Grade: 2D, strenuous half-day hike

Trailhead: Same as the Hike 77 trailhead. **D5.**

Introduction: Mile for mile, this very popular hike may be the most scenic one in the Park. The first part of this loop goes up the famous

Vernal Fall, from trail up to Clark Point

(or infamous) Mist trail—a steep, strenuous trail that sprays you with Vernal Fall's mist, which cools you on hot afternoons but makes the mostly bedrock route slippery and dangerous. Take raingear or, if it is a warm day, strip down to swimwear, since you can dry out on slabs above the fall. For best photos start after 10 A.M.

Description: Hike 77 tells you what to expect along your ascent to the Vernal Fall bridge. About 200 yards beyond the bridge you come to the start of your loop. Here the Mist trail continues upriver while the John Muir Trail starts a switchbacking ascent to the right. This is the route taken by those with horses or other pack stock. We'll go up the Mist trail and down the John Muir Trail. You can, of course go up or down either, but by starting the loop up the Mist trail, you stand less chance of an accident. Hikers are more apt to slip or to twist an ankle descending than ascending, and the Mist trail route to Nevada Fall has ample opportunities for mishaps.

In swimsuit or raingear, start up the Mist trail and soon, rounding a bend, receive your first spray. If you're climbing this trail on a sunny day, you're almost certain to see one, if not two, rainbows come alive in the fall's spray. The spray increases as you advance toward the fall, but you get a brief respite behind a large boulder. Beyond it, complete your 300-plus steps, most of them wet, which guide you up through a verdant, spray-drenched garden. The last few dozen steps are under the shelter of trees; then, reaching an alcove beneath an ominous overhang, you scurry left up a last set of stairs. These, protected by a railing, guide one to the top of a vertical cliff. Pausing here you can study your route, the nearby fall, and the river gorge. The railing ends near the brink of Vernal Fall, but unfortunately, people venture beyond it, and every year it seems that one or more are swept over the fall. Sunbathers, trying to reach the far side of Emerald Pool, which lies just above the brink, may underestimate the danger of the river's slippery rocks and the danger of its treacherous current. Don't be taken in.

Plunging into the upper end of chilly Emerald Pool is churning Silver Apron. Late in the summer when the Merced's flow is noticeably down, one is tempted to glide down this watery chute into Emerald Pool. This is hazardous, for one can easily crash on some boul-

Liberty Cap and Nevada Fall

ders just beyond the end of this silvery chute. Rivers are not to be taken lightly. You'll see a bridge spanning the narrow gorge that confines the Silver Apron, and this structure is our immediate goal. The trail can be vague in this area, due to use paths, but the correct route leaves the river near the pool's far (east) end, and you'll find outhouses here. After a brief climb south, the trail angles east to a nearby junction. From it a view-packed trail climbs almost ½ mile to Clark Point, where it meets the John Muir Trail. We, however, stay low and curve left over to the Silver Apron bridge. Beyond it we have a short, moderate climb up to a broad bench which was once the site of La Casa Nevada. Opened in 1870 it was managed by Albert Snow until 1891, when a fire burned the main structure to the ground.

Spurred onward by the sight and sound of plummeting Nevada Fall, you climb eastward, soon commencing a series of more than two dozen compact switchbacks. As you ascend them, Nevada Fall slips out of view, but you can see towering Liberty Cap. The climb ends at the top of a joint-controlled gully where, on brushy slopes, we once again meet the John Muir Trail (with outhouses just up it—see **Hike 79**).

From this junction hikers descending from Tuolumne Meadows, Clouds Rest, Half Dome, and Merced Lake join us as we head southwest toward nearby Nevada Fall. Along this stretch you may notice boulders—rich in large, blocky feldspar crystals—that contrast strongly with the local bedrock. These boulders are *erratics*— that is, rocks left by retreating glaciers which were here perhaps as recently as 13,500 years ago. Near the Merced River are patches of bedrock that have been polished, striated, and gouged by the last glacier.

Just a few yards before the Nevada Fall bridge you can strike northwest on a short spur trail down to a viewpoint beside the fall's brink. This viewpoint's railing is seen from the fall's bridge, thereby giving you an idea where the trail ends. Don't stray along the cliff's edge and, as said earlier, respect the river—people have been swept over this fall too. Standing near the tumultuous brink of the Merced River, you can look across its canyon—minimally eroded by glaciers—to *unglaciated* Glacier Point. Vernal Fall, which lies just beyond Emerald Pool, plunges over a vertical wall that is perpendicular to the steep one Nevada Fall plunges over. This part of the canyon contains major fracture planes, or joint planes, which account for the canyon's angular landscape.

From the Nevada Fall bridge we strike southwest, immediately passing more glacier polish and erratic boulders, and shortly ending a gentle ascent at a junction just beyond a seeping spring. Here we meet the Glacier Point-Panorama trail, and those descending from Glacier Point (**Hike 87**) join us here for a descent to Happy Isles along the John Muir Trail. This starts with a high traverse that provides an ever-changing panorama of domelike Liberty Cap and broad-topped Mt. Broderick—both testaments to the ineffectiveness of glacial erosion. As you progress west, Half Dome becomes prominent, its hulking mass vying for your attention. Eventually you descend to Clark Point, where you meet a scenic connecting trail that switchbacks down to Emerald Pool. If you enjoyed the Mist trail, you can visit it again by first descending this lateral, but remember to be careful while descending the Mist trail.

Backpackers, packers, and those wishing to keep dry continue down the John Muir Trail, which curves south into a gully, switchbacks down to the base of spreading Panorama Cliff, then switchbacks down a talus slope. Largely shaded by canyon live oaks and Douglas-firs, it reaches a junction with a horse trail (no hikers allowed) that descends to the Valley's stables. Continue a brief minute more to a junction with the Mist trail, turn left, and quickly reach the Vernal Fall bridge, from which you retrace your steps.

HIKE 79

HAPPY ISLES TO LITTLE YOSEMITE VALLEY

Distance: 7.9 miles semiloop trip

Grade: 2D, moderate 2-day hike

Trailhead: Same as the Hike 77 trailhead. **D5.**

Introduction: Many a backpacker has spent his or her first night in the "wilderness" of Little Yosemite Valley. Indeed, more backpackers camp in it than in any other Yosemite backcountry area. Perhaps too, more bears visit it than any other backcountry area. During the summer this area is patrolled by rangers stationed near the backpackers camp.

Description: Follow **Hike 78** up the Mist trail or John Muir Trail to a junction northeast of the

Liberty Cap's long east rib

brink of Nevada Fall. If you take the latter, you will add 1.0 mile. From this brushy junction you climb up a gully that is generally overgrown with huckleberry oak. From its top you quickly descend into forest cover and reach a fairly large 'swimming hole' on the Merced River. Though chilly, it is far enough above the river's rapids to provide a short, refreshing dip. A longer stay would make you numb. Beneath lodgepole and Jeffrey pines, white firs, and incense-cedars we continue northeast along the river's azalea-lined bank, then quickly encounter a trail fork. The left fork climbs and then descends the low east ridge of Liberty Cap. It is a 'shortcut' to the Half Dome trail, but the amount of climbing it requires offsets the little distance you'll save on it. Therefore, you might keep right on the main trail and go a short half mile to another junction, from where the John Muir/Half Dome trail branches north while the Merced Lake trail continues east. On the short stretch north to the left fork, you pass first a large backpackers camp with bearproof storage boxes, then outhouses, and beyond them a spur trail northeast over to a rangers' camp.

Some nearby landmarks—all off trail—make interesting side trips: Liberty Cap, Mt. Broderick, Lost Lake, and the Diving Board. After starting on the "shortcut" trail you can head west up the low east ridge of Liberty Cap and, *if careful*, quite safely reach its summit without climbing shoes or a rope. Mt. Broderick is another matter. You have to know how to use a map and how to climb. Some hikers may also want to bring a rope. Its summit, however, provides better views than does Liberty Cap's, particularly of Nevada Fall. Both of these "domes" are merely high points on the down-canyon end of ridges, and as such are typical of tropical landforms. Their asymmetry has very little to do with glaciation, for the amount of planing down their back sides and plucking away their steep down-canyon faces has been absolutely minimal. You can see similar "domes" in the unglaciated southern Sierra.

Don't get lost looking for Lost Lake, a swamp at the east base of Mt. Broderick. Trapped between moraines left by a glacier receding up-canyon perhaps only 13,500 years ago, this "lake" has been slowly filling with sediments dominated by windblown silt and pollen. Lost Lake will appeal to the naturalist but probably not to anyone else. Beyond Lost Lake one can climb to the steep-faced Diving Board, which in my opinion offers the best of all possible views of Half Dome's giant, intimidating northwest face. Good mountaineering sense and cross-country ability are prerequisites for this brushy ascent. From the low saddle just west of Lost Lake, descend sufficiently west down a gully before starting your climb. Small cliffs await those starting too soon. Be sure to study your route so you can find it when you descend. For any of these side trips you might consider first checking in with a ranger stationed in Little Yosemite Valley, then checking back when you have safely returned.

HIKE 80

HAPPY ISLES TO HALF DOME

Distance: 16.4 miles round trip

Grade: 4E, strenuous day hike

Trailhead: Same as the Hike 77 trailhead. **D5.**

Introduction: If I as a first-time visitor were allowed to make only *one* day hike in the Park, I would unquestionably choose this hike—the one that introduced me to Yosemite and fired my desire to "climb every mountain." Half Dome is certainly not for acrophobics, and if you are not in excellent condition, you'll want to spend a night in Little Yosemite Valley on your way up.

Description: Half Dome "is a crest of granite rising to the height of 4,737 feet above the Valley, perfectly inaccessible, being probably the only one of all the prominent points about the Yosemite which never has been and never will be trodden by human foot." So wrote Josiah D. Whitney—California's first prominent geologist—in his *1870 Yosemite Guide-Book.* Just five years later the impossible was accomplished, when George Anderson labored for weeks drilling a row of holes up to the "inaccessible" summit, reached on October 12, 1875. In the 1990s, *hundreds* reach the summit virtually every sunny summer *day,* climbing a frightening cable stairway that lies close to the original ascent route. The dome is being

Half Dome's cable route

loved to death, and perhaps the day will come when the cables up it will be dismantled, leaving the fantastic summit views only to skilled rock climbers. If the route remains, it could use a parallel route—one to ascend; one to descend. The heavy up-and-down traffic on a single cable route is a potentially dangerous situation.

During midsummer, thunderstorms are common, though they usually don't expel their lightning bolts until midafternoon. Therefore, you should plan to reach the summit and leave it by early afternoon. Depending on your hiking ability, you should plan to start from Happy Isles at 6 or 7 A.M. if you intend to do this as a day hike, or by 9 A.M. if you're starting from Little Yosemite Valley.

Follow **Hike 77** up to the Vernal Fall bridge, then the first part of **Hike 78** up to the junction just beyond Nevada Fall; or stay on the John Muir Trail from the bridge, following the last part of **Hike 78** in reverse. As in **Hike 79** climb east to the west end of Little Yosemite Valley, meet a trail fork, and take either path. Where they rejoin, you've not yet expended half the energy required to reach the summit.

After 1⅓ miles of forested ascent you leave the John Muir Trail (**Hike 51** in the downhill direction), which climbs east to Tuolumne Meadows, and you continue up the Half Dome trail. After 0.6 mile you meet a spur trail that goes about 280 yards east to a spring—your last chance for water (treat it!). The trail bends west just before reaching a saddle, which is worth the minor effort for a viewful rest stop. The trail next climbs through a forest of red firs and Jeffrey pines instead of white firs and incense-cedars. Half Dome's northeast face comes into view and, topping a crest, you get a fine view of Clouds Rest and its satellites, the Quarter Domes, the latter accessible by a somewhat brushy cross-country ascent from the saddle. Between them and us, previous glaciers spilled into Tenaya Canyon. The shoulder of Half Dome, west of and above you, never was glaciated.

You now have a traverse, which reveals more views, including Tenaya Canyon, Mt. Watkins, Mt. Hoffmann, and much of the upper Merced River basin. This traverse ends all too soon at the base of Half Dome's shoulder, where a sign warns of the potential lightning hazard. Even when thunderstorms are miles away, static electricity can build up on the summit. Out of a clear blue sky a charge can bolt down the cable, throwing your arms off it—or worse. If your hair starts standing on end, beat a hasty retreat!

Almost two dozen short switchbacks guide us up the view-blessed ridge of the dome's shoulder and, near the top, a cable lends additional aid. A real danger on this section is loose gravel, which could prove fatal if you fell off the trail at an exposed spot. Topping the shoulder you are confronted with the dome's intimidating cable pair, which definitely cause some hikers to retreat. (Usually the cables are put up around mid-May and removed in early October.) The ascent starts out gently enough, but it too quickly steepens almost to a 45° angle. On this stretch, first-timers often slow to a snail's pace, clenching both cables with sweaty hands. Looking down, you can see that you *don't* want to fall.

The rarefied air certainly hinders your progress as you ascend, but eventually an easing gradient gives new incentive and soon you are scrambling up to the broad summit area about the size of 17 football fields. With caution most hikers proceed to the dome's high

Hiker at brink of Half Dome's summit

point (8,842 feet), located at the north end, from where they can view the dome's over-hanging northwest point. Stout-hearted souls peer over the lip of this point for an adrena-line-charged view down the dome's 2,000-foot-high northwest face, perhaps seeing climbers ascending it. In the past a few folks liked to camp overnight to view the sunrise, but in 1993 camping became banned ostensi-bly in order to protect the small population of Mt. Lyell salamanders (accumulating human feces may have been the real reason). Sharing the summit are golden-mantled ground squir-rels. One of these squirrels, begging for food, may have followed you up the cables, staying close enough to you to avoid becoming the prey of a sharp-eyed hawk.

From the broad summit of this monolith, which originated in the late days of the dinosaurs, you have a 360° panorama. You can look down Yosemite Valley to the bald brow of El Capitan and up Tenaya Canyon past Clouds Rest to Cathedral Peak, the Sierra crest, and Mt. Hoffmann. Mt. Starr King—a dome that rises only 250 feet above you—dominates the Illilouette Creek basin to the south, while the Clark Range cuts the sky to the southeast. Looking due east across Moraine Dome's sum-mit, one sees Mt. Florence, whose broad form hides the Park's highest peak, Mt. Lyell, behind it.

HIKE 81

HAPPY ISLES TO MERCED LAKE

Distance: 28.2 miles round trip

Grade: 5E, moderate 3-day hike

Trailhead: Just east of the day-use parking lot in Curry Village, drive 0.2 mile southeast along the shuttle-bus road to a short spur road branching right to a backpackers' parking lot. **D5.**

Introduction: Best done in three days with overnight stops at Little Yosemite Valley and Merced Lake, this hike is often done in two by energetic weekend hikers. Its route, up a fan-tastic river canyon, is one of the Sierra's best.

Description: See **Hike 65** for the first ½ mile east to a stream-gaging station along the east bank of the Merced River. **Hike 77** describes the route to the Vernal Fall bridge; then you follow the last part of **Hike 78** in reverse up the John Muir Trail to Nevada Fall. The last 1¼ miles along this section are very scenic, with views of Half Dome, Mt. Broderick, Liberty Cap, Nevada Fall, and the Merced River canyon. Beyond the Nevada Fall bridge you soon meet the end of the Mist trail (risky for backpackers), then climb up and over a minor ridge into western Little Yosemite Valley, as described in the first part of **Hike 79**.

You leave the northbound John Muir Trail to embark on a shady 2-mile stroll, following the Merced Lake trail through the broad, flat valley. The valley's floor has been largely buried by glacial sediments, which like beach sand make one work even though the trail is level. Progressing east through Little Yosemite Valley, we stay closer to the base of glacier-polished Moraine Dome than to the Merced River, and along this stretch you can branch off to riverside campsites that are far more peaceful than those near the John Muir Trail junction, which tends to be a "Grand Central Station." The valley's east end is graced by the presence of a beautiful pool—the receptacle of a Merced River cascade. Leaving the camps of the picturesque area, we climb past the cascade and glance back to see the east face of exfoliating Moraine Dome.

Your brief cascade climb heads toward the 1,900-foot-high Bunnell Point cliff, which is exfoliating at a prodigious rate. Rounding the base of a glacier-smoothed dome, unofficially called the Sugar Loaf, you enter shady Lost Valley, in which no fires are allowed. At the valley's east end, switchback up past Bunnell Cascade, which with the magnificent canyon scenery can easily distract one from the real

danger of this exposed section of trail. Although the scenery may overpower you, past glaciers, which completely buried Bunnell Point, were powerless to effectively erode this part of the canyon. They overtopped the point by several hundred feet, yet their massive thicknesses, exerting over 100 tons per square foot on the lower slopes, failed to transform this canyon from a **V** to a **U** shape.

Just beyond the **V** gorge, the canyon floor widens a bit, and in this area we bridge the Merced River. Our up-canyon walk soon reaches a series of more than a dozen switchbacks that carry us up 400 feet above the river—a bypass route necessitated by another **V** gorge. Our climb reaches its zenith amid a spring-fed profuse garden, bordered by aspens, which in midsummer supports a colorful array of various wildflowers. Alpine lily, monk's hood, and arrow-leaved senecio grow chest-high, as if to divert our attention from the many smaller, though equally beautiful, wildflower species.

Beyond this glade you soon come out onto a highly polished bedrock surface. Here

Merced Lake and a view east up Lewis Creek and Merced River canyons

you can glance west and see Clouds Rest—a long ridge—standing on the horizon. Now you descend back into tree cover, and among the white boles of aspens brush through a forest carpet of bracken ferns and cross several creeklets before emerging on a bedrock bench above the river's inner gorge. From the bench you can study the features of a broad, hulking granitic mass opposite you whose south face is bounded by an immense arch. A "hairline" crack along its east side indicates that a major rockfall is imminent. Traversing the bench, you soon come to a bend in the river and at it bridge the Merced just above the brink of its cascades. Strolling east, you soon reach the west end of spacious Echo Valley, and proceed to a junction at its north edge.

Here, near an Echo Creek campsite, is the start of an alternate, less dramatic, high route you could take on your return back to Little Yosemite Valley. When your up-canyon route was built in 1931, the old High trail to Merced Lake fell into disuse, for it is almost a mile longer and climbs 750 feet more. It also has less water, fewer campsites, and fewer views. On the plus side, it does provide access to the rewarding summit of Moraine Dome (see **Hike 51**). This alternate route to Merced Lake climbs about 450 feet, passing a moraine about midway to a junction with the Echo Creek trail (**Hike 52**). It then branches west for a shorter climb to a broad granitic surface. Across bedrock it winds briefly down to a stagnant lakelet. Beyond it you get an incredible view— one that justifies the effort—of the glacier-smoothed slabs and walls that bound the Merced River canyon.

Leaving the broad surface, the High trail makes a brushy ascent to an ephemeral creek, crosses it, and on gentle bedrock slopes goes through a bouldery moraine. This feature, which you can trace west, is only one of many lateral moraines left high on the river canyon's north wall by the last glacier as it melted back up-canyon. The tremendous views soon disappear. You then begin a mile of exhilarating walking through a forest of Jeffrey pines, lodgepoles, and white firs which shade patch after patch of vivid-green bracken ferns. Still in forest you climb slightly, cutting across the crests of two lateral moraines just before a junction with the John Muir Trail. About 150 yards north up this trail, beyond yet another moraine crest, you'll find the south end of the Forsyth trail, and a two-minute walk along it will get you to a good Sunrise Creek campsite. From this vicinity this alternate return route from the High-trail junction coincides with the John Muir Trail, following the last part of **Hike 51** down to Little Yosemite Valley.

But with Merced Lake our first goal, we immediately bridge Echo Creek, strike southeast through burned-but-boggy Echo Valley, and climb east past the Merced River's largely unseen pools to Merced Lake's west shore. Don't camp here, but rather continue past the north shore to the Merced Lake High Sierra Camp and the adjacent riverside campground, about 9¼ miles beyond the John Muir Trail junction in Little Yosemite Valley. Be sure to use the bearproof storage boxes. Eighty-foot-deep Merced Lake, being a large one at a moderate elevation, supports three species of trout: brook, brown, and rainbow.

Chapter 11

Trails south and east of the Glacier Point Road

Introduction: This chapter, like Chapter 6, is one of contrasts, ranging from 3250 feet at the bottom of the Alder Creek trail, outside the Park, up to 11,180 feet at Red Peak Pass. All of the Park's plant communities are found within this altitudinal range. Along Hikes 82, 83, and 92, few hikers will be met, but at Ostrander and Royal Arch lakes, Hikes 84 and 86/91 respectively, camping space may be at a premium. This chapter is unique in that it has a network of trails through a grove of giant sequoias (Hike 93); no such trail system exists at the Park's two other groves (Hikes 18 and 19). Although thousands of persons visit this chapter's Mariposa Grove each week during summer, the vast majority ride trams. The few who explore the grove on foot are richly rewarded.

Supplies and Services: Wawona is the "urban" center for this area, having a large, historic hotel, a store, a gas station, and other amenities. In addition to a golf course, the hotel has a pool, but the natural pools on the South Fork Merced River are more enjoyable and get more use. Some of these are located just up from the river's covered bridge, as well as in spots upriver, while some are located beside and downriver from stretched-out Wawona Campground.

Just north of the river the Chilnualna Road branches east from the Wawona Road—the main road—and it takes you past the History Center and its stables (with rides available) to North Wawona, a private in-Park settlement with additional food and lodging.

North of the Wawona area you'll reach the start of the Glacier Point Road at a signed junction. At this road's end at Glacier Point you can buy snacks, film, and various tourist-oriented items.

Food, lodging, gas, and most supplies are also available in Fish Camp, a small Highway 41 settlement just 2 miles south of the Park's south entrance station. Oakhurst, a sprawling town about 13½ miles south of this settlement, has virtually everything.

Wilderness Permits: If you want to reserve a permit, see the "Wilderness permits" section on page 59. However, only Ostrander Lake (Hike 85) is likely to reach its quota of backpackers, and then only on summer weekends. Therefore, most backpackers will probably get their permits in person at the Wawona District Office. This is at the end of a short road that branches right from the Chilnualna Road immediately past the Pioneer Yosemite History Center.

Left: Merced Peak, from switchback at 8480 feet in Merced Peak Fork canyon (Hike 89)

Campgrounds: For Hikes 83-89, stay at Bridalveil Creek Campground, whose entrance is found along the Glacier Point Road. For Hikes 82 and 90-93, stay at Wawona Campground, about one mile north of the Wawona Hotel. Both are often full. An alternate to Wawona Campground is the small Summerdale Campground, about ½ mile north of the settlement of Fish Camp.

HIKE 82

BISHOP CREEK VIA ALDER CREEK TRAIL

Distance: 6.3 miles round trip

Grade: 2C, moderate half-day hike

Trailhead: On the Wawona Road 3.9 miles north of the Wawona Campground entrance and 280 yards west of the Alder Creek crossing; also 7.4 miles south of the Glacier Point Road junction. **C6.**

Introduction: Your descent to Bishop Creek can be one of the Sierra's most pleasant springtime hikes, though by early summer the creeks run dry and temperatures soar. Most of this trail's length is across rolling topography carpeted with one of my favorite plants, mountain misery; nowhere else in the Park will you see such a spread of this low, aromatic shrub. Despite its sticky nature, it is a favorite food of deer. Another bush to look for is the large whiteleaf manzanita, easily recognized by its smooth, red bark and its gray-green leaves. The quiet forest shading these bushes is a classic ponderosa-pine forest, though incense-cedars and black oaks prevail here and there, and occasionally a multitrunked foothill (gray) pine will be seen. In late May or early June you're likely to see many wildflowers blooming, including Indian pink, mountain dogbane, soap plant, milkweed, miner's lettuce, small larkspur, and cinquefoil. Birds-foot, wood, and bracken ferns add spice to the carpeted forest floor, and at Bishop Creek alders, azaleas and creek dogwoods provide an interesting contrast. Most of these herbs, shrubs, and trees were used by the local Indians either for food, drink, or medicine or for basketry, bows, or shelter.

Mountain misery carpets the floor of a ponderosa-pine/Mariposa-manzanita woodland

Description: From the road's bend near a cut through weathered granite, your trail drops below the Wawona Road and parallels it northwest. The trail quickly widens along an abandoned road, which it momentarily leaves. After about ½ mile of traversing, it begins a long drop to the South Fork Merced River. About 1.2 miles from your trailhead, you leave the Park and in the Sierra National Forest descend 0.8 mile to a springtime creek. In a short ¼ mile beyond it we climb to a low ridge, on which you'll find about a half dozen Indian mortar holes, perhaps covered with black-oak leaves, just a few yards west of the trail. From the ridge you have a steady descent, one that winds in and out of gullies as it drops about 550 feet to the banks of Bishop Creek. From there you could continue down to the South Fork Merced River—a total drop of almost 800 feet along a dry, steep 1.4-mile course. However, the steepness, heat, and springtime ticks for many people make the descent not worth it.

HIKE 83

BRIDALVEIL CREEK CAMP-GROUND—WAWONA LOOP

Distance: 30.3 miles semiloop trip

Grade: 6E, moderate 3-day hike

Trailhead: Bridalveil Creek Campground (see Hike 72 trailhead). Park at the campground's *far* end. **D5.**

Introduction: Sparkling lakes, deep canyons, and alpine crests are *not* found along this hike—but then, neither are the backpacking crowds. This is a hike for those who love quiet trails. Although most of it is forested, you will pass through areas that have been burned in lightning-caused forest fires. The trees are regenerating, and until they cast sufficient shade, shrubs and wildflowers will grow in greater abundance.

Description: From the campground's far end, our trail climbs only about 200 feet in the first 3 ⅓ miles, an excellent way to start a backpack hike. Although white firs and red firs are pre-

sent, they are greatly overwhelmed by a super-abundance of lodgepole pines along this creek-side stretch. After about 1.6 miles of it—on a ridge above nearby Bridalveil Creek—we join a trail that comes 1.7 miles from the Glacier Point Road (the **Hike 84** trailhead). A 1987 fire—one of several in the drainage—caused moderate damage to the forest here. The trail keeps above the creek for a short distance, then curves over to a moderate-size camp along the creek's tributary. Like others we'll meet, this one can have lots of mosquitoes before late July. A two-minute walk upstream from the camp ends at the tributary's ford, and on the east bank we meet our second junction, 0.7 mile past the first. A sometimes obscure trail to the left climbs a short mile east to the Ostrander Lake trail (**Hike 84**).

Turning right, climb gently south for a mile to the tributary's upper basin. In it your climb becomes first moderate and then steep as you struggle briefly up to a nearby crest that separates the unglaciated Alder Creek drainage from the Bridalveil Creek drainage, which was glaciated only at its highest elevations. Jeffrey pines yield to red firs as you traverse slopes over to a junction near a broad saddle. The trail you'll return on climbs east to here from Deer Camp, down to the west. Starting southeast, you quickly cross the broad saddle and enter the Chilnualna Creek drainage, which also was glaciated only at its highest elevations. Now you begin a rolling, gentle 1¼-mile descent that goes through several small meadows, all with abundant corn lilies. Just before you reach the next junction, your trail touches the east edge of long Turner Meadows, about 6 miles from your trailhead, and here you can make a fair camp.

At the junction you veer right, hop Turner Meadows creek, and then your old trail climbs unnecessarily 300 feet up to a ridge (originally, *horses* did the climbing, not hikers, so ups and downs were not an issue). On this moderate, shady ascent one has a crest view of glaciated-but-subdued Buena Vista Peak, to the east. You then start a 3,800-foot drop to the Wawona area. On it, western white pines quickly yield to their cousins, sugar pines, while farther down red firs yield to the closely related white firs. A shrubby black oak appears at about 7,540 feet elevation, near the top of its altitudinal range. Perhaps only on Smith Peak (**Hike 17**) can you find a specimen a couple of hundred feet higher. This oak is just past a secondary crest, and from it we plunge down to a creeklet, then make an equally long drop to its larger counterpart. From its verdant banks one has an easy ½-mile descent to a junction just above Chilnualna Creek. Here, near the confluence of this creek and its southbound tributary, you can find a suitable spot to spend your first night, about 9¼ miles from your trailhead. You may want to first view Chilnualna Fall, just downstream, but be extremely careful if you do, for the rock can be treacherously slippery.

After a possibly memorable sunset and a good night's sleep, descend the trail 4.0 scenic miles to its end, following the description of **Hike 90** in reverse. Then, gradually descending west, walk 1⅓ miles along a road that goes through the private inholding of North Wawona, which has supplies, food, and lodging. Your next trail, the Alder Creek trail, begins about ⅓ mile beyond the settlement's school, and this trailhead is about 300 yards before the Wawona District Office, which dispenses information and wilderness permits. Before resuming your loop hike, you might consider a side trip to the Pioneer Yosemite History Center, which you enter just west of a junction with the district office's spur road. By walking 200–300 yards upstream from the center's covered bridge you'll discover some small pools in the South Fork Merced River that in summer afternoons are among the warmest "swimming holes" in the Park.

The Alder Creek trail begins about 100 yards east of a west-heading service road. At your low elevation temperatures often soar into the 80s by early afternoon, and water may be absent until Alder Creek, about 6 miles ahead. After a brief, initial, open climb north, your trail turns west to make an ascending traverse for ⅓ mile across small gullies. At the end of a 2¾-mile-long, mostly viewless ascent, you reach a mile-high junction, from which a steep trail descends ¾ mile to the heavily traveled Wawona Road.

Starting east, we begin a 2¾-mile rolling traverse in and out of gullies and around or over low ridges to a view of 100-foot-high Alder Creek fall below. Along the last mile or so of this section you may see railroad ties, which are the few tangible relics of a dark period in the Park's history. From the early days of World War I through the 1920s, the Yosemite Lumber Company laid railroad tracks in and around western Park lands to log some of the Sierra's finest stands of sugar pines. Ironically, some of this timber—more than 6 million board feet—was cut to use in the construction of Hetch Hetchy's O'Shaughnessy Dam, completed in 1923. More than ½ *billion* board feet were cut before 1930, when John D. Rockefeller, Jr. and the US Government split the cost of buying up the logging company's interests.

Beyond the fall our abandoned-railroad route approaches lushly lined Alder Creek, parallels it north gently upstream for 1¼ miles, then crosses it to reach a nearby junction. Here or elsewhere along Alder Creek you can make your second night's camp. From the junction a trail climbs north 1⅓ miles to an old logging road, which westbound goes about 1 mile to a junction with a spur road south, then 5 miles to the Wawona Road, ending about 50 yards south of the Yosemite West road junction. Limited parking is at the start of this signed Mosquito Creek trail, which makes an easy, nearly level hike worth taking before or after summer, when higher trails are under snow. Eastbound, you could follow the old logging road ½ mile to a trail's resumption, which climbs a little over 3 miles to the Bridalveil Creek Campground entrance. However, thick brush—the result of logging—makes this shorter route undesirable.

The recommended route angles to the right at the Alder Creek junction, immediately refords the broad creek, and then climbs east for 1¾ miles, paralleling a murmuring tributary. This white-fir-shaded stretch ends at Deer Camp, a roadend flat along the fringe of the former logging area. You can camp here, but it lacks esthetics. Beyond it your trail continues east and, typical of old trails, it winds and switchbacks all too steeply up most of a 1,100-foot ascent. Midway up it, views expand, providing an overview of the Alder Creek basin. After about 1¼ miles of climbing, we top a crest, then momentarily descend to a usually flowing creeklet. Should you want to camp in this vicinity, do so at the nearby crest top if mosquitoes are abundant. Leaving the creeklet we climb around a meadow—rich in sedges, willows, and corn lilies—then make a final short push southeast up to a junction near a saddle. From it retrace your first day's steps 4.9 miles back to the trailhead.

HIKE 84

GLACIER POINT ROAD TO OSTRANDER LAKE

Distance: 12.7 miles round trip

Grade: 3C, easy 2-day hike

Trailhead: From a signed junction with the Wawona Road drive 8.9 miles up the Glacier Point Road to a turnoff on your right. This parking area is 1.3 miles past the Bridalveil Creek Campground spur road. **D5.**

Introduction: Ostrander Lake, being the closest lake to the Glacier Point Road, is the objective of many summertime weekend backpackers. It is also popular in winter and spring with cross-country skiers.

Description: The first half of our hike is easy— a gentle ascent through a forest that is interspersed with an assortment of meadows. Start along a former jeep road and soon encounter the first of several areas of lodgepole forest badly burned in a 1987 fire. Farther up, on Horizon Ridge, you'll see a forest burned in a

1994 fire. Note the difference that seven years of regrowth makes. Just ⅓ mile from the trailhead we cross a sluggish creek, then amble an easy mile to a ridge junction. From it a short lateral drops to Bridalveil Creek—possibly a difficult June crossing—then climbs equally briefly to the Bridalveil Creek trail (**Hike 83**).

From the junction our route contours southeast past unseen Lost Bear Meadow, and after a mile makes a short ascent east up along a trickling creek to its crossing. Just beyond the ford our road curves west to a nearby junction with a second lateral to the Bridalveil Creek trail. Though we are now about halfway to Ostrander Lake, we've climbed very little, and from this junction we face 1,500 feet of vertical gain, mostly through burned forests. Nevertheless, some trees survived, and they indicate the former (and future) forest type.

The steepening road climbs east through a mixed forest, then climbs more gently south across an open slab that provides the first views of the Bridalveil Creek basin. You then curve southeast into a Jeffrey-pine stand, before climbing east through a white-fir forest. These firs are largely supplanted by red firs by the time you top a saddle that bisects Horizon

Ostrander Lake, nestled in a cirque at the west end of Horse Ridge

Ridge. Climbing southeast up that ridge, your road passes through a generally open stretch decked with lupines, sulfur flowers and, surprisingly, sagebrush. About 400 feet above your first saddle the road switchbacks at a second one, then curves up to a third. From it the road makes a momentary descent southeast before bending to start a short, final ascent south into unburned forest surrounding Ostrander Lake. Near this bend we get far-ranging views across the Illilouette Creek basin. We can see the tops of Royal Arches and Washington Column and, above and east of them, North, Basket, and Half domes. Behind Half Dome stands the Park's geographic center, broad-topped Mt. Hoffmann. Reigning over the Illilouette Creek basin is Mt. Starr King and its entourage of lesser domes. To the east and northeast the jagged crest of the Clark Range cuts the sky.

Beyond the short, final ascent south we drop in several minutes to Ostrander Hut. When it is snowbound, cross-country skiers can stay in it, if they've first obtained reservations from the Valley's Wilderness Center (see Chapter 1). The hut is on a rocky glacial moraine left by a glacier that retreated perhaps 16,000 years ago. Behind it, lying in a bedrock basin, is 25-acre, trout-populated Ostrander Lake. Here, camping is good along the west shore.

Ostrander Hut, built atop a moraine

HIKE 85

OSTRANDER LAKE-MONO MEADOW LOOP

Distance: 19.6 miles loop trip

Grade: 4D, moderate 2-day hike

Trailhead: From a signed junction on the Wawona Road, drive 10.1 miles up Glacier Point Road to a forested saddle with a parking area on your right. **D5.**

Introduction: Like the previous hike, this one is a good one for weekends. Being a loop trip, it can be walked in either direction. It is described counterclockwise because the 2¼-mile cross-country stretch is easier to hike and follow in that direction.

Description: Park at the Mono Meadow trailhead, then walk west down the Glacier Point Road for 1.2 miles to the **Hike 84** trailhead. From it follow that hike 6⅓ miles up to the north shore of Ostrander Lake. you can spend the night here or at the Hart Lakes, about 1½ miles to the east.

To begin your cross-country route to those lakes, start from the northeast shore of Ostrander Lake and go southeast on a diagonal upslope. If you're on course, you should approach the north shore of a pond after about ¼ mile of hiking. After reaching this check point, you now strike east for an easier ¼-mile ascent to the north shore of a shallow lakelet—not a desirable camping area. Beyond the lakelet's east end you soon curve northeast and climb 200 vertical feet up to a ridge, which you ascend southeast for about 200 yards. Then you make a ⅓-mile traverse, having distant views across the Illilouette Creek basin, to a view of the Hart Lakes. A gully descends southeast to the larger Hart Lake, but it is choked with brush. Even if you stay just north of the gully, chinquapin bushes still cause some problems down to this larger lake. Rimmed with lodgepoles, Labrador tea, and red heather, it harbors mosquitoes through late July, but should have pleasant camping after that. A tent helps before then. In the early morning you may find the lake's placid surface occasionally broken by leaping rainbow trout.

Leave the larger Hart Lake at its northeast corner and go northeast about 250 yards to the east side of a low summit, then begin a moderate descent north toward soon-sighted Edson Lake. Midway between the Hart Lakes and this lake you'll reach open granite slabs across which you can diagonal northeast to a moraine, and the Buena Vista trail. This trail runs along the moraine's crest for more than 300 yards before making a noticeable drop west from it. On this trail you follow the first part of **Hike 86** in the reverse direction, first descending almost 7 miles to an intersection with the Mono Meadow trail, then ascending it 3 miles southwest to the Mono Meadow trailhead.

Largest Hart Lake and Horse Ridge

HIKE 86

MONO MEADOW TO BUENA VISTA AND ROYAL ARCH LAKES

Distance: 30.4 miles round trip

Grade: 6E, easy 4-day hike

Trailhead: Same as the Hike 85 trailhead. **D5.**

Introduction: The subalpine lakes nestled around Buena Vista Peak can be reached from North Wawona—Hike 91—or from three trailheads along the Glacier Point Road. This hike starts from one of these trailheads and visits five of the peak's lakes. Although this route is slightly longer than Hike 91, it requires 20% less climbing effort. Also see Hike 94 for a little-used route to these lakes.

Description: At the trailhead, shaded by magnificent red firs, ancient Bridalveil and Illilouette drainage glaciers once joined, just barely overtopping today's forested pass—according to François Matthes, who in 1930 produced a "classic" US Geological Survey Professional Paper 160 on Yosemite Valley and environs. Interestingly, none of the ancient glacial deposits he mapped in these drainages existed, except in his imagination. Nevertheless, some still appear on the Park's 1989 geologic map. Looking for nonexistent glacial deposits, we start our trail with a steady, moderate descent north, followed by an easing gradient east to lodgepole-fringed Mono Meadow. Until mid-July you may face 200 yards of

Half Dome and Mt. Starr King, from slabs above Edson Lake

muddy freshets and meadow bogs before you reach the narrow meadow's east edge. During this period, desperate hikers try to circumvent the mire, and several paths may spring up to confuse you. The real trail crosses the meadow on a 120° bearing, and it becomes obvious once you're within the forest's edge.

Beyond the meadow your Mono Meadow trail crosses a low divide, then makes a generally viewless, easy descent to a major tributary of Illilouette Creek. Here, 1½ miles from your trailhead, is your first possible campsite. You ford the tributary at the brink of some rapids, and in early season this ford could be a dangerous one. From the tributary you have a short though unnecessary climb, with 200 feet of elevation gain. The climb does have some merit, for at the crest and on your descent east from it you're rewarded with views of North, Basket, and Half domes, Clouds Rest, and Mt. Starr King. After a descent through a fir forest you emerge on an open slope with a thin veneer of *grus*, or granitic gravel. On the slope you descend straight toward Mt. Starr King, the highest of the Illilouette Creek domes, and immediately after the view disappears, you reach a junction with the Buena Vista trail, which links Glacier Point with the Buena Vista Peak area (the end of **Hike 89** briefly describes this trail north to Glacier Point).

You turn right and go just 40 yards up-canyon to a second junction, from where the Mono Meadow trail goes 300 yards east past campsites to ford broad Illilouette Creek. From it the trail climbs a slope veneered with glacial outwash—stream deposits from the last glaciers that existed up-canyon—then it crosses a bedrock bench with a veneer of grus. In "classic" Professional Paper 160, Matthes said this grus was sediments of an ancient, glacial lake. Actually this gravel, as elsewhere in glaciated *and* unglaciated granitic lands, is nothing more than weathered granitic bedrock. Real lake sediments are mud, not gravel. Of more interest to the hiker is that this spacious bedrock bench is suitable for camping. You can protect your food from bears if you can find a deep crack in bedrock just downstream from the camps, and stick your food in it. If the crack is narrow enough or deep enough bears won't be able to reach your food. **Hike 89,** descending Illilouette Creek from Merced Pass, traverses through this camping

Clouds building over bleak Buena Vista Lake

area, then follows the Buena Vista trail northwest toward Glacier Point.

From the junction before the creek crossing our route heads southeast up the Buena Vista trail. Over much of the route up toward Buena Vista Peak the vegetation has been burned by several large, natural fires. Usually a burn is quite unsightly for a year or two, but wildflowers often abound in one, and after several years brush and young trees soften the visual effect. In 1¼ miles we come to a creeklet with a fair camp on its west bank. The trail's gradient gradually eases, then you cross a broad divide and in ¼ mile angle sharply left to descend along the edge of a sloping meadow. Beyond it are aspens that hide a step-across creek. Just a few minutes' walk east of it you cross a slightly larger creek, then make a gentle ascent southeast across sandy soils to steep slopes above Buena Vista Creek. Camping is poor along the west bank, but good—and isolated—above the east bank. Fallen trees may provide access across the bouldery creek to these sites.

Soon our trail leaves Buena Vista Creek, curves southwest, and climbs moderately in that direction for 1½ miles to a ford, between two meadows, of diminutive Edson Lake creek. From a poor campsite the trail ascends along a moraine crest, then in one mile leaves it to angle southeast up to a higher crest. Where your trail makes this sudden angle left, you can leave it and contour ⅓ mile west over to a campsite at shallow Edson Lake. Our trail follows the higher moraine crest southwest for more than 300 yards, finally leaves the burned area, and then makes a ¼-mile, view-packed descent to Hart Lakes creek. From where the trail leaves the crest, you can continue cross-country southwest up it, soon diagonal up slabs, and then climb south up to the Hart Lakes. This is the reverse of the last part of **Hike 85**.

From brush-lined Hart Lakes creek we make a short contour over to Buena Vista Creek, with a small campsite on its east bank. After ½ mile of moderate ascent you cross a creek that bends northeast, then continue south up a slightly shorter ascent to a recrossing of that creek. Immediately beyond you cross its western tributary, then follow this stream south briefly up to two ponds, from

Reflections in Grouse Lake

which you switchback up a cirque wall with ice-shattered blocks to a crest junction. **Hike 91**, ascending from North Wawona, now joins our route for a loop around the lakes of Buena Vista Peak. The first lake we encounter, about ⅓ mile southeast from the junction, is rather bleak Buena Vista Lake, which has rainbow and brook trout. Nestled on a broad bench at the base of the cool north slope of Buena Vista Peak, this lake is the highest and coldest one we'll see. It does, however, have at least two good, if somewhat exposed camps. In threatening weather, camp lower down.

Royal Arch Lake is well named

Starting at the lake's outlet, take short switchbacks up to a broad, viewless pass, from where one can climb ¾ mile up a gentle ridge to Buena Vista Peak for an unrestricted panorama of the Park's southern area. From the pass we descend 2 easy, winding trail miles to a favorite lake on this loop, Royal Arch Lake, which lies below a broad, granitic arch. This lake, like Buena Vista Lake, has rainbow and brook trout. Just past the outlet is an excellent, popular campsite. For more solitude head cross-country ¾ mile west to less attractive Minnow Lake, which has brook trout.

Leaving Royal Arch Lake, we parallel its outlet creek for ½ mile, then angle south across slabs to a junction. Here we meet the route of **Hike 94,** which starts northwest from Chiquito Pass, crosses the South Fork Merced River and climbs to Buck Camp, a ranger station about 1½ miles from our junction.

Turning right, we descend west toward Johnson Lake, reaching good campsites along its northwest shore in just ¾ mile—with hordes of mosquitoes in early season. You don't see large Crescent Lake, but on meeting its inlet creek, about ⅓ mile beyond a meadowy divide, one can walk 150 yards downstream, passing a fair camp before reaching the lake's shallow, trout-filled waters. You might visit or camp near the lake's south end, for from its outlet you can peer into the 2,800-foot-deep South Fork Merced River canyon.

Beyond Crescent Lake's inlet creek our trail quickly turns north, passes a small creekside meadow, and then climbs more than 150 feet to a second broad divide. From it we descend into the headwaters of a Chilnualna Creek tributary. Your moderate-to-steep gradient ends when you approach easily missed Grouse Lake. Look for a use trail that descends about 100 yards to a fair campsite on the north shore of this shallow, reedy lakelet.

Lodgepoles and red firs monopolize the slopes along your 2-mile descent from this lake down to a hillside junction. From it, hikers completing **Hike 91** head west down-canyon to their trailhead. Hikers on the second day of that hike join us for a short northwest stretch, first up over a nearby divide, then down more than 400 feet to Chilnualna Creek. Just above its north bank is a good, medium-size campsite, and just beyond that is another trail junction. From it **Hike 91** trekkers climb east. Should you want to visit the Chilnualna Lakes,

take this 5.3-mile trail up past them to the crest junction where **Hike 91** first joined our route, then backtrack 13.1 miles to your trailhead. This route is 10.0 miles longer than the following route, including its 1.2-mile walk along the Glacier Point Road back to the trailhead.

Spurning the longer option, we head northwest from Chilnualna Creek. During midsummer, our gently ascending traverse is brightened by the orange sunbursts of alpine lilies, growing chest-high along the wetter parts of our trail. As we near Turner Meadows we encounter a trail junction from which **Hike 83** departs southwest down to the Wawona area.

You now backtrack along the first part of that hike, first ascending past and through a series of "Turner Meadows," then topping a forest pass to quickly meet a trail descending to Deer Camp. You, however, keep right, traverse to a crest and descend to a tributary of Bridalveil Creek. But before reaching Bridalveil Creek, you meet a junction, turn left and then cross the tributary creek. Along it you momentarily pass a moderate-size campsite and then in ½ mile reach another junction. The main trail continues 1.6 miles northwest to Bridalveil Creek Campground, but we veer right, drop to nearby Bridalveil Creek, ford it, and make an equally short climb up to the Ostrander Lake trail—a closed jeep road. In 1½ miles this northbound route ends at the Glacier Point Road, beside which we walk 1.2 miles east to our trailhead.

HIKE 87

GLACIER POINT TO YOSEMITE VALLEY VIA NEVADA AND VERNAL FALLS

Distance: 9.1 miles one way

Grade: 2C, moderate day hike

Trailhead: Same as the Hike 75 trailhead. **D5.**

Introduction: This is the most scenic of all trails descending to the floor of Yosemite Valley. Either take a bus up to Glacier Point or have someone drop you there and meet you down at Camp Curry.

Description: From the early 1870s until January 1968, a large pile of embers was pushed off Glacier Point at evening darkness to create the renowned Firefall—a glowing "waterfall." Quite a spectacle. Then from the early 1970s until June 1990, people in the chilly early morning hours would take running leaps from this vicinity out into space. This hang gliding was also quite a spectacle. However, one reason for establishing the Park was to protect its natural lands, and you can see a spectacular part of them by making the short pilgrimage out to nearby Glacier Point before starting Hike 87.

Just east of the entrance to the Glacier Point parking lot Hike 87 starts south up a signed trail that quickly forks. The Pohono Trail, **Hike 75**, veers right, but we veer left, climbing a bit more before starting a moderate descent. A switchback leg helps ease the grade, and then we descend, often with views. A 1987 natural fire blackened most of the forest from near the trailhead to just beyond the upcoming Buena Vista trail junction, but most trees survived. In open areas, black oaks are thriving, and shrubs have regenerated with a vengeance. Between charred trunks are occasional

great views of Half Dome, Mt. Broderick, Liberty Cap, Nevada Fall, and Mt. Starr King. After 1⅔ miles and an 800-foot drop, our Glacier Point-Panorama trail meets the Buena Vista trail. Over 2.2 miles this first heads up-canyon to Illilouette Creek, then leads up along it to intersect the Mono Meadow trail (**Hike 86**).

Our trail branches left and switchbacks down to a spur trail that goes a few yards to a railing. Here, atop an overhanging cliff, you have an unobstructed view of 370-foot-high Illilouette Fall, which splashes down over a low point on the rim of massive Panorama Cliff. Behind it Half Dome rises boldly while above Illilouette Creek Mt. Starr King rises even higher. In ¼ mile your trail descends to a wide bridge, wisely placed upstream. Still, wading in the creek could carry you swiftly downstream and over the fall.

Your trail soon passes just above the brink of Illilouette Fall, and gravels here are remnants of a thick accumulation that choked the creek when the uppermost part of the last glacier formed a low ice-dam across its mouth. The trail then starts a major climb along the slopes just above Panorama Cliff. It first climbs

Glacier Point view: Tenaya Canyon, Half Dome, and Mt. Lyell above Little Yosemite Valley

Illilouette Fall

past this vicinity is a superlative panorama extending from Upper Yosemite Fall east past Royal Arches, Washington Column, and North Dome to Half Dome. Our forested, moderate climb ends after 200 more feet of elevation gain, and then we descend gently to the rim for some more views, contour east, and have even more, these dominated by Half Dome, Mt. Broderick, Liberty Cap, Clouds Rest, and Nevada Fall. Your contour ends at a junction with the Mono Meadow trail, which climbs southwest over a low ridge before descending to Illilouette Creek.

A fresh, Tioga-age lateral moraine descends northwest across the junction. François Matthes, in his "classic" 1930 paper, mapped many ancient lateral moraines above this one, but no one has been able to find any of them—ascend any of the slopes and see for yourself. Worth an ascent from this junction is a visit to the Starr King Lake environs, to the southeast and about 1300 feet above you. The cross-country route 1½ miles up to the west edge of the bench holding the lake is strenuous but straightforward, and is not exposed. From any of three low summits along the north edge of the bench one has stellar views of Mt. Starr King, Half Dome, Moraine Dome, and the features of Little Yosemite Valley that lie below them. Starr King Lake, although of ample dimensions, is so shallow that you can wade entirely across it. Sometimes in late summer it dries up, so if you want to camp here but find it dry, head ¼ mile southeast from the lake to a gully with a spring-fed creek.

Beyond the trail junction Hike 87 makes a mile-long, switchbacking, generally viewless descent to a trail split, each branch descending a few yards to the John Muir Trail. You'll descend along it, as described in the last part of **Hike 78**, but first walk over to the nearby brink of roaring Nevada Fall. Alternately, you could descend the Mist trail, a shorter route, which begins a few hundred yards northeast of Nevada Fall. Being shorter, it is also steeper, and is potentially dangerous for those who try to descend it too rapidly. This wet route is described in the opposite direction in the first part of **Hike 78**. From the reunion of the John Muir and Mist trails, walk but a minute to the Vernal Fall bridge, then follow **Hike 77** in reverse down to the Happy Isles shuttle-bus stop. From it you can ride or walk west to Camp Curry, the Valley's east hub of activity.

briefly along its rim, then switchbacks away, soon returning near Panorama Point. The former viewpoint was in part undermined by a monstrous rockfall that broke loose during the winter of 1968–69. The rest of the viewpoint could break loose at any time. About ⅓ mile

HIKE 88

GLACIER POINT TO MERCED AND WASHBURN LAKES

Distance: 53.2 miles semiloop trip

Grade: 7G, moderate 6-day hike

Trailhead: Same as the Hike 75 trailhead. **D5.**

Introduction: Along this route you'll make a thorough examination of the Merced River above Yosemite Valley. The length of this route gives you an appreciation for the magnitude of its past glaciers, at least one having extended as far down-canyon as the El Portal area by the Park's west border.

Description: As in **Hike 87** you make a scenic excursion 5.4 miles to the John Muir Trail. Some backpackers making this loop prefer to start from Happy Isles, and though their hike to our junction is 2.3 miles shorter, it involves 1000 more feet of climbing—something to consider with a full pack on your back. In a few minutes from where you hit the John Muir Trail, you reach Nevada Fall, then in an equally short time reach the upper end of the Mist trail. From here you follow **Hikes 79** to Little Yosemite Valley, then **Hike 81** to campsites near the east shore of Merced Lake, a long though relatively easy 16.0 miles from your Glacier Point trailhead. If you travel to this lake in one day, at that pace you'll do the entire circuit in four. Most hikers, however, should plan on six, spending nights in Little Yosemite Valley, at Washburn Lake, along the High trail, at Merced Lake, and again in Little Yosemite Valley.

From campsites near the east shore of Merced Lake, you climb around a low transcanyon rib, down which the Merced River shoots to a churning pool. Beyond the rib you have a level ¾-mile stroll past lodgepoles and aspens to a junction beside the Merced Lake Ranger Station. Descending to it is the Lewis Creek trail, named for the multibranched creek we bridged just before this junction. We'll be starting a 23.9 mile loop from this junction and will complete it along the last part of the Lewis Creek trail, which can also be followed up to Volgelsang High Sierra Camp and beyond down to Tuolumne Meadows (**Hike 56**). Don't hike this loop in the reverse direction, for though it involves the same amount of climb-

A giant arch on a dome, one mile southwest of Echo Valley

ing, the climbing comes in larger steps. The described route has a much more gradual ascent.

Starting southeast from the junction we skirt along the edge of a broad, flat canyon floor which, like the next 7½ miles, is dominated by lodgepoles. The ½-mile width of the canyon floor leads one to expect its sediments to extend more than 200 feet down to bedrock. One would expect to see a deep "Merced Lake" here, but not even a pond exists. At best a swampy lake may have existed after the last glaciers retreated up-canyon, which may have disgorged prodigious sediments in their voluminous outwash to fill it in by about 13,500 years ago.

About ¾ mile south from the junction we rejoin the Merced River at a point where a bedrock dam cuts across it, forming pools both above and below it. Just upstream is another bedrock dam and then we see a large, smooth slab on the canyon's southwest wall which, like other similar sites, in the past has borne avalanches. As your trail's gradient changes from level to a gentle ascent, junipers, Jeffrey pines, and white firs become prominent. Mule ears, found in abundance on volcanic soils, merely dot the slopes here, and at a large tributary aspens radiate their own charm. Immediately beyond this tributary, the Merced River cascades through a small gorge, and beside it you'll find ochre-stained slabs—the artwork of soda springs. Climbing onward, note a progression toward dryness as expressed in a sequence from bracken fern to chinquapin to huckleberry oak and ultimately to sagebrush. Next, a river cascade treats you, followed by a long, tempting pool, which lies just below a rocky moraine. You then pass an even larger pool, beside a trail blasted in bedrock, immediately before reaching bedrock-dammed Washburn Lake.

In Washburn Lake's cold waters—at least 86 feet deep—brook and rainbow trout await the skillful angler. The lake's north shore has been a popular camping area, still, most of the lake's campsites are along the lake's south end. Here, incoming sediments are slowly filling in the lake—a process that should be accomplished in about a half-million years. However, long before then, perhaps in the next few thousand years, a glacier will advance down-canyon and eradicate the lake sediments left after the last one retreated. By the lake's inlet, notice the plant succession south from the shore. Sterile, newly deposited sand covers the shore, but a few feet back, sedges take hold. Farther back, willows start to shade them out and these in turn are shaded out by lodgepoles and aspens. Until late July, mosquitoes can plague campers here, and before then use the rocky north-end campsites.

Beyond the lake, whose basin was buried under as much as 3000 feet of ice in past glaciations, we hike up-canyon, soon noting a cleft in our canyon's west wall—the result of erosion along a large, straight fracture. Momentarily the trail approaches the Merced River, where you may see a good campsite 150 yards below a very photogenic fall. Continuing southeast, you leave most backpackers for an excursion into the upper reaches of the Merced River. In ½ mile your trail bends east, and beyond a tumultuous cascade it gradually levels off, curves south, and passes a packer campsite about 40 yards before bridging the Merced River near its confluence with the Lyell Fork.

More cascades are passed as you make an effort south up the Merced Peak Fork canyon,

Calm, early morning waters of Washburn Lake; Peak 11370 in distance

Fletcher Creek and Hike 56 run along the east (right) side of Babcock Dome

whose east wall has one exposure of very massive dikes. Beyond this view we soon bridge the fork beside another packer camp, then switchback eastward across open slopes. Along this ascent you see the two summits of Mt. Florence, above the Lyell Fork canyon to the north-northeast, and the two summits of Merced Peak, above a cross-country route to the south-southwest. Once in the Triple Peak Fork canyon, about 4 miles beyond Washburn Lake, the trail first climbs for ½ mile. It then makes a very gentle 2¼-mile climb across glaciated slabs and through a thinning lodgepole forest to a riverside junction. From here **Hike 89** climbs to Red Peak Pass and **Hike 98** descends from the pass to our junction. The area of our riverside junction is a scenic one to camp in, but if you're making this hike in six days, you should plan to camp higher up.

Look for a log hereabouts to cross the wide tributary of Triple Peak Fork; then, back on the trail, head southeast to a quick ford of the fork. From the ford your trail makes a gentle ascent south, paralleling the unseen fork for ½ mile to the start of a switchbacking climb northeast. Here is the place to leave the trail for an easy ½-mile cross-country jaunt up to seldom-visited Turner Lake. At 9540 feet elevation, it is the only nearby lake you'll find where campfires are legal. All the others we'll approach lie above the 9600-foot contour—stoves only. The 550-foot climb northeast is generally a viewless one, due to the lodgepoles and hemlocks, though you may get an occasional view north of the Mt. Florence ridge and

of the Matthes Crest, in the distance west of it. Your climb ends on a small flat below the west spur of unseen Isberg Peak. From here, beside a tall cairn, **Hike 98** continues up to Post Peak Pass. For a campsite, you may want to follow that route for ⅓ mile, then traverse ¼ mile east to a fairly large, unnamed lake, whose northwest shore is bordered with protective lodgepole pines.

Our hike, however, proceeds north from a cairn along the High trail, quickly reaching a step-across creek that, if followed upstream for an easy ¾ mile, leads to a treeline lake. Following blazes north, you descend to a shallow, glaciated trough, then climb up to three ephemeral creeklets. From these you could hike ⅓ mile cross-country up to a small subalpine lake. Your ascent yields to a contour, then to a descent to a trickling creeklet, from which you climb to a low nearby saddle and then descend once again to another creeklet. A lake lies on a bench about ¼ mile east of it, but the climb to it is quite steep. In about ½ mile your high-altitude traverse, shaded by lodgepoles and hemlocks, crosses Foerster Creek, then about ¾ mile farther, after you briefly ascend the second of two gently descending ridges, you can leave the trail for a ¼-mile contour east to a lovely little lake. This cross-country route begins about 30 yards before the trail makes a short, steep descent into a gully. Rather than camp on the fragile shoreline vegetation—which one should never do—camp just west of the lake.

Beyond the gully our trail undulates to a forested crest. From this crest you can look back and see the twin summits of rusty, metavolcanic Isberg Peak and the pointed summit of gray, granitic Post Peak. You can also identify slightly rusty Triple Divide Peak. West of it stands dark-gray, metamorphic Merced Peak, then the varicolored peaks of the Clark Range. In the distant northwest rise Clouds Rest and Mt. Hoffmann, while east of them stands the Park's highest massif—the Mt. Lyell complex.

Leaving the bouldery crest, you descend into the deep, glaciated Lyell Fork canyon via dozens of short switchbacks—one with an excellent viewpoint—then eventually reach the seasonally powerful Lyell Fork, bordered by mountain hemlocks. This is the northernmost locality in which you'll want to set up your third night's camp. No camping space is found at the ford, so either follow the tumbling stream a couple of hundred yards downstream or about ⅓-⅔ mile upstream. If you want to head upstream, leave the trail about 200 yards beyond the Lyell Fork, where it starts a traverse northwest. The trail here might be hard to follow for a short distance, so watch for ducks and blazes.

Soon starting a westward climb, you pass four large junipers, which add contrast to your typically pine-hemlock landscape. Beyond a conspicuous notch you get a revealing panorama of the Clark Range and the expansive bench below it, which borders the rim of the deep Merced River gorge. This "gorge within a canyon" topography has previously been interpreted as the result of two distinct major uplifts in the Sierra Nevada. However, the canyon below us lies *parallel* to the Sierra crest, and therefore its river's gradient would not have been increased by any uplift. We now know that these inner gorges are very tens of millions of years old. Despite having massive glaciers flow down them, they have been only slightly modified. (See the end of **Hike 10** for evidence of virtually no erosion in the last 10 million years in the Tuolumne River canyon, where glaciers were as much as 4000 feet thick.)

After the view we re-enter forest and cross a small Mt. Florence creek at the base of its splashing waterfall. From it you climb past joint-controlled slabs, ascending almost 500 feet over a mile's course to a bouldery summit. Along the ascent to this forested summit you come to a viewpoint that provides the trail's best panorama of the upper Merced River canyon, from Peak 11210 (about one mile east of us) south to Triple Divide Peak and then north along the entire Clark Range. The trail, which has climbed unnecessarily, now descends ½ mile to a second Mt. Florence tributary, with

Foerster Creek Lake near sunset

camping potential, then climbs an equal distance to a slope below unseen Cony Crags, which you saw from points south of the Lyell Fork.

With no more major climbing to come until after Nevada Fall, you can enjoy the trail's course, which ducks down into a shallow-but-glaciated side canyon with a creekside campsite, then beyond it switchbacks more than 30 times down to a junction in Lewis Creek canyon. Here you join **Hike 56** for a considerable descent to the Merced Lake Ranger Station, at the end of your loop. Midway along this descent you pass a junction with the Fletcher Creek trail, the return route of **Hike 56**. From the ranger station you backtrack to Merced Lake and Echo Valley, then, as in **Hike 81**, decide which of two routes to take to Little Yosemite Valley. Beyond this valley and Nevada Fall you soon retrace the steps of **Hike 87** back to your trailhead at Glacier Point.

HIKE 89

GLACIER POINT TO MERCED, WASHBURN, AND OTTOWAY LAKES

Distance: 48.6 miles loop trip

Grade: 6F, moderate 5-day hike

Trailhead: Same as the Hike 75 trailhead. **D5.**

Introduction: The Park's trails exceed 11,000 feet in only three places: Donohue Pass (11,056–Hike 58), Parker Pass (11,100–Hike 60), and Red Peak Pass (11,180–Hikes 89 and 98). This hike reaches the highest—Red Peak Pass—by ascending the spectacular Merced River canyon. From the pass, which cleaves the multihued Clark Range, the route follows the shallow Illilouette Creek canyon—a very relaxing stretch—back to the trailhead.

Description: The first 23.8 miles are the same as the first part of **Hike 88**. In that hike you start from Glacier Point, spend your first night in Little Yosemite Valley, hike past Merced Lake, and spend your second night at Washburn Lake. Hiking up-canyon on your third day, you should reach a junction in upper

Triple Peak Fork canyon at or before noon. Here **Hikes 88** and **98** branch east to immediately cross the fork.

Our trail angles west, begins a moderate ascent, and in a few minutes climbs steeply up a short, straight gully. Above it the trail climbs moderately for about a 250-foot elevation gain, then rolls southwest across granitic benches. These, like the gully, are angular, and they were formed as a result of weathering and erosion along the many joints, or fractures, in the granitic landscape. The smooth, generalized contour lines of the Merced Peak map area are misleading, for there are many small ups and downs.

With more than half of your multiday hike behind you, you soon begin a switchbacking course northwest up to a granitic crest that divides the Triple Peak Fork from the Merced Peak Fork. Although the crest does support lodgepoles, mountain hemlocks, and whitebark pines, the forest cover is thin enough to permit views of many of the peaks that rim the upper Merced River basin. From the crest you have a moderate though reasonably short descent to the two-branched Merced Peak Fork. You could camp in this vicinity or else hike cross-country ⅔ mile gently downstream to a shallow lake.

The trail to a second crest—one that separates the Merced Peak and Red Peak forks—has interesting nearby features and pleasant tree-filtered views to divert one from the effort of the climb. We reach the second crest at a broad saddle that conveniently holds a scenic lakelet, which makes a good place for an extended stop. Having a fair number of

A feldspar dike arcs toward slabs stained by soda springs, below Washburn Lake

By early fall, Merced Peak's "glacier" can all but disappear; view from Red Peak Pass

conifers, its surrounding slopes provide your last wind-shielded campsites this side of Red Peak Pass. Rather than climb toward that pass, the trail first makes an unnecessary descent north from the lakelet, then turns southwest to climb. Here, at the start of the climb, you could descend cross-country northwest to Red Devil Lake. About ½ mile distant, its lengthy, intricately winding shoreline provides the best near-treeline campsites.

Our trail, which until now has been across granitic terrain, enters a metamorphic one as it climbs to a broad bench. On it you pass two sizable, windswept ponds, neither one having desirable camping. In midsummer, lowly wildflowers abound on this bench, attracting many pollinating insects that in turn may end up as food for resident yellow-legged frogs or altitude-transcending Brewer's blackbirds.

Leaving the bench, you climb northwest past the last holdout of whitebark pines, then switchback southwest up a bleak alpine ridge. On it you have unobstructed views of the greater part of the upper Merced River basin. Tufts of sedge cluster around almost every available crack, and occasional wildflowers catch your eye as you struggle in a thin atmosphere up past tiny tarns toward a ragged, notched crest. Your trail, which soon becomes a series of short, steep switchbacks, heads for Red Peak Pass, which may be snowbound well into summer. When the switchbacks are not under snow, their rocky nature can easily turn your ankle if you take a careless step.

Along your ascent to Red Peak Pass you might notice a small glacial moraine—a remnant of the Little Ice Age—lying at the edge of the Red Peak cirque. It may look like a collection of boulders that slid down Red Peak, but its large blocks are gray, not red, as they would be if they came from that peak. Rusty talus boulders, derived from the peak, do rest atop the moraine, whose gray blocks came from the south.

At Red Peak Pass you have views as far as Matterhorn Peak, along the Park's north rim. Closer, Mt. Lyell crowns the upper Merced River basin and is flanked on the northwest by Mt. Maclure and on the southeast by Rodgers Peak. Twin-peaked Mt. Florence breaks the horizon west of this trio while east of all of them the dark, sawtooth Ritter Range pokes above the Park's eastern crest boundary. Below the peaks lies a broad upland surface that is cleft by the 2000-foot-deep Merced River canyon. Turning south, you have a tunneled, almost lifeless view of dark-gray Merced Peak, its western outliers, and rockbound Upper Ottoway Lake.

By late summer 1977, after two dry years, the Merced Peak snowfield had completely disappeared. When John Muir first saw it in the autumn of 1871, it was an active snowfield, that is, a small glacier. Muir was not the first to see a Sierran glacier, but he was the first to recognize one. On July 2, 1863, William Brewer and Charles Hoffmann—both members of Josiah D. Whitney's Geological Survey of California—climbed the Lyell Glacier and almost reached the summit of Mt. Lyell. However, several feet of fresh snow covered the glacier and perhaps because of that they saw no crevasses. In his journal Brewer wrote:

A great glacier once formed far back in the mountains and passed down the valley [Lyell Canyon], polishing and grooving the rocks for more than a thousand feet up on each side, rounding the granite hills into domes. It must have been as grand as any that are now in Switzerland. But the climate has changed, and it has entirely passed away. There is now no glacier in this state—the climate conditions do not exist under which any could be formed.

In *The Mountains of California* John Muir disagrees. Muir was familiar with the characteristics of a glacier, as is revealed in the following passage of his 1871 discovery of the Merced Peak glacier:

I observed a series of small terminal moraines ranged along the south wall of the amphitheater, corresponding in size and form with the shadows cast by the highest portions. The meaning of this correspondence between moraines and shadows was afterward made plain. Tracing the stream back to the last of its chain of lakelets [the one above Upper Ottoway Lake], I noticed a deposit of fine gray mud worn from a grindstone, and I

at once suspected its glacial origin, for the stream that was carrying it came gurgling out of the base of a raw moraine that seemed in the process of formation. Not a plant or weather-stain was visible on its rough unsettled surface. It is from 60 to over 100 feet high and plunges forward at an angle of 38°. Cautiously picking my way, I gained the top of the moraine and was delighted to see a small but well-characterized glacier swooping down from the gloomy precipices of Black Mountain [Merced Peak] in a finely graduated curve to the moraine on which I stood. The compact ice appeared on all the lower portions of the glacier, though gray with dirt and stones embedded in it. Farther up [at the firn line] the ice disappeared beneath coarse granulated snow. The surface of the glacier was further characterized by dirt bands and the outcropping edges of the blue veins, showing the laminated structure of the ice. The uppermost crevasse, or 'bergschrund,' where the névé was attached to the mountain, was from 12 to 14 feet wide, and was bridged in a few places by the remains of snow avalanches. Creeping along the edge of the schrund, holding on

Lower Merced Pass Lake is fairly scenic

with benumbed fingers, I discovered clear sections where the bedded structure was beautifully revealed. The surface snow, though sprinkled with stones shot down from the cliffs, was in some places almost pure, gradually becoming crystalline and changing to whitish porous ice of different shades of color, and this again changing at a depth of 20 or 30 feet to blue ice, some of the ribbon-like bands of which were nearly pure, and blended with the paler bands in the most gradual and delicate manner imaginable. . .

After this discovery I made excursions over all the High Sierra, pushing my explorations summer after summer, and discovered that what at first sight in the distance looked like extensive snowfields, were in great part glaciers, busily at work completing the sculpture of the summit-peaks so grandly blocked out by their giant predecessors.

On August 21 [1872] I set a series of stakes in the Maclure Glacier, near Mount Lyell, and found its rate of motion to be little more than an inch a day in the middle, showing a great contrast to the Muir Glacier in Alaska, which, near the front, flows at a rate of from five to ten feet in twenty-four hours.

Dome 7730, along the alternate route about one mile west of Mt. Starr King, displays a human face under proper lighting

Thus Muir can be credited with the first discovery of Sierran glaciers.

From Red Peak Pass your descent to Lower Ottoway Lake—the ideal place to spend your third night—is a two-stage descent, each with more than two dozen switchbacks. The initial descent may appear to be lifeless—only cold granitic rocks and gravel—but closer inspection reveals the presence of alpine sedges and wildflowers. These are present in sufficient quantity to permit pikas to thrive up to the very pass itself. A high, nasal voice often gives away the presence of these diminutive, short-eared members of the rabbit family. They are preyed on by the short-tailed weasel, a small voracious predator that dons a white coat in the winter.

Our first descent stage ends just above a pond and adjacent Upper Ottoway Lake. Neither of these cold, shimmering jewels has suitable camping, but you can make an interesting side trip over to them and then east up into the deep cirque that once held Muir's glacier. Today only its moraines exist, which show the size of the once-living snowfield.

Our second stage begins with a moderate descent west followed by the usual short switchbacks. On this descent many wildflowers are seen, including paintbrush, penstemon, monkey flower, baby elephant heads, columbine, phlox, leptodactylon, cinquefoil, yarrow, senecio, aster, and daisy. Sagebrush, heather, and dwarf whitebark pines appear before you reach the eastern arm of Lower Ottoway Lake. A slab above its northeast shore makes a good sunbathing area after a quick dip in its cold waters. Anglers can dangle lines for a tasty rainbow-trout meal. You'll find the best camps under lodgepole and whitebark pines above the lake's northwest shore. The lake makes an ideal base camp for exploring the Merced Peak environs.

Back on the trail, you leave the lake and parallel Ottoway Creek west, and after ⅔ mile hopefully find a log to cross it. Then you ramble southwest up and down a glaciated landscape for 1¾ miles, crossing Illilouette Creek before reaching a junction with the Illilouette Creek trail. From it you can start south up along the east bank of a creek, cross it after a minute's walk, and reach very good campsites along the west shore of Upper Merced Pass Lake. As elsewhere, bears may visit this lake (and Lower Ottoway Lake), but here there are enough deep, bear-proof cracks to hide your food in. (Before you drop your food sack in a deep crack be sure you'll be able to retrieve it.)

Hike 98 descends north from Merced Pass to our trail junction and then it climbs northeast up to Red Peak Pass. Our hike, however, descends northwest along the Illilouette Creek trail, passing unseen Lower Merced Pass Lake. To avoid mosquitoes at this relatively warm, shallow lake with a water-choked spongy shore, camp on the granitic ridge west of the lake. Below this nearby lake, your trail crosses several creeklets and in places may be hard to follow, so look for blazes on lodgepoles. About 1¾ miles below the last trail junction you cross to the east bank of Illilouette Creek, which you then parallel for 3¾ miles. You can find several places to camp along the creek's east bank, or if you cross to the west bank, even better ones.

Where the canyon's late-Pleistocene moraines force Illilouette Creek west over toward Buena Vista Creek, you continue northwest, cross the crests of five low moraines, and drop to a tributary of the Clark Fork, which has several good campsites above its south bank. These sites, about 7 miles from your trailhead, are a good choice for your fourth night on the trail.

From the camps look for a log to cross the Clark Fork, and engage an easy 1¼-mile traverse through a pleasant Jeffrey-pine/white-fir forest to a junction. Before reaching it, however, you pass some nearby boulders—one the size of a house—that fell from a dome north of here hundreds of years ago. Near these boulders and beyond, you'll see some evidence of 1970s and later forest fires that scar much of the landscape in the Illilouette Creek basin.

From the junction you can reach your trailhead at Glacier Point by two ways. Keeping right, you can make a high traverse to the Glacier Point-Panorama trail, then reverse the first part of your first day's hike. This alternate route adds about 600 feet of climbing and a little more than 2 miles to your total hiking effort, but is worth it to those who enjoyed the spectacular Panorama Cliff traverse.

Our hike's regular route branches left at the junction, immediately crosses a spring-fed creeklet, then starts down the partly burned slopes. Our moderate ridge descent ends on a gravelly, open slope above Illilouette Creek. From here the Mono Meadow trail climbs north 2⅓ miles back up to the trail we had earlier branched away from, while a use trail heads briefly ahead (west) toward some good, near-creek campsites. Your route turns south, descends the glacial outwash sediments to adjacent Illilouette Creek, and on its sandy, fly-infested north bank you find more camps. A tent comes in handy here as long as a bear doesn't rip it apart. Hang your food on a bear cable if there is one available.

After a usually wet creek crossing, you reach this busy area's most popular camps, above the creek's south bank. Beyond them we hike a minute to a junction with the Buena Vista trail (**Hike 86**) and a few yards farther reach a junction with the westbound Mono Meadows trail (also **Hike 86**). The westbound trail climbs 3.0 miles up to the Glacier Point Road. Our route, the northbound Buena Vista trail, descends along Illilouette Creek, climbs up to the Glacier Point-Panorama trail, and then ascends it for a total of 3.8 miles to our trailhead at Glacier Point. Because camping is prohibited within 4 trail miles of Glacier Point, you can't camp along this entire stretch. However, several places make fine rest stops.

HIKE 90

NORTH WAWONA TO CHILNUALNA FALLS

Distance: 8.1 miles round trip

Grade: 2D, moderate day hike

Trailhead: At the east end of the Chilnualna Road. The Chilnualna Road starts in the Wawona area immediately north of the bridge across the South Fork Merced River. On it you drive past the Pioneer Yosemite History Center

A small, boulder-drilled natural bridge

and a nearby fork right to the Park's district office. In 0.1 mile another road forks left, and just beyond it, on the right, is a small parking area for the Alder Creek trail, located ½ mile along your main road. This northbound trail begins roughly 100 yards east of the road forking left. You then drive east 1¼ miles farther, to a short road branching down to a large parking area. This road is located only 100 yards before the pavement on Chilnualna Road ends. Ahead, a dirt road descends to bridge Chilnualna Creek, while a paved road curves northwest. From the parking area a trail climbs about 100 yards north-northeast to the actual trailhead. If you have stock, you will have to head about 250 yards up the paved road curving northwest to a road climbing north. Ascend this ¼ mile to its second switchback, from where a horse trail climbs about 280 yards east to the end of the foot trail. **C6.**

Introduction: Not all Yosemite waterfalls are found in Yosemite Valley; several are located along Chilnualna Creek. As in the Valley, the severely hanging canyon of Chilnualna Creek above the highest fall originated *not* in response to glaciers deeply eroding the South Fork Merced River canyon. Rather it slowly originated as the river eroded downward for some 50 million years under warm, wet climates, which existed until 33 million years ago.

Description: The hikers' trail starts as a gently ascending dirt road, quickly giving way to a footpath that heads up Chilnualna Creek almost to its 25-foot-high fall. When the creek's flow is *slow*, hikers *with some climbing skill* can follow the creek several hundred yards up to a fairly large swimming hole, at the base of another fall. Most stick to the trail, which becomes steep and potentially dangerous, especially when wet. Soon it reaches the horse trail, and on that you climb to cross a manzanita-clothed ridge before entering a forest of ponderosa pines and incense-cedars. A few open spots allow one to survey the Wawona area to the south, Wawona Point to the southeast, and Wawona Dome to the east. Then, climbing east, you reach Chilnualna Creek in ¼ mile, and hike up along it another ¼ mile. If you need water, get it before the trail leaves the creek. In mid and late summer the ascent can be hot and dry.

On a moderately graded trail you now climb more than a dozen switchbacks of various lengths up into a cooler forest before making a fairly open traverse southeast toward the main Chilnualna Fall. Here you see the entire length of the fall, which churns for hundreds of feet down a deep, confining chute. Your trail comes to within a few yards of the fall's brink, but due to loose gravel and lack of a protective railing, you should not venture any closer to it.

Not far above Chilnualna Fall proper is an upper fall, a 60-foot-high cascade that is quite impressive in early season. To get around this fall and its small gorge, your trail switchbacks north, then curves south above the lip of the gorge. Views extending over the forested Wawona area are left behind as you reach a trail junction. Just below this junction and also below the main trail east of it are several good campsites. From the junction **Hike 91** follows the trail, climbing generally northeast up Chilnualna Creek, while **Hike 83** follows the trail that descends south to here from Turner Meadows.

While *cautiously* investigating the Chilnaulna Fall area, you might look for a small natural bridge below and just downstream from the trail junction. The stream was deeply undercutting a granite slab while at the same time its boulders were drilling a pothole through the slab. Eventually the slab was drilled completely through, and the creekside rim of the pothole stands today as a small bridge.

HIKE 91

NORTH WAWONA TO ROYAL ARCH, BUENA VISTA, AND CHILNUALNA LAKES

Distance: 28.3 miles semiloop trip

Grade: 5E, moderate 4-day hike

Trailhead: Same as the Hike 90 trailhead. **C6.**

Introduction: Glaciers originating on the slopes of Buena Vista Peak descended north, south, and west, then retreated to leave about a dozen small-to-medium-size lakes. This hike visits seven of these plus dashing Chilnualna Fall—one of the Park's highest falls outside Yosemite Valley.

Description: Hike 90 guides you up through a changing forest to campsites—a possible first night's stop—in an area around a trail junction near a south-flowing tributary of Chilnualna Creek. From that tributary your trail makes a short, steep ascent northeast, then traverses southeast. Soon reaching Chilnualna Creek, you'll find additional campsites along both its banks.

After crossing to the southeast bank, you head upstream, then veer away from the creek to make a short, moderate ascent to a low gap. Past it you enter a damp meadow—an early-season mosquito haven—then climb for a mile, paralleling the usually unseen creek at a distance before intersecting its tributary, Grouse Lake creek. Generally a jump-across creek, it can be a 20-foot wide, slippery-slab ford in June. Now just above 7,000 feet, you feel the effects of a higher elevation as well as see them—as expressed in the predominance of stately red firs and occasional lodgepole pines. Before reaching a junction after a ¾-mile ascent, note your first trailside western white pines.

At the junction we join **Hike 86** for a short northwest stretch, first up over a nearby divide, then down more than 400 feet to Chilnualna Creek. Just above its north bank is a good, medium-size campsite, and just beyond that is another trail junction. Here we turn right while **Hike 86** continues ahead, bound for Turner Meadows and the Glacier Point Road.

Eastbound, make a moderate ¼-mile ascent, followed by a gentler one that goes 1¼ miles along the lodgepole-shaded bank of Chilnualna Creek. After a ¼-mile walk along

Glaciated bedrock slopes above Johnson Lake

this gentler stretch, you'll find an acceptable campsite. At the end of the stretch you cross the seasonal creek that drains the middle and northern Chilnualna Lakes. We go a few yards along the larger creek that drains the southern and eastern Chilnualna Lakes, then leave it to cross a nearby bouldery ridge that is a recessional moraine left by a Tioga-age glacier about 13,500 years ago. At its maximum, about 20,000 years ago, this glacier calved icy blocks over the brink of Chilnualna Fall, as did some earlier glaciers.

Young glacial evidence in the form of moraines, erratics, and polish is often seen along the remaining 1⅔-mile, shady climb to the waist-deep southern Chilnualna Lake. Being so shallow, it is one of this route's warmest lakes for cooling off in. The best of the Chilnualna Lakes is also the least visited: the lake at the base of Buena Vista Peak's western shoulder, about ½ mile east-southeast of our trailside lake. A more-frequented lake is the middle one, which is easier to reach. From the far end of our lake, head ¼ mile up its inlet creek to a small pond, then walk due north over a low ridge to the middle lake. From it one can easily regain the trail by continuing north—no need to drop along its outlet creek.

Leaving the trailside lake and its fair west-shore campsite, climb over a low, bouldery morainal ridge, skirt a small meadow, and cross the middle lake's ephemeral creek. Past it you curve clockwise over to the northern lake's outlet creek, parallel it upward, and then, just ¼ mile before the lake, cross over to the north bank. Upon reaching the shallow, narrow lake you find a good campsite among red firs and western white pines. If weather is threatening, camp here rather than climb east to the exposed pass.

At that 9040-foot-high pass, about a ¾-mile winding ascent from the northern lake, we meet the Buena Vista trail. Now we follow most of the second half of **Hike 86** as it goes past Buena Vista, Royal Arch, Johnson, Crescent, and Grouse lakes. You may want to visit all of them, and you should plan to spend at least a day in this scenic glacier-lake area. A little more than 2 miles west of Grouse Lake you'll leave **Hike 86** where you first met it, and descend the way you came—past Chilnualna Fall. An exhilarating alternate conclusion—for *competent, experienced* hikers only—is to start

from Crescent Lake and descend its Crescent Creek cross-country down to the South Fork Merced River, then follow that about 4½ rugged miles west to where a use trail becomes prominent. Onward, take this trail and then a road west to your trailhead, about 1¼ miles farther.

<hr>

HIKE 92

WAWONA HOTEL TO MARIPOSA GROVE

Distance: 16.2+ miles round trip

Grade: 4D, strenuous day hike

Trailhead: In Wawona, take the eastbound road that goes along the south side of the South Fork Merced River. This first passes a parking area on the right, then soon reaches an RV dump station on the left. Continue east 160 yards farther to a road branching right, west-southwest. Make a tight turn onto it and follow it to where it curves south and almost levels off. The trail begins immediately before the road crosses the high point of a west-dropping ridge. **C6.**

Introduction: Though almost all Mariposa Grove visitors drive to it, one can also walk to it. This hike describes the forested pathway to the Mariposa Grove of Big Trees (giant sequoias)—or Wawona, as the Indians called them.

Description: Your trail, initially part of the Two Hour Ride Trail, begins eastward as a dusty horse trail locally adorned with excrement, urine, and flies. You quickly pass an old, abandoned canal, climb to a crest, and in a short mile reach a crest fork. To the left, a broad horse path descends to a summer camp. From it the broad horse path climbs southeast back up to a junction with our trail. This junction is reached after a second short, dusty mile, most of it right along the forested crest. Views of large Wawona Meadow are generally poor or nonexistent. From the saddle where the broad horse path rejoins our trail, we turn south to briefly descend to within 40 yards of noisy, paved Wawona Road, where there is parking for several vehicles. Starting from here cuts 1.9 miles, each way, from the total distance.

Here the Two Hour Ride Trail leaves us, crossing Wawona Road to loop back to the Wawona area. Now on a much less used, generally horse-free route, we climb east up a steepening ridge before veering south up to a usually flowing creek, 1.7 miles beyond the horse trail. Our trail maintains its moderate gradient as it next climbs south above the headwalls of two eroding, enlarging bowls. Then in ½ mile it begins to switchback up to a broad-crest junction with a ridge trail, about 6¼ miles from your trailhead.

The most direct way from here to the heart of the sequoia grove—its museum—is the following 1.3-mile route. Head 0.8 mile northeast up the Outer Loop Trail to a junction in a fairly level area, branch right and go about 150 yards southeast to cross the grove's tram road, continue 0.2 mile east on another trail, then branch left onto another trail that winds about 250 yards eastward to the museum.

The preferred way is longer, making a 3.7-mile loop. Start south on the Outer Loop Trail, which soon begins a winding, rolling traverse ½ mile southwest over to a junction with a northeast-climbing trail, then leads 0.1 mile farther to another junction. Branch left, leaving the Outer Loop Trail, to traverse ½ mile to the tunneled California Tree, then in 50 yards reach the famed Grizzly Giant. From it a trail climbs 250 yards north to a crossing of the tram road. This road makes an initial climb southwest to a switchback, from which a minor trail drops southeast, then climbs briefly to a trail paralleling the tram road northwest. You keep to the main trail and make a winding, 400-foot ascent for ¾ mile to the tram road. From here you'll see the museum, and hiking toward it, you first start north on a trail that quickly reaches a junction, from which you wind about 250 yards eastward to the museum. Complete the loop hike by following the previous paragraph in reverse. There are other trails, some worth taking, some not, but all adding to your distance. These are mentioned in **Hike 93**. Along it you'll thoroughly explore the giant sequoias and their interesting natural history.

A sequoia cone

HIKE 93

MARIPOSA GROVE OF BIG TREES

Distance: 6.9 miles loop trip; other routes possible

Grade: 2C, moderate half-day hike

Trailhead: From the Park's south entrance station drive east 2.1 miles up to road's end at the Big Trees parking lot. Be forewarned that by mid-morning it can be full. During summer and early fall, take the free shuttle bus that leaves from the Wawona Store, just northwest of the Wawona Hotel. **D6.**

Introduction: Near the southwest end of the parking lot is an information kiosk in which visitors can get introduced to the Mariposa Grove while waiting to take the tram. The tram ride gives you an instructive, guided tour of the grove's salient features and, at its stops, you can step off, explore the immediate area, and then get on the next tram. However, by hiking you get a more intimate experience with the giant sequoia and associated plants and animals.

Description: Two trails leave from the eastern, upper end of the parking lot. The northern one is the Outer Loop Trail, which makes a switch-backing climb 0.6 mile north to a junction with a trail east, then a winding traverse 0.6 mile northwest to a junction with a trail down to Wawona (see **Hike 92**). Our route is the southern one, which actually starts at the kiosk and runs along the edge of the parking lot. On this nature trail you momentarily parallel the tram road east before crossing a creeklet and the road. The signs along this trail not only identify

Visitors are dwarfed by the Grizzly Giant

the notable sequoias, but also educate you on their natural history, including such items as bark, cones, fire, reproduction, and associated plants and animals.

One point worth elaborating is how difficult it is for a sequoia to successfully replace itself. For a seed to become a tree first there must be a fire, which removes humus to expose mineral soil. Then for the seedling to survive, there must be adequate soil moisture. In the last 15 million years, summers generally have been too dry, and almost invariably seedlings died before fall rains arrived. Before then, summers were wetter, especially before 33 million years ago. Today, a seedling is likely to survive only if first there has been a ground fire and then if there has been a heavy snowpack so that the soil will stay moist through the summer. Fortunately, a sequoia can live to 2000+ years in age, producing over a *half billion* seeds in this time, and only one seed is required to replace the parent. The oldest known sequoia—the Muir snag, in the Kings River's Converse Basin

Grove—is estimated to have lived for about 3500 years. Sequoias survive today because they have "all the time in the world" to wait for proper regenerative conditions.

At the tram-road crossing lies the Fallen Monarch, largely intact, including its roots. Note that they grew in shallow soil, because bedrock lies only a couple of feet down. Unfortunately, occasional severe winds can topple a tree before it reaches old age. From the south side of the road your nature trail climbs ¼ mile east before crossing the road. At this spot stand the Bachelor and the Three Graces. In a similar distance your trail reaches the Grizzly Giant. Like the Leaning Tower of Pisa, this still-growing giant seems ready to fall any second, and one wonders how such a top-heavy, shallow-rooted specimen could have survived as long as it has. Though it's the largest tree in the Park—and probably the oldest at almost 3,000 years—there are at least 25 specimens elsewhere larger than it. It has a trunk volume of about 34,000 cubic feet, compared to about 52,500 cubic feet for the largest, the General Sherman, in Sequoia National Park's Giant Forest Grove. The Grizzly Giant has enough timber to build about 20 homes, but fortunately sequoia wood is very brittle, shattering when a tree falls—a feature that saved it from being logged into oblivion.

Heading north from the east end of the enclosure circling the Grizzly Giant, we reach in 50 yards the California Tree, also enclosed, but with a path through it. It once had a deep burn, which was cut away in 1895 so that tourists could ride a stage through it. Beyond this tree a trail traverses ½ mile west to the Outer Loop Trail. We, however, take an ascending trail that parallels the tram road

The Mariposa Grove Museum, situated in a Brobdingnagian forest

The fire-scarred Clothespin Tree

This guide's suggested route from the junction is to start on a trail a few paces away, which descends north about 90 yards to a junction with an east-west trail (along the most direct way to the Mariposa Grove Museum in **Hike 92**). This winds about 250 yards eastward, skirting below restrooms and then passing a west-heading nature trail before reaching the museum, with an adjacent water fountain. In the museum you will find information and displays on the giant sequoia, its related plants and animals, and the area's history. From just east of it you could take a trail ⅓ mile east up to the tram road, beside which you'd spy the lower end of the Fallen Wawona (Tunnel) Tree, which toppled during the late winter or spring of 1969. This 2,200-year-old giant, like many others, had a fire-scarred base, and it was enlarged in 1881 for first stagecoaches and much later automobiles to pass through it. An old timer is one who remembers waiting in a long line while each car drove through, stopping to have a passenger get out and photograph the momentous event. Today, the tree is not much to look at.

The suggested route continues from the museum momentarily east along the tram road to a bend. Here is the amazing Telescope Tree, which has been hollowed out by fire. Inside it you can look straight up to the heavens. Despite its great internal loss, this tree is still very much alive, for its vital fluids—as in all trees—are conducted in the sapwood, immediately beneath the thick bark. The heartwood is just dead sapwood whose function is support.

From the back side of the tree you take a trail that climbs 50 yards to the Upper Loop Trail, mentioned earlier. On it you hike ⅓ mile counterclockwise to pass just above the Fallen Wawona Tree, then continue about 250 yards to a crest saddle. Just 40 yards east of it is the Galen Clark Tree, a fine specimen named for the man who first publicized this grove and later became its first guardian. From the saddle a road branches from the tram-road loop, and on it you make an easy climb ½ mile to Wawona Point. No sequoias grow along this route, probably because of insufficient ground water. From the point you see the large, partly man-made meadow at Wawona, to the northwest, and the long, curving cliff of Wawona Dome, breaking a sea of green, to the north.

north for 250 yards before crossing it. Our trail then climbs to a nearby switchback from where a lightly used trail winds southeast down to an old road. We start north and quickly reach a lackluster trail that traverses northwest to the tram road, from where another trail, equally lackluster, descends southwest to the Outer Loop Trail. Additionally a switchbacking one climbs northeastward to a loop in the upper part of the tram road.

Our trail gains 400 feet elevation climbing to the same spot, starting north and then going briefly east before switchbacking to wind northwest to the upper end of the switchbacking trail, the junction being about 15 yards from the tram road. Here too is the Upper Loop Trail, which parallels the tram road counterclockwise as both circle the upper grove. (Although our area is called the Mariposa Grove, it is really two groves, a lower one, which includes the Grizzly Giant and trees below it, and an upper one, which mostly is encircled by the Upper Loop Trail.)

View straight up the Telescope Tree

After returning to the crest saddle, descend west along the Outer Loop Trail, which takes you down almost 3 essentially viewless, sequoia-less miles to the parking lot. The descending trail winds westward about 0.7 mile to a junction. From here a connecting trail goes about 270 yards southeast down to the tram road and the adjacent west end of the nature trail. Onward the Outer Loop Trail descends about 200 yards to a second connecting trail, the one mentioned in **Hike 92**, descending about 150 yards southeast to cross the grove's tram road. We continue 0.8 mile southwest on the Outer Loop Trail down to the junction on a broad ridge from where one could follow **Hike 92** in reverse 6¼ miles down to Wawona. Instead, we start south on the Outer Loop Trail, which soon begins a winding, rolling traverse ½ mile southwest over to a junction with a northeast-climbing trail, then walk 0.1 mile farther to another junction, the eastbound trail from it leading to the California Tree and the Grizzly Giant. Unless you want to make another visit to them (and add about ½ mile to your hike) continue southward ½ mile down to the parking lot.

Chapter 12

Trails of Yosemite's Southeastern Backcountry

Introduction: This section explores the back ways into southeastern Yosemite. As roads in the Sierra National Forest were steadily upgraded—particularly Forest Route 7 (old Road 5S07)—more and more hikers discovered—and returned to—this scenic area. The Chain Lakes and the lakes of the southwest part of Ansel Adams Wilderness already rival many of the Park's better-known lakes in popularity. Much of the landscape is lodgepole-pine forest, but around Fernandez, Post Peak, and Isberg passes, the vegetation shifts to subalpine. Truly alpine Red Peak Pass, at 11,180 feet elevation, is the highest trail point in the entire Park. Two of this section's natural attractions are not found anywhere else in the other sections: a broad, scenic subalpine plateau and an unbelievable mottled-granite landscape—both seen along Hikes 98 and 100.

Supplies and Services: Oakhurst, at the crossroads of Highways 41 and 49, has just about everything you'll need for a backcountry hike. Closer to the trailheads is a settlement at the south end of Forest Route 7 (Beasore Road), just above the north shore of Bass Lake. Here in Pines Village are cafes and restaurants, a market, a gas station, and tourist-oriented businesses. After driving 13.5 miles north up Forest Route 7, you'll reach Jones Store, with a few but very pertinent food items. Also selling food plus other assorted items is the Minarets Pack Station, located on Road 5S88 (see the third trailhead description in Hike 97). This large pack station, located near Miller Meadow, serves the western part of Ansel Adams Wilderness and the southeastern part of Yosemite National Park.

Wilderness Permits: Get one at the Forest Service office (559-658-7588) in the Yosemite-Sierra Visitors Center, located in downtown Oakhurst. For Hikes 99 and 100 you can get one at the Clover Meadow Ranger Station, located close to their trailheads. Permits are also available at the Mariposa-Minarets Ranger District Office (559-877-2218), located in the tiny settlement of North Fork, but for most people this is out of the way.

Campgrounds: If you are driving up late at night, you might want to stop at Chilkoot Campground, 4 miles up Forest Route 7. Otherwise, use Upper Chiquito Campground for Hikes 94-96. You branch left from Forest Route 7 about one mile beyond a junction with Road 5S04, opposite Globe Rock. For Hikes 97-98 use Bowler Group Camp if you are in a group or else use Clover Meadow Campground. Both are mentioned in Hike 97's trailhead information. For Hikes 99-100 use Granite Creek Campground, mentioned in Hike 99's trailhead information.

HIKE 94

ROYAL ARCH LAKE VIA CHIQUITO PASS

Distance: 19.6 miles round trip

Grade: 4E, moderate 2-day hike

Trailhead: From the Highway 49 junction in Oakhurst, drive north on Highway 41 for 3.5 miles up to a junction with Road 222. Follow this east 3.5 miles to a fork, veer left and continue east 2.4 miles on Malum Ridge Road 274 to a junction with *north*-climbing Forest Route 7, or Beasore Road. (South, Beasore Road descends briefly to Pines Village, just above the north shore of Bass Lake.) Paved Forest Route 7 climbs north 4.0 miles to Chilkoot Campground, then it climbs to an intersection at Cold Springs Summit, 7.4 miles beyond the campground. Road 6S10 (an alternate, 0.2-mile-longer route to Cold Springs Summit) heads west from this intersection, winding 5.5 miles over to a junction near Kelty Meadow, mentioned in the next paragraph. From the summit, Forest Route 7 winds 8.6 miles, going past Beasore Meadows, Jones Store, Muglers Meadows, and Long Meadow before coming to a junction with Road 5S04, opposite Globe Rock, 20.0 miles from the start of Forest Route 7. Turn left and drive up the road 2.4 miles to a signed trailhead atop a small, flat ridge area. *Trail mileages for Hikes 94-96 are based from this trailhead.* From it a trail climbs 2.9 miles to Chiquito Pass. **E6.**

A lesser known route gets you to a trail that drops to Chiquito Pass in only 0.8 mile—a 2.1-mile saving each way. This higher, later-opening alternate route is a mile shorter to drive than the one just described but, being on narrower roads, takes a little more time to drive. Starting from the Highway 49 junction in Oakhurst, you drive north on Highway 41 3.5 miles up to Road 222, then continue 0.6 mile past it to a right turn onto Forest Route 10 (Sky Ranch Road). After climbing 11.4 miles from Highway 41, this meets a junction near Kelty Meadow, mentioned above, from where one can veer right toward Cold Springs Summit. You, however, veer left, driving 1.7 mile north to a junction with Road 6S07, on the left, which descends 8.2 miles west to Highway 41 at the southern fringe of the town

of Fish Camp. This rocky road has one potentially bad creek ford and is not recommended for automobiles.

Your road curves right and immediately passes the entrance to Fresno Dome Campground. Just 1.5 miles past your junction with Road 6S07 a road branches left toward the Star Lakes area. Beyond this junction you could get lost. At *most* junctions your road is the wider, obvious one. (Because new logging spurs may be built, this guide will mention only the important junctions.) Your road divides after 3.1 miles past the Star Lakes junction, and you curve left and wind 0.9 mile up to another junction. Here you keep right, on the level, rather than climb left, and drive 4.5 miles to a major junction. If you're on the correct road you should cross two saddles, pass Lost Lake (on your right) and a trail to Grizzly Lake (on your left). A rockslide area along this 4.5-mile stretch sometimes releases boulders that temporarily block the road—the only real gamble with this route.

From the major junction with a wide road branching left, our wide road traverses 2.7 miles, veers right around a descending ridge and in 0.5 mile reaches a spur road branching left. Follow this road 0.4 mile to a turnaround at its end, 26.7 miles from Highway 41. From here a short trail descends to Chiquito Pass. In early season you may not be able to drive it all the way. The main road goes 0.4 mile to an unofficial camping area, with tables and spring, then 0.6 mile to a turnaround. **E6.**

Introduction: The shortest way in to Royal Arch Lake is along this route from Chiquito Pass—only 7.6 miles from the alternate trailhead. Perhaps because the hiker has to first drive about an hour along dirt roads, this route is spurned in favor of routes from North Wawona (**Hike 91**) or from the Glacier Point Road (**Hike 86**). Each approach to Royal Arch Lake and other lakes around Buena Vista Peak has its own merits.

Description: On a flat area atop a granitic ridge, our well-signed Chiquito Lake trail traverses northwest away from curving Road 5S04. Jeffrey pines largely dominate the broken forest cover, and often grazing beneath them are cattle. These may be with us on and off until we leave Sierra National Forest at Chiquito Pass. About ⅓ mile from our trailhead we cross a short-lived creeklet, then climb moderately an equal distance to a junction with a long-abandoned trail. Progressing northwest from it, you have an easy traverse that takes you past another creeklet and over to the bank of Chiquito Creek. Now your climbing begins in earnest as you gain about 500 feet over a short-mile ascent up a large, dusty lateral moraine. Hikers descending this occasionally steep Chiquito Lake trail sometimes take shortcuts, resulting in confusing paths, but these always quickly rejoin the main trail, should you be led astray. Fortunately your unrelenting ascent is usually shaded by red firs and by western white, Jeffrey, and lodgepole pines.

The climb is essentially over when the moraine gives way to a small bedrock knoll. After traversing for a few minutes beyond it, you drop to ford seasonally wide Chiquito Creek. Once across it you crest the top of a low moraine and arrive at a spacious campsite—one of several—along the south shore of disappointing Chiquito Lake. Were Chiquito Lake not dammed, it would be little more than a waist-deep swamp. Even with the dam it is little better, its tainted waters attracting both cows and mosquitoes. Should you for some reason decide to camp beneath lodgepoles by this sedge-lined lake, bring a tent and treat the water.

Just beyond, at the lake's southwest corner, we take a path 250 yards west to a junction with the alternate route mentioned in the trailhead description. Those taking it join us for a ⅓-mile walk north over to Chiquito Pass, where we leave the grazing cows and their muddy shoreline environment behind. Note that Chiquito Pass, signed 8039 feet in elevation, sits atop a long, multicrested moraine. A Tioga-age glacier that once spilled over Chiquito Pass and down the upper Chiquito Creek drainage, left this moraine as it retreated from this vicinity about 16,000 years ago. Except for its ridgecrests and mountaintops, the entire South Fork Merced River basin, north of us, lay under a sea of ice during these and earlier glacial times. Your 500-foot ascent was up an eastern lateral moraine left during the Tioga glaciation, which was cold and wet enough to create a glacierette on the north slopes of Quartz Mountain, near the alternate trailhead.

Just within the fence—and Yosemite National Park—at Chiquito Pass, the trail splits. **Hikes 95** and **96** go right, northeast,

Globe Rock

along the moraine, while we go left and descend northwest away from this bouldery, multicrested feature. Our descent into a red-fir/lodgepole-pine forest momentarily abates at wide Spotted Lakes creek, which in early season you cross on large boulders. Leaving its banks of alders, willows, and wildflowers, you continue on a lesser gradient, your trail curving west to cross the South Fork Merced River at Gravelly Ford. A medium-size camp exists on each bank, and to get from one to the other you'll probably have to wade unless a large log is handy.

After leaving the gravelly banks, climb up a low, dry, sagebrush-clothed slope, then curve down to the west end of rightly named Swamp Lake. Beyond it is a wet meadow, which like the lakelet sires hordes of mosquitoes that last well into August. This is unfortunate, for in July and early August it has also one of the better assemblages of tall, water-loving wildflowers. Leaving the wet flat for better-drained, less-mosquitoed slopes, we climb northwest one mile up a gradually steepening trail. The gradient becomes an exhausting one just before you top a gravelly, boulder-strewn moraine ridge. From it you plummet down to diminutive Givens Creek, only to climb again. After an easy ⅓ mile of climbing you meet a little used though perfectly good trail that goes 3½ miles east to a junction with the Chain Lakes-Moraine Meadows trail. About 2¾ miles east along this trail you'd find a short spur trail that descends a few hundred yards to a cold, bubbly, rust-stained soda spring similar to the ones in Tuolumne Meadows.

Starting west, we go but 60 yards before a sometimes faint trail branches right. Staying out of sight, it parallels our conspicuous trail ¼ mile before it climbs northwest an equal distance to a main trail. On that trail one can hike northeast 1.6 miles to a junction with the Givens Lake trail. **Hike 96** returns along this route from Givens Lake.

From the junction with the sometimes faint trail we climb 0.6 mile west to the above mentioned main trail, first crossing a glacier-polished ridge before meeting the junction atop a second ridge. Leaving this ridge, one descends southwest through a red-fir-dominated forest interspersed with sunlit, grassy openings. Lodgepoles and Jeffrey pines increase in number westward, and then you climb northwest to the meadowy environment of Buck Creek. Just west of it and south of the main trail stands Buck Camp Ranger Station—the summer "headquarters" for patrols through the South Fork Merced River basin. Its network of trails, though usually well signed, can confuse unprepared novice backpackers, for prominent landmarks are absent.

A mile-long slog, first along and through wet, sloping meadows, confronts you beyond Buck Camp. You end this moderate-to-steep 720-foot climb in a fairly deep ridge cleft where views are blocked by red firs and western white pines. An equally steep trail segment, descending almost ½ mile west, ends at the Buena Vista Peak loop trail. Here we turn right and make an easy ascent ¾ mile up to an excellent campsite at the southwest corner of beautifully backdropped Royal Arch Lake. As in Hikes 86 and 91 you could make a circuit of the Buena Vista Peak lakes. The last part of **Hike 86** describes this loop from Buena Vista Lake south past Royal Arch, Johnson, Crescent, and Grouse lakes, while the last part of **Hike 91** describes the rest of this loop past the Chilnualna Lakes.

HIKE 95

CHAIN LAKES VIA CHIQUITO PASS

Distance: 16.5 miles round trip

Grade: 3D, easy 2-day hike

Trailhead: Same as the Hike 94 trailhead. **E6.**

Introduction: Reached in three hours from the standard trailhead and only two from the alternate one, these lakes receive considerable backpacking pressure. Only the long road to each trailhead prevents them from being overrun. The charm of middle Chain Lake draws the crowds while the shore of upper Chain Lake provides a base camp for peakbagging mountaineers.

Description: The route up to the Yosemite National Park boundary at Chiquito Pass is described in **Hike 94**. Leaving it, head northeast and pass a stagnant pond trapped between the crests of two bouldery, brushy moraines. The one on our left stays with us for a full ½ mile before we cross it and make a slight descent to a flat-floored forest. In early summer, several creeks and creeklets are flowing, and then the traverse can be a muddy one that hikers hurry along to evade a marauding horde of mosquitoes so typical of this shady, damp environment.

The last creek crossing is the widest, and beyond it you have a mile-long ascent up to a small, moraine-dammed meadow. From it one could contour east cross-country over to a creek draining Spotted Lakes. However, these lakes are best reached by starting from the end of a jeep road that traverses the southwest slopes of Red Top. From this road, which ends 4.4 miles beyond the Chiquito Pass trailhead, you have only a 1½-mile cross-country hike to these trout inhabited lakes. Furthermore, from the end of an east branch of this jeep road you can reach the summit of Red Top in less than a mile's ridgecrest hike. This rusty peak, composed largely of ancient, metamorphic rocks, contrasts with our granitic trailside landscape.

From the moraine-dammed meadow we climb a short ½ mile up to a low point on a glacier-polished ridge, cross it, and make a rolling, short-mile traverse northeast to a trail junction on the north bank of boulder-choked Chain Lakes creek. From it, **Hike 96** follows the creek downstream. We turn right, upstream, and hike east on a moderate-to-steep trail up to shallow lower Chain Lake, at about 8950 feet elevation. This fairly warm lake is too shallow for swimming, but is heavily fished. Its trout may periodically die, though it can be repopulated from the middle lake's trout. Camps here are inferior to those by the deeper middle lake.

From the outlet of the moraine-rimmed lower lake, your trail climbs over a low ridge and drops to a *de facto* north-shore foot trail at the lake's far end. Next, you make a short, fairly steep ascent up along a creek to picturesque, island-dotted middle Chain Lake. The warm bedrock islands are easily reached, particularly from the excellent oversized camp along the lake's southwest shore. To reach that camp, cross the lake's *two* outlet creeks and then follow a primitive path along the west shore. This 20-foot-deep lake is a classic sub-alpine lake, rimmed with lodgepole pines, western white pines, and mountain hemlocks understoried with Labrador tea, red heather, western blueberry, and dwarf bilberry. The last two plants, both huckleberries, produce edible berries in late summer, after the crowds have left, and then the birds, bears, and golden-mantled ground squirrels have a feast.

Beyond the middle lake the trail is less traveled. It climbs steeply to the bouldery crest of a moraine, winds over to a stagnant pond, and drops south to a photogenic lakelet. Near this lakelet the trail may divide and reunite, and then it briefly climbs to deep upper Chain Lake. Cold, windswept, and rock-rimmed, it offers marginal camping but it is a good staging area for experienced mountaineers planning to climb slopes up to Gale Peak and the Park's southeast boundary crest. Anglers may have a better chance up here than down at heavily fished middle Chain Lake.

Gale Peak reflected in Middle Chain Lake's tranquil water

SOUTH FORK MERCED RIVER SEMILOOP

Distance: 23.4 miles semiloop trip

Grade: 5E, easy 3-day hike

Trailhead: Same as the Hike 94 trailhead. E6.

Introduction: While many hikers follow the beaten path to the Chain Lakes, to Breeze Lake, or to the Buena Vista Peak lakes, far fewer take the path to Givens Lake, which is visited along this hike. Givens Lake, lying on a bench below Moraine Mountain, has the most incredible moraine assemblage to be found at any of the Park's lakes. For those interested in glacial geology, these moraines alone make the hike worthwhile.

Description: Follow the first part of **Hike 94** up to Chiquito Pass (or down to it, if you take the alternate route), then follow **Hike 95** up to middle Chain Lake, which is 7.4 miles by the longer, regular route. On the second day backtrack to the junction mentioned in Hike 95 and make a moderate-to-steep descent along Chain Lakes creek. In ⅓ mile the trail veers north to a nearby junction with a lateral trail heading west to the Chiquito Pass-Buck Camp trail (**Hike 94**). This westbound lateral descends ¾ mile to a spur trail, which descends a few hun-

dred yards south to a cold, bubbly, rust-stained soda spring that is similar to the ones in Tuolumne Meadows. Beyond the spur trail the lateral trail drops and climbs across ground moraines and bedrock slabs, terminating in 2¾ miles.

Rather than take this alternate route to Givens Lake (as briefly described in **Hike 94**), we continue north on a winding, rolling path, first passing a couple of stagnant ponds. From bedrock benches and slabs we see forested Moraine Mountain, a broad mass to the northwest. Nearing the South Fork Merced River, note that the landscape becomes gentler—almost flat—and the lodgepoles, being ideally suited to it, completely exclude red firs and western white pines from the forest's cover.

Above the south bank of the South Fork you'll find a medium-size camp that is good by late July, after mosquitoes diminish. Once you ford the South Fork, you'll find a similar camp, used by equestrians, 90 yards downstream. From the bank you head north through one of the Moraine Meadows, which is more of a forest than a meadow. In 200 yards you come to an east-west trail and now join followers of **Hike 98** for a 1½-mile traverse west. After walking ½ mile along it, you pass through a bedrock gap, then soon swing northwest down into a small though impressive gully with straight, vertical walls. About ⅓ mile farther, cross a small creek that descends from slopes below Merced Pass, then in a like distance

Givens Lake and its moraine, which blankets a bedrock ridge

climb southwest to a junction, passing a crescentic pond midway. From here, those following **Hike 98** depart north, bound for Merced Pass.

Among red firs, western white pines, and lodgepole pines we start southwest, drop into a gully, curve into a larger one, and then climb more than 300 feet to a forested, boulder-strewn pass along the southeast base of Moraine Mountain. A cross-country ascent up it is easy, but trees prevent summit views.

From the pass we descend past a wet meadow, rich in corn lilies, then continue to gradually drop as we cut across slopes down to a lower saddle. Here you'll see a faint, ducked path—your route—climbing northwest up a broad ridge. Just ¼ mile up it you reach a wet meadow in which one could lose the tread. It heads at a 250° bearing across the meadow, turns north, and in a ¼-mile stretch crosses three prominent lateral moraines before ending at the northeast shore of Givens Lake. What makes these lateral moraines prominent is not their height (which isn't great) but rather the way they stand out so sharply above the bedrock bench they lie upon. The innermost moraine curves around Givens Lake, enclosing its bedrock basin as what appears to be an amazingly leakproof earthfill dam. Actually, youthful moraines such as this one are very leaky; the lake is dammed by a very low bedrock ridge buried beneath the moraine. All three of these moraines were left as the Tioga-age glacier, which once covered the South Fork basin and extended almost to Wawona until about 20,000 years ago, retreated to oblivion by about 15,000 years ago. You'll find the best campsite near the blunt peninsula at the lake's south end. Spend your second night at this shallow, relatively warm lake, perhaps getting in a good swim and catching one or more rainbow trout before the sunlight fades on Moraine Mountain.

The next morning retrace your steps back to the saddle and then make a mile-long 600-foot descent southwest through a red-fir forest to lodgepole-lined Givens Meadow creek. After crossing it—on large, upstream boulders in early season—curve west and soon parallel the creek's south bank for a brief spell. Leaving the south bank of the creek, you swing southwest on a short ascent to a wide gap. On it

your trail passes *through* a tiny, seasonal pond that lies due west of a minor summit.

About 250 yards past this low summit, you reach the first of two paths that leave our wider trail just before a shallow saddle by an exfoliating cliff. We take the first path, which soon merges with the second; then we descend southeast in a short, fairly steep ½ mile to a junction with an east-west trail. West, it climbs 0.6 mile to a junction with the trail we recently left. East, we go 60 yards to a junction. You could continue east, taking this lateral trail over to the Chain Lakes-Moraine Meadows trail for a second visit to middle Chain Lake. Our hike, however, reverses the first part of Hike 94 for a 3.1-mile walk southeast to Chiquito Pass. From that pass retrace your steps to the trailhead.

VANDEBERG-LILLIAN LAKES LOOP

Distance: 12.6 miles semiloop; side trips extra

Grade: 3D, easy 3-day hike

Trailhead: Follow the Hike 94 trailhead description 20 miles up Forest Route 7 to the junction with Road 5S04, opposite Globe Rock. Continue along your road, an obvious route, 7.5 miles to a junction with Road 5S86. This junction is 0.4 mile past the Bowler Group Camp entrance and 100 yards *before* Forest Route 7 crosses Ethelfreda Creek. Your first of three trailheads lies at a road's end parking area above Norris Creek, 1.9 miles up this road. Be aware that there may be a rough creekbed crossing about ½ mile before the parking area. This trailhead provides the shortest mileage for any hike along the Lillian Loop trail. It is also the start of a trail to Norris Lake and the Jackass Lakes, the latter being worthy goals. **F6.**

The second trailhead—*the one from which the trail mileages of Hikes 97 and 98 are based*—is at the end of Road 5S05. This forks left only 100 yards *after* Forest Route 7 crosses Ethelfreda Creek. Take Road 5S05 2.3 miles to the trailhead and its large turnaround/parking area.

Dark, metamorphic Madera Peak stands above granite-rimmed Lady Lake

Former logging operations have added spurs to this road, but you should have no problem finding the trailhead. By starting at it you hike 0.6 mile farther in each direction than you would from the first trailhead. **F6.**

The third trailhead is in the Clover Meadow area. On Forest Route 7 drive east from the Road 5S05 fork, passing Road 5S88, which branches south 0.4 mile to Minarets Pack Station and then in 250 yards reaches a junction. Here, 30 miles from the start of Forest Route 7, you meet the end of Forest Route 81, a.k.a. Minarets Road, ascending 52 paved miles north from North Fork. From the junction, drive northeast 1.8 miles on Road 5S30 to a junction at the Clover Meadow Ranger Station. Turn left here, get your permit (if you haven't gotten one in advance), then continue past the station about 0.3 mile to the Clover Meadow Campground entrance. Midway along your road the Fernandez trail starts from its south (left) side. You can also locate this trail at the far end of the campground. This trail climbs 1.4 miles west to the north side of the parking area at the second major trailhead. **F6.**

Introduction: If you are in shape, you could hike this entire circuit in one day without overexerting yourself. However, it is so scenic that three days are recommended—sufficient

time to visit Lady, Chittenden, Staniford, and Rainbow lakes. Visiting all four of these desirable lakes lengthens your route to 21.1 miles and changes its classification to a 5E, moderate 3-day hike.

Description: From the second trailhead at the end of Road 5S05, you start west up the Fernandez trail, passing through a typical mid-elevation Sierran forest: white fir, Jeffrey pine, lodgepole pine, and scrubby huckleberry oak. After ⅓ mile of gentle ascent across morainal slopes, you reach the lower end of a small meadow and meet a junction at its west side. From it a trail meanders almost a mile to the vicinity of the first trailhead before climbing up to Norris Lake and the Jackass Lakes. Beyond the junction your trail's gradient becomes a moderate one, and red firs quickly begin to replace white firs. The forest temporarily yields to brush—huckleberry oak, chinquapin, greenleaf manzanita, and snow bush—as we struggle up short, steep switchbacks below a small, exfoliating "dome." Now entering Ansel Adams Wilderness, we have a steady ½-mile pull up to a near-crest junction with a steep, mile-long trail from the first trailhead. If you come up this short, exhausting route, remember this junction, for if it is not properly signed it can be easy to miss as you later descend the Fernandez trail.

We continue a moderate ascent up the Fernandez trail for only a few more minutes, then reach a crest junction. If you are following **Hike 98** and are in a hurry, you can keep right, staying on the Fernandez trail. Although this lakeless route bypasses the best part of Hike 97, it will save you 2.4 miles in your ascent to Fernandez Creek.

Heading west toward peaks and lakes, we veer left and start up the Lillian Loop trail. This trail's first 2 miles are generally easy. Conifers shade your way first past a waist-deep pond, on your right, then later past two often wet, moraine-dammed meadows—both mosquito havens. Then the trail climbs to a bedrock notch in a granitic crest. On the crest you arc around a stagnant pond, then make a short descent to a junction above Madera Creek. If you plan to camp at very popular Vandeberg Lake, you could leave the trail here and descend southwest to find some campsites along its east shore.

From the junction the right branch—for horses—descends north to Madera Creek, then circles counterclockwise ⅓ mile to rejoin the left branch above the lake's west shore. We take the left branch, curving above good-to-excellent campsites along the lake's north shore. From them, steep, granitic Peak 9852, on

Madera Peak's northeast ridge, is reflected in the lake's placid early morning waters.

Where the two trail branches of the loop trail reunite, you start a 250-yard climb up bedrock to a trail junction at the edge of a lodgepole flat. Here a spur trail takes off south and climbs gently to moderately up to a large campsite on the north shore of granite-rimmed Lady Lake. On the east-shore moraine that juts into the lake, you'll find an even better campsite, though not quite as large. This lake's irregular form, speckled with several boulder islands, makes it a particularly attractive lake to camp at or to visit, especially since it is back-dropped by hulking, metamorphic Madera Peak. Like all the lakes you might visit along this hike, Lady Lake has trout. Because it is shallow, it is a good lake for swimming from late July through mid-August.

Beyond the Lady Lake trail junction your Lillian Loop trail crosses the lodgepole flat, then climbs a couple of hundred feet up fairly open granitic slabs. On them you can stop and appreciate the skyline panorama from the Minarets south to the Mt. Goddard area in Kings Canyon National Park. During past glaciations virtually all of this panorama except for high crests and mountain peaks was under ice.

Descending northwest from a ridge on a moderate-to-steep gradient, you reach, in ¼

Youths relaxing and fishing at the largest of the Staniford Lakes

mile, an easily missed junction, if it is not well-signed. Here, close to a Staniford Lakes creek, one can start a mile-long climb up to cliff-bound Chittenden Lake. (If you miss this junction, then you probably wouldn't be able to follow the obscure trail to that lake anyway.) Where this trail curves from northwest to southwest at the lower end of a small, wet meadow, you could follow an equally obscure trail ¼ mile northwest up to extremely shallow Shirley Lake, which is not worth most hikers' efforts.

The last slabby trail section to Chittenden Lake is so steep that equestrians rarely visit it. Chittenden may be the most beautiful of all the lakes in this part of Ansel Adams Wilderness, though Lady and Rainbow lakes offer competition. Although Chittenden's water usually does not rise above the low 60s, the lake's three bedrock islands will certainly tempt some swimmers. If there are more than two backpackers in your group, don't plan to camp at this fairly deep lake, for flat space is really at a premium.

On the Lillian Loop trail, you go north only about 200 yards past the Chittenden Lake trail junction before you see a Staniford lake. A waist-deep, grass-lined lakelet, this water

body, like Shirley Lake, is best avoided. After a similar distance you'll come to a trailside pond atop a broad granitic crest. In this vicinity you can leave the trail, and on your third optional excursion descend southeast briefly cross-country on low-angle slabs to the largest of the Staniford Lakes. This is certainly the best lake to swim in, and if any sizable lake along this route will warm up to the low 70s in early August, it will be this one. The great bulk of the lake is less than 5 feet deep, its only deep spot being at a diving area along the west shore.

More ponds are seen along the north-bound Lillian Loop trail before it dips into a usually dry gully. It then diagonals up along a ridge with many glacier-polished slabs. You soon cross the ridge, then quickly descend to Lillian Lake's outlet creek, which drains southeast into Shirley Creek. A short walk upstream ends at the lake's low dam and an adjacent, lodgepole-shaded area that once comprised the largest campsite in this part of the wilderness. Since camping is prohibited within 400 feet of the northeast shore, be inventive and try elsewhere. Being the largest and deepest lake you'll see along this hike, Lillian Lake is also the coldest—not good for swimming.

View southwest toward Sing Peak, from Lillian Lake's outlet

However, its large population of trout does attract anglers.

With our basic hike now half over, we leave the lake's outlet and descend a mile east past lodgepoles, hemlocks, western white pines, and red firs down to a two-branched creek with easy fords. The Lillian Loop trail ends in ¼ mile, after a short, stiff climb over a gravelly knoll. Here, at a junction on a fairly open slope, we rejoin the Fernandez trail. **Hike 98** describes this trail from this point upward.

Your fourth optional side trip ascends this trail one mile northwest up to a junction, from which the Rainbow Lake trail first wanders ¾ mile northwest to that prized lake. This trail may become vague on bedrock slabs where it bends from southwest to northwest, and unsuspecting hikers may continue southwest down toward Lillian Lake, 400 feet below, before realizing their error. The correct route ends at a large, former camp 50 yards above Rainbow Lake. Today, camping is prohibited within ¼ mile of the lakeshore. One can cross this multilobed lake by swimming from island to island.

From the Lillian Loop-Fernandez trails junction, those descending **Hike 100** join us as we descend ⅓ mile east on the Fernandez trail to a linear gully, follow it a bit, then drift over to the crest of a moraine. After its end you soon engage a few short switchbacks near some junipers, and here get a good view of much of your basin's landscape.

Below the switchbacks the Fernandez trail descends ½ mile to a trail junction. If you were to follow the trail north 70 yards to a crest saddle, you would see that it forks into the Post Creek trail (left) and the Timber Creek trail (right). The Post Creek trail ends after a 1.9-mile climb to a packer camp on the West Fork of Granite Creek. Just below this spot is the creek's confluence with Post Creek, and a faint trail—essentially cross-country—more or less parallels this creek northward 1½ miles to the Post Peak Pass trail (**Hike 100**). The Timber Creek trail climbs about 5¾ miles up to the Joe Crane Lake trail (**Hike 99**).

From the junction the Fernandez trail descends briefly past lodgepoles and junipers to a gravelly flat along the north bank of Madera Creek. This spacious flat is well suited for camping, and from it you can inspect the dark plug of olivine basalt, above you, which was once part of the throat of a cinder cone.

Glaciers removed the cinders but were too feeble to erode the lava. On the flat you may see an old trail heading east, the former Walton trail, which crossed Madera Creek about 250 yards below the Fernandez trail ford, which once provided an alternate route to our trailhead. With that goal in mind, cross the creek and ascend about 500 feet on the Fernandez trail, our ridge ascend ending after a brief contour southeast to a wilderness-boundary junction with the start of the Lillian Loop trail. From it retrace your steps back to your trailhead.

FERNANDEZ-RED PEAK-POST PEAK PASSES LOOP

Distance: 48.0 miles semiloop trip

Grade: 6F, moderate 6-day hike

Trailhead: Same as the Hike 97 trailhead. **F6.**

Introduction: Along this double-loop hike you cross four major divides and sample lakes in the Granite Creek, South Fork Merced River, Illilouette Creek, and Merced River basins. On one divide you cross Red Peak Pass, at 11,180 feet the highest pass in Yosemite National Park.

Description: On your first hiking day follow **Hike 97** either to the large Staniford lake or ⅔ mile farther to Lillian Lake. Then, on the second day, head east to the Fernandez trail junction mentioned in that hike. From that point we make a mile-long, winding climb northwest up granite slabs through an open forest to a meadowside trail junction immediately below a low gap. From here a trail, described in **Hike 97**, climbs 1½ miles up to rewarding Rainbow Lake. We, however, keep to the Fernandez trail, climbing ½ mile north to a broad crest, then traversing ¾ mile northwest to a junction. Early on this traverse you recognize the Park boundary's two named summits, broad Triple Divide Peak and narrow Post Peak. At the junction, above the south bank of Fernandez Creek, a trail branches right, eventually climbing to Post Peak Pass. We'll descend on that trail, which is described in **Hike 100**.

Keeping to the Fernandez trail, you immediately pass a good campsite, on your left, jump across Fernandez Creek, and above its north bank meet a connecting trail that briefly descends to a meadow and the Post Peak Pass trail. More campsites are found near this meadow. Our Fernandez trail climbs west and after ½ mile it switchbacks high above Fernandez Creek to offer down-canyon views. These disappear as you curve right into a bowl and meet a trail that makes an exhausting ¼-mile climb to Rutherford Lake. If you make this side trip, you'll find the best camps along the east shore, about 200 yards beyond the south-end dam. Another dam is at the lake's northeast bay.

Beyond the Rutherford Lake trail you face a two-stage ascent to Fernandez Pass. Short switchbacks elevate you 200 feet to a broad, shallow gap, from which you descend into a large, granitic bowl. After crossing its sub-alpine meadow, you begin your second stage—far more taxing—which climbs by more than two dozen switchbacks 450 feet almost up to an unnamed crest saddle. From the saddle, which is well dressed with white-bark pines and mountain hemlocks, the view west is surprisingly unimpressive. However, from our trail the view east is quite impressive, ranging over much of the Granite Creek basin and extending to the Ritter Range and the central Sierra Nevada crest. From the saddle you traverse south ¼ mile across generally open slopes, heading toward a fin on the boundary ridge just yards before dropping to 10,175-foot Fernandez Pass. This is named for Sergeant Joseph Fernandez, who with Lieutenant Harry Benson and others explored, mapped, and patrolled the Yosemite backcountry in the 1890s. They also planted trout, starting a practice that continued without serious question until the 1970s, when biologists began to study the ecological effect of fish in the high country.

At the pass, decked with ragged hemlocks, lodgepoles, and whitebark pines, your views are far more restrictive than from the previous saddle. You may note an old trail that drops northeast down a gully to the granitic bowl. Though still used by many hikers, this trail was abandoned decades ago because of its steepness and the long-lasting snowfield that lingered in much of the gully. Unlike our overly engineered ascent to the pass, our descent is steep, dropping 600 feet along an old trail to a junction. Along this descent you see Breeze Lake, where you should spend your second night.

From the junction, follow a winding path toward this lake. Midway to it, the path may become vague along the west shore of a pond, but continue upward, soon entering a straight, joint-controlled gully that takes you to deep, rockbound Breeze Lake. Being larger than average and also lying in a cirque below the slopes of towering Gale Peak, the lake often lives up to its name. A few small campsites can be found along the lake's north and west shores.

On your third morning, return to the main trail and start west down the canyon. Midway to a chest-deep lake and its shallower neighbor, you pass some giant mountain hemlocks and mature lodgepoles—among the best to be seen in the Park. During the afternoon the

Lower Ottoway Lake and Merced Peak

Approaching Post Peak Pass, you have a view back at a broad, open expanse

deeper lake can provide a refreshing swim, and its shore makes a good spot for a trail break. From these small lakes your descent along morainal ground quickly steepens, then you cross the lakes' creek for an easing descent to the wildflowered banks of the South Fork Merced River. Once on its north bank—sometimes reached by a ford—you walk a viewless mile along a rolling trail to a junction in Moraine Meadows. By walking south 200 yards through the lodgepole-invaded meadow, you can reach the South Fork, which has a medium-size camp above its south bank and a similar one 90 yards downstream on its north bank.

Hike 96 joins our route at the Moraine Meadows junction, and continuing west on our trail, we pass through a bedrock gap after ½ mile, then soon swing northwest down into a small though impressive gully with straight, vertical walls. About ⅓ mile farther, we cross a small creek, then in a like distance climb southwest to a junction, passing a crescentic pond midway. Here, those following **Hike 96** turn left, bound for Givens Lake.

Bound for Merced Pass, we turn right and contour north ½ mile to the wildflowered creek we crossed earlier, crossing it twice more. A short, steep climb then ensues, bringing you up to a small meadow, at whose head you cross the now trickling creek. With the pass now more or less in sight, you climb easily over to your final creek crossing—hardly worth noting—then make a final, short push up to 9295-foot Merced Pass. Lodgepoles and western white pines totally preclude any view, so, after catching your breath, descend ¾ mile to a creek that drains Upper Merced Pass Lake. Just before this creek you can traverse east across slabs to the nearby lake, which is blessed with very good campsites.

Above the northeast bank of the lake's outlet creek, we come to a junction from which **Hike 89** descends northwest down Illilouette Creek canyon. We now follow part of that hike in reverse, climbing about 2.6 miles to the northwest shore of Lower Ottoway Lake, to spend our third night. On day four, continue backtracking along Hike 89, climbing 2.1 miles breathlessly up to alpine Red Peak Pass before making a generally descending, 6.6-mile trek to a trail junction beside a tributary of the Triple Peak Fork of the Merced River.

After spending your fourth night somewhere in this vicinity, cross the tributary as in **Hike 88,** using a nearby log, if available. On a trail you then quickly reach and cross the Triple Peak Fork. From this easy crossing your trail makes a gentle ascent south, paralleling the unseen tributary for ½ mile to the start of a switchbacking climb northeast. This 550-foot climb is generally a viewless one, due to lodgepoles and hemlocks, though you can get an occasional view north of the Mt. Florence ridge and of the Matthes Crest, in the distance west of it. Your climb ends on a small flat below the west spur of unseen Isberg Peak. Here, 1⅔ miles from the Triple Peak Fork, you leave **Hike 88** and head south from a tall cairn. In ⅓ mile you enter a broad, open expanse—an awesome landscape of a sort not seen anywhere else along Yosemite's trails. From the northwest edge of this expanse you could traverse ¼ mile east to a fairly large, windswept lake with a sandy beach along its north shore. Protective lodgepole pines shelter a campsite near it.

On your open trail you see a pond lying immediately west of the unseen lake, then soon enter a grove of struggling lodgepoles growing on rocky ground. Venturing beyond this grove is unwise in threatening weather, for you won't find any protective cover until you cross Post Peak Pass and descend *below* Porphyry Lake.

From the grove our trail gradually curves left, and looking back, we have a startling view: we seem to be at land's end, with the world dropping off beyond our broad, alpine surface. Starting to climb, one can scan an entire stretch of crest from Isberg Peak clockwise to Triple Divide Peak. After a moderate ascent for a 200-foot gain, we arrive at a meadowy junction to which **Hike 100,** from visible Isberg Pass, descends. Now you follow that hike, first ⅓ mile generally east up to a crest saddle, then south along the crest to Post Peak Pass. Hike 100 descends past Porphyry Lake, and you should spend your last trail night well below it, perhaps at Post Creek or Fernandez Creek. The next day, hike out to your trailhead via the Fernandez trail, as described in the last part of **Hike 97**.

CORA AND JOE CRANE LAKES VIA ISBERG TRAIL

Distance: 18.6 miles round trip

Grade: 4D, moderate 2-day hike

Trailhead: As in the description of the route to the third Hike 97 trailhead, drive 30 miles northeast up Forest Route 7 to a junction with Road 5S30, located just 0.2 mile east of a spur road south to the Minarets Pack Station. Ahead, the main paved route is Forest Route 81, an alternate road to this junction. Drive 1¾ miles northeast on Road 5S30 to the Clover Meadow Ranger Station, and get your permit there if you haven't gotten one in advance. Then continue about 1⅓ miles on your road to a crossing of West Fork Granite Creek, usually possible in early July (ask first at the R. S.), and take your road downstream about 1.1 miles to the trailhead parking, near the Granite Creek Campground entrance. **F6.**

Introduction: Granite Creek Campground, by your trailhead, was designed with equestrians in mind. Because your trailhead is one of the most remote in the Sierra Nevada—a 1½-hour drive from the nearest settlement, Bass Lake— there are relatively few hikers. Beyond Cora Lakes, a favorite with packers, you'll have most of the glaciated, subalpine scenery to yourself. If your time is limited to one or two days, then middle Cora Lake is a worthy goal in itself. It is 9.2 miles, round trip.

Description: The trail starts across a lodgepole flat, then climbs to a slightly higher one along which we approach bouldery East Fork Granite Creek. The creek's large boulders, like our flat's gravels, were left by a retreating glacier. During past glaciations almost the entire Granite Creek basin (both forks) lay under ice. Only the metavolcanic summit of Timber Knob, high above Cora Lakes, rose above the sea of ice, which extended continuously to Mt. Goddard, in northern Kings Canyon National Park, about 42 miles southeast of us.

After paralleling the East Fork for a few minutes, you begin to climb through a predominantly fir forest and soon enter a poorly defined side canyon. In it you cross and then recross its diminutive creek, whose bed has oversize boulders, deposited by a glacial stream, not by the existing creek. Near its head the canyon becomes a well-defined gully, which you ascend to a forested divide separating a 7842-foot-high knoll from the south end of the Post Peak-Timber Knob crest. From the divide you circle clockwise, passing many firs and a few aspens before climbing high on the wall of a deep box canyon. Just before some deep, parallel furrows—one confining the cascading East Fork—you see pyramidal Squaw Dome, 6 miles to the south, and also broad, gentle Kaiser Ridge, on the far horizon behind it.

At the brink of one furrow we enter Ansel Adams Wilderness, spot a creekside campsite, and hike up a shallow, forested canyon past unseen Green Mountain, just to the east. About 3 miles from our trailhead we come to another campsite, this one by a junction with the Stevenson trail. This trail immediately crosses the East Fork, then gives rise to other trails that radiate across the upper San Joaquin River basin. These routes are favorites with equestrians, including the route to Devils Postpile and Reds Meadow.

Still on the Isberg trail, you curve left for a brief upstream hike, and may see an old trail that once went southwest toward the Strawberry Tungsten Mine. An often plentiful supply of mosquitoes tends to discourage camping by this bank.

After making the typically wet ford of the East Fork, you go but 35 yards east to a bend. A less-used, ½-mile lateral trail continues straight ahead over to the Stevenson trail. If you start across it, you're likely to see a packer camp not far south from it. The broader Isberg trail angles north from this lateral and soon makes a short, steep climb that fortunately yields to a gentle ¾-mile ascent through a verdant, rich forest growing on deep, morainal soils. Your ascent ends just after you cross Cora Creek and arrive at the southeast corner of middle Cora Lake. Camping is prohibited within 400 feet of this shore, but good sites are along the north shore. The lake is shallow, making it warm and excellent for swimming, yet it is deep enough to support trout.

Beyond middle Cora Lake you make a short, dusty climb to the top of a low volcanic ridge, which still exists despite some 2 million years of repeated glacier attacks on it. As everywhere else in the range, the evidence here testifies to the inefficacy of glacial erosion. From the ridge an even shorter descent takes you to a junction with the eastbound Chetwood trail. If you are hiking only to middle Cora Lake, but would like an alternate route back, you can take this easy trail 2¼

Yosemite boundary crest, from meadow by East Fork Granite Creek

Post Peak above treeline Joe Crane Lake

miles over to the Stevenson trail, then go ½ mile southwest down that trail to the East Fork and the Isberg trail. The total distance of this semiloop hike is 11.1 miles.

Although you now leave most equestrians and backpackers behind, you may meet cattle, which in some summers are still brought up to graze in this wilderness. Your 2.4-mile hike northwest to the Joe Crane Lake trail is an amazingly easy one. At first your trail hugs the base of a volcanic plateau, keeping just above wet meadows. After 1.1 miles you pass the meadow-bordered site of Knoblock Cabin, just past your first view of Isberg and Post peaks. You could camp by the meadow's end, by which you cross East Fork Granite Creek. However, better camping lies along its west bank. After a mile of fairly easy ascent, you cross Joe Crane Creek, and about ¼ mile beyond it reach the Joe Crane Lake trail. **Hike 100** continues up-canyon along the Isberg trail, bound for Sadler Lake and Isberg Pass.

Mountain hemlocks temporarily dominate the shady, well-graded climb of 300 feet up the lower part of the Joe Crane Lake trail. Then, in more-open terrain, it contours south before bending southwest gently up to a slab at the base of a descending ridge. Here you'll see a trail branching left down to nearby Joe Crane Creek—the Timber Creek trail. From it your trail climbs more than 500 feet to Joe Crane Lake. Above the lake's east shore is a lodgepole-shaded packer site. A smaller camp lies on the lake's southwest shore. Certainly the packer camp is more desirable, for from it you can watch the sun's first rays illumine

Post Peak, a scene exquisitely reflected in the lake's tranquil waters. Whether you come here for the view, the peace, the trout, or a swim (temperatures at best in the low to mid 60s), you're almost certain to be pleased.

GRANITE CREEK FORKS LOOP

Distance: 29.6 miles loop trip

Grade: 5E, moderate 3-day hike

Trailhead: Same as the Hike 99 trailhead. **F6.**

Introduction: Those wanting to make a longer, more scenic loop than Hike 99 should try this loop. It crosses three alpine passes, entering Yosemite National Park for just under a mile between the first two. It then descends to the Porphyry Lake environs, which geologists and nongeologists alike will admit is one of the strangest landscapes to be found in the entire Sierra Nevada.

Description: As in **Hike 99,** climb 4.6 miles up the Isberg trail to middle Cora Lake, then continue on an easy ascent 3.1 miles to the Joe Crane Lake trail junction. Keeping to the Isberg trail, we leave Hike 99 as we make an easy up-canyon climb ⅔ mile to a ford of East Fork Granite Creek. Now a multistage climb to Isberg Pass begins. Up at around 9000 feet elevation, short, steep switchbacks can tire hikers. If you stop and rest, you might look to the west and try to determine the rate of recovery of a lodgepole grove that in the '70s was mowed down by a snow avalanche from the west. The gradient abates after more than 300 feet of precious altitude gain, and after a relaxing ¼-mile creekside ascent you reach a junction with a trail to McClure Lake. This trail immediately fords the creek, then skirts the south shore of Sadler Lake, and climbs ½ mile to that cold, deep lake. A massive cliff encircles most of McClure Lake, but its esthetic appeal is offset by a dam on the lake's outlet. Furthermore, the tightly rimmed lake has no flat space for adequate camping.

Better camping is found at Sadler Lake, which the Isberg trail reaches in less than 200 yards beyond the McClure Lake trail junction. Our trail curves to the lake's north shore, along which no camping is allowed within 400 feet of it. Try small sites, such as one near the inlet on the lake's west shore or ones on level spots on bedrock slopes just above the lake. These sites are the last good ones until Post Creek. Sadler Lake, though fairly large, is extremely shallow—barely chest-deep.

From the north shore of Sadler Lake the trail starts its second steep ascent, making feeble efforts to switchback up the slopes. As before, after 300 feet of ascent the gradient eases and at a sharp bend left, you may find a sign pointing toward alpine McGee Lake, unseen on a broad bench ½ mile to the northeast. Now you climb southwest, reaching a ridge that dams shallow, bedrock-lined lower Isberg Lake. On the short descent to the north

shore of this lake you'll probably note some giant erratics, looking as fresh as on the day a glacier dropped them. You could camp among lodgepoles north of the lake, but the sites are definitely inferior to those at Sadler Lake.

If you haven't done so already, don your dark glasses for the climb south up the lake's inlet creek, leave it, and pass a large mountain hemlock before reaching the McClure Lake vista, on a barren, granitic ridge. From it you see the deep lake lying at the base of a forbidding cliff. A moderate climb, made difficult by thinning air, takes us ¼ mile west up to truly alpine, 10,900-foot-high upper Isberg Lake. The trail keeps its distance from the lake's shore in order to avoid its fragile alpine turf. It then does a remarkable thing: it zigzags more than two dozen times, climbing more than 300 feet northwest *away* from Isberg Pass. From the top of this climb you have nearly a ½-mile traverse over to 10,520-foot Isberg Pass.

An old trail used to climb from upper Isberg Lake directly southwest up to the pass, much as did an old trail up to Fernandez Pass (**Hike 98**). The old Isberg trail, however, wasn't painfully steep, nor was it in a snowbound gully. And, being entirely across solid bedrock, it posed no danger to either hiker or environment. I recommend that you leave the lower switchbacks and head cross-country directly up the old route to the pass. But if you are on horseback, then by all means keep to the switchbacking trail.

Leaving Isberg Pass and its prostrate whitebark pines, we enter Yosemite National

Sadler Lake and the Yosemite National Park crest boundary

Park and actually climb a bit, going from ledge to ledge, before dropping ½ mile on an irregular course to a trail junction. Near the trail junction you can scan most of the upper Merced River basin, rimmed by a spectacular alpine crest. The Clark Range borders the basin to the west, the Cathedral Range to the north, and the Park's boundary crest to the east. With map and compass you can identify many peaks, including Mt. Hoffmann and Tuolumne Peak on the distant skyline about 18 miles northwest.

From the junction **Hike 98** joins your route as you climb ⅓ mile up to an unnamed saddle—at 10,620 feet—on the boundary crest. As at Isberg Pass, you now have a view of the Ritter Range, but also one of upper Ward Lake, below you, and much of the enormous San Joaquin River basin. Staying at or near the crest, you traverse south for ½ mile, getting high from the spectacular views as well as from the rarefied air. At last you climb almost to the top of Post Peak's northern satellite, then drop to desolate, 10,750-foot Post Peak Pass. Despite its height, its orientation prevents one from having the far-ranging views found along the crest traverse.

Our trail descends from Post Peak Pass via short, very steep switchbacks that force us to constantly brake. Be careful on this descent, for there are many loose boulders and this is no place for an injury. After dropping more than 550 feet, you skirt across bedrock benches above the east shore of tiny Porphyry Lake. The lake—a home for yellow-legged frogs—is a suitable place to rest your aching knees. Camp space, however, is nonexistent.

This area looks like it came down with a very bad case of measles. And not just the lakeshore. The "outbreak" spreads across hundreds of acres, dotting the landscape with countless thousands of dark, tightly packed, beachball-size spheres. Nowhere else in the Sierra will you find such a landscape. One explanation for this phenomenon is that the "beachballs" are quartz-diorite inclusions in a matrix of rock known as the "granite porphyry of Post Peak." The lighter-colored granite porphyry, which has quartz and feldspar crystals in a fine-grained groundmass, intruded a mass of quartz diorite about 98-100 million years ago. The intrusive process broke the quartz diorite into thousands of angular blocks, and the molten granite, before it solidified, began to melt the blocks, the way water melts ice

cubes floating in it. Because the molten-granite pluton intruded the solid quartz-diorite pluton at a relatively shallow depth, the granite cooled faster than usual. Had the intrusion taken place at the usual, greater depth, the quartz diorite might have been greatly or completely melted, and a typical granitic landscape would have developed.

The "beachballs" stay with us for at least ⅓ mile south of Porphyry Lake, and we leave them only after our moderately descending Post Peak Pass trail crosses a gully and takes on a gentler gradient. Now the trail makes a 1½-mile traverse south through wet meadows before entering a lodgepole forest. In it you soon start down the snout of a giant lateral moraine, briefly angle east, then descend ¾ mile southwest to Post Creek. Crossing to the west bank of Post Creek, you'll find an adequate campsite. It would be rated "good" were it not for the abundance of mosquitoes. A tent is highly desirable here.

The route climbs southwest from the Post Creek camp, cutting through a low divide after ¼ mile, then descending toward a reedy lake. On the short descent to it you'll see some more exposures of intruded quartz diorite. Your trail skirts along the southeast shore of the small lake, though at its outlet a second trail briefly descends the north bank, only to climb back up the south bank. Take this trail when the first is flooded. From the lake's southwest end you can continue a few yards in that direction and make camp—away from most of the mosquitoes—on a low divide. Leaving this gap, the

"Beachball" landscape near Porphyry Lake

trail drops southwest ¼ mile, crossing a creekbed immediately before a junction with the Slab Lakes trail. This primitive trail, which is essentially cross-country along its last ¾ mile, climbs 2⅓ miles to the two treeline lakes. They can serve as a staging area for a strenuous but safe ascent up Triple Divide Peak.

Just 50 yards west of the trail junction you cross the main Slab Lakes creek—one of three parallel washes—then momentarily enter a small meadow. Camps can be found among lodgepoles near the confluence of Slab Lakes creek and Fernandez Creek, as well as up Fernandez Creek. At the meadow's southwest end we meet Fernandez Creek, with a trail ascending each bank. Cross the creek and climb 250 yards up to a junction with the Fernandez trail. On this trail you hike 1¼ miles southeast over to a junction with the Rainbow Lake trail, then continue for another mile down to a junction with the Lillian Loop trail. This 2¼-mile stretch is described in the first paragraph of **Hike 98.**

From your junction you can take a highly scenic, lake-blessed alternate route by following the first half of **Hike 97,** described in the opposite direction, along the Lillian Loop trail. You'll end at the Fernandez trail parking area, from which you follow the shorter regular route.

This route leaves the Lillian Loop trail junction and descends the Fernandez trail, as in the second half of **Hike 97,** first for 1.8 miles down to a gravelly flat along the north bank of Madera Creek, suitable for camping, then climbs moderately south for a mile before traversing about ⅓ mile over to a junction with the start of the Lillian Loop trail. Keep on the Fernandez trail, descending southeast about 0.2 mile to a trail branching south, then continuing your course for about 1¼ miles down to a trail branching west over toward the first, these two meeting at the end of Norris Creek Road (an alternate trailhead for Hike 97). Now you make a gentle descent ⅓ mile east to the Fernandez trail trailhead and parking area at the end of Road 5S05. From the north side of the parking area you descend 1.4 miles, passing Clover Meadow Campground just minutes before reaching the Clover Meadow Ranger Station. From it you follow the main road, 5S30, 230 yards northeast to the start of the Mammoth trail's pleasant, mile-long route northeast that takes you to lower Granite Creek Campground. A ⅔-mile walk north up its road gets you to the Granite Creek Campground road and your vehicle. About 120 yards before this junction, a horse bridge crosses Granite Creek. Beneath it you can clean up in chilly, potholed pools. However, watch your step on the adjacent slippery, smooth rock.

Recommended Reading and Source Materials

(The entries marked * are very technical and are intended
for readers with experience in the subject area.)

General

Browning, Peter. 1991. *Place Names of the
Sierra Nevada.* Berkeley: Wilderness
Press, 264 p.

Browning, Peter. 1988. *Yosemite Place
Names.* Lafayette, CA: Great West
Books, 256 p.

Medley, Steven P. 1994. *The Complete
Guidebook to Yosemite National Park.*
El Portal: Yosemite Association,
112 p.

Muir, John. 1894 (1977). *The Mountains of
California.* Berkeley: Ten Speed
Press, 400 p.

Muir, John, and Galen Rowell. 1989. *The
Yosemite.* San Francisco: Sierra Club,
223 p.

Robertson, David. 1984. *West of Eden: A
History of the Art and Literature of
Yosemite.* El Portal: Yosemite
Association, 174 p.

Backpacking and Mountaineering

Arce, Gary. 1996. *Defying Gravity: High
Adventure on Yosemite's Walls.*
Berkeley: Wilderness Press, 194 p.

Beck, Steve. 1995. *Yosemite Trout Fishing
Guide.* Portland, OR: Amato Publications, 158 p.

Darvill, Fred, Jr. 1998. *Mountaineering
Medicine.* Berkeley: Wilderness
Press, 110 p.

Graydon, Don, and Kurt Hanson, eds.
1997. *Mountaineering: The Freedom of
the Hills.* Seattle: The Mountaineers,
528 p.

King, Clarence. 1972 (1997).
Mountaineering in the Sierra Nevada.
Lincoln: University of Nebraska
Press, 320 p.

Rowell, Galen A., ed. 1974. *The Vertical
World of Yosemite.* Berkeley:
Wilderness Press, 207 p.

Secor, R.J. 1992. *The High Sierra: Peaks,
Passes, and Trails.* Seattle: The
Mountaineers, 368 p.

Winnett, Thomas. 1987. *The Tahoe-
Yosemite Trail.* Berkeley: Wilderness
Press, 112 p.

Winnett, Thomas, and Melanie Findling.
1994. *Backpacking Basics.* Berkeley:
Wilderness Press, 134 p.

Winnett, Thomas, and Kathy Morey.
1998. *Guide to the John Muir Trail.*
Berkeley: Wilderness Press, 112 p.

History

Brewer, William H. 1930 (1974). *Up and
Down California in 1860-64.* Berkeley:
University of California Press,
583 p.

Bunnell, Lafayette H. 1880 (1990).
Discovery of the Yosemite in 1851. El
Portal: Yosemite Association, 314 p.

Farquhar, Francis P. 1965. *History of the*

Sierra Nevada. Berkeley: University of California Press, 262 p.

Muir, John. 1911 (1990). *My First Summer in the Sierra*. San Francisco: Sierra Club, 208 p.

Reid, Robert L. 1983. *A Treasury of the Sierra Nevada*. Berkeley: Wilderness Press, 363 p.

Russell, Carl P. 1968 (1992). *100 Years in Yosemite*. El Portal: Yosemite Association, 267 p.

Sanborn, Margaret. 1989. *Yosemite: Its Discovery, its Wonders and its People.* El Portal: Yosemite Association, 289 p.

Geology

Alley, Richard B. 2000. The Two-Mile Time Machine: Ice Cores, *Abrupt Climate Change, and Our Future.* Princeton, NJ: Princeton University Press, 229 p.

*Bateman, Paul C. 1992. *Plutonism in the Central Part of the Sierra Nevada Batholith, California.* US Geological Survey Professional Paper 1483, 186 p.

Bateman, Paul C., and Clyde Wahrhaftig. 1966. "Geology of the Sierra Nevada." In *Geology of Northern California* (Edgar H. Bailey, ed.). California Division of Mines and Geology Bulletin 190, p. 107-172. [Classic article on the Sierra Nevada, but now extremely dated.]

Bowen, Oliver E., Jr., and Richard A. Crippen, Jr. 1997. "California's Mother Lode Highway." *California Geology.* v. 50, nos. 2-6. [Geology along Highway 49.]

Clark, William B. 1970. *Gold Districts of California.* California Division of Mines and Geology Bulletin 193, 186 p.

Cox, Allan, and Robert B. Hart. 1986. *Plate Tectonics: How It Works.* Oxford: Blackwell Scientific Publications, 392 p.

*Foster, David A., and C. Mark Fanning. 1997. "Geochronology of the northern Idaho batholith and the Bitterroot metamorphic complex: Magmatism preceding and contemporaneous with extension." *Geological Society of America Bulletin,* v. 109, p. 379-394.

*Graymer, Russell W., and David L. Jones. 1994. "Tectonic implications of radiolarian cherts from the Placerville Belt, Sierra Nevada Foothills, California: Nevadan-age continental growth by accretion of multiple terranes." *Geological Society of America Bulletin,* v. 106, p. 531-540.

*Greene, David C., Richard A. Schweickert, and Calvin H. Stevens. 1997. "Roberts Mountains allochthon and the western margin of the Cordilleran miogeocline in the Northern Ritter Range pendant, eastern Sierra Nevada, California." *Geological Society of America Bulletin,* v. 109, p. 1294-1305.

Gutenberg, Beno, John P. Buwalda, and Robert P. Sharp. 1956. "Seismic explorations on the floor of Yosemite Valley, California." *Bulletin of the Geological Society of America, v.* 67, p. 1051-1078.

Harland, W. Brian, and others. 1990. *A Geologic Time Scale 1989.* Cambridge: Cambridge University Press, 263 p.

*Harwood, David S. 1991. *Stratigraphy of Paleozoic and Lower Mesozoic Rocks in the Northern Sierra Terrane, California.* US Geological Survey Bulletin 1957, 78 p.

*House, Martha A., Brian P. Wernicke, and Kenneth A. Farley. 1998. "Dating topography of the Sierra

Nevada, California, using apatite (U-Th)/He ages." *Nature,* v. 396, p. 66-69.

*Howell, David G., ed. *Tectonostratigraphic Terranes of the Circum-Pacific Region.* Houston: Circum-Pacific Council for Energy and Mineral Resources, 585 p.

Huber, N. King. 1981. *Amount and Timing of Late Cenozoic Uplift and Tilt of the Central Sierra Nevada, California—Evidence from the Upper San Joaquin River Basin.* US Geological Survey Professional Paper 1197, 28 p. [Foremost paper on Sierran uplift; but outdated.]

Huber, N. King. 1987. *The geologic story of Yosemite National Park.* US Geological Survey Bulletin 1595, 64 p. [Good bedrock geology; poor uplift and glacial geology.]

Jones, David L. 1997. "Uplift of the Sierra Nevada: fact or fancy?" *Guide to the Geology of the Western Sierra Nevada: Sacramento to the Crystal Basin. Northern California Geological Society.*

*Lahren, Mary M., and Richard A. Schweickert. 1994. "Sache Monument Pendant, central Sierra Nevada, California: Eugeoclinal metasedimentary rocks near the axis of the Sierra Nevada batholith." *Geological Society of America Bulletin,* v. 106, p. 186-194.

Matthes, François E. 1930. *Geologic History of the Yosemite Valley.* US Geological Survey Professional Paper 160, 137 p. [The widely acclaimed classic on Yosemite Valley, but completely outdated.]

Matthes, François E. 1950. *The Incomparable Valley.* Berkeley: University of California Press, 160 p. [Popular account of the above, and equally outdated.]

*McNulty, Brendan A., Weixing Tong, and Othmar T. Tobisch. 1996. "Assembly of a dike-fed magma chamber: The Jackass Lakes pluton, central Sierra Nevada, California." *Geological Society of America Bulletin,* v. 108, p. 926-940.

Molnar, Peter. 1990. "The Rise of Mountain Ranges and the Evolution of Humans: a Causal Relation?" *Irish Journal of Earth Sciences,* v. 10, p. 199-207. [A serious spoof of the widespread geomyth of recent uplift of the world's ranges.]

*Oldow, John S., and others. 1989. "Phanerozoic evolution of the North American Cordillera; United States and Canada." In *The Geology of North America; An Overview* (The Geology of North America, Volume A, Albert W. Bally and Allison R. Palmer, eds.). Boulder: Geological Society of America, p. 139-232.

*Ruddiman, W.F., and H.E. Wright, Jr. 1987. *North America and Adjacent Oceans During the Last Deglaciation* (The Geology of North America, Volume K-3). Boulder: Geological Society of America, 501 p.

Schaffer, Jeffrey P. 1997. *The Geomorphic Evolution of the Yosemite Valley and Sierra Nevada Landscapes: Solving the Riddles in the Rocks.* Berkeley: Wilderness Press, 388 p. [The only comprehensive source on Sierran uplift and glaciation based solely on field evidence.]

Shelton, John S. 1966. *Geology Illustrated.* San Francisco: W.H. Freeman, 434 p. [Perhaps the best geology text ever written; a true classic.]

Wahrhaftig, Clyde. 1965. "Stepped topography of the southern Sierra Nevada." Geological Society of America Bulletin, v. 76, p. 1165-1189. [Another outdated classic, negated

by its own evidence, but nevertheless awarded geomorphology's
highest honor, the Kirk Bryan
award.]

Geologic Maps

Alpha, Tau Rho, Clyde Wahrhaftig, and
N. King Huber. 1987. *Oblique map
showing maximum extent of 20,000-
year-old (Tioga) glaciers, Yosemite
National park, central Nevada,
California.* US Geological Survey
Map I-1885. [Considerably underes-
timates the lengths and thicknesses
of these glaciers.]

Bailey, Roy A. 1989. *Geologic map of the
Long Valley caldera, Mono-Inyo
Craters volcanic chain, and vicinity,
eastern California.* US Geological
Survey Map I-1933. [Some glacial
deposits are misdated.]

Bateman, Paul C. 1992. *Pre-Tertiary
bedrock geologic map of the Mariposa
1° by 2° quadrangle, Sierra Nevada,
California; Nevada.* US Geological
Survey Miscellaneous Investigations
Series Map I-1960.

Bateman, Paul C., and others. 1983.
*Geologic map of the Tuolumne
Meadows quadrangle, Yosemite
National Park, California.* US
Geological Survey Map GQ-1570.

Bateman, Paul C., and Konrad B.
Krauskopf. 1987. *Geologic map of the
El Portal quadrangle, west-central
Sierra Nevada, California.* US
Geological Survey Map MF-1998.

Calkins, Frank C., and others. 1930
(1985). *Bedrock geologic map of
Yosemite Valley, Yosemite National
Park, California.* US Geological
Survey Map I-1639.

Chesterman, Charles W. 1975. *Geology of
the Matterhorn Peak Quadrangle,*
*Mono and Tuolumne Counties,
California.* California Division of
Mines and Geology Map Sheet 22.

Dodge, F.C.W., and L.C. Calk. 1987.
*Geologic map of the Lake Eleanor quad-
rangle, central Sierra Nevada,
California.* US Geological Survey
Map GQ-1639.

Huber, N. King. 1983. *Preliminary geologic map of the Pinecrest quadrangle, central Sierra Nevada, California.* US
Geological Survey Map MF-1437.

Huber, N. King, and C. Dean Rinehart.
1965. *Geologic map of the Devils
Postpile quadrangle, Sierra Nevada,
California.* US Geological Survey
Map GQ-437.

Huber, N. King, Paul C. Bateman, and
Clyde Wahrhaftig. 1989. *Geologic
map of Yosemite National Park and
vicinity, California.* US Geological
Survey Map I-1874. [Dates on
metamorphic rocks are poor; glacial
deposits are inaccurate.]

Kistler, Ronald W. 1966. *Geologic map of
the Mono Craters quadrangle, Mono
and Tuolumne Counties, California.* US
Geological Survey Map GQ-462.

Kistler, Ronald W. 1973. *Geologic map
of the Hetch Hetchy Reservoir quadrangle, Yosemite National Park, California.*
US Geological Survey Map
GQ-1112.

Peck, Dallas L. 1980. *Geologic map of the
Merced Peak quadrangle, central Sierra
Nevada, California.* US Geological
Survey Map GQ-1531.

Stewart, John H., John E. Carlson, and
Dann C. Johannesen. 1982. *Geologic
map of the Walker Lake 1° by 2° quadrangle, California and Nevada.* US
Geological Survey Map MF-1382A.

Wagner, D.L., and others. 1981. *Geologic
map of the Sacramento quadrangle,
scale 1:250,000.* California Division
of Mines and Geology Regional

Geologic Map Series, Map No. 1A.
Wahrhaftig, Clyde. 2000. *Geologic map of the Tower Peak quadrangle, central Sierra Nevada, California.* US Geological Survey Map I-2697.

Biology

_____. 1996. *Sierra Nevada Ecosystem Project, Final Report to Congress* (Vol. I: Assessment Summaries and Management Strategies, 209 p. Vol. II: Assessments and Scientific Basis for Management Options, 1528 p. Vol. III: Assessments, Commissioned Reports, and Background Information, 1101 p.). Davis: University of California, Centers for Water and Wildland Resources.

Barbour, Michael, and others. 1993. *California's Changing Landscapes: Diversity and Conservation of California Vegetation.* Sacramento: California Native Plant Society, 246 p.

Botti, Stephen J., and Walter Sydoriak. 2001. *An Illustrated Flora of Yosemite National Park.* El Portal: Yosemite Association, 484 p.

Edelbrock, Jerry, and Scott Carpenter, eds. 1990. *Natural Areas and Yosemite: Prospects for the Future* (Yosemite Centennial Symposium Proceedings). El Portal: Yosemite Association, 667 p.

Gaines, David. 1992. *Birds of Yosemite and the East Slope.* Lee Vining: Artemisia Press, 352 p.

Gibbens, Robert P., and Harold F. Heady. 1964. *The Influence of Modern Man on the Vegetation of Yosemite Valley.* Berkeley: University of California Division of Agricultural Sciences Manual 36, 44 p.

Grater, Russell K., and Tom A. Blaue. 1978. *Discovering Sierra Mammals.* El Portal: Yosemite Association, 174 p.

Hartesveldt, Richard J., and others. 1975. *The Giant Sequoia of the Sierra Nevada.* Washington, D.C.: National Park Service, 180 p.

Harvey, H. Thomas, Howard S. Shellhammer, and Ronald E. Stecker. 1980. *Giant Sequoia Ecology: Fire and Reproduction.* Washington, D.C.: National Park Service Scientific Monograph Series No. 12, 182 p.

*Hickman, James C., ed. 1993. *The Jepson Manual: Higher Plants of California.* Berkeley: University of California Press, 1400 p.

Horn, Elizabeth L. 1998. *Sierra Nevada Wildflowers.* Missoula, MT: Mountain Press, 215 p. [This contains over 220 photographs of common shrubs and wildflowers. It is a good introduction for those who prefer plant identification by photos rather than by keys.]

Jameson, E.W., Jr., and Hans J. Peeters. 1988. *California Mammals* (California Natural History Guide 52). Berkeley: University of California Press, 403 p.

Klikoff, Lionel G. 1965. "Microenvironmental influence on vegetational pattern near timberline in the central Sierra Nevada." *Ecological Monographs,* v. 35, p. 187-211.

Leopold, A. Starker, and others. 1951. *The Jawbone Deer Herd.* Sacramento: California Division of Fish and Game, Game Bulletin 4, 139 p.

McGinnis, Samuel M. 1984. *Freshwater Fishes of California* (California Natural History Guide 49). Berkeley: University of California Press, 316 p.

Niehaus, Theodore F., and Charles L. Ripper. 1981. *A Field Guide to Pacific States Wildflowers* (Peterson Field Guide 22). Boston: Houghton Mifflin, 432 p.

Ornduff, Robert. 1974. *An Introduction to California Plant Life* (California Natural History Guide 35). Berkeley: University of California Press, 152 p.

Peterson, Roger Tory. 2001. *A Field Guide to Western Birds* (Peterson Field Guide 2). Boston: Houghton Mifflin, 432 p.

Petrides, George A., and Olivia Petrides. 1998. *A Field Guide to Western Trees*. Boston: Houghton Mifflin, 308 p.

Sawyer, John O., and Todd Keeler-Wolf. 1995. *A Manual of California Vegetation*. Sacramento: California Native Plant Society, 471 p.

Sibley, David Allen. 2000. *(National Audubon Society's) The Sibley Guide to Birds*. New York: Alfred A. Knopf, 544 p. [The *new* bird authority.]

Stebbins, Robert C. 1985. *A Field Guide to Western Reptiles and Amphibians (Peterson Field Guide 16)*. Boston: Houghton Mifflin, 360 p.

Storer, Tracy I., and Robert L. Usinger. 1964. *Sierra Nevada Natural History*. Berkeley: University of California Press, 374 p. [A classic, but somewhat dated, especially in geology.]

Watts, Tom. 1973. *Pacific Coast Tree Finder*. Berkeley: Nature Study Guild, 62 p.

Weeden, Norman F. 1996. *A Sierra Nevada Flora*. Berkeley: Wilderness Press, 259 p.

Willard, Dwight, 1994. *Giant Sequoia Groves of the Sierra Nevada: A Reference Guide*. 372 p. [Self-published, excellent, but unfortunately out of print. A real collector's item.]

About the author

Jeffrey P. Schaffer has hiked and climbed in Yosemite since his early college days in 1962. Studying biology, geography and geology for 14 years at the University of California, he earned three degrees, and in Yosemite he has done original research in all three fields. While working on the first edition of this guidebook, he realized there were serious errors in the interpretation of how Yosemite Valley was formed, and this ultimately led him to write the first new interpretation since 1930, *The Geomorphic Evolution of the Yosemite Valley and Sierra Nevada Landscapes*. His work in this area includes, with the aid of Dr. Ben Schifrin, a complete remapping of the trails of Yosemite National Park and vicinity.

Index

Numbers in *italics* indicate photographs.